T0337389

Strategic Human Resource Management

This book provides a comprehensive and up-to-date study in strategic human resource management (SHRM). It aims to provide students and practising managers with an in-depth view of essential concepts and techniques in the area in a highly readable and understandable form. It focuses particularly on practical applications, examples and cases that students and HR managers can utilize in gaining insights into the subject. The book serves two important purposes: providing an academically rigorous study and offering an insightful and user-friendly pedagogy. It includes:

- opening stories
- new terms and concepts
- questions for discussion
- HR anecdotes
- caselets and 'news grabs'

Feza Tabassum Azmi is Professor at the Department of Business Administration, Faculty of Management Studies and Research, Aligarh Muslim University, Aligarh, India. Her primary area of interest is strategic human resource management. Her research papers have been published in various journals including *International Journal of Human Resource Management, European Business Review, International Journal of Commerce and Management, Singapore Management Review*, and *Philippines Management Review*, among others.

Strategic Human Resource Management

Text and Cases

Feza Tabassum Azmi

CAMBRIDGE
UNIVERSITY PRESS

University Printing House, Cambridge CB2 8BS, United Kingdom

One Liberty Plaza, 20th Floor, New York, NY 10006, USA

477 Williamstown Road, Port Melbourne, vic 3207, Australia

314 to 321, 3rd Floor, Plot No.3, Splendor Forum, Jasola District Centre, New Delhi 110025, India

79 Anson Road, #06–04/06, Singapore 079906

Cambridge University Press is part of the University of Cambridge.

It furthers the University's mission by disseminating knowledge in the pursuit of education, learning and research at the highest international levels of excellence.

www.cambridge.org
Information on this title: www.cambridge.org/9781108482318

First published 2019

Printed in India by Nutech Print Services, New Delhi 110020

A catalogue record for this publication is available from the British Library

ISBN 978-1-108-48231-8 Hardback
    978-1-108-71195-1 Paperback

To Nabeel and Aliza

Contents

List of Figures   *xi*
List of Tables   *xiii*
Preface   *xv*
Acknowledgements   *xix*

PART I   The Framework of Strategic Human Resource Management

1. Concept of Strategic Human Resource Management   **3**
Chapter Overview   3
Learning Objectives   3
Opening Story: General Electric's Journey to 'Imagination at Work'   3
Conceptual Background   5
Models of SHRM   7
Characteristics of SHRM   18
SHRM Framework   21
Emerging HR Scenario   23
Chapter Summary   32
Exercises and Discussion Questions   33
Caselet: Strategic HR at Colgate-Palmolive   33
Notes   35

PART II   Context of SHRM

2. Environment of SHRM   **41**
Chapter Overview   41
Learning Objectives   41
Opening Story: India's Economic Growth   41
Business Environment: An Introduction   42
The Systems Concept   43
Business Environment and SHRM   44
External Environmental Factors   45
Internal Environmental Factors   71
Chapter Summary   74
Exercises and Discussion Questions   75
Caselet: Reliance Jio—The Game Changer?   75
Notes   77

3. Technology and HRM   **80**

Chapter Overview   80

Learning Objectives   80

Opening Story: Kumbh Mela Goes Hi-tech   80

Technological Environment   81

Trends in the Nature of Work   82

IT and HRM   84

Impact on HR Sub-Systems   86

Impact on HR Culture and Structure   89

Challenges and Opportunities   97

Social Media and HR   98

Internet of Things, Big Data, and HR   101

Chapter Summary   105

Exercises and Discussion Questions   105

Caselet: Circular Organization at Harley-Davidson Motor Company   105

Notes   107

PART III   Strategy Formulation

4. Strategy Formulation and HRM   **111**

Chapter Overview   111

Learning Objectives   111

Opening Story: Rethinking the Role of HR   111

Strategic Management Process   112

Importance of Human Resources to Strategy   114

Integration of Strategy and HRM   115

Strategy Formulation and Planning   116

Typology of Integrated HR Systems   117

Chapter Summary   122

Exercises and Discussion Questions   122

Caselet: Strategic HR Integration at The Walt Disney Company   123

Notes   125

5. Workflow Analysis and Strategic Job Analysis   **127**

Chapter Overview   127

Learning Objectives   127

Opening Story: The Future of Work   127

Future of Work and Talent Management   128

Workflow Analysis   130

Job Design, Job Redesign, and Job Analysis   133

Understanding Job Analysis   135

Strategic Job Analysis   139

Strategic Job Analysis and Dejobbing   142

Competency Profiling and Strategic Job Modelling   143

Chapter Summary   149

Exercises and Discussion Questions 149
Caselet: Job Remodelling at Tata Motors 150
Notes 153

PART IV Strategy Implementation

6. Strategic Human Resource Planning and Staffing **157**
Chapter Overview 157
Learning Objectives 157
Opening Story: Strategic Manpower Planning in Indian Armed Forces 157
Strategic Human Resources Planning (SHRP) 159
SHRP Process 160
Strategic Staffing 164
Strategic Recruitment 165
Strategic Recruitment and Realistic Job Preview 181
Strategic Selection 182
The Selection Mechanism 187
Placement and Induction 197
Chapter Summary 200
Exercises and Discussion Questions 201
Caselet: Mirakle Couriers: Driving Social Change 201
Notes 203

7. Strategic Training and Development **205**
Chapter Overview 205
Learning Objectives 205
Opening Story: Barbie Doll's Journey 205
From Training to Learning 206
Organizational Learning 207
The Learning Framework 208
Learning and Knowledge Management 209
The ADDIE Model 210
The Employee Learning Matrix 219
Unlearning and Relearning 221
Career Planning and Development 222
Promotions and Succession Planning 224
Chapter Summary 228
Exercises and Discussion Questions 229
Caselet: How Toyota Learns to Excel 229
Notes 231

8. Performance Management and Compensation **232**
Chapter Overview 232
Learning Objectives 232
Opening Story: Evolving Performance Management Paradigm 232
Performance Appraisal 234

Weaknesses of Performance Appraisal System   239
Performance Appraisal to Performance Management   239
Appraisal Feedback and Counselling   245
Potential Appraisal   246
Compensation and Rewards   247
Traditional Compensation System   248
Strategic Compensation   249
Executive Compensation   259
Designing an Effective Compensation Strategy   261
Chapter Summary   264
Exercises and Discussion Questions   265
Caselet: Performance Management and Rewards at Tata Consultancy Services   265
Notes   267

9. Employee Relations, Engagement, and Termination   **268**
Chapter Overview   268
Learning Objectives   268
Opening Story: Industrial Relations Reforms in India   268
Employee Relations   269
Trade Unionism   271
Collective Bargaining   272
Employee Participation in Management   274
Employee Engagement   276
Employee Retention and Termination   280
Chapter Summary   285
Exercises and Discussion Questions   286
Caselet: Employee Relations and Engagement at Taj Hotels   286
Notes   288

PART V   Strategy Evaluation

10. Strategic HR Evaluation   **291**
Chapter Overview   291
Learning Objectives   291
Opening Story: HR and Finance—Marriage on the Clouds   291
Measuring HRM   292
Approaches to HRM Evaluation   293
Evaluating HR Subsystems   296
Evaluating the HR System   303
Strategic HR Evaluation: Challenges   304
HR Analytics   305
Chapter Summary   308
Exercises and Discussion Questions   309
Caselet: Valuing Human Resource at Infosys   309
Notes   311
Index   313

Figures

1.1	The Michigan Model	10
1.2	The Harvard Model	12
1.3	Strategic HRM Framework	21
1.4	Ulrich's Typology of HR Roles	26
2.1	The Systems Concept	44
2.2	Major Employment and Labour Laws in India	61
2.3	Environmental Profile of India: A Snapshot	68
3.1	The 4-I Principle	90
3.2	Hierarchy versus Hyperarchy	94
3.3	Organization Design—Phases of Evolution	96
4.1	Organizational and HR Planning Typology	120
5.1	Workforce of the Future—The Competing Forces Shaping 2030	130
5.2A	Workflow of an Organization	131
5.2B	Workflow of HR Department	132
5.3	Example of Job Description and Job Specification	137
5.4	Uses of Job Analysis	138
5.5A	Competency Mapping of HR Manager's Job	145
5.5B	Competency Levels for HR Manager's Job	145
5.6	Skill Matrix at BP	147
6.1	Change in Recruitment Advertisements	171
7.1	The Learning Iceberg	208
7.2	Employee Learning Strategy Matrix	219
7.3	The Forgetting Matrix	221
8.1	Performance Appraisal versus Performance Management: Timelines	241
8.2	360-Degree Appraisal	243
8.3	Strategic Compensation	249
9.1	Employee Engagement Typology	277
10.1	Framework for HR Evaluation	293

Tables

1.1 Traditional versus Strategic HRM   6
1.2 Instrumental versus Humanistic Approach   13
1.3 Miles and Snow's Typology (HRM Systems)   16
1.4 Management Levels and HR Roles   27

2.1 India's Relative Rank in Economic Indices   51

5.1 Traditional versus Strategic Job Analysis   142

6.1 Recruitment Sources and 3L Principle   181
6.2 Traditional Preview and Realistic Job Preview   182
6.3 RVU of Common Selection Tools   197

7.1 Training versus Learning   207

8.1 Performance Appraisal versus Performance Management   240

9.1 Industrial Disputes in India   270

Preface

With the ever-escalating challenges of the business environment, the corporate world is fast realizing the importance of human resource (HR) as an inimitable strength for attaining sustainable advantage. This has given place to the idea that human resource management (HRM) needs to be aligned to the strategic management (SM) process of the organization. The integration of the above two disciplines is termed as strategic human resource management (SHRM).

Academic debates around the 1980s and early 1990s suggested the need to integrate SM and HRM closely. These debates highlighted the growing strategic nature of the HR function. The concept of SHRM became popular in the 1980s with the development of two models that talked about integrating strategy and HRM, namely the *Michigan Model* and the *Harvard Model*. Academic writings in SHRM started to emerge after this, but it was only by the end of the 20th century that the practice gained popularity and momentum among practitioners.

In recent times, SHRM has become a well-accepted concept and practice. Today, HR is seen as potential contributors to the realization of the organization's vision. It is interesting to note that HR departments are now considered to be investment centres rather than cost centres. HR executives are today considered as important strategic partners. The increasingly important role that HR managers are playing today is exemplum of the fact that SHRM has arrived. There now exists empirical evidence that documents the contribution of the strategic HR approach to organizational performance.

Despite the increasing importance of SHRM, there is still a paucity of texts on SHRM in the context of emerging economies, more specifically in the Indian context. The volatile and dynamic business environment of emerging markets warrants an increasing focus on valuing HR and linking HR issues with strategic imperatives. Keeping in mind the fact that India is one of the fastest growing emerging markets today, this book is expected to provide insights into the fast-evolving SHRM terrain.

Almost all B-schools and universities offering management courses teach papers related to the area of HRM. However, the dearth of books on SHRM makes the task of teachers and students quite challenging in terms of obtaining relevant and contextual matter on the subject. In the absence of a comprehensive book on SHRM, especially in the context of emerging economies, the current book hopes to fill a wide gap in the market.

The book seeks to provide a comprehensive and up-to-date text in the area. It aims to provide students and practicing managers with a comprehensive view of essential concepts and techniques in the area in a highly readable and understandable form. This book particularly focuses on practical applications, examples, and cases that practitioners can utilize in gaining insights into the subject in order to carry out their HR-related responsibilities. The book serves two important purposes: to provide an erudite source that is high on academic rigour and has comprehensive coverage, while at the same time being a book that is simple, readable, and user-friendly. Academic work of other authors, wherever cited, has been appropriately mentioned in the references.

For the ease of structuring and for brevity, the book has been divided into five parts. The five parts have been further subdivided into ten chapters.

PART I: THE FRAMEWORK OF STRATEGIC HUMAN RESOURCE MANAGEMENT

The first part of the book deals with the conceptual framework of SHRM. The evolution and concept developments in the area are traced and discussed.

Chapter 1: Concept of Strategic Human Resource Management

The *first* chapter deals with the concept of SHRM. Various models and schools of thought in the area are presented. The nature and characteristics of SHRM are discussed. The chapter highlights the emerging HR scenario and the different roles that HR managers are playing.

PART II: CONTEXT OF SHRM

The second part of the book deals with the context of SHRM. It discusses the environmental and technological factors that impact HR systems and strategies.

Chapter 2: Environment of SHRM

In the *second* chapter, the nature and concept of a business environment is discussed. The components of macro and micro business environments and how they affect HR practices are highlighted. Various trends and emerging dimensions of the business environment of relevance to HRM are pointed out.

Chapter 3: Technology and HRM

The *third* chapter focuses on the emerging trends in the workplace vis-à-vis the technological environment. It introduces the concept of e-HR and highlights how various HR sub-systems are getting transformed due to IT. It also highlights how traditional organizational structures are giving way to more flexible and amorphous organizational forms.

PART III: STRATEGY FORMULATION

The third part of the book highlights the concepts and issues related to the strategy formulation phase vis-à-vis HRM.

Chapter 4: Strategy Formulation and HRM

The *fourth* chapter delves into the role of the HR function in the SM process and vice versa. It highlights the importance of HR to strategy. It also discusses the various approaches to integration of strategic planning and HRM.

Chapter 5: Workflow Analysis and Strategic Job Analysis

The *fifth* chapter focuses on discussing the concepts of workflow analysis and job analysis. Further, it carries out a discussion on the difference between traditional and strategic job analysis. Themes such as dejobbing, strategic job modeling, and competency mapping are discussed.

PART IV: STRATEGY IMPLEMENTATION

Part four of the book is concerned with developing an understanding of how HR sub-systems are aligned with strategy. It discusses the process of strategy implementation vis-à-vis HRM. It highlights how strategic design of HRM sub-systems is different from that of traditional processes, usually seen in textbooks on HRM.

Chapter 6: Strategic Human Resource Planning and Staffing

The *sixth* chapter deals with strategic human resource planning (SHRP). It involves linking business strategies to future manpower needs and laying down HR plans. Thereafter, the concept of strategic staffing is discussed, involving a detailed discussion of strategic recruitment, selection, and placement.

Chapter 7: Strategic Training and Development

The *seventh* chapter focuses on strategic training and development. It discusses the concepts of organizational learning and unlearning as broad themes of strategic training and development. Further, it delves into a discussion on career planning and development as well as succession planning.

Chapter 8: Performance Management and Compensation

The *eighth* chapter discusses the concepts of performance appraisal and performance management. It focuses on the need to move from performance appraisal to performance management. Further, the concepts of compensation and rewards are also discussed. Various types of strategic compensation systems are examined.

Chapter 9: Employee Relations, Engagement, and Termination

The *ninth* chapter deals with the idea of employee relations, engagement, and termination. Issues related to trade unions, collective bargaining, and employee participation in management are highlighted. The meaning and significance of employee engagement are then discussed along with the typology of engagement. Thereafter, issues related to retention and employee termination are covered.

PART V: STRATEGY EVALUATION

The last part of the book is a reflection of the SHRM philosophy, *'what can't be measured, can't be managed'*. This part deals with a discussion of measures and techniques that can help evaluate the HRM function.

Chapter 10: Strategic HR Evaluation

The *tenth* and last chapter discusses the concept of strategic HR evaluation. Various approaches and techniques of HR evaluation are highlighted. Methods of evaluation of an individual HRM subsystem as well as the HRM system as a whole are examined. The concept of HR analytics and its use in strategic HR evaluation is also taken up.

Key features of the book

- Every chapter starts with a brief chapter overview and learning objectives so that the reader can make out how the chapter will help in enhancing his/her understanding of SHRM.
- The actual contents of the chapter begin with an opening story that sets the background for the chapter. The opening story features an example or illustration that sets the tone for the chapter.
- Content of each chapter is clearly and logically arranged under different headings and subheadings. This provides a flow to the topics discussed so as to lend clarity to the reader.

- In order to make the text meaningful and interesting, the content in each chapter is supported with relevant figures and tables that are sequentially numbered.
- Each chapter ends with a chapter summary in bullet form for a quick recapitulation of the chapter contents.
- Chapters are followed by a small caselet for reflection and discussion. These caselets are intended to further link the subject matter with real-world problems and situations.
- Each chapter features a news item box titled as 'news grab' that focuses on a recent news item related to the concept being discussed in the chapter. This is specially done to link the theoretical aspects with actual developments taking place around us. This projects the practical value of the book as different from merely a theoretical text.
- Each chapter contains an HR anecdote to make the text interesting to read.
- Chapters end with questions for discussion and relevant notes/references.
- The book intends to be based not merely on theoretical concepts but on evidence-based HRM. It, thus, uses examples, cases, illustrations, research and empirical data, and news items to acquaint the reader with the actual scenario existing in the corporate world and to develop a thorough grounding in HR developments.
- *New topics and concepts*   The book introduces dozens of new and emerging topics and concepts in HR, not generally discussed in conventional books and writings on HRM. Some of these concepts are hyperarchy, velcro, and ambidextrous organizations as new organizational forms; dejobbing and strategic job modeling in the light of job analysis; bodyshopping, temping, and boomerang hiring as recruitment options; reliability and validity of the selection process; organizational learning, unlearning, and relearning; career plateaus; social media and HR; variable pay and employee stock option plans; Big Data, Internet of Things, and HR analytics; and balanced scorecard and HR scorecard. These concepts help introduce the emerging trends in the HR arena.

The above features make the book very easy to comprehend and interesting to read, without compromising on its academic rigour and value.

It is worth noting that SHRM is a dynamic and evolving field. Some facts, concepts, cases, and examples cited in the book may change by the time the reader gets to read the book. This is a natural course of a discipline's growth.

Acknowledgements

First of all, I thank the Almighty God for providing me the patience and will to complete this book.

I deem it my privilege to express my profound sense of gratitude to my revered teachers for providing constant encouragement and support. I am thankful to all the teaching and non-teaching staff at the Department of Business Administration, Aligarh Muslim University, Aligarh, India, with whom I have worked for several years now and who are part of my academic journey. I must acknowledge the role that my students have played, over the years, in shaping my thoughts and motivating me to be an eager learner always.

I wish to place on record my gratitude for the anonymous reviewers of the book for providing inputs that helped me in refining the present work. I would also like to thank all the authors and scholars whose works I have referred to in the book.

I am extremely thankful to the editorial and publishing team at Cambridge University Press for their support and continued interest in the book. It is because of their efforts and dedication that this book got published in this form. Special thanks to Anwesha Rana, Associate Commissioning Editor, Cambridge University Press, for her support in getting this book published. Thanks to Aniruddha De, Senior Production Editor, Cambridge University Press, for his keen involvement during the publication of this book.

This study could not have been possible without the support of my family. I am thankful to all my family members who have been a constant source of encouragement for me. I owe special thanks to my father who inspired my quest to read and write. Thanks are due to all friends and well-wishers for their encouragement and concern regarding the progress of the work. I must acknowledge the support of my husband, Naved, who was more concerned than me about the work and whose stringent deadlines finally led to the timely completion of this book. I owe my deepest gratitude to my son, Nabeel, and daughter, Aliza, my greatest teachers and source of happiness.

The Framework of Strategic Human Resource Management

Part I

THE FRAMEWORK OF STRATEGIC HUMAN RESOURCE MANAGEMENT
Chapter 1: Concept of Strategic Human Resource Management

Part II

CONTEXT OF SHRM
Chapter 2: Environment of SHRM
Chapter 3: Technology and HRM

Part III

STRATEGY FORMULATION
Chapter 4: Strategy Formulation and HRM
Chapter 5: Work Flow Analysis and Strategic Job Analysis

Part IV

STRATEGY IMPLEMENTATION
Chapter 6: Strategic Human Resource Planning and Staffing
Chapter 7: Strategic Training and Development
Chapter 8: Performance Management and Compensation
Chapter 9: Employee Relations, Engagement, and Termination

Part V

STRATEGY EVALUATION
Chapter 10: Strategic HR Evaluation

CHAPTER 1

Concept of Strategic Human Resource Management

Chapter Overview

In this chapter, we will discuss the meaning and concept of strategic human resource management (SHRM). Various models and schools of thought in the area of SHRM are presented. The nature and characteristics of SHRM are also discussed. The chapter also sketches a picture of the emerging human resource (HR) scenario and the changes taking place in the field of human resource management (HRM). The different types of HR roles are also discussed. In the end, the challenges facing new age HR departments are highlighted.

Learning Objectives

1. To develop an understanding of the basic concept of SHRM and its different models and schools of thought
2. To gain insights into the changes taking place in the field of HRM and the consequent changes in the roles and responsibilities of HR managers
3. To understand the challenges that HR departments and HR managers have to face in this changing scenario

OPENING STORY

General Electric's Journey to 'Imagination at Work'

John F. Welch, Jr., the iconic leader of General Electric (GE), gave new directions to the company when he took over as chairman and chief executive officer (CEO) in 1981. Welch embarked on an imposing challenge: building a revitalized 'human engine' to animate GE's formidable 'business engine'.

At that time, GE was already one of the world's largest corporations built around 14 distinct businesses—including aircraft engines, medical systems, engineering plastics, major appliances, NBC television, and financial services. Soon after he became CEO, Welch articulated GE's now-famous strategy of 'number one or number two globally'.

His programme had two central objectives. First, he championed a company-wide drive to identify and eliminate unproductive work in order to energize GE's employees. He developed procedures to speed up decision cycles, move information through the organization, provide quick and effective feedback, and evaluate and reward managers on qualities such as openness, candour, and self-confidence to create a lean and efficient organization. Second, and perhaps of even greater significance, Welch was instrumental in leading a transformation of attitudes at GE—to release 'emotional energy' at all levels of the organization and encourage creativity and feelings of ownership and self-worth.

His ultimate goal was to create an enterprise that could tap the benefits of global scale and diversity without the stifling costs of bureaucratic controls and hierarchical authority. This requires a transformation not only of systems and procedures, he argued, but also of people themselves.

A few years later, a leading business magazine printed an article about GE that listed its businesses and the fact that it was truly number one or number two in virtually all of them. Welch remarked then, 'Ten years from now, we want magazines to write about GE as a place where people have the freedom to be creative, a place that brings out the best in everybody. An open, fair place where people have a sense that what they do matters, and where that sense of accomplishment is rewarded in both the pocketbook and the soul. That will be our report card.'

Source: Adapted from N. Tichy and C. Charan (1989), Speed, simplicity, self-confidence: an interview with Jack Welch, *Harvard Business Review*, September–October.

The journey thus far ...

Jack Welch is seen as one of the most influential leaders of the corporate world. He firmly believed that good business leaders create a vision, articulate the vision, passionately own the vision, and relentlessly drive it to completion.

Welch believed in winning by involving people at all levels. He was convinced that everyone onboard is valuable and needs to be given a sense of ownership. All human resource (HR) functions, such as training, compensation, and rewards, need to be changed to make people change. They need to be linked to overall strategic direction.

After more than 23 years, in 2003, General Electric Co. decided to change its well-recognized slogan, 'We Bring Good Things to Life', to launch a new campaign with the tagline 'Imagination at Work' in a major effort to overhaul the company's image and emphasize people power. The beliefs are a set of principles, such as accountability and autonomy, designed to change employee and management mindset and make everyone focus on delivering results to customers and determine GE's success.

Aon Hewitt, the global HR and consulting company, ranked GE first on its annual *Global Aon Hewitt Top Companies for Leaders* list in 2014. GE was ranked number 10 on Forbes' *World's Most Valuable Brands List* in its 2016 rankings.

GE's website states

'At GE, our relentless quest for progress has fueled 130 years of innovation. We believe that our people are our most powerful catalysts for growth and innovation. By investing in our employees, we not only build careers, we drive progress. Because when one person grows, we all grow—and together, we all rise. As a result of this commitment, GE invests more than $1 billion each year in employee development worldwide.' Jeff Immelt, CEO, says, 'We have the ambition to lead the next generation of industrial progress.'

CONCEPTUAL BACKGROUND

GE's story is reflective of how people power can transform a company into a world-class enterprise. The concept of SHRM is essentially based on this principle of people power.

SHRM is basically concerned with the integration of HRM with the strategic management process. It is defined as a set of techniques that enables interventions to be made within the business in order to improve performance.[1] The term 'strategic human resource management' is now widely used in management literature. In general, SHRM is the effective application of human resources to meet an organization's strategic objectives.

Chris Hendry and Andrew Pettigrew stated that in SHRM, there are two themes that overlap: the term 'strategic' and 'human resources'.[2] It connotes integrating HRM with business strategy. According to them, there are four underlying meanings in the concept of SHRM:

1. The use of strategic planning
2. A coherent approach to the design and management of personnel systems based on workforce strategy and often underpinned by a broad 'philosophy'
3. Matching HRM activities and policies to some explicit business strategy
4. Seeing the people of the organization as a 'strategic resource' for the achievement of 'competitive advantage'

Definitions of SHRM vary, but most authors agree that it seeks to gain competitive advantage by managing human assets through an integrated, synergistic set of HR practices that both complements and promotes the overall business strategy.[3] SHRM is largely about integration and adaptation. Its concern is to ensure that (*a*) HR management is fully integrated with the strategy and the strategic needs of the firm, (*b*) HR policies cohere both across policy areas and across hierarchies, and (*c*) HR practices are adjusted, accepted, and used by line managers and employees as part of their everyday work.[4] From a 'constituency-based' perspective, it is argued that HR academics and practitioners have embraced SHRM as a means of securing greater respect for HRM, thereby enhancing their status and prestige within organizations.[5]

However, there is divergence of views on the nature of integration. Definitions of SHRM range from it being an HR system that is tailored to the demands of the business strategy[6] to it being the pattern of planned HR activities intended to enable an organization to achieve its goals.[7] In the first definition, HRM is a reactive management field, whereas in the latter definition, it has a proactive function in which HR activities actually create and shape the business strategy.

The basic premise underlying SHRM is that organizations adopting a particular strategy require HR practices that suit that strategy. HRM must flow from and be dependent on the organization's corporate strategy. HR planning includes strategic goals and objectives.[8] These definitions, however, tend to emphasize the implementation role of HR. On the other hand, several scholars believe that in order for SHRM to be effective, HR practices must be effectively integrated with all phases of the strategic planning process.[9]

Despite differences in definitions, it can nevertheless, be emphasized that a traditional or non-strategic approach to HRM is separate from business, reactive, short-term, and of no interest to the board of directors. On the other hand, SHRM is the close linking of HR planning with strategic initiatives of the firm. HRM in organizations has often appeared to be disjointed and haphazard, giving little consideration to the organization's strategy. The growing proactive nature of the HR function and its importance to organizations has led to the emergence of SHRM. Today, HR is seen as potential contributors to the creation and realization of the organization's goals. It is interesting to note that the HR department is now considered to be a potent powerhouse for strategic management. Table 1.1 highlights the differences between traditional HRM and modern-day strategic HRM.

Table 1.1 Traditional versus Strategic HRM

	Traditional HRM	Strategic HRM
Beliefs	Conformity	Can-do outlook
Guidelines	Contracts and rules	Vision and mission
Objectives	Organizational interest	Organizational and individual interests
Scope	Personnel department	General managers
Methodology	Technical, specialist	Professional, managerial
Approach	Segregated, staff function	Systems approach
Functions	Traditional, administrative	Modern, developmental
Nature	Short-term, constrained	Evolving strategic role
Thrust	Monitoring	Nurturing
Status	Implementer, reactive	Formulator, proactive
Role	Attain goals	Design goals

Some scholars have described SHRM as an outcome, while others have described it as a process. Patrick M. Wright and Gary C. McMahan consider SHRM as the pattern of planned HR deployments and activities intended to enable a firm to achieve its goals.[10] Thus, SHRM can be seen as an organizational system designed to achieve sustainable competitive advantages through people. As a process, SHRM can be seen as a mechanism of linking HR practices to business strategies. Karen Legge notes that strategy formulation and implementation are inextricably entangled in a continuous, formative, and adaptive process.[11] Considering both process and outcome, Catherine Truss and Lynda Gratton define SHRM as the linkage of HR functions with strategic goals to improve business performance.[12]

SHRM is a process that involves the development of HR strategies that are integrated vertically with the business strategy and horizontally with one another. It deals with people issues that affect or are affected by the strategic plans of the organization.[13] SHRM has gained importance as there is research evidence to prove that it contributes to firm performance and competitive advantage. The HRM function, once responsible for record-keeping and maintenance, has evolved into a strategic partner.[14]

Based on the above discussion, it can be concluded that SHRM is basically concerned with the integration of HRM with the strategic management process. In general, it is about the effective application of human resources to meet an organization's strategic objectives.

There is divergence of views on the nature of integration. While some definitions focus on tailoring HR systems to the demands of the business strategy, others focus on developing patterns of planned HR activities intended to enable an organization to achieve its goals. Despite differences in definitions, SHRM is seen as the close linking of HR with strategic imperatives of an organization.

MODELS OF SHRM

Various scholars have identified taxonomies of schools of thoughts and models in SHRM. Researchers have linked SHRM with firm performance and effectiveness. Broadly speaking, one of the following three ways to examine the effectiveness of HR practices on firm performance can be identified: contingency, universalistic, and configurational.[15]

- **Contingency perspective**   Contingency theorists argue that, in order to be effective, an organization's HR practices must be consistent with the organization's business strategy.
- **Universalistic perspective**   Researchers in the universalistic perspective are micro-analytical in nature and posit that some HR practices are always better than others and that all organizations should adopt these practices.
- **Configurational perspective**   Configurational theories are concerned with how the pattern of multiple independent variables is related to a dependent variable, that is, how systems of HR practices lead to better performances.

David Guest terms universalistic, contingency, and configurational perspectives as external fit (HRM as a strategic integration), internal fit (HRM as an ideal set of practices), and configurational fit (HRM as bundles-internal and external fit), respectively. Guest classifies the configurational approach by dividing it into two further approaches. One is the 'fit-as-bundles' approach, which assumes that a multiplicative pattern of particular HRM practices brings out synergistic effects on performance. The second approach is the 'fit-as-gestalt' approach, which implies that combinations among HRM practices are additive rather than multiplicative.[16]

Daniel A. Verreault and Mary Anne Hyland club the above into two categories, namely the 'strategic approach' and the 'systems approach'. The strategic approach implies achieving 'fit' between HRM and strategy, that is, vertical fit. The systems approach focused initially on the relationship between individual HRM practices and organizational performance and later on a set of HRM practices and performance, that is, internal fit. This approach was identified earlier as the 'universalistic' approach and later as 'configurational'.[17]

John Purcell considers two major perspectives to SHRM: best fit (contingency) and best practices (universalistic and later configurational) approach.[18] Others like John Storey distinguish between hard (strategy as a determinant of HRM) and soft (employee commitment as a determinant of HRM) dimensions of SHRM.[19]

Based on these classifications, two major schools of thought in SHRM can be identified: the *best fit* school or contingency approach and the *best practices* school or universalistic and configurational approach.

The Best Fit School

The best fit perspective focuses essentially on the HR–strategy link. It is, therefore, also called the strategic approach or contingency approach. It is based on the premise that organizational effectiveness is contingent on ensuring a fit between corporate strategy and HRM.

The issue involving the link between strategy and HR revolves around the debates in strategic management between Igor Ansoff and Henry Mintzberg and between Michael Porter and C. K. Prahalad.[20] These debates highlight the differences in approaches to strategic management. Their debate revolves around the issue whether strategy formulation and implementation are separate. The differences pin upon the planning versus learning hypothesis giving rise to two streams of research:

- *Strategic Management Literature*   This is the classical or traditional stream, with its focus on strategic content, which assumes strategy-making as a rational, formal-analytical, and planning process.
- *Organization Theory Literature*   This is the behaviour-based stream, with its focus on process, which emphasizes strategy-making as a learning process.

The traditional strategic management approach assumes that strategy formulation and implementation are separate functions. The top management of the company formulates a comprehensive strategy, which is then implemented by the lower level staff. This stream characterizes strategic decision-making as a rational process, as suggested by Igor Ansoff and others, that attempts to fit an organization with its environment. The logic of the formal-analytical view of strategic planning rests on an 'ends-ways-means' model: establish corporate objectives (ends); given those objectives, develop a strategy (ways) for attaining them; and then marshal the resources (means) necessary to implement this strategy. This rational decision-making is concerned with the content or 'what' of strategy and has nothing to do with how to achieve it.

As an alternative to the 'rational-outcome' view, other writers like Mintzberg have drawn attention towards the rationality of the 'process', that is, how outcomes are actually achieved. The organization theory literature, which is the behaviour-based stream, focuses on the process and sees strategy-making as a learning process. Strategic decision-making in a learning organization takes shape in an entrepreneurial fashion—bottom-up. The learning approach is based on a means-ways-ends sequence. A company begins by investing in its capabilities and encourages its managers to exploit ways to achieve its ends.

Organization theory supports the resource-based view (RBV) of the firm. Resource-based theory owes much of its genesis to a remarkable book by a University of London Professor of Economics, Edith Penrose, in 1959.[21] Penrose conceptualized the firm as a collection of productive resources. To have the potential to generate sustained advantage, resources must meet the criteria of value, rarity, inimitability, and originality or non-substitutability. Together, this is called the 'VRIO' framework. This work was later rediscovered by several others.[22]

A popular expression of the RBV is associated with the work of C. K. Prahalad and Gary Hamel, who argue that competitive advantage stems from building core competencies.[23] HRM can be valued not only for its role in implementing a given competitive scenario, but for its role in generating strategic capability. These theories uphold the importance of employees. Scholars like Ansoff and Mintzberg, however, have documented that although the two approaches to strategic management differ, their use is not mutually exclusive, as companies tend to employ both approaches.

Two divergent approaches to SHRM can be identified based on the above two approaches to strategic management: *instrumental approach*, which draws upon the traditional rational-outcome model of strategic management to view HRM as something that is driven by corporate strategy, and *humanistic approach*, which utilizes the latter organizational process theory to emphasize the reciprocal relationship between strategic management and HRM.

Both these schools/approaches talk about fit between strategy and HRM. They are also called contingency schools because they assume that HRM is contingent on organizational strategy. Both approaches, however, look at the strategy–HRM fit from different perspectives.[24]

Instrumental Approach to SHRM

This approach draws upon the 'rational-outcome' model of strategic management to view HRM as something that is driven by and driven directly from corporate, divisional, or business level strategy, and geared almost exclusively to enhancing competitive advantage. The instrumental approach places emphasis firmly on human *resource* management. It basically talks about the concept of *one-way fit* between HRM and business strategy by prescribing the design of HRM policies in the light of strategy. This is referred to as 'hard' HRM.

Thus, taken from this perspective, HRM is concerned with the integration of HR issues into business planning. The *Michigan model* of HRM is an example of the instrumental approach.

The Michigan Model

The Michigan model of HRM has originated from the writings of C. Fombrun, Noel Tichy, and M. A. Devanna, who discussed it in a detailed fashion in their book titled *Strategic Human Resource Management*, published in 1984.[25] The model is called the 'matching model' because it depicts the relation between HRM and organizational strategy. The model shows how activities within HRM can be unified and designed in order to support the organization's strategy. It is divided into two parts: the first part shows HR–strategy integration and the second depicts the HR cycle. The first part depicts that organizational effectiveness is achieved by ensuring a tight fit between corporate/business strategy and HRM strategy. The model emphasizes a 'tight fit' between organizational strategy, organizational structure, and HRM. It argues that all issues associated with HR should be derived from strategy. The second part of the model shows how HR functions, such as selection, appraisal, development, and reward, can be mutually geared to produce the required type of employee performance. It basically talks of the concept of one-way fit between HRM and business strategy by prescribing the design for HRM policies in the light of strategy. Figure 1.1 depicts the Michigan model.

The Michigan model is seen as a harder, less humanistic approach to HR. The hard model of HRM emphasizes the quantitative, calculative, and business strategic aspects of managing resources.

Managerial implications of the model

The model is focused on individual and organizational performance. It concentrates on managing human assets to achieve strategic goals. It requires that personnel policies, practices, and systems are not only consistent with the business objectives of the firm but should also have coherence among various sub-systems of HRM. The influence of the hard version has encouraged the development of measurable criteria in HRM (for example, profit per employee, added value per employee, and costs per employee).

Figure 1.1   The Michigan Model

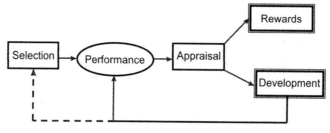

Part A: HRM–Strategy integration Process

Part B: The HR Cycle

Source: Adapted from C. J. Fombrun, N. M. Tichy, and M. A Devanna (1984), *Strategic human resource management* (New York: John Wiley).

The matching model has been criticized on various grounds. The model is considered simplistic in nature. It has also been criticized because of its dependence on a rational strategy formulation approach and because of the nature of the one-way relationship with organizational strategy. It fails to perceive the potential for a reciprocal relationship between HR strategy and business strategy. There is the claim of excessive 'unitarism'. The so-called unitary frame of reference describes an approach towards people as a unit within which managerial authority is taken to be legitimate and ultimate. It hardly leaves any room for stakeholders to voice their opinions.

Thus, from this viewpoint, HRM appears as something that is 'done to' passive human resources, rather than something that is 'done with' active human beings. In many respects, humanistic variants of HRM can be seen as a response to many of these criticisms.

Humanistic Approach to SHRM

This approach utilizes 'process' theory to emphasize the reciprocal nature of the relationship between strategic management and HRM, and the latter's role in ensuring that competitive advantage is achieved through people, and not at their expense. These approaches are closely associated with what has become known as the Harvard School of HRM. As the humanistic label implies, the emphasis is on the 'soft' aspects of HRM. The emphasis is on *'human'* resource management. This leads to a less prescriptive and more people-centred approach than that found in instrumental orientations.

The Harvard Model

The *Harvard Model*, proposed by Michael Beer, Bert Spector, P. Lawrence, Quinn Mills, and Richard Walton of Harvard University in 1984 through their book *Managing Human Assets*, is another significant model of SHRM.[26] The model recognizes the different stakeholder interests that impact HRM policy choices.

The type of HRM policies and practices an organization prefers should be dependent on its organizational vision, mission, strategy, goals, and objectives. The model, presented in Figure 1.2, argues that HR policies are to be influenced by two significant considerations:

1. *Situational factors*   This includes the internal and external environment factors such as labour market conditions, societal values, business strategies, and technology that will influence HRM policies.
2. *Stakeholders' interests*   The stakeholders influence HRM policies. They include management, employees, unions, and government agencies.

Further, the model classifies HRM policies and practices into four themes:

- *HR flows*: Recruitment, selection, placement, promotion, appraisal and assessment, promotion, termination, and so on
- *Reward systems*: Pay systems, non-monetary recognition schemes, and so on
- *Employee influence*: Clarification of responsibility, authority, hierarchy, and delegation of powers
- *Work systems*: Definition of work and alignment of people

The above HR practices are centred on four Cs as described below:

- *Competence* of employees: Competence creates a positive attitude towards learning and development and, thereby, gives employees the versatility in skills and the perspective to take on new roles and jobs as needed.

Figure 1.2   The Harvard Model

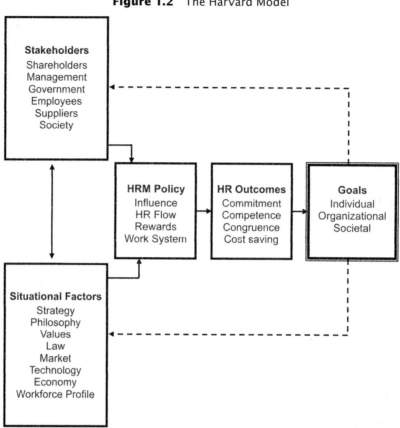

Source: Adapted from M. Beer, B. Spector, P. R. Lawrence, D. Q. Mills, and R. E. Walton (1984), *Managing human assets* (New York: The Free Press).

- *Commitment* of employees: Commitment means that employees will be motivated to 'hear, understand, and respond' to management's communications relating to the organization of work.
- *Congruence* between the goals of employees and the organization: There must be congruence between and among various HRM policies as well as practices in operation.
- *Cost effectiveness* of HRM practices: Cost effectiveness means that 'the organization's HR costs have been kept low'. HRM policies must be evaluated in terms of costs and benefits.

Managerial implications of the model

This model offers three significant insights for practice. First, HRM policies should be defined keeping in view the environmental factors and stakeholders' concerns. In other words, there must be a good fit between an organizational environment and HR policies. Second, such HRM policies and practices must have a goal to achieve employee commitment, competence development, coherence among themselves, and embrace cost-effective methods. Third, HRM that stems from environmental factors and is drawn based on four Cs will result in employee and organizational effectiveness. This is a soft model as it is based on stakeholders' concerns and their commitment to organizational goals.

The model is different from the Michigan model because it talks about the concept of the *two-way fit* between HRM and business strategy as it takes into consideration employee interests. While the Michigan model is called the reactive model in which strategy drives HR, the Harvard model is a proactive model in which HR is involved in strategy formulation. Table 1.2 presents the differences between the instrumental and humanistic approaches.

Even the Harvard model has been criticized for not clearly explaining the complex relationship between strategy and HRM. Although the model is primarily analytical, there are prescriptive elements leading to potential confusions; for example, 'HR outcomes' box, where desirable outcomes are identified, leading to fixation with only certain outcomes.

There can be no standard theory of HRM but, rather, a need for analytical knowledge of basic principles. Scholars have concluded that even if the rhetoric of HRM is 'soft', the reality is almost always 'hard', with the interests of the organization often prevailing.[27]

Although clear distinctions exist between the soft and hard models of HRM, they need not be mutually exclusive, when it comes to a strategic orientation, but can be complementary. SHRM requires a balance of emphasis. Adopting and balancing both hard and soft HR initiatives is the way out.[28]

Table 1.2 Instrumental versus Humanistic Approach

Instrumental Approach	Humanistic Approach
Drawn from Michigan Model	Drawn from Harvard Model
Hard version	Soft version
Emphasis on human 'resource'	Emphasis on 'human' resource
Rational-outcome model	Process model
Organizational goals	Organizational and individual goals
HRM to be driven by corporate strategy	HRM to drive and be driven by corporate strategy
One-way link	Two-way link
Reactive	Proactive
Quantitative and calculative	Qualitative and intuitive
HRM is things 'done to' HR	HRM is things 'done with' HR
Unitarist orientation	Pluralist orientation
HR as implementer	HR as formulator and implementer

While the above two schools fall under the best fit schools of thought, there is another broad school of thought in SHRM, namely the best practice school.

The Best Practice School

The best practice school is different from the best fit school in its approach. Both schools essentially talk of a strategic approach to HRM. However, the focus of best fit theorists is on integrating HR practices with the organization's business strategy, whereas best practice theorists focus on the relationship between HRM practices and organizational performance. This approach was identified earlier as the 'universalistic' approach and later as the 'configurational' approach.[29]

Research has found evidence to support the thesis that HRM leads to increased organizational performance.[30] SHRM has become more central to management literature owing to this link.

Universalistic Perspective

Researchers in the universalistic perspective are micro-analytical in nature and emphasize that certain HR practices are always better than others and that all organizations should adopt these practices for enhanced productivity and performance. The best practices approach advocates universal HR practices, that is, they have an effect on business performance regardless of the context in which they are applied. These practices are also called 'high performance work practices' (HPWP), 'high commitment work practices' (HCWP), 'high involvement work practices' (HPWP), or simply 'best practices'.

The most influential best practice set is associated with the seven practices identified by Jeffrey Pfeffer, namely employment security, selective hiring, self-managed team, pay contingent on company performance, extensive training, reduction of status differences, and sharing information.[31] John E. Delery and D. Harold Doty identify seven 'best practices'—internal career opportunities, formal training systems, appraisal measures, profit sharing, employment security, voice mechanisms, and job definition.[32] M. A. Huselid identified thirteen HRM practices.[33] Others included practices such as teams, job rotation, quality circles, employee empowerment, communication, partnership, and innovation.

The universal perspective is not without its critics. Organizations that do not adopt best HR practices can also generate greater returns. The universal school does not address the role of strategy as a contingency. Another controversy involving this issue is whether there exists a set of 'best practices' that are universally effective across contexts and industries. Several best practices have failed in a number of cultures.

Configurational Perspective

Configurational theorists focus on a pattern of multiple variables related to a dependent variable, that is, how systems of HR practices, rather than individual HR practices, lead to better performances.

Effects of HR practices are multiplicative rather than additive and, hence, it can be said that HR practices affect performance when used in certain configurations. Thus, researchers in this area believe that any effect of HR practices lies in the architecture of the system, not in the so-called best practices. This view articulates a 'strategic bundle' of HRM practices, which interact to provide synergistic results.[34]

These configurations are assumed to be ideal-type constructs.[35] SHRM is seen as the pattern of planned HR deployments and activities, thus suggesting their inclination towards a configurational view, calling for a 'horizontal integration' of the various HR activities.[36] According to this perspective, SHRM requires coordinated HR activities across the various sub-functions. The configurational approach combines internal and external fit, which is seen as the basis for maintaining and increasing performance. Many scholars have provided topologies of HRM systems or have developed ideal-type employment systems in line with the configurational perspective.[37]

David P. Lepak and Scott A. Snell propose a framework that depicts the various HR architectures focusing on internalizing or externalizing (such as make or buy) employment. They examined the characteristics of HR configurations in four different employment modes (namely knowledge-based, job-based, contract work, and alliance). Each employment mode was found to be associated with a particular HR configuration (namely commitment-based, productivity-based, compliance-based, and collaborative).[38]

Jeffrey Sonnenfeld and Maury Peiperl also propose a framework classifying organizations as club, academy, fortress, and baseball team depending on corporate and HR strategies. However, they maintain that firms should exhibit one model type of system.[39]

Arthur (1992) makes a distinction between HRM practices that can be labelled as control- or commitment-oriented. Control-oriented HRM systems focus on cost reduction and improvement in efficiency, whereas commitment HRM systems emphasize employee development and trust. It is a continuum where the HRM dimensions differ with respect to their orientation. The HRM systems are bundles of coherent HRM practices, characterizing the SHRM approach.[40]

Raymond Miles and Charles Snow have developed combinations of HR practices suited for different firm strategies, which is by far the most popular typology. Miles and Snow observed four basic types of strategic behaviour and organizational characteristics that they call defender, prospector, analyser, and reactor. Defenders operate in a narrow domain and protect it aggressively. They achieve this with a high degree of efficiency through centralized decision-making. The basic strategy of defenders is to 'build' or 'make' human resources. The role of HR may be limited to file maintenance or record keeping. It is characterized by an administrative linkage. Prospectors are virtually the opposite of defenders. They continually search for new products or markets. Their domain is broad and unstable. Prospectors need a decentralized market-based design with employee participation. Prospectors require that the HR department be proactive and involved in strategic decisions. Prospectors typically 'buy' in talent. Analysers are a hybrid of defenders and prospectors. Analysers are expected to have greater HR–strategy integration in order to design HR practices to strike a balance between the two strategies. Reactors lack a consistent strategy. Miles and Snow's typology depicted in Table 1.3 has been used very often in empirical research.[41]

Table 1.3 Miles and Snow's Typology (HRM Systems)

HRM Systems	Type A (Defender)	Type B (Prospector)	Type AB (Analyser)
Basic Strategy	Building human resource	Acquiring human resource	Allocating human resource
Recruitment, Selection, and Placement	Emphasis: 'make' Little recruitment above entry level, selection based on merit	Emphasis: 'buy' Recruiting at all levels, selection may involve pre-employment psychological testing	Emphasis: 'make and buy' Mixed recruiting and selection approaches
Training & Development	Skill building, extensive training programmes	Skill identification and acquisition, limited training programmes	Skill building and acquisition, extensive training programmes
Performance Appraisal	Process-oriented, identification of training needs, individual/group performance evaluation, time series comparisons	Results-oriented, identification of staffing needs, divisional/corporate performance evaluation, cross-sectional comparisons	Mostly process-oriented, identification of training and staffing needs, individual/group/divisional performance evaluation, mostly time series and some cross-sectional comparisons
Compensation	Oriented towards hierarchy, internal consistency, cash-oriented, driven by superior–subordinate differentials	Oriented towards performance, external competitiveness, incentives-oriented, driven by recruitment needs	Mostly oriented towards hierarchy, some performance considerations, internal consistency, external competitiveness, cash-and incentives-oriented

Source: Adapted from R. E. Miles and C. C. Snow (1984), Designing strategic human resource systems, *Organizational Dynamics 13*(1): 36–52.

Randall S. Schuler and Susan E. Jackson's blending strategies also speak of the same idea. They talk of three competitive strategies that organizations, when adapted to HR issues, can use to gain competitive advantage: innovation, quality-enhancement, and cost reduction. They showed how business strategy, proposed by Michael Porter, is blended with corresponding employee role behaviour and HRM practice. Thus, HRM could then be seen as a menu of strategic choices. Schuler and Jackson found modest differences in HR priorities between firms in the growth versus maturity stages and pursuing differentiation versus cost strategies.[42]

John Purcell suggests how employee characteristics and resourcing can be matched to the strategic position in terms of the Boston Consulting Group matrix. For *wildcat/question-mark* organizations, employees need to be willing to work in a variety of areas. For *star* organizations, a high degree of individualism is required, with careful selection to employ the best. *Cash cow* organizations need order and stability, and, thus, need employees who will not 'rock the boat'. Finally, in *dog* organizations, the emphasis will be on reducing surplus labour in order to cut costs.[43]

L. Dyer and G. W. Holder identify three types of HR systems, namely inducement, investment, and involvement. The inducement HR strategy (centralized and low-cost) is likely when the environment is based on price. The investment HR strategy (partially centralized and creativity driven) is likely in environments based on differentiation. The involvement strategy (decentralization and flexible) is suitable for highly competitive markets.[44]

Likewise, Peter A. Bamberger and Ilan Meshoulam produced an orthogonal model offering four distinctive approaches to HR strategy formulation. On the vertical axis, strategies are distinguished by the extent to which the organization is focused on outputs or processes. The horizontal axis represents the extent to which the HR strategies rely on internal or external skills. The resulting 2 × 2 matrix provides four forms of HR strategy: 'commitment' characterized by a reliance on internal labour and output orientation, 'free agent' distinguished by reliance on external labour and output orientation, 'paternalism' focusing on internal labour and process, and, finally, 'secondary strategy' focusing on process and external labour. [45]

Several other such frameworks of configurations of practices also exist. Researchers have found evidence of organization-level outcomes and groups or bundles of HR practices.[46] One of the major limitations of the configurational perspective, however, is that different authors have presented different bundles and configurations of HR practices. Researchers in configurational theory invoke idealist HRM systems. The field tends to ignore the ways in which national or cultural differences influence HRM. It is too simplistic to think that one type of HR strategy and employment relationship will be appropriate for all employees.

Reconciling the Different Views

Broadly speaking, one of the following three approaches to SHRM can be found: contingency, universalistic, and configurational. Based on these classifications, two major schools of thought in SHRM can be identified: the *best fit* school or contingency approach and the *best practices* school or universalistic and configurational approach. Furthermore, two divergent approaches to SHRM can be identified under the *best fit* school: *instrumental approach*, which draws upon the traditional rational-outcome model of strategic management to view HRM as being driven by corporate strategy and *humanistic approach,* which utilizes organizational process theory to emphasize the reciprocal relationship between strategic management and HRM. The *Michigan model* of HRM is an example of the instrumental approach, whereas the *Harvard model* of HRM is based on the humanistic approach. The best practice school is slightly different from the best fit school in its approach. The best practice theorists focused more on the relationship between HRM and organizational performance. This approach was initially identified as the 'universalistic' approach and later as the 'configurational' approach.

The best practice and best fit hypotheses are not in conflict but simply operate at different levels. Pfeffer's system of best practices is sometimes included in universalistic and sometimes in configurational school. Miles and Snow's typology sometimes is interpreted both as a contingency and a configurational theory. Thus, it can be concluded that the different schools are, in fact, complementary. Organizations adopt different approaches depending on their priorities and specific contexts.

CHARACTERISTICS OF SHRM

As can be understood from the example above, SHRM is largely concerned with 'integration' or 'fit'. SHRM is concerned with establishing two types of fit, namely vertical and horizontal fit.[47]

Vertical Fit

It is concerned with ensuring integration of HRM with the strategic management process. The key aspects of a vertical fit are:

- The organizational vision is used to provide an overarching frame of reference for laying down the HR vision and plan.
- HRM activities are designed keeping the organization's strategy in mind.
- Organizational strategy is also designed keeping in mind HR issues.
- Top-level strategic teams include HR head or executives.
- Inputs about HR are considered an integral part of the organizational strategy.
- Top management takes special interest in HR issues and strategies.
- There is existence of a comprehensive exchange and feedback mechanism between the senior managerial team and the HR department.
- Senior HR executives are provided training in general managerial skills.

Horizontal Fit

Horizontal fit is concerned with ensuring integration at the same level. This involves two types of fit—internal and external fit.

Internal Fit

It involves integration between the various HRM sub-functions or sub-systems, such as staffing, compensation, and training. The key features of internal fit are listed below:

- The HR vision helps integrate all the HRM activities.
- HR policies, such as recruitment, training, and reward, are consistent with each other. There is a common vision that runs across these sub-functions. All HRM activities are, thus, integrated and coherent with each other.
- An information sharing mechanism between HR sub-areas exists.
- A coordinating mechanism between HR sub-functions is established.

External Fit

This is concerned with the integration between HRM and other functional areas, for example, marketing, finance, and operations. The key aspects are:

- Consistency of HR activities with other functional activities is established by aligning all functional areas with the organizational vision and strategy.
- All managers are in some way HR managers, as they all deal with people issues.
- HR decisions are taken jointly with managers of other areas.
- Managers of other areas are actively involved in HR activities, such as recruitment, selection, training, appraisal, and compensation.

At Google, the HR team, better known as 'People Operations team' has revolutionized HR the same way Google has revolutionized search engines. Google is known for its innovative strategy to find, grow, and keep the remarkable assemblage of talent known as Googlers. These Googlers are the champion of Google's culture and values, partnering with business leaders to help them build an excellent organization. HR is seen as a business partner and all HR activities are integrated with overarching business strategies. Google's culture can be seen as an example of SHRM philosophy.

Therefore, we can say that SHRM is an approach to managing human resources that supports long-term business goals and outcomes. It does not operate independently within a silo. It interacts with the other departments within an organization in order to attain the goals of the organization. SHRM is seen as a partner in organizational success.

Based on the above discussion, the characteristics of SHRM can be identified:

1. **SHRM is an integrative approach to people management**   The HR strategy adopted by a firm should be integrated with the firm's corporate strategy. The key idea behind overall strategic integration is to coordinate the human resources in such a way that it contributes to carrying out its strategy. This will help an organization attain synergy.
2. **SHRM is a generalist approach to people management**   SHRM is not the sole responsibility of HR departments but also of other agents, such as top and line managers. Thus, all managers are people managers. It is expected that managers at all levels, irrespective of their departments or functional areas, will take interest in HR issues.
3. **SHRM is a comprehensive approach to people management**   A strategic approach to human resources is concerned with all of the firm's employees. It is concerned with designing HR strategies keeping all the departments and units in mind. It looks at the HR function from a broad perspective rather than considering HR issues as part of a narrow technical domain.
4. **SHRM focuses on competitive advantage**   HR strategy is meant to attain competitive advantage. Definitions of SHRM vary, but most scholars agree that it ultimately seeks to gain competitive advantage by managing human assets through an integrated, synergistic set of HR practices that both complements and promotes the overall business strategy.

5. **SHRM considers employees as most important**   Various scholars have testified to the intrinsic worth of HR as valuable organizational assets. HR is potentially the most vital source of sustainable competitive advantage for organizations. An organization's HR is the most valuable organizational asset.

6. **SHRM has a long-term focus**   Conventional HRM is not aligned to business needs and has a short-term focus. Traditionally, HRM policies were designed on an *ad hoc* basis, depending on needs. SHRM, on the other hand, has a long-range focus.

7. **SHRM focuses on customers—internal and external**   The external customer is someone who buys a company's goods or services and pays for it. Internal customers, from the perspective of SHRM, are employees who avail the services of the HR department, which in turn is utilized to create a deliverable for the external customers. Satisfied internal customers help build satisfied external customers.

8. **SHRM has a market and environmental focus**   Strategic human resource decisions explicitly recognize the threats and opportunities in each area and attempts to capitalize on the opportunities while minimizing the chances of threats. The market and environmental forces impact HR strategy. SHRM emphasizes laying down HR policies with an external market focus rather than a traditional inward focus.

9. **SHRM elevates the status of the HR function**   SHRM implies that HR professionals are at the centre of the organization today. While it has been argued that the status of HR managers has risen, HR department is being viewed as an important department. This requires that HR managers adopt a business partner role. In many companies, the head of HRM sits on the board of directors. This has elevated the status of HR functions in modern-day business organizations.

10. **Administrative and strategic HRM are inextricably intertwined**   Under the SHRM philosophy, HRM exists at various levels. This view is based on the idea that all functions of HR have some strategic element. Management levels are usually classified into three categories—strategic, managerial, and operational levels. SHRM activities can be associated with these levels.

11. **SHRM is a combination of hard and soft models**   The Michigan model advocates that organizational effectiveness is achieved by ensuring a tight fit between corporate strategy and HRM. The Harvard model recognizes different stakeholder interests and environmental factors that help shape HR strategies. Although the first is a *hard* approach (strategy as a determinant of HRM); the second is a *soft* dimension (employee interests also as a determinant of HRM). SHRM is an amalgamation of both hard and soft models.

12. **SHRM focuses on the measurement of HRM activities**   SHRM focuses on the philosophy *'what can't be measured, can't be managed.'* The importance of HR as firm assets was appreciated by the accounting profession. It has also led to development of models on planning, forecasting and auditing of HR. Measurable criteria and techniques, such as profit per employee, added value per employee, costs per employee, and training cost-benefit analysis, have evolved over time.

Various methods and techniques of measuring the HR function are discussed in the last part of this book.

SHRM FRAMEWORK

SHRM is understood as the pattern of planned HR activities intended to enable an organization to create and shape the business strategy. It talks of a two-way fit between corporate strategy and HR strategy. This is based on the 'proactive' fit approach. The emphasis shifts from viewing HRM as the implementer of organizational strategy to an active participant in strategy formulation.

Figure 1.3 depicts the framework for SHRM.

Figure 1.3   Strategic HRM Framework

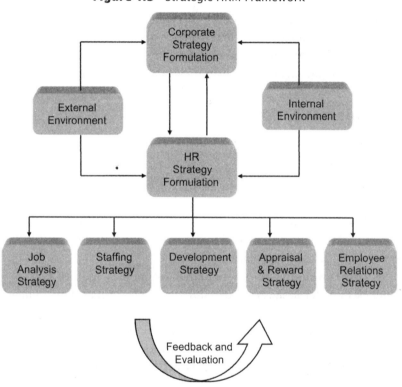

The figure indicates that the overall HR strategy flows from the business strategy and at the same time affects the business strategy. The model shows HR strategies being integrated with corporate strategies. Both corporate and HR strategy influence each other. HRM is viewed in the larger organizational context. HR department has a vision, envisaged in line with organizational vision. HR activities are aligned with this HR vision. This in turn generates specific HR strategies in key areas. As can be seen from Figure 1.3, HR-strategy formulation becomes a part of corporate strategy formulation phase. HR executives are seen as formulators and not just implementers of strategies.

Strategy Formulation

The strategy formulation phase involves laying down the strategic direction. Here corporate strategy and HR strategy are designed together. The strategy formulation phase requires:

- Lay down organization and HR vision
- Set corporate and HR objectives
- Outline corporate strategy and HR strategy to attain objectives
- Undertake business and planning
- Approve the vision, objectives, strategy, and plans and set common agenda

The process takes place under the influence of the internal and external environments of the organization. Assumptions about likely internal and external changes impact both corporate strategy as well as HR strategy. The probability of occurrence of these changes and the intensity of their likely impact on the organization determines the course of strategies.

Strategy Implementation

The broad and overarching corporate vision and HR vision serve as the basis for designing strategies in different sub-areas of HRM:

- **Job Design**   It requires arranging tasks, responsibilities, authority for different roles in light of strategic imperatives.
- **Staffing**   It is important to attune recruitment and selection policies, methods and techniques to suit the organizational strategies in order to staff the organization with 'right' people and 'right' set of competencies.
- **Training and Development**   Development strategies require providing learning opportunities to foster strategy linked skills, attitudes, behaviours, competencies, and knowledge.
- **Performance Management and Reward**   Evaluation of individual, group and unit performance should be done in light of organizational strategy. Monetary and non-monetary incentives to employees should be linked to the performance and contribution to the strategic goals.
- **Employee Relations**   Employee relations involve encouraging healthy human relations so as to create synergy for the attainment of vision and commitment to a common ideology.

Strategy Evaluation

Once strategies have been designed, it is necessary to put in place a well-founded mechanism for feedback and follow-up. The evaluation of strategies is an important component of SHRM. It involves:

- Highlighting the contribution of HR strategy to the bottom line
- Promotion of HR function as a critical and not support activity

- Ensuring accountability in resource utilization
- Demonstrating the role of HR in accomplishment of organization vision
- Assessing and demonstrating the deliverables and benefits of HR strategy

For the success of SHRM, it is of utmost significance that HR executives should ensure the deliverables of HRM are well known. Companies with well-structured and strategically-linked HR practices have improved organizational performance. It is the responsibility of HR executives to ensure that the results that are yielded by HRM activities are well known, so as to provide evidence of the benefits of the strategic role of HRM. Bringing about the SHRM perspective mandates putting in place a strong architecture for corporate strategy and HRM integration to take place. Furthermore, the organization structure and culture of the organization should also be compatible with the proposed strategies.

An important aspect of this framework is the fact that although it depicts strategy formulation and implementation as different phases, in reality, the two may not be separate functions. The traditional approaches to strategy emphasized a formulation-implementation dichotomy. SHRM is based on the philosophy that formulation and implementation are not classified into a clearly delineated dichotomy. Strategic decision-making takes place in a collaborative fashion. Any dichotomy is for the purpose of clarity in depiction of phases only and is not exemplum of the process.

It is important to understand that the SHRM framework as presented in Figure 1.3 is only a simplified depiction of its process and various phases. SHRM in real life does not usually take the form of a simplistic, well-articulated, and linear process that flows logically and seamlessly from the business strategy. Implementing SHRM is a more complex process than depicted by diagrammatic frameworks or theoretical matrices. The framework only serves as a visual representation of the components and activities that occur in the process. In reality, the implementation of the framework involves many more dimensions. All these components and dimensions of SHRM have been discussed in detail in the succeeding chapters in the book.

EMERGING HR SCENARIO

The nature of HRM is evolving with the change in competitive market environment and the realization that HR must play a more strategic role in the success of an organization. To understand the emerging HR scenario better, we will highlight the features of the new age HR departments and the changing HR roles.

New Age HR Departments

SHRM implies that HR professionals are at the centre of the organization today. Consequently, HR departments are changing their focus from administrative roles to strategic roles, from a narrow specialist approach to a generalist approach, and from counting activities to presenting outcomes. The new age HR department is learning to work more closely with employees helping them to better meet the corporate and business goals. In general, HR is increasingly becoming a part of the top-level strategic decision-making team. Rather than just sitting in their closed offices and handling day-to-day administrative work, HR is now getting involved in decision-making and making a contribution to the company as a whole.

In addition, a closer relationship with managers at all levels in the company is making it easier for the HR department to take part in crucial business operations and corporate matters. HR departments, in a number of organizations, are now called the Corporate HR department, Strategic HR department, and so on. This symbolizes their new strategic role as being different from their traditional administrative role. For instance, HR was earlier an independent function at Cadbury India. Now, it is integrated with the corporate strategy and is called the 'HR & Corporate Strategy' department. Similarly, Sam Walton, Wal-Mart's founder, placed so much value on his employees that he called Wal-Mart's HR department 'The People Division' and his employees as 'associates'.

Another important development taking place in HR is witnessed in the upward movement of HR executives in organizational hierarchy. HR managers today occupy important positions, such as director, vice-president, general manager (GM) of HR, and chief human resources officer (CHRO). A growing number of organizations today have senior HR executives as members of the board of directors or as part of senior-level decision-making teams. Many companies now embrace the role of HR at the boardroom table, reflected by the increasing use of the term 'chief human resources officer'. HR directors have a key role in SHRM if they are on the board or in the top management team. They are there to envision how HR strategies can be integrated with the business strategy, prepare strategic plans, and oversee their implementation.

Further, to foster greater coherence in the HR unit, a large number of organizations have moved to a flat structure of their HR departments. The department is now organized in a team-based design, in sharp comparison to traditional personnel departments where sub-units responsible for recruitment, training, compensation, and so on were segregated into separate compartments with little coordination between them. In majority of the Fortune 500 companies, the head of the HRM is an officer (usually a vice president) who answers directly to the CEO.

With the emergence of SHRM, HR managers are expected to devote more time and effort on strategic responsibilities. Consequently, HR departmental functions are being examined to determine if outside providers can perform them more efficiently and at lower cost than when done internally. In most big organizations, administrative HR functions are being outsourced to external providers. This helps save time and money and focuses the attention of HR managers on more important issues.

Another significant trend affecting HR departments is extensive automation of the HR function and widespread prevalence of electronic HR or e-HR. An important part of HR management is to deliver HR services in a cost-effective and efficient manner. Information technology (IT) is currently affecting HR delivery systems. Information systems are fast replacing manual record keeping and processing of HR data.

Looking at the widespread influence of automation and e-HR, various dimensions of the application of IT in HRM have been discussed in different chapters of this book.

Changing HR Roles

Traditionally, HR professionals have been seen as 'company morale officers' or 'discipline officers' who do not understand the business realities of the organizations and do not contribute measurably to the strategic success of the business. Specialist HR positions traditionally have focused on routine administrative responsibilities. In some organizations, the role was confined to maintaining industrial relations while in some others it dealt with hiring and pay-related activities.

It is vital for HR professionals to represent employee issues and concerns in the organization. However, just being an effective employee advocate is not sufficient. Instead, the HR professionals must be strategic contributors, partners with operating managers, administratively efficient, as well as cost-effective. Leading firms in competitive environments now have world-class HRM departments.

It is interesting to note that the HR department is now considered to be a potent powerhouse for strategic management. Apocryphal tales of HR executives graduating from mere organizers of company picnics to strategic decision makers are exemplum of the increasingly intrinsic and vital role that HR assumes in the present scheme of things.

Typologies of HR Roles

Research on the characteristics of specialist HR positions prior to 1990s has tended to identify only traditional HR activity. However, recently, HR managers have become strategic partners. Recent developments have provided HR managers with the opportunity to move from their typecast administrative roles to becoming strategic partners.

Various authors have presented typologies of HR roles. John Storey has developed a typology based on: (*a*) action orientation (interventionary versus non-interventionary) and (*b*) choices (strategic versus tactical). These lead to the following HR roles: (*i*) *advisors* (consultants to general management), (*ii*) *handmaidens* (services to line) (*iii*) *regulators* (formulate employment rules), and (*iv*) *change makers* (facilitate business needs).[48]

Susan E. Jackson and Randall S. Schuler talk of six HR roles: *partnership* (knows the business), *change facilitator* (long-term vision), *enabler* (builds commitment), *strategic* (strategic decisions), *innovator* (skills needed in the future), and *monitoring* (hard and soft data).[49] Various other scholars have identified following HR roles to become prominent: business person, shaper of change, strategist, talent manager, assets manager, and cost controller.

The typology developed by Dave Ulrich is by far one of the most popular ones. He highlighted the roles of HR professionals in his path breaking work, *Human Resource Champions: The Next Agenda for Adding Value and Delivering Results*, published in 1997. He describes a multi-faceted approach to delivering HR services that meets the needs of both employees and employers, and positions HR as a significant contributor to organizational success.[50]

His model of HR roles is based on two dimensions or axes to highlight various HR roles:

   I. Strategy versus operations
  II. Process versus people

The first axis reflects the demands of a current/operational/tactical versus a future-oriented/ strategic orientation. The second axis consists of a focus on people on the one end of the axis and a focus on process at the other. Ulrich's framework is the most popular framework on HR roles and is used widely by academicians in the HRM literature.

Based on these two dimensions, four types of HR roles can be envisaged: (*a*) *administrative expert* (design HR processes), (*b*) *employee champion* (upholding employee concerns), (*c*) *change agent* (managing transformation and change), and (*d*) *strategic partner* (aligning HR with strategy). The latter two roles are strategic in nature. Figure 1.4 illustrates this typology.

Figure 1.4   Ulrich's Typology of HR Roles

Source: Adapted from D. Ulrich (1997), *Human resource champions* (Boston, MA: Harvard Business School Press).

Ulrich's model of HR roles serves as a valuable framework for understanding the complex synergies that HR professionals have to develop to perform the operational and strategic jobs, keeping in mind both people and processes to gain competitive advantage.

Levels and Domains of HR Roles

HR managers perform various roles at different levels. Management issues are divided into three levels—strategic, managerial, and operational. HRM activities associated with these levels may also be identified.[51] Table 1.4 depicts these levels of HR roles. As can be seen from the table, all functions of HRM have three levels of tasks and roles.

The strategic role emphasizes that HR management becomes a participant in the strategic decision-making process. The primary issues of concern here include developing an understanding of business issues, attuning HR policies to the organization's strategy, managing human resources in an international context, and dealing with mergers and acquisitions. Managerial activities are tactical in nature and involve a medium-term time frame. This may involve carrying out recruitment and selection, training employees, resolving safety problems, and administering wages and salaries. Typically, the managerial role requires HR professionals to identify and implement HR programmes and policies in the organization. The administrative or operational role of HR management refers to tasks of routine, short-term nature. This may involve work such as maintaining employee records and files, compiling HR-related databases, processing employee benefits claims, implementing leave policies, and compiling and submitting reports. The focus is on performing these activities efficiently.

Table 1.4 Management Levels and HR Roles

Level	Priorities	Recruitment and Selection	Benefits and Rewards	Performance Appraisal	Training and Development	Career Planning
Strategic (Long term)	Ensure vertical integration, lay down HR vision, create strategies, chalk out future plans	Specify the characteristics of people needed in the long term	Determine how rewards will be linked to business strategy	Make early identification of potential, develop appraisal system	Plan developmental exercises for people to run future businesses	Develop long-term systems to manage individual needs
Managerial (Medium term)	Ensure horizontal integration, create HR plans, show HR deliverables	Validate the selection criteria, develop recruitment plans	Set up medium-term compensation and benefit plans	Set up systems that relate current conditions and future potential	Establish management development programmes	Identify career paths, provide career development
Operational (Short term)	Implement strategies, hire and fire, manage payroll, train, maintain HR records	Plan and set up recruitment and selection systems	Administer wage and salary programme	Set up appraisal system and controls	Provide for specific on- and off-the-job training	Fit individuals to specific jobs, plan career

Source: Adapted from M. A. Devanna, C. J. Fombrun, and N. M. Tichy (1981), Human resource management: A strategic approach, *Organizational Dynamics* 9(3): 51–67.

HR managers play a major role as drivers of business strategy today. They are playing a strategic role in their organization. However, HR managers also perform managerial and administrative or operational HRM activities. Apart from the above roles, HR managers play various other roles too, such as facilitators of employee-related issues, linking pin between lower and top-level people, communicators, resource allocators, organizers, leaders, and consultants.[52]

Apart from traditional areas, HR managers play a key role in various emerging domains like international expansions and mergers and acquisitions.[53] HR managers play a major role in quality management initiatives by providing training, facilitating change, empowering employees, instituting team-based reward systems, and communicating to workers their role in quality. They are significant drivers of change management and organizational learning initiatives. HR managers play a key role in engendering organizational learning capability.[54]

The example of Oil and Natural Gas Corporation Limited (ONGC) merits discussion here. ONGC is a flagship company of India and has the unique distinction of having in-house service capabilities in all the activity areas of exploration and production of oil and gas. In the mid-1990s, ONGC undertook an organization transformation exercise in which HR took a lead role as a change agent by evolving a communication strategy to ensure involvement and participation among employees in various work centres. HR measurement parameters have been incorporated since 1994–1995 to systematically and scientifically evaluate the effectiveness of HR systems.

Role of Functional Area Managers in HR

Decentralization of responsibilities to functional managers has been viewed as a key characteristic of SHRM. The idea is to integrate HR with other functions such as marketing, finance, and operations. The word devolution or devolvement has been used in this context. Devolution has been defined as the reallocation of personnel tasks to functional area managers. With the emergence of SHRM, the line–personnel relationship has changed. Line managers or functional area managers are spending more of their time on HR activities, such as selection, training, appraisal, and employee relations. Functional managers are aligning with HR managers to carry out HR tasks and activities.

Managers throughout organizations are responsible for managing and leading people. Therefore, the effective management of human resources is integral to any manager's job. Thus, cooperation between HR managers and other functional area managers is critical to organizational success. This cooperation requires a regular interface between the HR department and other managers within the organization.

It is clear that line managers are now spending more time on HR issues. However, the responsibility for HRM appears to vary between line managers and HR managers from organization to organization. In many organizations, HRM is still the responsibility of HR departments. In some organizations, functional managers are expected to be involved in HRM but the authority to make final decisions on HR by them is missing. In several others, functional managers generally take up responsibility for work force expansion and reduction.

The ability and willingness of functional managers to carry out HR tasks remains a challenge. Managers dealing with HR issues have little training for it. Of course, reducing the administrative workloads of functional area managers and maintaining good relations with HR are means to develop greater devolution. Line managers need to be involved in HRM in the true sense for effective HRM and cross-functional area integration to take place.

Role of Top Managers in HR

Top-level managers provide visionary leadership, define purposes and values, and set the organization's direction. They develop the overall business strategies and ensure that functional strategies for marketing, product development, operations, IT, and HR are designed and implemented in ways that provide sustained support to the achievement of business goals.

Research and surveys on strategic HR have examined the critical importance of the CEO, top management team, and board of directors in HR issues.[55] When top executives consider HR as a source of competitive advantage, they tend to support HR–strategy integration. Often, the low expectations by top management concerning the strategic contributions of the HR function contribute to the limited attention to HR issues.

The influence of top management on HRM policies and practices cannot be ignored. Top management's support leads to higher effectiveness of the HR department and helps it to play a strategic role. The role of the CEO and senior managers in developing capabilities of employees is crucial. Top management can help in identifying appropriate strategies to create sustainable competitive advantage through HR efforts. Scholars agree that top management is the most powerful force facilitating the adoption of SHRM. The level of HR–strategy integration is found to be stronger when the top management views employees as a strategic resource.

For instance, the People Division at Wal-Mart actively collaborates with top executives to reduce the risk of business failure and drives company's success through people. Employees at Wal-Mart are the common organizational bridge that ties all of Wal-Mart's strategies and tactics together to insure the achievement of the company's aggressive goals. The only way the company's executives can accomplish their seven overarching strategies (price, operations, culture, key item/products, expenses, talent, and service) is by aligning their business strategies with their HR practices.

Non-linear and Lateral Moves

SHRM has engendered a generalist orientation in organizations. Consequently, lateral moves and shifts have become common and there is greater interaction between HR and other managers. Career progression today is not always defined as a salary increase or a change in job title in the same department, but more importantly an opportunity to develop one's skills and get involved in varied activities spanning across boundaries.

With massive changes taking place in the HR arena, an interesting phenomenon has taken roots. HR executives are moving beyond HRM and are leveraging their growing generalist orientation to take up other assignments. These assignments range from heading the HR department to heading business units to steering the company as CEOs.

Many organizations have HR generalist roles today. The HR generalist is typically assigned to one or more business units, such as marketing, production, or supply chain, and serves as the initial point of contact for all people issues. The generalist is responsible for securing and aligning all human capital to help the business unit achieve its strategic and operational objectives. The responsibilities of an HR generalist vary widely, ranging from strategic initiatives, such as designing business processes or modifying organizational structures, to sometimes routine administrative tasks, such as responding to employee inquiries or preparing payrolls.

The generalist usually works well in a matrix organizational structure and reports to the head of the business unit he/she is assigned to. Although the generalist is expected to address many requests independently, he or she must rely on the HR specialist functions such as staffing or compensation for designing initiatives. HR generalist roles may involve higher levels of compensation and status. This is true if the move involves a promotion to a higher level, such as from 'manager-training' to 'vice president-human resources'. As a generalist, one is exposed to all aspects of HR. In addition, one is exposed to many strategic and tactical business challenges. The job also provides a significant amount of 'identity'. A generalist works closely with the business and is involved in all aspects of HR from end-to-end. Working as a generalist allows one to learn more about the business.

Although it may not be easy for specialist HR executives to transition into such roles, the move can be beneficial for both the executive and the company. Generalist experience is likely to expand the HR executive's skill set and career options. HR generalists are increasingly being asked to assume strategic responsibilities and are held accountable for improving organizational performance. However, such moves are not without career risks, as specialists and generalists have quite different roles.

Apart from occupying HR generalist positions, many HR executives are moving to other departments or units in pivotal roles. In a lateral move, the employee's job responsibilities change giving the employee new opportunities. Looking at its benefits, organizations are marketing the lateral move as a development opportunity rather than as a parking spot. It gives the HR manager a chance to expand skills and career path opportunities. Lateral moves impart agility and cross-functional expertise to HR managers and helps them make significant strategic contributions. In a lot of organizations today, HR executives are shifted to other departments, such as marketing, operations, and even finance.

In addition, an increasing number of HR executives are occupying top positions and are today GMs and CEOs of their companies. Historically, heads of HR have not been contenders for the CEO's post as they were perceived to be lacking in financial acumen and business knowledge. However, today HR heads are ready for the transition to the top job, now that organizations are open to the idea of CEOs from HR. The popular perception that HR and business are incompatible with each other because business is about numbers and results and HR is about people is outdated. Financial acumen and technological savviness have become hygiene factors for CEOs today, and their prowess is determined by their people management skills. The commonly accepted fact is that you cannot grow a business, form a joint venture, or make an acquisition, if you cannot handle the people issues.

As HR professionals gain credibility for their business skills, handling large HR budgets, and driving complex organizational strategy, they have been able to fight the perception of being weak in matters related to finance and lacking the execution focus that is the hallmark of a successful CEO. Today, there are many heads of HR who manage their function as business heads. Being in HR gives one an overall view of the organization because one is not bound by one's function/role. The biggest strength of HR professionals is their high emotional intelligence (EI) and people connect.

Swiss executive recruiter Ellie Filler observed that for years, many HR chiefs reported to the chief operations officer (COO) or chief financial officer (CFO) and complained that they lacked real influence in the C-suite. Today, they often report directly to the CEO, serve as the CEO's key adviser, and are even occupying the CEO's position. She began noticing significant changes in the roles of CHROs. To explore this phenomenon, she teamed up with Dave Ulrich from the University of Michigan. By comparing various executive roles within large corporate structures, they made a surprising discovery: CHROs possessed behaviours and management skills that were more closely linked with CEOs than with any other group. They observed that CHROs make great CEOs.[56]

Both GM and Xerox Corporation have had CEOs who spent time in the HR departments. James Smith, who became CEO at Thomson Reuters, earlier worked in HR. In India too, the trend has been similar. Several CEOs and company heads have been HR professionals earlier. K. Ramachandran became CEO at Philips India after working in HR at the same company. Pratik Kumar, CEO at Wipro Infrastructure Engineering, was earlier in Wipro's HR department. The transition of these leaders from HR to CEO roles indicates that the career progression is reflective of a new trend—one that is expected to change the playing field for HR professionals. Running an HR department is seen as an excellent developmental step. With changing organizational dynamics and technical competence being easy to replicate, the strengths that HR professionals bring to the table are becoming increasingly valuable to businesses.

Another change that is happening is that the HR head in a company today need not be an HR specialist. Instead, he could be a talent from line function, such as finance or marketing. The heads of HR at several companies, such as Infosys, TCS, Satyam Marico, Crompton Greaves, Cadbury, and Nerolac, were not career HR professionals. For instance, T. V. Mohandas Pai was a member of the board and director–human resources at Infosys. He earlier served as the CFO at Infosys. Many companies differentiate between operational and strategic HR. Although the operational aspect of HR is being handled by traditional HR executives, the strategic part is being given a business dimension by introduction of people from non-HR streams. In some companies, traditional HR activities are outsourced and strategic activities are performed by HR executives.

HRM, as a function, is evolving with changing imperatives of the competitive market environment. John Boudreau and Peter Ramstad, authors of *Beyond HR*, state that HR needs to move beyond its traditional 'soft' approach to embrace 'a new decision science talentship'. This requires HR to, among other things, adopt a far more differentiated approach to investing in talent, and make far greater use of 'talent analytics', a rigorous framework of HR-related measures, to better manage and evaluate an HR strategy.[57]

PWC, in a pathbreaking report titled *Workforce of the Future: The Competing Forces Shaping 2030* (2017), highlights how automation and 'thinking machines' are replacing human tasks and jobs, and thereby changing the skills that organizations are looking for in their people. These momentous changes raise huge HR challenges. Workers will need to learn new skills—'re-tooling' will become the norm. Unique human traits, such as EI, creativity, and innovation, will become more valuable than ever before. HR managers' role will change tremendously. It will compel redesigning traditional 'one-size-fits-all' HR programmes to deliver uniquely targeted learning and development frameworks and remodelled jobs and capabilities.[58]

If HRM wants to create added value for the company, it has to become a full strategic partner with the business to achieve strategic goals.

HR Anecdote
The Owl and the Field Mouse

A little field mouse was lost in a dense forest. Unable to find his way out, he finally spotted a wise old owl sitting in a tree. The mouse pleaded, 'Please help me wise old owl to find my way out of this wood'.

'Easy', said the owl, 'Grow wings and fly out, just as I do.'

'But how can I grow wings?' asked the mouse.

The owl looked at him haughtily, sniffed disdainfully, and said, 'Don't bother me with the details, I only decide the policy.'

The above story is reflective of the reality in many companies. The dichotomy in strategy formulation and implementation undermines the true spirit of strategic management. The best strategy is one which takes an integrative bottom-to-top approach. This involves incorporating HR inputs in the strategic decision-making process. This interaction helps develop strategies that have an in-built action plan for implementation too.

Source: Adapted from http://www.businessballs.com/stories.htm.

News Grab
New study stresses importance of human capital management

The Confederation of Indian Industry (CII) in association with risk management company Willis Towers Watson released a study, *The State of Human Capital Risk in India*, which emphasizes the importance of human capital. The study is based on views of nearly 100 chief executive officers, chief human resource officers and other senior executives in India spanning industry sectors. The study states that corporate leaders today are more likely to realize that human capital can make or break the sustained viability and success of their business and must make it a priority. Pointing out that human capital risk (HCR) management is only going to grow in importance, the report finds that three out of four respondents plan to invest additional resources in HCR management over the next five years. They realize that at the root of many strategic and operational risks is the mismanagement of HCR. The study finds that 62% companies indicate HCR to be an urgent board-level concern. It suggests that till just a few years back 'managing HCR' rarely figured on the agenda of a firm's board, but today Indian company boards are recognizing their crucial role in matters around human capital.

Source: LiveMint, New study stresses importance of human capital management, 26 April 2016, retrieved from https://www.livemint.com.

CHAPTER SUMMARY

- SHRM refers to the integration of HRM with the strategic management process.
- The three approaches to examine the effectiveness of HR practices on firm performance are contingency, universalistic, and configurational approaches.

- Two major schools of thought in SHRM can be identified: the best fit school or contingency approach and the best practices school or universalistic and configurational approaches.
- The best fit school can be categorized into two divergent approaches to SHRM: Instrumental approach based on the Michigan model and the humanistic approach based on the Harvard model.
- The best practice theorists focused on the relationship between individual or systems of HRM practices and organizational performance.
- SHRM is largely concerned with 'integration' or 'fit'. SHRM is concerned with establishing two types of fit, namely vertical and horizontal fit.
- In the present changing context, the HR professional has evolved to become a strategic business partner.
- An important characteristic of SHRM is the increasing involvement of functional area managers and top managers in HR activities.
- Lateral moves and shifts have become common and there is greater interaction between HR and other managers.

EXERCISES AND DISCUSSION QUESTIONS

1. Describe the changing nature and status of HRM. What factors have led to these changes?
2. Why is the support of line and top management critical to the effective functioning of HRM practices in an organization? Highlight how participation of functional and top managers in HRM has increased in recent times.
3. Taking any company of your choice, gather relevant data about the company and discuss the following points:
   i. the broad corporate strategies and HR practices of the company
   ii. whether HR practices have been aligned with corporate strategies
   iii. the key roles played by HR managers

   Discuss the approach to HRM followed in the company, whether it is traditional/administrative or strategic in nature. Provide examples to substantiate your answer.

CASELET

Strategic HR at Colgate-Palmolive

Colgate-Palmolive Company (C-P) is a global company with sales of over $5 billion that recently received new 'marching orders'. The new CEO developed and communicated a new strategic direction for the company based on what he called his 'corporate initiatives'. Among other things, the new strategy emphasized concentrating on new products, being the low-cost producer, and simplifying businesses and people management procedures. It also focused on changing structures, pushing decision-making downward, promoting entrepreneurial action, and improving morale and motivation. The new strategy was aimed at making Colgate a leaner, more responsive competitor in its global markets and in focusing the company more clearly on health-related products.

Consistent with this new strategy, several steps were taken. Four major businesses were divested, including two sports and recreation companies. A major reorganization took place, which merged two levels of senior management. HR programmes at C-P got a new mandate to help Colgate achieve its new goals.

The programmes laid out for Colgate provide a glimpse of how HRM today is being pressed to get involved in strategic management. At C-P, HRM was directed by the CEO to develop and execute programmes designed to create a company culture that would achieve the following:

- Encourage a spirit of teamwork and cooperation among business units in working towards common objectives, with emphasis on acknowledging and rewarding individual and unit excellence.
- Foster entrepreneurial attitudes among the managers and innovative thinking among all employees.
- Emphasize the commonality of interest between the employees and shareholders.

To that end, numerous HRM programmes had to be designed. For example, the company's executive incentive compensation plan was redesigned to place more emphasis on individual performance and achieving operating targets. Employee benefits were redesigned to make them more flexible and responsive to employees' needs. The bottom line was that by implementing these programmes, HRM helped refocus employee efforts in a manner that contributed to the extension of Colgate's strategic plan.

Soon, C-P topped the list of the 25 best big companies for work–life balance. C-P offers some great employee benefits, such as flexible work hours, telecommute options, and nearby back-up childcare centres, which is a nice perk for work-at-home parents. As a result, C-P has a high rate of employee retention, which is a testament to their work culture. Colgate truly is a world of opportunity. To support employee development and job satisfaction, Colgate proudly offers global career opportunities and access to world-class training and education programmes. Colgate encourages employees to expand their professional horizons. Attracting, developing, and retaining exceptional people is a priority for the company. C-P has a two-pronged approach to developing people.

- Individual development planning (IDP): Colgate IDPs enable employees to partner with their managers to identify skills, behaviours, and knowledge needed to achieve specific goals
- Succession planning: Colgate relies on global succession planning to identify and develop a continuous stream of the next two to three generations of Colgate leaders

One major problem that C-P is facing in the current scenario is how to sustain organizational excellence in a perpetually disruptive job market. With large scale turnover taking place across all industries and retiring baby boomers in the western world, getting a good supply of people is a challenge and C-P is learning to grapple with that challenge currently.

C-P managers realize the need for an even more coherent HR-strategy integration. Colgate is a truly global company being globally diversified in over 120 countries in all continents. As such, it is important to attract, develop, and retain people of all backgrounds, cultures, and nationalities. Building this global mindset and cultural sensitivity in the people is critical to their business survival and to the family's satisfaction while operating abroad. This requires having superior communications up, down, and across the organization, and to have values in place that encourage cooperation, sharing of information, and joint decision-making.

There is a need to integrate people, processes, and functions along a common theme. It must begin by developing the competencies, getting senior management commitment, communicating the intent and encouraging everyone, from the administrative staff to the most senior staff to come together. This certainly requires establishing processes which bring forth and tap the ability of all employees to contribute effectively. Effective change management must be in place to manage the transition from where the organization is now to where it needs to be. All this brings forth the extremely crucial role of the HR team. Getting the team geared up is the key.[59]

Questions for Discussion

1. Which approach or model of SHRM is evident from the case? Discuss.
2. What does the company need to do to gear up its HR team in order to cope with the challenges discussed in the end?

NOTES

1. C. J. Fombrun, N. M. Tichy, and M. A. Devanna (1984), *Strategic human resource management* (New York, NY: John Wiley).
2. C. Hendry and A. Pettigrew (1986), The practice of strategic human resource management, *Personnel Review 15*(5): 3–8.
3. See, for instance, L. Gratton, V. Hope-Hailey, P. Stiles, and C. Truss (1999), *Strategic human resource management: Corporate rhetoric and human reality* (Oxford: Oxford University Press); M. A. Huselid, S. E. Jackson, and R. S. Schuler (1997), Technical and strategic human resource management effectiveness as determinants of firm performance, *Academy of Management Journal 40*(1): 171–188.
4. R. S. Schuler (1992), Strategic human resources management: Linking the people with the strategic needs of the business, *Organizational Dynamics 21*(1): 18–32.
5. P. Bamberger and I. Meshoulam (2001), *Human resource strategy: Formulation, implementation and impact* (Thousand Oaks, CA: Sage Publications); J. Pfeffer and G. Salancik (1977), *The external control of organizations: A resource-dependence perspective* (New York, NY: Harper & Row).
6. R. E. Miles and C. C. Snow (1984), Designing strategic human resource systems, *Organizational Dynamics 13*(1): 36–52.
7. P. M. Wright and G. C. McMahan (1992), Theoretical perspectives for strategic human resource management, *Journal of Management 18*(2): 295–320.
8. J. B. Arthur (1992), The link between business strategy and industrial relations systems in American steel minimills, *Industrial and Labor Relations Review 45*(3): 488–506; W. B. Werther, Jr., and K. Davis (1996), *Human resources and personnel management* (New York, NY: McGraw-Hill).
9. N. Bennett, D. J. Ketchen, and E. B. Schultz (1998), An examination of factors associated with the integration of human resource management and strategic decision-making, *Human Resource Management 37*(1): 3–16; Boxall, P. F. and J. Purcell (2003), *Strategy and human resource management* (Basingstoke, UK: Palgrave Macmillan).
10. P. M. Wright and G. C. McMahan (1992), Theoretical perspectives for strategic human resource management, *Journal of Management 18*(2): 295–320.

11. K. Legge (1995), *Human resource management: Rhetorics and realities* (Chippenham, UK: Macmillan Business).

12. C. Truss and L. Gratton (1994), Strategic human resource management: A conceptual approach, *The International Journal of Human Resource Management 5*: 663–686.

13. M. Armstrong (2000), *A handbook of human resources management techniques* (London, UK: Kogan Page).

14. As evidenced by M. A. Huselid (1995), The impact of human resource management practices on turnover, productivity, and corporate financial performance, *Academy of Management Journal 38*(3): 635–672; R. S. Schuler and S. E. Jackson (1987), Linking competitive strategies with human resource management practices, *Academy of Management Executive 1*(3): 207–219; P. M. Wright, T. M. Gardner, L. M. Moynihan, and M. R. Alien (2005), The relationship between HR practices and firm performance: Examining causal order, *Personnel Psychology 58*: 409–446.

15. J. E. Delery and D. H. Doty (1996), Modes of theorizing in strategic human resource management: Tests of universalistic, contingency, and configurational performance predictions, *The Academy of Management Journal 39*(4): 802–835.

16. D. Guest (1997), Human resource management and performance: A review and research agenda, *The International Journal of Human Resource Management 8*(3): 263–276.

17. D. A. Verreault and M. A. Hyland (2005), Evidence for increasing the focus on strategic risk in HRM audits, *Managerial Auditing Journal 20*(5): 524–543.

18. J. Purcell (1999), Best practice and best fit: Chimera or Cul-De-Sac, *Human Resource Management Journal 3*(9): 26–41.

19. J. Storey (1992), The part played by senior and middle line managers in the management of human resources, in *Developments in the management of human resources*, ed. J. Storey (Oxford, UK: Blackwell Publishers).

20. For the debates in strategic management between Ansoff and Mintzberg and between Porter and Prahlad on planning versus learning as the basis for strategy formulation and implementation, see H. I. Ansoff (1965), *Corporate strategy* (New York, NY: McGraw Hill); H. I. Ansoff (1991), Critique of Henry Mintzberg's the design school, *Strategic Management Journal 12*: 449–461; H. Mintzberg (1987, July–August), Crafting strategy, *Harvard Business Review 65*(4): 66–75; H. Mintzberg (1990a), The design school, reconsidering the basic premises of strategic management, *Strategic Management Journal 11*(3): 171–195; H. Mintzberg (1990b), Strategy formation: Schools of thought, in *Perspectives on strategic management*, ed. J. W. Fredrickson, pp. 105–236 (New York, NY: Harper Business); H. Mintzberg (1991), Learning & planning: Reply to Igor Ansoff, *Strategic Management Journal 12*: 463–466; G. Hamel and C. K. Prahalad (1989), Strategic intent, *Harvard Business Review 67*(3): 63–76; G. Hamel and C. K. Prahalad (1993), Strategy as stretch and leverage, *Harvard Business Review 71*(2): 75–84; M. E. Porter (1985), *Competitive advantage: Creating and sustaining superior performance* (New York, NY: The. Free Press); M. E. Porter (1991), Towards a dynamic theory of strategy, *Strategic Management Journal 12*(S): 95–117.

21. E. T. Penrose (1959), *The theory of the growth of the firm* (New York, NY: Wiley).

22. J. B. Barney (1991), Firm resources and sustained competitive advantage, *Journal of Management 17*(1): 99–120; B. Wernerfelt (1984), A resource-based theory of the firm, *Strategic Management Journal 5*(2): 171–180.

23. C. K. Prahalad and G. Hamel (1990, May–June), The core competence of the corporation, *Harvard Business Review 68*(3): 79–91.

24. D. Goss (1995), *Principles of human resource management* (London, UK: Routledge).

25. C. J. Fombrun, N. M. Tichy, and M. A. Devanna (1984), *Strategic human resource management* (New York, NY: John Wiley).

26. M. Beer, B. Spector, P. R. Lawrence, D. Q. Mills, and R. E. Walton (1984), *Managing human assets* (New York, NY: The Free Press).

27. D. Guest (1995), Human resource management, trade unions and industrials, in *Human resource management: A critical text*, ed. J. Storey (London, UK: Routledge).

28. C. Mabey, G. Salaman, and J. Storey (1998), *Human resource management: A strategic perspective* (Oxford, UK: Blackwell).

29. Delery and Doty, Modes of theorizing in strategic human resource management; P. M. Wright, B. B. Dunford, and S. A. Snell (2001), Human resources and the resource-based view of the firm, *Journal of Management* 27(6): 701–721.

30. P. F. Boxall (1995), Building the theory of comparative HRM, *Human Resource Management Journal* 5(5): 5–17; M. A. Huselid and B. E. Becker (1996), Methodological issues in cross-sectional and panel estimates of the human resource-firm, *Industrial Relations* 35: 400–422.

31. J. Pfeffer (1998), Seven practices of successful organizations, *California Management Review* 40(2): 96–124.

32. J. E. Delery and D. H. Doty (1996), Modes of theorizing in strategic human resource management: Tests of universalistic, contingency, and configurational performance predictions, *The Academy of Management Journal* 39: 802–835.

33. M. A. Huselid (1995), The impact of human resource management practices on turnover, productivity, and corporate financial performance, *Academy of Management Journal* 38(3): 635–672.

34. J. P. MacDuffie (1995), Human resource bundles and manufacturing performance: Organizational logic and flexible production systems in the world auto industry, *Industrial and Labor Relations Review* 48(2): 197–221.

35. B. E. Becker and B. Gerhart (1996), The impact of human resource management on organizational performance: Progress and prospects, *Academy of Management Journal* 39(4): 779–801.

36. P. M. Wright and G. C. McMahan (1992), Theoretical perspectives for strategic human resource management, *Journal of Management* 18(2): 295–320.

37. Arthur, The link between business strategy and industrial relations, 488–506; Miles and Snow, Designing strategic human resource systems, 36–52.

38. D. P. Lepak and S. A. Snell (1999), The human resource architecture: Toward a theory of human capital allocation and development, *Academy of Management Review* 24(1): 31–48.

39. J. Sonnenfeld and M. Peiperl (1988), Staffing policy as a strategic response: A typology of career systems, *Academy of Management Review* 13(4): 588–600.

40. Arthur, The link between business strategy and industrial relations, 488–506.

41. Miles and Snow, Designing strategic human resource systems, 36–52.

42. R. S. Schuler and S. E. Jackson (1987), Linking competitive strategies with human resource management practices, *Academy of Management Executive* 1(3): 207–219.

43. J. Purcell (1992), The impact of corporate strategy on human resource management, in *Human resource strategies*, ed. G. Salaman (London, UK: Sage Publications).

44. L. Dyer and G. W. Holder (1988), A strategic perspective of human resource management, in *Human resource management: Evolving roles and responsibilities*, ed. L. Dyer, pp. 1–45 (Washington, DC: Bureau of National Affairs).

45. P. Bamberger and I. Meshoulam (2001), *Human resource strategy: Formulation, implementation and impact* (Thousand Oaks, CA: Sage Publications).

46. M. A. Youndt and S. A. Snell (2004), Human resource configurations, intellectual capital and organizational performance, *Journal of Management XVI*(3): 337–360.

47. C. A. Lengnick-Hall and M. L. Lengnick-Hall (1988), Strategic human resource management: A review of the literature and a proposed typology, *Academy of Management Review 13*(3): 454.

48. Storey, The part played by senior and middle line managers.

49. S. E. Jackson and R. S. Schuler (2000), *Managing human resources: A partnership perspective* (Cincinnati, OH: South-Western College).

50. D. Ulrich (1997), *Human resource champions* (Boston, MA: Harvard Business School Press).

51. R. Anthony (1965), *Planning and control systems: A framework for analysis* (Boston, MA: Division of Research, Graduate School of Business Administration, Harvard University); M. A. Devanna, C. J. Fombrun, and N. M. Tichy (1981), Human resource management: A strategic approach, *Organizational Dynamics 9*(3): 51–67.

52. S. Ghoshal and C. Bartlett (1995), Building the entrepreneurial organization: The new organizational processes, new managerial tasks, *European Management Journal 13*(2): 139–155.

53. I. Björkman and A. Søderberg (2006), The HR function in large-scale mergers and acquisitions: The case study of Nordea, *Personnel Review 35*(6): 654–670.

54. P. Senge (1990), *The fifth discipline: The art and practice of learning organization* (London: Century Business).

55. C. D. Fisher and P. Dowling (1999), Support for an HR approach in Australia: The perspective of senior HR managers, *Asia Pacific Journal of Human Resources 37*(1): 1–19; J. Purcell (2001), The meaning of strategy in human resource management, in *Human resource management: A critical agenda*, ed. J. Storey, pp. 59–77 (London: Thomson Learning).

56. E. Filler and D. Ulrich (2014), Why chief human resources officers make great CEOs, *Harvard Business Review*, December, pp. 20–22.

57. J. Boudreau and P. Ramstad (2007), *Beyond HR: The new science of human capital* (Boston, MA: HBR Press Book).

58. PWC (2017), Workforce of the future: The competing forces shaping 2030, retrieved from www.pwc.com/people.

59. With inputs from https://www.colgatepalmolive.co.in.

Context of SHRM

Part I

THE FRAMEWORK OF STRATEGIC HUMAN RESOURCE MANAGEMENT
Chapter 1: Concept of Strategic Human Resource Management

Part II

CONTEXT OF SHRM
Chapter 2: Environment of SHRM
Chapter 3: Technology and HRM

Part III

STRATEGY FORMULATION
Chapter 4: Strategy Formulation and HRM
Chapter 5: Work Flow Analysis and Strategic Job Analysis

Part IV

STRATEGY IMPLEMENTATION
Chapter 6: Strategic Human Resource Planning and Staffing
Chapter 7: Strategic Training and Development
Chapter 8: Performance Management and Compensation
Chapter 9: Employee Relations, Engagement, and Termination

Part V

STRATEGY EVALUATION
Chapter 10: Strategic HR Evaluation

CHAPTER 2

Environment of SHRM

Chapter Overview

In this chapter, we shall learn about the nature and concept of business environment and its various components. Issues related to how the components of a business environment affect organizations and human resource (HR) policies and practices are discussed. Various trends and emerging dimensions of the business environment with relevance to human resource management (HRM) are also highlighted.

Learning Objectives

1. To understand the concept and relevance of business environment
2. To identify the features and components of business environment
3. To understand in detail the external and internal environmental forces and their implications for HRM
4. To identify the emerging trends in the environmental forces and how they are likely to alter the HR context

OPENING STORY

India's Economic Growth

The national portal of the Government of India mentions that India has emerged as the fastest growing major economy in the world, according to the International Monetary Fund (IMF). It is the world's sixth largest economy by nominal gross domestic product (GDP) and the third largest by purchasing power parity (PPP). The Indian economy grew at 7.7 per cent in the first three months of 2018. India has one of the fastest growing service sectors in the world, with an annual growth rate above 9 per cent since 2001.

Advantage India

Major strengths of India are as follows:

- World's largest democracy with 1.2 billion people
- Stable political environment and responsive administrative setup
- Well-established judiciary to enforce rule of law
- Land of abundant natural resources

- India's growth will start to outpace China's within 3–5 years and, hence, will become the fastest-growing major economy with 9–10 per cent growth over the next 20–25 years
- India is coming up with investor-friendly policies
- India's economy is likely to grow five-fold in the next 20 years
- It has a large pool of skilled manpower with a significant English-speaking population
- India has a demographic dividend—it is a young country with a median age of 30 years
- India has a huge untapped market potential
- Progressive simplification and rationalization of direct and indirect tax structures
- Robust banking and financial institutions

Success stories

Overseas investors are looking at India as an attractive investment destination owing to the prospects of high returns. A number of corporates and multinational corporations (MNCs) from all over the world have established businesses in India and have expanded over the years.

India has witnessed a number of success stories—both Indian and multinational firms have registered higher profits, increased turnover, and higher sales over the years. This has induced them to reinvest profits and inject fresh capital into their processes in order to reap the benefits of the Indian growth story. Global players have benefited from their operations in India and have made expansion plans for the country.

The reform process initiated during the early 1990s has begun to show its impact, and India is taking huge strides in the course of growth and development. However, recognizing that there is no room for complacency, Indian policy makers are moving ahead with due caution and at the same time, integrating India with the global economy. According to the World Bank, India's economic environment is promising and its growth prospects are strong.

Source: https://india.gov.in/india-business-portal.

BUSINESS ENVIRONMENT: AN INTRODUCTION

The opening story clearly indicates that India's environment has undergone a paradigm shift. The Indian economy is on a robust growth trajectory and boasts of a stable annual growth rate, rising foreign exchange reserves, and booming capital markets, among others. Narendra Modi, Prime Minister of India, has launched the *Make in India* initiative with an aim to boost the manufacturing sector of Indian economy. This initiative is expected to increase the purchasing power of an average Indian consumer, which would further boost demand and, hence, spur development, in addition to benefiting investors. Besides, the government has come up with the Digital India initiative, which focuses on three core components: creating digital infrastructure, delivering services digitally, and increasing digital literacy. The government of India has prioritized sustainability as the key aspect of India's development. To achieve this, the government aims to encourage education, skill development, digital connectivity, and entrepreneurship in a sustainable manner. All these initiatives will play a vital role in driving the Indian economy and will fuel positive changes in the environment of India.

An environment can be defined as anything that surrounds a system. Therefore, the business environment refers to all the forces that surround the business organization. These forces affect the decisions, strategies, processes, and performance of the business. While some of these factors or forces may have a direct influence over the business firm, others may operate indirectly. Thus, business environments may be defined as the total surroundings, which have a direct or indirect bearing on the functioning of a business.

Organizations do not exist in a vacuum. They exist in an environment. Business environment refers to the conditions, circumstances, and influences that affect the organization's ability to achieve its objectives. The term *business environment* connotes factors that are beyond the control of the business and which affect the functioning of a business enterprise. The environmental factors influence almost every aspect of a business. Every decision that an organization takes is affected by the changes taking place in its environment. Policies in different areas, such as marketing, HR, operations, or finance, are impacted by environmental forces. The success of every business depends on adapting itself to the environment within which it functions. Hence, it is important for an organization to scan and analyse the various components of the business environment.

The relationship between business organizations and their environment can be explained through the systems concept.

THE SYSTEMS CONCEPT

A system is a group of interacting, interrelated, or interdependent elements forming a complex whole. A system is a unit that consists of several sub-units or sub-systems and is itself part of a larger system. A system can be seen as a regularly interacting or interdependent group of items forming a unified whole. All parts or components of a system must be closely coordinated and properly integrated, so that the entire system is a unified whole and it can accomplish common objectives as planned.

Each system is a part of its environment, called 'suprasystem'. Environment includes all those factors external to a system that affect it and are uncontrollable to a large extent. There is constant interaction between a system and its environment. The impact of these environmental factors is so powerful on the functioning of a system that it is almost impossible for a system to exist without taking them into account.

A business enterprise is a system. The environment of a business system, for instance, includes all those economic, legal, technological, political, and social factors that influence its functioning but are outside its control and purview to a great extent. It consists of various sub-systems that operate in a balanced, coordinated, and integrated manner to make the whole as a business system. These sub-systems or sub-units are the various departments, divisions, and so on.

Every sub-system has its own set of systems—for example, the production sub-system comprises processes, supply chain, inventory management, quality control, and so on. A marketing sub-system may comprise the marketing sub-units responsible for product, price, sales, promotion, and distribution. Therefore, it can be said that the organization is a system comprising several sub-systems. This may also be called the **internal environment** of an organization.

The organization is itself part of a larger system. This is called the **external environment**. External environment refers to all the external forces within which an organization operates and may be classified as *micro environment* or *macro environment*. A micro environment is the smaller, direct, and immediate external environment. It includes customers, suppliers, lenders, creditors, and direct intermediaries. A macro environment is the larger, indirect, and distant external environment. It includes economic, political, legal, social, cultural, and technological environmental factors.

A business system involves 'input–output conversion' process. The essence of this process lies in the fact that a business system takes inputs (such as materials, equipment, human effort, technology, and information) from the external environment and transforms those (through organizational and managerial processes) to produce the final output (such as goods and services) for the external environment.

Figure 2.1 shows the systems concept as applied to business organizations.

Figure 2.1   The Systems Concept

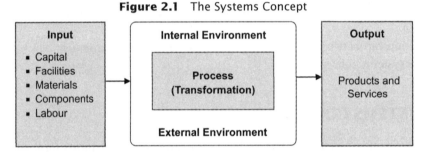

Systems theory has brought a new perspective for managers to interpret patterns and events in their organizations. In the past, managers typically focused only on their own functional area. The problem was that an organization would have departments that may be operating well by themselves but did not integrate well together. Departments or units were often working in isolation or many times at cross purposes due to lack of integration. Consequently, the organization suffered as a whole. An important element of the systems concept is the idea of 'synergy'. It means that the whole is greater than the sum of its parts. In organizational terms, synergy means that departments within an organization cooperate and interact more closely. Of late, managers have recognized the need for integrating the various departments or units of the organization.

BUSINESS ENVIRONMENT AND SHRM

There is a close and continuous interaction between an organization and its environment. This interaction helps a business firm in making policies and using its resources more efficiently and effectively. The business environment is multifaceted, complex, and dynamic in nature and has a far-reaching impact on the survival and growth of the business. Proper scanning, analysis, and understanding of the environment helps businesses determine the direction and goals for the enterprise, identify areas for growth and expansion, detect threats and opportunities, identify strengths and weaknesses, get a pulse of the market and industry, and lay down appropriate strategies.

Traditionally, HR practitioners and academics have neglected HRM's environmental context, preferring to concentrate on its administrative and technical aspects. This is consistent with criticisms of traditional personnel management orientation for its narrow focus on functional matters, such as routine hiring and firing issues. Despite the obsession with strategy, HRM theories have a fundamental weakness of having a myopic vision that fails to look beyond the boundary of the firm.

The business environment in reality impacts the HRM function on a daily basis. Strategic HRM (SHRM) policies and programmes operate in a complex environment comprising several elements both inside and outside the firm. A business environment has a bearing on the functioning of various HR activities. In order to function effectively, HR managers need to pay attention to rapid changes taking place in the organization's environment. These changes present challenges that require HR programmes to be designed to meet those challenges. In order to formulate HR strategies, managers need first to scan the environment and identify major threats and opportunities.

As discussed in the previous chapter, SHRM is largely concerned with 'integration' or 'fit'. SHRM is concerned with establishing two types of fit, namely vertical and horizontal fit. Vertical fit deals with the integration of HRM with the strategic management process (which takes into account environmental impact on strategy). Horizontal fit is concerned with ensuring integration at the same level. This involves two types of fit—internal and external fit. Internal fit involves integration between the various HRM sub-functions or sub-systems—for example, staffing, compensation, and training. External fit is concerned with the integration between HRM and other functional areas—for example, marketing, finance, and operations. This supports the idea of synergy within a system.

It is important to understand the components of the environment and the impact they have on HR strategies and policies.

EXTERNAL ENVIRONMENTAL FACTORS

The external environment refers to all the external forces within which an organization operates and may be classified as a *macro environment* and *micro environment*. A macro environment is the larger, indirect, and distant external environment. It includes economic, political, legal, social, cultural, and technological environmental factors. These factors affect an organization indirectly. For instance, a change in government may affect an organization indirectly through new policies. A micro environment is the smaller, direct, and immediate external environment. It includes customers, suppliers, lenders, creditors, and direct intermediaries. Micro environmental factors affect an organization directly. For instance, changes in a competitor's employee compensation strategy are likely to affect an organization directly.

Macro environment

Macro environmental factors typically include economic, political, legal, social, cultural, and technological environmental factors. In this section, we shall discuss the major components of the macro environment and their implications for HR strategies and policies.

Economic Environment

The economic environment refers to all those components of the environment that signify the nature of the economy and the current stage of advancement of the economy. These may include the economic system, economic structure, economic indicators, economic growth, standard of living, economic policies, economic cycles, demand and supply, markets for goods, capital market, money market, financial market, industrial structure, trading mechanisms, export–import scenario, and so on.

Three important dimensions of an economic environment need to be highlighted:

- Economic Structures
- Economic Systems
- Economic Policies

Each of these dimensions is discussed in detail below.

Economic Structures

The economic structure refers to the economic conditions of a nation signified by a set of economic factors that include gross domestic product (GDP), pace of economic growth, per capita income, markets for goods and services, availability of capital, foreign exchange reserve, growth of foreign trade, strength of capital market, and so on. It is a term that describes the changing balance of output, trade, income, and employment in different sectors of the economy—ranging from primary (farming, fishing, mining, and so on) to secondary (manufacturing and construction industries), to tertiary and quaternary sectors (tourism, banking, software, and so on). It defines the level of advancement of an economy. It is the classification of a country according to the proportion of output produced by the primary, secondary, and tertiary sectors.

Economic structure has been traditionally categorized in terms of developed, developing, and less developed or underdeveloped economies. However, these classifications are only indicative in nature and do not imply any true categorization. According to the United Nations (UN), there is no established convention for the designations of 'developed' and 'developing' countries. It notes:

> *The designations 'developed' and 'developing' are intended for statistical convenience and do not necessarily express a judgment about the stage reached by a particular country or area in the development process.*[1]

The IMF too notes that the development concept needs defining, but unfortunately no simple definition exists. In the *New Palgrave: A Dictionary of Economics* overview article on 'development economics', Clive Bell used 'pioneers' and 'latecomers' as an organizing framework, given that newly independent countries started out poor in a world in which there were already rich countries. Economic development was seen as a process where latecomers catch up with pioneers.[2]

While classification schemes are convenient for analysis and communication, each one comes with a set of limitations, biases, and cultural overtones. This could suggest that a developing–developed country dichotomy is too restrictive and that a classification system that goes beyond this dichotomy could better capture the diversity in development status across countries. There is no official guideline regarding which country may be considered developed. While some countries, such as the United States, Canada, and Japan, are clearly classified as developed, in the case of countries such as Malaysia and Russia, it may not be appropriate to fit them into the construction of a dichotomous classification framework.

A classification system organizing countries based on their level of development is termed as *development taxonomy* and the associated criterion or parameter is called the *development threshold*. Based on the generally agreed taxonomies, developed countries are also called advanced countries, industrialized countries, more developed countries (MDCs), global north countries, first world countries, and post-industrial countries. The terms used for developing countries are less developed countries (LDCs) or non-industrialized nations.

The IMF identifies 37 advanced economies and all others are considered 'emerging market and developing economies'. It uses a flexible classification system that considers (*a*) per capita income level, (*b*) export diversification (so oil exporters that have high per capita GDP would not make it to the list of advanced economies because around 70 per cent of their exports are oil), and (*c*) degree of integration into the global financial system.[3]

The UN has no formal definition of developed or developing countries, but still uses the term for monitoring purposes and classifies as many as 159 countries as developing. Under the UN's current classification, all of Europe and Northern America, along with Japan, Australia, and New Zealand, are classified as developed regions, whereas all other regions are developing. The UN maintains a list of the least developed countries, which are defined by gross national income (GNI) per capita as well as measures of human capital and economic vulnerability. The country classification system of the United Nations Development Programme (UNDP) is built around the human development index (HDI), which was launched together with the *Human Development Report (HDR)* in 1990.[4]

The Organization for Economic Cooperation and Development (OECD), which is an international economic organization of 34 countries founded in 1961 to stimulate economic progress and world trade, considers its members as the 'developed countries club'.[5]

The World Bank uses GNI per capita as an indicator to classify countries. Each year on 1 July, the World Bank revises the analytical classification of the world's economies based on estimates of GNI per capita for the previous year. The updated GNI per capita estimates are also used as input to the World Bank's operational classification of economies that determines lending eligibility. The World Bank identifies 74 countries as high-income countries. These have been generally referred to as the developed world. The low- and middle-income groups taken together are referred to as the developing world.

The United States, Canada, Japan, Australia, New Zealand, and most countries in northern and western Europe are considered developed, along with Hong Kong, Singapore, and South Korea. In terms of international trade statistics, Israel is also treated as a developed country. Some of the high-income countries in the World Bank's classification that are neither 'advanced' nor 'developed' include the Bahamas, Croatia, Kuwait, Latvia, Oman, and Saudi Arabia.

Various other classifications and categorizations of countries have been developed by leading world bodies. A category of countries called emerging and developing economies are identified by the IMF on the basis of economic outlook. Newly industrialized countries (NICs) are nations with economies more advanced and developed than those in the developing world but not yet with all signs of a developed country. NIC is a category between developed and developing countries, and it includes Brazil, China, India, Malaysia, Mexico, the Philippines, South Africa, Thailand, and Turkey. Big emerging market (BEM) economies are Argentina, Brazil, China, Egypt, India, Indonesia, Mexico, Poland, Russia, South Africa, South Korea, and Turkey. BRIC refers to the combination of Brazil, Russia, India, and China. The acronym was first coined in 2001 and prominently used in a thesis of the Goldman Sachs investment bank. The economies of the BRIC nations are rapidly developing and by 2050 are expected to eclipse most of the current richest countries of the world. Usually, any country that is neither a developed country nor a failed state is classified as a developing country.

LDCs are also referred to as underdeveloped countries sometimes. Underdeveloped countries are least income countries. To moderate the euphemistic aspect of the word 'underdeveloped', international organizations have started to use the term *less economically developed country* (LEDC) for the poorest nations. That is, LEDCs are the poorest subset of LDCs. This also moderates the wrong tendency to believe that the standard of living in the entire developing world is the same. A number of poor countries have experienced prolonged periods of economic decline. Such countries are classified as least developed countries.

Countries with an inconsistent record of development, such as most countries in Africa, Central America, and the Caribbean (except Jamaica) and a few countries from Southeast Asia (Laos and Cambodia), fall into this category. Countries with long-term civil war or large-scale breakdown of rule of law or countries classified as failed states (such as Afghanistan, Haiti, Somalia, Rwanda, Myanmar, and Vietnam) or non-development-oriented rules (such as Madagascar, Nepal, and Niger) also fall into this classification. They sometimes also have low resources and low economic development.

International Development Association (IDA) is the part of the World Bank that helps the world's poorest countries. LEDCs are IDA-eligible countries—that is, countries that have a per capita income of less than $1,195 and lack the financial ability to borrow from the World Bank. IDA loans are deeply concessional, interest-free loans and grants for programmes aimed at boosting economic growth and improving living conditions. Blend countries are eligible for IDA loans because of their low per capita incomes but are also eligible for International Bank for Reconstruction and Development (IBRD) loans because they are financially creditworthy.[6]

It is important to note that the 2016 edition of world development indicators (WDIs) by the World Bank states that the classifications are becoming less relevant, and with the focus of the sustainable development goals (SDGs) for the whole world, we should start phasing out the terms *developed* or *developing* from publications and databases. Therefore, in WDI 2016, there is no longer a distinction between developing countries (defined in previous editions as low- and middle-income countries) and developed countries (previously, high-income countries). Regional groupings (such as East Asia) are now based on geographical coverage rather than a subset of countries that were previously referred to as developing.

The World Bank states that the terms *developed* and *developing* are tricky and should be used cautiously. The usage of the terms can be made for statistical convenience only, making it clear that one is not judging the development status of any country. Further, it is interesting to note that economies are changing dramatically; thus, any classification is only temporary and subject to limitations.[7]

In this book too, any allusion to a country as developed or developing is only indicative and does not suggest any judgement on the economic status of a country.

Parameters to Map Economic Structures

In the absence of a methodology or consensus regarding the level of development, different institutions have developed different parameters. A number of generally accepted indicators have been used by world bodies to study economic structures and the 'relative' level of development of countries. Some of these indices or parameters are:

- **GNI per Capita**   As discussed, until now, developed economies were considered to be those that have high income per capita whereas developing economies were grouped in the low- to middle-income bracket. New thresholds to define income levels are determined at the start of the World Bank's fiscal year in July. For the 2019 fiscal year, low-income economies are defined as those with a GNI per capita of $995 or less in 2017; lower middle-income economies are those with a GNI per capita between $996 and $3,895; upper middle-income economies are those with a GNI per capita between $3,896 and $12,055; and high-income economies are those with a GNI per capita of $12,056 or more. The classification includes all World Bank members, plus all other economies with populations of more than 30,000. According to the World Bank, the term *country*, used interchangeably with *economy*, does not imply political independence but refers to any territory for which authorities report separate social or economic statistics. The estimates are calculated using the *World Bank Atlas Method.*[8]

  According to the UN, some high-income group (HIG) countries may also be developing countries. For instance, despite being HIGs, the OPEC countries in the Middle East depend overwhelmingly on oil production and export (notably Saudi Arabia). In many cases, per capita income is also skewed. Thus, a high-income country may be classified as either developed or developing.

- **GDP**   Another indicator of economic structure development is GDP. Developed economies have higher GDP as compared to developing countries. However, when using GDP as an indicator of developed status, one must take into account how some countries have achieved a (usually temporarily) high GDP through natural resource exploitation without developing industries or services necessary for development. For instance, Nauru, which is considered the world's smallest island nation in the Central Pacific, has recorded an exceptionally high

GDP, though it relies mainly on phosphate extraction. Likewise, the Bahamas, Barbados, Antigua, and Barbuda depend overwhelmingly on tourism. These countries, although rich, cannot be called developed in the real sense. At the same time, some countries have a high GDP, yet do not qualify as developed countries on account of high population, which tends to lower their per capita income. For instance, India is among the top 10 countries by nominal GDP; however, the per capita income of India (that is, the GDP/population) is quite low.

- *HDI*   HDI is a composite statistic used to rank countries by the level of 'human development' by the UNDP. The index was developed in 1990 by Pakistani economist Mahbub ul Haq and Indian economist Amartya Sen. It is a composite index of three indices measuring countries' achievements in longevity, education, and income. The index rating ranges from 0 to 1. Longevity is measured by life expectancy at birth. For education, a proxy is constructed by combining measures of actual and expected years of schooling. The income measure used in the HDI is GNI per capita, with local currency estimates converted into equivalent US dollars using PPP. Developed economies have a high HDI.

  In the *HDR of 1990,* countries were divided into low, medium, and high human development countries using threshold values 0.5 and 0.8. In the *HDR of 2009*, a fourth category—very high human development—was introduced with a threshold value of 0.9. While there is a strong correlation between high HDI and prosperity of the economy, the UN points out that the HDI accounts for more than income. A few examples are Italy and the United States. Despite a relatively large difference in GDP per capita, both countries rank roughly same in terms of HDI. Developing countries are reported to have an inconsistently varying HDI score and per capita income, but are in a phase of economic development.

- *Dominant Service Sector*   Developed economies are usually those where the tertiary (services) and quaternary sectors dominate. The quaternary sector of the economy is an extension of the three-sector theory (primary–agricultural, secondary–manufacturing, and tertiary–service) of industrial evolution. It principally concerns intellectual services—information generation, information sharing, consultation, education, research, and development. Countries with advanced economic structures exhibit advances in the development of the service and quaternary sector.

- *High Level of Industrialization*   Another indicator of economic structure is the level of industrialization. For a country's development, its industrial base must be strong. Industrialization is not only a major value-producing activity but also generates employment. Developing countries have a developing industrial base. These countries have not achieved a significant degree of industrialization relative to their populations and, thus, have in most cases, a medium to low standard of living. However, the term 'industrialized country' may sometimes be ambiguous, as industrialization is an ongoing process that is hard to define and measure.

- *Democracy and Welfare Capitalism*   Developed nations are characterized by national democracy and industrial democracy. The economically advanced or developed nations are characterized by welfare capitalism. This type of capitalism seeks to ensure economic security, independence, stability, and opportunity.

- *Market Orientation*   Market orientation and privatization are also seen as hallmarks of development of the economic structure. The market-oriented economies of the mainly democratic nations in the OECD also fall under developed countries, although some OECD countries are not HIGs.
- *Stock Market Development*   Stock market development is another indicator of the robustness of any country's economic structure. The Financial Times–London Stock Exchange (FTSE) group classifies countries as advanced based on stock markets. FTSE reviews the quality of market criteria for all stock markets included in the FTSE index on the basis of the ease, cost, and security of underlying investment transactions.

Table 2.1 presents India's relative ranking in terms of GDP, GDP per capita, and HDI based on recent available data.

Table 2.1   India's Relative Rank in Economic Indices

Rank	GDP (Nominal) Rankings	(US $)	GDP (Nominal) Per capita Rankings	(US $)	Human Development Index Rankings	HDI Index
1.	United States	19,390,604	Luxembourg	104,103	Norway	0.944
	European Union	17,277,698	Macau	80,893		
2.	China	12,237,700	Switzerland	80,190	Australia	0.935
3.	Japan	4,872,137	Norway	74,505	Swizerland	0.930
4.	Germany	3,677,439	Iceland	70,057	Denmark	0.923
5.	United Kingdom	2,622,434	Ireland	69,331	Netherlands	0.922
6.	*India*	2,597,491	Qatar	63,506	Germany	0.916
7.	France	2,582,501	United States	59,532	Ireland	0.916
8.	Brazil	2,055,506	Singapore	57,714	US	0.915
9.	Italy	1,934,798	Denmark	56,308	Canada	0.913
10.	Canada	1,653,043	Australia	53,800	New Zealand	0.913
-	-	-	*India* (138)	1940	*India* (130)	0.609

Sources: The World Bank, *World Development Indicators, 2017,* www.worldbank.org; United Nations Development Programme, *Human Development Report 2015—Sustaining Human Progress: Reducing Vulnerabilities and Building Resilience,* retrieved from hdr.undp.org/en/content/human-development-index-hdi.

Note: Several economies not considered to be sovereign states (that is, non-sovereign entities, former countries, dependent territories, or special groupings) are not ranked but are listed for comparison. For instance, Macau (considered as Special Administrative Region of the People's Republic of China) ranks second in terms of GDP (nominal) per capita.

Economic Systems

An economic system is the system of production, distribution, and consumption of goods and services of an economy. An economic system can be defined as a set of methods and standards by which a society decides and organizes the allocation of limited economic resources to satisfy unlimited human wants. The economic system is composed of people and institutions, including their relationships to productive resources, such as through the convention of property. Economic systems are the means through which countries and governments distribute resources and trade goods and services. They are used to control the factors of production, including labour, capital, entrepreneurs, physical resources, and information resources.

Economic systems fall into one of three categories: capitalist (market) economy, socialist (command) economy, and mixed economy:

- *Capitalist (Free-Market) Economy*   Capitalist economies are also called 'laissez-faire' or free-market economies. It is also called a 'hands off' system due to the government's non-interference in the marketplace. In a free-market economy, national and state governments play a minor role. Instead, consumers and their buying decisions drive the economy. The absence of central control and planning is one of the major features of this economic system. The role of the government in a market economy is to simply ensure that the market is stable enough to carry out its economic activities properly. It provides access to valuable goods and services, rewards initiative, generates wealth, and creates a higher standard of living. Typical examples of a free-market economy are the United States, Canada, and countries in the European Union (EU).

- *Socialist (Planned) Economy*   Command economy or socialist economy is a government-controlled planned economy. In a government-regulated economy, the market plays little to no role in production decisions. This kind of system is also called the 'hands on' system due to the government's hands in the affairs of the economy. A planned economy is also sometimes called a command economy. All major decisions related to the production, distribution, commodity, and service prices are made by the government. All resources are publicly owned with the intent of minimizing inequalities of wealth, among other social objectives. It helps establish an egalitarian society with lesser gap between haves and have nots. Some examples of a planned economy are the erstwhile USSR, China, Yugoslavia, Vietnam, Cuba, and North Korea.

  It is important to note that the terms 'socialism' and 'communism' are often used interchangeably. There exists a difference between the two. Socialism generally refers to an economic system, while communism generally refers to both an economic and a political system. As an economic system, socialism seeks to manage the economy through deliberate and collective social control. Communism, however, seeks to manage both the economy and the society by ensuring that property is owned collectively, and that control over the distribution of property is centralized in order to achieve both classlessness and statelessness.

- *Mixed Economy*   A mixed economic system combines features of the market and command economy. Many economic decisions are made in the market by individuals. However, the government also plays a role in the allocation and distribution of resources. In a mixed economy, there is flexibility in some areas and government control in others. Mixed economies include both capitalist and socialist economic policies and often arise in societies that seek to balance a wide range of political and economic views, such as India and Russia, to some extent. At the time of independence, India was influenced by socialist ideologies. However, it has gradually adopted certain free-market principles in order to accelerate economic growth.

Economic Policies

Economic policy refers to the actions taken by governments for the benefit of the economy. It covers the systems for setting levels of taxation, government budgets, money supply, interest rates, national ownership, international trade, and related areas of economic activity. All business activities and operations are directly influenced by the economic policies framed by the government from time to time. The common types of economic policies are as follows:

- *Industrial Policy* The industrial policy of a country is its official strategic effort to encourage the development and growth of the industrial/manufacturing sector as well as other sectors of the economy.
- *Fiscal Policy* It includes government policy with respect to budgeting, public expenditure, taxation, and public debt. Through these policies, the government tries to regulate the economy. For instance, taxes are a fiscal policy tool because changes in taxes affect the consumer's income, and changes in consumption lead to changes in real GDP. Likewise, public expenditure can have a direct effect on the level of economic activity. A reduction in public spending can reduce the level of economic activity through the reverse operation of the expenditure multiplier. By adjusting government spending, the government can influence economic output. Public debt is a sound fiscal weapon to fight against inflation and deflation. Fiscal policy helps to stabilize the economy.
- *Monetary Policy* Monetary policy is the process wherein the government of a country, through the monetary authority (generally, a central bank), controls the supply of money in the economy with its control over interest rates to maintain price stability and achieve high economic growth. It includes all the activities and interventions that aim for the smooth supply of credit to the business and give a boost to the trade and industry. Central banks use a number of tools to shape monetary policy. The instruments of monetary policy are of two types: quantitative tools (for example, bank rate policy, open market operations, and reserve ratios) and qualitative or selective tools. They are meant to regulate the overall level of credit in the economy through commercial banks.[9]
- *International Trade Policy* Trade policy is a set of rules and regulations that are intended to change international trade flows, particularly imports and exports. Trade policy defines standards, goals, rules, and regulations that pertain to trade relations between countries. A country's trade policy includes the taxes imposed on import and export, inspection regulations, and tariffs and quotas. It aims at increasing exports and bridging the gap between export and import. Trade policies can assume varying dimensions and scope, depending on the number of parties involved in the policies, namely national trade policy (for citizens), bilateral trade policy (to regulate trade between two nations), and international trade policy (global trading policies).

- ***Foreign Investment Policy***   Recently, there is a growing trend towards globalization, whereby large multinational firms often have investments in a variety of countries. Many see foreign investment in a country as a positive sign and as a source for future economic growth. A foreign investment policy aims at regulating the inflow of foreign investment in various sectors for speeding up industrial development and taking advantage of modern technology. The foreign investment policy lays down the rules for both direct and indirect investment. Today's era of globalization depends on sound trade policies to reflect market changes, establish free and fair trade practices, and expand the possibilities for booming international trade.

Implications of Economic Environment for HRM

The economic structure of a country affects the HRM policies of business organizations. Economic conditions are directly related with labour market and labour supply, which subsequently affect the recruitment and selection patterns of the organizations. Per capita income and GDP influence the minimum wage rate, which is part of the compensation and benefits. It also has an impact on the way companies hire and the bargaining power that they exercise vis-à-vis the labour market. Labour cost tends to be higher in developed countries on account of labour being skilled and educated. The quality of labour available differs from country to country depending on the level of economic development. HRM practices are, thus, inextricably linked with the relative economic prosperity of the country.

Economic systems also influence HRM strategies and HRM approach. In free-market economies, companies have far greater freedom in terms of HRM decision-making. On the other hand, in restrictive and planned economies, HRM policy-making is largely governed by the state, with corporations having little or no control over HR decisions. The level of deregulation and decentralization at the workplace is dependent on the overall freedom in the economic environment of a country. Industrial democracy is a product of national democracy.

Economic forces impinge on demand for labour and the types of labour required. They determine how people are recruited, trained, or retrained. However, with hypercompetitive conditions in some markets, the pressure is focused on competing firms to retain labour and reskill it. Organizations have to adjust their HR policies and practices accordingly. The stage of advancement of the economic environment of a country determines the primary demand for goods and services. This primary demand affects derived demand for labour. Derived demand is the demand for a factor of production or intermediate good that occurs as a result of the demand for another intermediate or final good. Therefore, the demand for labour or HR is a derived demand from the demand for goods and services.

Economic policies and economic trends like inflation and deflation affect the distribution of income and wealth. These factors influence the wage and salary levels of an organization. They also impact the amount of money and resources companies commit for recruitment, training, and other HR needs. For instance, primary demand for goods and services in the market affects the derived demand for labour. Therefore, when markets are facing an economic boom, it tends to foster investment and spending, thereby leading to more demand for labour. Thus, economic conditions have a profound impact on HR budget. Economic conditions influence the financial health of the organization.

Due to globalization and increased cross-border trading, there is greater movement of labour today. One consequence is that skilled professional workers can work anywhere and are not geographically constrained, resulting in firms having to adjust their recruitment and HR policies to this market situation. The mobility and migration of labour depends on a country's integration with the rest of the world. Brain drain often takes place from developing to developed countries. For instance, it is common in India for engineering and IT professionals to move to Western countries, mainly the United States, in search of jobs. There are also significant changes in the structure of the economy, with increased activity in the service sector today. This has implications for education and training policy generally and for the employment prospects of existing and potential workers. Service workers have different training requirements and development needs.

Economic instability impacts HRM practices adversely. In times of instability or crisis, companies are forced to cut down their HR expenditure. People do not have as much money to spend in an economic downturn and tend to be much more selective in what they buy or services they use. This means some industries, such as those producing luxury items or non-essential services, sell less and may even have to lay off some staff. They often start maintaining basic in-house training programmes instead of paying external trainers. Sometimes, they are even forced to cut down their training and other HR expenditures, such as employee incentives and benefits.

Politico-legal Environment

Politico-legal environmental factors refer to a country's political system, political structure, type of government, governmental activities and ideology, political conditions, role and strength of opposition parties, legal structure and systems, nature of law, role of political institutions, and so on. Political and economic environments are closely interlinked. For instance, an increase or decrease in tax, though an economic policy, could be an example of a political element. Different governments follow different ideologies and this influences their economic policy as well. The political environment is perhaps among the least predictable elements in the business environment. A cyclical political environment develops, as democratic governments have to pursue re-election every few years. Pressure groups tend to change government policies. Government priorities and need for political expediency change from time to time.

Two important and interlinked dimensions of the politico-legal environment need discussion in this context:

- **Political system and nature of polity**   It refers to the nature of politics, type of government and governance, government ideologies and philosophy, role of opposition, party system, government mechanism, and institutions, and so on.
- **Types of laws and legal framework**   It refers to the legal structure and systems, nature of law, role of executive, legislature, judiciary, and so on.

Each of these components is discussed in detail below.

Political system and nature of polity

Each society must have a political system in order to maintain law and order and a systematic and recognized procedure for allocating a nation's resources. Decisions have to be made about the duties and responsibilities of citizens and also about the rights and privileges. If the society is to be orderly, people must obey the rules that are made. The political institution determines and enforces the laws and punishes those who disobey them. As societies become developed and more complex, political systems will also develop. Shmuel N. Eisenstadt has classified the functions of a political system as legislative, decision-making, and administrative.[10] Almond and Coleman have described that the main function of a political system is to maintain the integration of society by determining norms.[11]

In all modern states, governmental functions have greatly expanded with the emergence of the government as an active force in guiding social and economic development. In countries with a command economy, the government has a vast range of responsibilities for many types of economic behaviours. In these countries, the government owns or regulates businesses and industries. Even in free-market economies such as the United States some level of government regulation, for example, the use of credit controls to prevent economic fluctuations, is now accepted with relatively little questioning.

Scholars and researchers have identified various types of political systems. *Anarchy* refers to the complete lack of a political system. In fact, anarchy, being a state of disorder, cannot be considered a true political system. *Authoritarian* governments are characterized by absolute or blind obedience to formal authority, as against individual freedom. Dictatorships are examples of authoritarianism. *Totalitarianism* is the most extreme form of authoritarianism because it controls all aspects of life. Mussolini's Italy, Hitler's Nazi Germany, and Stalin's Soviet Union are often quoted as examples of totalitarian states. *Oligarchy* is a form of government in which there is a 'rule by a few'. It is a form of power structure in which power effectively rests with a small number of people by virtue of royalty, wealth, family ties, corporate, religious, or military control. Privately owned, Russia-based MNCs (including producers of petroleum, natural gas, and metal) have, in the view of some analysts, led to the rise of Russian oligarchs at one point.

Monarchy is a government controlled by a king or queen, determined by a predisposed line of sovereignty. There are two main types of monarchy that differ based on the level of power held by the individual or family currently in power. Absolute monarchy exists when the monarch has no or few legal limitations in political matters. An absolute monarchy works like a dictatorship in that the king has complete rule over his country. Constitutional monarchies, which are more common, exist when the monarch retains a distinctive legal and ceremonial role but exercises limited political power. The most familiar example of a monarchy is the constitutional monarchy that exists in the United Kingdom.

Democracy is a form of government in which the citizens create and vote for laws directly or indirectly via representatives. In its broadest sense, democracy is a way of life in which an individual feels free to act within accepted boundaries of norms and equal in terms of his/her rights. People participate in the government through the representatives they elect.[12] Most countries today have a democratic system.

Democracy is classified into direct or indirect democracy. In direct democracy, all eligible citizens have direct and active participation in political decision-making. Athenian democracy is unique to direct democracy. Within modern-day representative governments, certain electoral tools such as referendums, citizens' initiatives, and recall elections are referred to as forms of direct democracy. For instance, citizens of the United Kingdom decide to leave the EU through a referendum that was held on 23 June 2016. In most modern democracies, citizens remain the sovereign power but political power is exercised indirectly through elected representatives. This is called indirect or representative democracy. If the head of state is also democratically elected, it is called a democratic republic. The most common mechanisms involve elections of the representatives through adult suffrage.

The most prevalent system is the parliamentary system. In this type of system, as in India, the nation is composed of small units or states. Each unit elects members of parliament from a list of candidates. After elections, the party with the majority of members forms the government and chooses the prime minister and cabinet. In a system like that of the United States, members of the legislature hold their office for a certain fixed term. After elections, a majority party is determined, which forms the government. Another common system involves a legislature composed of one party. Such systems are common in communist nations, such as the erstwhile USSR and China.

Nearly all modern states today provide for some distribution of governmental authority on a territorial basis due to administrative necessity. Systems in which the grant of power may be exercised at the will of the central government are termed unitary systems. Systems in which a balance is established between two autonomous sets of governments, one national and the other provincial or state, are termed federal. A great majority of all the world's nation-states are unitary systems, including Bulgaria, France, the Netherlands, Japan, Poland, Romania, the Scandinavian countries, Spain, and many of the Latin American and African countries. Of the eight largest countries in the world by area, seven—Russia, Canada, the United States, Brazil, Australia, India, and Argentina—are organized on a federal basis (China, the third largest, is, however, a unitary state).

Business organizations need to approach the study of governmental systems with great caution. Often political systems having the same kind of legal arrangements and using the same type of governmental machinery may function very differently. For instance, India and the United Kingdom are both parliamentary democracies but there are fundamental differences between the two systems in terms of the constitution, functioning of the government, customs, traditions, and practices. All these differences make the two countries disparate in terms of chalking out business strategies by any corporation.

At the same time, business organizations confront an ever-changing and evolving political environment. In many parts of the world, there have been continuing experiments with new constitutions and political structures. The 20th century witnessed remarkable changes in political systems and structures. The paradigm shifts that occurred in the world's political systems during this period have been remarkable. Monolithic empires disintegrated, small nation-states emerged, several wars transformed the international order, new ideologies emerged, democracy swept the world, and new political systems emerged. The rise of new political order and the involvement of citizens in governmental activity led to innumerable social, economic, and technical developments. Even in the 21st century, transformations in political systems continue, the most noticeable one being what is called the Arab spring.

Types of laws and legal framework

Law is a body of rules recognized and maintained by the state to regulate human behaviour and conduct. It is a set of rules determined and enforced by a sovereign political authority. Law can be described as a system of rules and regulations that a society recognizes as binding on its citizens and violation of which attracts punitive action. Law is not only important for an orderly social life but also essential for the very existence of a society. Law may be defined as a set of rules that regulates human conduct. It is created and maintained by the state. Law is seen as the manifestation of the concept of sovereignty; it is a preserver of the social order and an embodiment of a nation's ideals.

The important functions of law are to maintain order and establish standards and norms of behaviour. It is also meant to protect civil liberties and rights and provides a framework to resolve disputes and deliver justice. Laws provide equality and uniformity in the system. Because laws apply equally to all citizens, they help maintain impartiality and an egalitarian order.

The most important feature of a good law is that it should apply equally and uniformly to all citizens, irrespective of any criteria. Furthermore, law should be easily comprehensible and understood by everyone. It should be practical yet simple. At the same time, it should be enforceable and easy to put into effect. Laws should be stable yet progressive. In India, the parliament has the power to amend laws to make them relevant in the changing times by following a prescribed procedure, as laid down in the constitution.

The law of any country is derived from various sources. Some of these sources may be the history and background of a country, national conventions and practices, international conventions, treaties, agreements, judicial decisions and orders, laws of other nations, and religious scriptures. Laws can also be the result of public activism. For instance, the Right to Information (RTI) Act in India, which came into effect from 2005, is believed to be the outcome of years of struggle and public activism to infuse transparency in the public system.

The Institutions of Politico-legal System

In a democratic political setup, there are three institutions, which together constitute the total political environment: (*a*) the legislature, (*b*) the executive, and (*c*) the judiciary.

- **Legislature**   The characteristic function of all legislatures is the making of law. In most systems, however, legislatures also have other tasks, such as selection of the government, criticism and keeping a check on the government, supervision of administration, impeachment of executive and judicial officials, and determination of election procedures. In most countries, legislatures usually consist of members chosen by the people of the country. Legislatures differ strikingly in their size, the procedures they employ, and legislative power. In size, the British House of Commons, with more than 600 members, is among the largest legislative bodies. Bicameral legislatures are common in many countries, particularly those with a federal system of government, such as India. Unicameral legislatures are typical in those with a unitary system of government, such as New Zealand and Denmark.

The parliament is the supreme legislative body of the Republic of India. Parliament is a bicameral body with two houses: the Rajya Sabha (council of states) and the Lok Sabha (house of the people). The president, in his role as the head of legislature, has full power to summon or prorogue either house of Parliament. The president exercises these powers upon the advice of the prime minister and his council of ministers.

- **Executive**   Generally speaking, the executive arm of the government executes the laws created by the legislature. Executives are government officials who participate in the determination and direction of government policy. They include heads of state, government leaders, and cabinet members and ministers. In presidential systems, such as in the United States, the president is both the political head of the government and the ceremonial head of state. In parliamentary systems, such as in the United Kingdom or India, the prime minister is the political head, while a monarch (in the United Kingdom) or elected president (in India) serves as the head of state. In mixed presidential–parliamentary systems, such as France, the president serves as head of state but also wields important political powers.

- **Judiciary**   Similar to legislators and executives, courts are major entities in the legal process. Judicial bodies promulgate rules of behaviour based on laws. Usually there are two judicial hierarchies, one dealing with civil and the other with criminal cases, each with a large number of local courts and one apex court at the national level. This is the pattern of judicial organization in India and the United Kingdom. In India, the constitution provides for a single integrated judicial system with the Supreme Court at the apex, high courts at the middle (state) level, and district courts at the local level. Reflecting the federal organization of its government, the United States also has two court systems: one set of national courts and 50 sets of state courts. In some countries, such as France, there is a double hierarchy, one that handles all civil and criminal cases and another that deals with administrative cases. In contrast, Germany, which is also federal in governmental organization, possesses only a single integrated court system.

Implications of Politico-legal Environment for HRM

The political environment can impact business organizations in many ways. This includes the political system, the government policies, and attitude towards the business community. All these aspects have a bearing on the strategies adopted by the business firms. The ideology of the political parties, mainly the ruling party, also influences business organizations and their operations. One may recall that the Coca-Cola Corporation has operated as a branch in India since the early 1950s. It had to wind up operations in the late 1970s due to strict foreign regulations in India. Coca-Cola was directed to continue its operations on the condition that its branch converted into an Indian company with 40 per cent foreign equity. On closer examination, it was clear that this directive was a tool to control the company.

Governments can alter their rules and regulations. This could, in turn, have an effect on business. The stability of the government also influences business and related activities to a great extent. It sends a signal of strength and confidence to various interest groups and investors. Lack of political stability in a country affects business operations. Political factors have the power to change results. Different aspects of government policy can affect businesses differently. Companies should be ready to deal with the implications of politics on their own functioning. Managers need to understand how different legislations can affect their activities. Therefore, business organizations must have the acumen to perceive the nature of political systems and likely changes carefully.

Organizations need to scan and analyse the political environment on a regular basis and design appropriate strategies, policies, and practices to suit the political system. An ongoing political development across the globe is large-scale privatization and globalization. Corporations need to address the legal requirements arising out of the impact of privatization on employment legislation or health and safety law. There is increasingly active government involvement in labour markets. This too provides both opportunities and threats to organizations as employers.

The legal framework of a country has a direct impact on HRM practices. The political and legal environment of a country gives birth to HRM practices. Each of the functions performed in the management of human resources right from employee recruitment to termination, is in some way affected by laws and regulations. Managers are expected to follow all laws and government regulations relating to HRM. Therefore, the legal framework decides the design and nature of different HRM practices.

The relationship between HR and the politico-legal environment is intricate. Most countries with advanced political systems have regulations dealing with employer–employee relationship, employment contract, employment protection and job security, discrimination legislation, welfare, health and safety at work, unfair dismissal and redundancy, working time, and working conditions. Legislation covering minimum working age, minimum wages, family friendly policy, occupational health and safety, strikes, retrenchments, and transfer and closure of undertakings are all fields of employment law. HR departments have to comply with these legal rules and implement them.

The labour laws and social security provisions of a country affect the workplace rules and benefits extended to employees. For instance, in India, we have numerous labour laws that affect HR policies at the workplace. There are laws determining employment contracts and standing orders governing workplace rules. Figure 2.2 presents a snapshot of some of India's major labour laws and constitutional provisions for employment.

Many HR issues are intrinsically linked with politico-legal developments. Any employment law changes must be reflected in company policy and incorporated by HR managers into their HR plan. Conventions and practices, such as reservations and lobbying, are also impacted by the nature of polity. For instance, in the United States, lobbying in government and power circles is a common practice. In India, reservation in jobs is a major HR issue affecting selection policies.

Political environment also influences the trade union movement, labour activism, and industrial democracy. It governs the overall HR and industrial relations (IR) philosophy of corporations. Most of the labour unions in India are affiliated to various political parties. Strikes and labour disputes often assume national significance owing to the active role of national-level trade unions. One can understand how the labour dispute at Maruti's Manesar plant in Haryana, India, in

2012, became an issue of national debate with the involvement of trade unions at higher levels. The Haryana government, at that time, had to intervene to bring about a third-party negotiation between workers and management.

Figure 2.2   Major Employment and Labour Laws in India

Service Conditions and Wages
- Payment of Wages Act, 1936
- The Payment of Wages (Amendment) Act, 2005
- Minimum Wages Act, 1948
- The Maternity Benefit Act, 1961
- Payment of Bonus Act, 1965
- Contract Labour (Regulation & Abolition) Act, 1970
- Bonded Labour System (Abolition) Act, 1976
- Child Labour (Prohibition & Regulation) Act, 1986—Amended in 2016

Occupational Health, Welfare and Safety
- Factories Act, 1948
- Industry-specific legislations: Plantation Labour Act, 1951; The Mines Act, 1952; Explosives Act, 1884; Dock Workers (Safety, Health & Welfare) Act, 1986; Building and Other Construction Workers (Regulation of Employment and Conditions of Service) Act, 1996, among others

Industrial Relations
- The Trade Unions Act, 1926
- The Trade Unions (Amendments) Act, 2001
- The Industrial Employment (Standing Orders) Act, 1946
- The Industrial Disputes Act, 1947

Social Security
- The Employees Compensation Act, 1923
- The Employees State Insurance Act, 1948
- The Employees Provident Fund & Miscellaneous Provisions Act, 1952—Amended in 1996
- The Payment of Gratuity Act, 1972
- Employees Liability Act, 1938

Employment and Training
- The Employment Exchanges (Compulsory Notification of Vacancies) Act, 1959
- Apprentices Act, 1961
- The Persons with Disabilities (Equal Opportunities, Protection of Rights, and Full Participation) Act, 1995

The Ministry of Labour and Employment, Government of India is responsible for regulations related to workers.

Today's manager must understand the regulatory system in order to function effectively in the framework of the political, legal, and regulatory environment. HRM policies and strategies should be in accordance with legal necessities. The differences in HRM practices results from the differences in legislations and regulations of different countries. An MNC will have differing HR strategies in each of its subsidiaries owing to national differences in political and legal systems.

Sociocultural Environment

A sociocultural environment refers to factors related to general society and social relations that affect a business organization. It includes factors such as the social structure, type of society, social strata, demographics, population composition, education, culture, traditions, beliefs, practices, customs, religions, language, and life styles. The social environment consists of the sum total of a society's beliefs, customs, practices, and behaviours.

Every society constructs its own social environment. If a business operates in a multicultural society, then the social environment is even more complicated because the environment will consist of diverse sub-populations with their own unique values, beliefs, and customs. Different societies have different cultures; however, it is important not to confuse the idea of *culture* with *society*. A culture represents the beliefs and practices of a group, while society represents the people who share those beliefs and practices. Neither society nor culture could exist without the other.

Certain important dimensions of the sociocultural environment that need to be highlighted are discussed below.

Social structure and type of society

The social structure and the values that a society cherishes have a considerable influence on the functioning of business organizations. Social behaviour is arranged in a structural form so as to enable the society to function in a coordinated manner. In this system, roles are always more stable than the role occupants themselves. It may be noted that the behaviours and living styles of people belonging to different social structures vary significantly. According to the *Encyclopedia Brittanica*, social structure is the distinctive, stable arrangement of institutions whereby human beings in a society interact and live together. Social structure is sometimes defined simply as patterned social relations and interactions between the members of a given social entity.[13]

At a larger level, social structure is the system of socio-economic stratification, for example, the class structure, social institutions, or other patterned relations between large social groups. At a smaller level, it is the structure of social ties between individuals, for example, family or affiliated organizations. The family is generally regarded as a major social institution and a locus of a person's social activity. Newer forms of families such as nuclear families, childless families, single parent families, and quasi-family units based on non-marital cohabitation are emerging. Family sizes are getting smaller and mobility is splitting up some families, but the family still remains as a functional social institution, especially in Eastern societies.

Societies differ in the way the social structure is classified and arranged. Different societies understand the concept of social structure in different ways. For instance, the concept of family differs from society to society. It is believed that relationships in the Eastern or occidental cultures are more family-centric. Family values have a strong influence on people in the East than the West. In Western societies, the self is given preference over family.

Demographics

Demographics are quantifiable characteristics of population. Demography refers to the size, structure, distribution of population, temporal changes in population, birth, migration, ageing, and death rates. Demographics tell about a population's characteristics. It may help in getting an idea about the composition of population in terms of age, race, gender, economic status, level of education, income level, employment, and domicile, among others. Demographic trends reveal developments and changes in human population. This data is often compared over time to identify major changes. The size, density, distribution, and growth rate of population have a direct bearing on the functioning of business organizations.

Education

An important dimension of the sociocultural environment is education and literacy. Education is the process of facilitating learning. Knowledge, skills, values, beliefs, and habits of a group of people are transferred to other people through teaching, training, research, or any other method. *Literacy* is traditionally understood as the ability to read and write. Its meaning has been expanded to include the ability to use language, numbers, images, and other means to understand and use basic aspects of life. The United Nations Educational, Scientific and Cultural Organization (UNESCO) defines literacy as the 'ability to identify, understand, interpret, create, communicate and compute, using printed and written materials associated with varying contexts. Literacy involves a continuum of learning in enabling individuals to achieve their goals, to develop their knowledge and potential, and to participate fully in their community and wider society'.[14]

Religion, beliefs, and customs

Religion can be explained as a set of beliefs concerning the cause, nature, and purpose of the universe, usually involving devotional and ritual observances, and often containing a moral code governing the conduct of human affairs. Many religions have narratives, symbols, and sacred histories that aim to explain the meaning of the existence of the universe. Religion helps people make sense of the world. It gives people faith in something eternal and everlasting. It provides motivation and binds people together. Belief is the state of mind in which a person thinks something to be the case. It is a feeling of being sure that someone or something exists or that something is true—a feeling that something is good, right, or valuable. Beliefs, in turn, give rise to customs. A custom is a traditional practice or usual way of doing something, followed by a social group or people. People within any cultural group are not homogeneous, even though they may hold many beliefs, practices, and institutions in common.

Lifestyle and preferences

A major sociocultural factor influencing businesses is lifestyle and preferences. The term 'lifestyle' can denote the interests, opinions, behaviours, and behavioural orientations of an individual, group, or culture. The term was originally used by Austrian psychologist Alfred Adler.[15] The term refers to a combination of determining intangible or tangible factors. Tangible factors relate specifically to demographic variables, whereas intangible factors concern the psychological aspects of an individual such as personal values, preferences, and outlooks. Lifestyle may often be an outcome of one's religion and sacred beliefs. A lifestyle typically reflects an individual's attitudes, way of life, values, or world view. Changing lifestyle can impact a firm in many different ways.

The Labour Market

An important component of the sociocultural environment is the labour market. A labour market can be seen in terms of the type, number, and quality of labour pool available. Labour market refers to a place where workers and employees interact with each other. A labour market in an economy functions on the principle of demand and supply of labour. Labour markets may be local or national or even international in their scope and are made up of smaller, interacting labour markets for different qualifications, skills, and geographical locations.

The traditional concept of labour markets can be understood through the following explanation:

Population = All the people (Eligible + Ineligible)
Ineligible = Those who cannot be employed, such as children, completely handicapped, or imprisoned persons
Eligible = Total labour force + Labour reserve
Total labour force = Armed forces + Civilian labour force
Civilian labour force = Unemployed persons + Employed persons
Labour reserve = People who are not currently working by choice or any other reason, such as college students, housewives, and retired people
Labour market = 'All eligible'

Traditionally, labour market was seen as a unit extending only to a small geographic area. Later, as worker mobility increased and so did the demand for high-skill talent, the scope and size of labour market extended nationally and even internationally. Now companies hire from across the world. Further, the definition of labour pool has extended to include even non-traditional forms of labour.

Some of these trends that have led to an extended definition of the labour market are discussed below.

- **Ageing global population** Profound changes to the demographic of working people are taking place. This is the phenomenon of ageing of population reflected in the shift in the distribution of a country's population towards older ages. Many countries are witnessing the middle age bulge reflected in the 'Pig in a Python' syndrome. Almost one in three companies expects the number of employees over the age of 60 to increase significantly by 2020, according to the latest study by the *Economist Intelligence Unit (EIU)*.[16] Managing this older workforce will pose a new set of challenges for employers, including healthcare provision and productivity issues.

Currently, India is not facing this problem as it has a vibrant young population base. It is an exception to the ageing phenomenon and is designated as a 'demographic outlier' by the UN. However, India is in the grip of an elderly population 'time bomb' according to a UN report which revealed its number of old people will triple by 2050. The report *Status of Elderly in Select States of India*, by the United Nations Population Fund, found the number of over-60s will increase from around 100 million today to more than 300 million by 2050 and warned the government to prepare for the additional strain this will put on families and health and welfare services. It also predicted that the number of over-80s will increase sevenfold.[17]

- **Potential labour reserve**   Due to the problem of ageing population, companies are trying to consider what changes they must introduce to have a more diversified workforce. This has led to increasing interest in tapping the non-traditional workforce and non-traditional employment practices. This may include housewives, college students, or even retired people. Due to widespread use of IT, many of these people are choosing to work on flexible arrangements that suit them.

- **Extended careers**   Companies are today offering options of extended career to people reaching their retirement ages. This is helping them retain the expertise, experience, and value of senior employees. It is quite likely that employees may wish to begin with a phased-in retirement, such as part-time or project-based employment or extending the time of retirement. Companies are also exploring opportunities to attract those employees who, in the past, discontinued their careers due to family commitments.

- **Increasing women in workforce and colleges**   Until modern times, social and cultural practices restricted women's active entry and participation in the workforce. However, owing to education, women's right movements, and increasing awareness among women themselves, the trend has changed. Women now make up almost half of American workers. They run some of the world's best companies. They earn almost 60 per cent of university degrees in America and Europe. In India too, the change is perceptible. In terms of sheer numbers, women's presence in the labour force has increased dramatically, from 30.3 million in 1970 to 72.7 million in 2011. Converted to percentages, it means that women made up 37.97 per cent of the labour force in 1970 compared to 47.21 per cent between 2006 and 2010. The 1970 census data showed very little participation from women as accountants, police officers, judges, physicians, and surgeons. However, the 2011 data shows women having a strong presence in high-esteem occupations.[18]

This has engendered a sense of equality, increasing household income, financial stability for families, higher self-esteem, and independence. There are macroeconomic benefits too due to female labour force participation. Gender equality has a positive correlation with per capita GDP, according to the World Economic Forum's 2014 *Global Gender Gap Report*.[19] The International Labour Organization (ILO) has also suggested that women's work may be the single most important factor in reducing poverty in developing economies.[20] The rise of women in workforce has brought in a new orientation in company outlook and policies.

- **Rise of knowledge workers**   The world is witnessing a change in the composition of workers in terms of skills and working profile. Business landscape has metamorphosed from a predominantly industrial and manufacturing base to a growing service sector. Consequently, the workforce has also evolved from their status of being blue collar workers to white collar workers to knowledge workers. A knowledge worker is one who applies knowledge and intellectual capital for work and who uses brain power rather than brawn power to get the job done. Knowledge workers prefer more autonomy and independence. They demand higher salaries and vie for better opportunities. These aspects make the management of knowledge workers a highly intricate function.[21] Peter Drucker once opined that knowledge worker productivity requires that the knowledge worker is both seen and treated as an 'asset' rather than a 'cost'.[22]
- **Shift in bargaining power**   The rise of knowledge or intellectual work has led to increasing power in the hands of the worker. Intellectual workers have relatively more control over their work than traditional workers owing to their capacity to deploy their intellectual capital and expertise to their work. Improvement in quality of labour owing to higher education and better skills has shifted the bargaining power from employers to employees.

Geert Hofstede's framework of national cultural is often used for cross-cultural understanding. It was forwarded after years of extensive cross-cultural research between 1967 and 1973. It describes the effects of a society's culture on the values of its members, and how these values relate to behaviour. It explains how values in the workplace are influenced by national culture. The model of national culture consists of six dimensions, namely power distance, individualism versus collectivism, masculinity versus femininity, uncertainty avoidance, time orientation, and indulgence versus restraint (this last dimension was added by Hofstede in 2010). The framework can be used to give a general overview and an approximate understanding of other cultures, what to expect from them, and how to behave towards groups from other countries.[23]

Implications of Sociocultural Environment for HRM

Sociocultural environment has significant implications for HR strategies. Every organization has its own culture, and employees tend to adjust themselves to that culture. However, organizational culture tends to be influenced by the national or regional culture. For instance, in countries with collectivism culture, hiring is mostly done in organizations internally, while in countries with individualistic cultures, hiring is done through external sources such as through advertisements or hiring agencies.

Natural culture and traditions may affect HRM activities in terms of transferring related national characteristics to the business. HR managers in MNCs work under the influence of local culture since it has a direct or indirect impact on HR activities. National culture and traditions need to be taken into consideration by firms while designing HR strategies or activities. Organizations should consider the values, traditions, norms, rituals, and expectations of society while laying down HRM policy and strategies. As shown by Hofstede, national culture is one of the important elements that determine organizational perspectives in establishing effective HRM practices.

Population-related metrics like the rate of population, literacy, and demographic composition too have a bearing on HR issues. High population figures may indicate easy availability of labour. This may encourage business enterprises to use labour-intensive techniques of production. Moreover, availability of skilled labour in certain areas may motivate firms to set up their units in such area—for example, a number of MNCs have set up their manufacturing base in India due to the easy availability of skilled manpower. Thus, a firm that keeps a watch on the changes in the demographic trends will be able to better attune its HR practices to suit such trends. Various HR policies like work–life balance have to be designed in the light of such demographic variables such as gender, marital status, and family type. Female workers have different demands and expectations from the workplace as compared to male workers. The increasing rate of women contributing to the workforce has led to more gender-specific HR policies.

Sociocultural environment influences the quality of workforce and their work orientation, ethics, and value system. HR managers will have to incorporate these differences when designing work and tasks. HR managers often are required to design such things as work schedules, working conditions, timings, holidays, and leave-related policies keeping the sociocultural differences in mind. The type of workforce impacts HR policies in various ways. Skilled and educated workforce has a higher bargaining power. Training programmes and training methods are also affected by the nature of workforce.

An important component of sociocultural environment is the concept of diversity. It is recognized that people have many dimensions to their personality—age, gender, race, colour, religion, education, experience, background, traits, and so on. Differences among people at work are both an advantage and a disadvantage. Groups made up of diverse people are more creative and are able to see different perspectives of an issue. Diversity leads to greater innovation, agility, flexibility in the workplace, and enhanced performance. Many countries require by law that organizations maintain balance in gender, racial, and ethnic diversity.

Technological Environment

Technological environment refers to the type of technology in prevalence, level of technological development and advancement, extent of automation, balance between capital- and labour-intensive technologies, technological research, development and innovations, demand and supply of technology, cost of technology, use and abuse of technology, technology life cycle, technological collaborations, technical know-how, and the safeguards vis-à-vis technology.

Changes in technology have become particularly significant in the post-millennium world. Technology is today seen as a decisive factor. Technology, more particularly information and communications technology, has transformed the way business is done today. The technological environment of a country affects the working of business organizations. Business organizations need to constantly scan the technological environment for changes taking place as these are likely to affect its working. The development in IT has made it possible for businesses to collect and store data and to analyse the available data to come up with meaningful conclusions and make informed decisions. Technology can catapult a business to success. At the same time, technological disasters can destroy a business.

The wave of technological transformation impacts HRM tremendously. Technology has transformed the way HRM activities are performed. There is a significant impact of technology, particularly information and communications technology, on the nature of organizational structure, culture, and employee behaviours. The HRM function can meet the challenge of becoming more strategic and future-oriented by leveraging IT. Technology has completely redefined the role of HR all over the world. Recent advances in technology have transformed nearly every aspect of HR, right from sourcing to performance management to career mapping. The world of technology and mobile computing has made the concept of traditional workplace a thing of past. It would offer numerous tools to better manage and engage talent in the organization. It is helping HR managers to shift their focus from managing workforce to driving profits to the company.

Technological environmental factors and the impact of IT on HRM merit a detailed discussion and have been covered separately in the next chapter.

Figure 2.3 presents a snapshot of the macro environment of India.

Figure 2.3 Environmental Profile of India: A Snapshot

General Profile
Area: 3.3 million sq. km
Location: The country is surrounded by the Bay of Bengal in the east, the Arabian Sea in the west, and the Indian Ocean to the south. India occupies a major portion of the Indian subcontinent.
Geographic Coordinates: Lying entirely in the northern hemisphere, the country extends between 8° 4' and 37° 6' latitudes north of the equator and 68° 7' and 97° 25' longitudes east of it.
Indian Standard Time: GMT + 05:30
Border Countries: Afghanistan, Pakistan, China, Bhutan, Nepal, Myanmar, and Bangladesh. Sri Lanka is separated from India by a narrow channel of sea, formed by the Palk Strait, and the Gulf of Mannar.
Coastline: 7,517 km
Climate: Tropical climate marked by relatively high temperatures and dry winters. There are four seasons (*a*) winter (December–February), (*b*) summer (March–June), (*c*) south-west monsoon season (June–September), and (*d*) post-monsoon season (October–November)
Terrain: The mainland comprises of four regions, namely the great mountain zone, plains of the Ganga and the Indus, the desert region, and the southern peninsula.
Natural Resources: Coal, iron ore, manganese ore, mica, bauxite, petroleum, titanium ore, chromite, natural gas, magnetite, limestone, gypsum, phosphorite, steatite, fluorite, and so on.

Political Profile
Country Name: Republic of India; Bharat Ganrajya
Capital: New Delhi
Government Type: Democratic republic with a parliamentary system of Government.
States and Union Territories: 29 states and 7 union territories.

Constitution: Came into force on 26 January 1950 and is the source of the legal system in the country.

Executive Branch: The President of India is the Head of the State, while the Prime Minister is the Head of the Government.

Legislative Branch: Lok Sabha and Rajya Sabha form both houses of the parliament.

Judicial Branch: The supreme court of India is the apex body of the Indian legal system, followed by other high courts, and subordinate courts.

Economic Profile

Gross Domestic Product (GDP): US$2,597,491. World rank: 7th (2017)

GDP Growth: 7.7% Q4 (2017–2018)

GDP Composition- Services: 54%; **Industry:** 29%; **Agriculture:** 17% (2016–2017)

Forex Reserves: US$405.8 billion, as on 13 July 2018.

Value of Exports: India's exports stood at US$303.4 billion (2017–2018)

Major Export Partners: EU, US, UAE, China, and Japan. India is also tapping newer markets in Africa and Latin America.

Exchange Rates: Indian rupees per US$—1 US$ = 68.49 INR (31 July 2018)

Fiscal Year: 1 April–31 March

FDI Inflows: US$377.068 billion (2017)

Ease of Doing Business Rank: 100 (2017)

Credit Rating: Baa2 **Outlook**: Stable (*Moody's*)

Major Sectors Attracting Highest FDI Equity Inflows: Services Sector (18 per cent), Construction Development (8 per cent), Computer Software and Hardware (7 per cent), Telecommunications (6 per cent), Automobile (5 per cent), Drugs and Pharmaceuticals (5 per cent), Chemical (4 per cent), and Trading (4 per cent).

Transportation in India—Airports: Airports Authority of India (AAI) manages 125 airports in the country, which includes 18 international aerodromes, 78 domestic ones, and 26 civil enclaves at defence airfields. **Railways:** The Indian Railways network is spread over 65,800 km, with 12,617 passenger and 7,421 freight trains each day from 7,172 stations plying 23 million travellers and 2.65 million tonnes of goods daily. **Roadways:** India's road network of 4.87 million km is the second largest in the world. With the number of vehicles growing at an average annual pace of 10.16 per cent, Indian roads carry about 65 per cent of freight and 85 per cent of passenger traffic. **Waterways:** 14,500 km **Major Ports of Entry:** Chennai, Ennore, Haldia, Jawaharlal Nehru Port Trust (JNPT), Kolkata, Kandla, Kochi, Mormugao, Mumbai, New Mangalore, Paradip, Tuticorin, and Vishakhapatnam.

Socio-demographic Profile

Population: 1,291,400,000 (2015–2016 est.)

Population Growth Rate: 1.29 per cent (2015 est.)

Religions: Hinduism, Islam, Christianity, Sikhism, Buddhism, and Jainism

Languages: Hindi, English, and at least 16 other official languages

Literacy: Total population: 74.04 per cent (provisional data—2011 census)

Males: 82.14 per cent **Females:** 65.46 per cent

Suffrage: 18 years of age; universal

Life Expectancy: 66.38 years (men), 68.7 years (women) (2013)

Source: India in Business, Ministry of External Affairs, Government of India, retrieved from http://indiainbusiness.nic.in/newdesign/index.php.

Micro environment

Micro environment refers to those factors with which business is closely related. These factors influence an organization more directly. Three important components of the micro environment are customers, competitors, and suppliers.

Customers

Customers of an enterprise are the buyers and users of its goods and services. There are different types of customers and include household, government, industry, commercial enterprises, and so on. The number and types of customers influence the working of an organization—for example, changing tastes and preferences of customers impact the policies and strategies that organizations adopt.

Competitors

Competitors are the rivals who may be providing similar product or services. Competing firms can influence business in a number of ways. They can do so by bringing new and cheap products in the market, by launching a new sales promotion scheme, or by bringing about product modification.

Suppliers and Lenders

Suppliers are the providers of raw materials, equipment, parts, materials, and anything else that is required for producing the final product. Like the customers, the suppliers also influence business. Strained supplier relations can affect a business organization adversely.

Implications of Micro Environmental Factors for HRM

An organization's micro environment affects its overall HR philosophy and approach to HR. Each of the components of the micro environment has an impact on HR strategies. These components affect the overall HR perspective and HR strategies.

Organizations exist to cater to the demands of their customers. Any change in customer needs or preference may warrant changing the product/service design or delivery. This may require fresh training of employees or even hiring new personnel. Thus, customers affect the policies of the HR department. This is more relevant in modern service-oriented economies where employees have a direct interface with customers. Today, companies are recognizing that HR plays a seminal role in building a customer-friendly culture. HR departments are focusing their efforts on improving customer satisfaction. They are designing HR activities to give employees the support they need to develop and nurture lasting relationships with customers.

Similarly, the actions of competitors also influence the business strategy and HR strategy of an organization. Rival firms can increase wages and salaries, bring about a change in working conditions, or offer better training programmes. All this will have a bearing on the HR strategies of an organization. Hence, business organizations are required to keep pace with their competitors by implementing suitable HR systems. Organizations also set HR benchmarks and standards against the performance of their competitors in order to keep pace or even outsmart their rivals. The approach to HR investment, thus, depends on competitor's strategies.

Suppliers too have an impact on the HR function. Suppliers of HR—colleges, universities, and employment agencies—directly affect the design of policies regarding recruitment, selection, training, and so on. Suppliers of raw materials or other inputs also determine how HR activities are designed. For instance, if a supplier starts supplying an energy-saving high-tech equipment that will make an organization's business process more efficient, the organization may be required to train its employees to operate the new equipment. This may necessitate bringing about a new training programme.

Thus, it is clear that entities in the micro environment affect HR policies and practices directly and indirectly.

INTERNAL ENVIRONMENTAL FACTORS

Various internal or organizational factors also affect the working of a business organization and its HR function.

Nature of Business and Industry

The nature of business is an important determinant of the nature of HR practices an organization adopts. HR strategies and practices differ on the basis of industry or sector to which a firm belongs. The skills and abilities of HR required depend on the nature of the industry. Companies depending on continuous technological development and innovation require high-tech knowledge workers. Manufacturing organizations will have an entirely different perspective to HR as compared to service organizations. Even within the same sector, there may be differences in HR strategies. HRM practices of automobile companies may be different from those of a company manufacturing computer equipment as HR practices vary according to manufacturing processes and techniques.

Organizational Mission and Strategy

Mission statements demonstrate the framework that firms operate in. It determines the HR policies too. The mission statement lays down the basic guidelines for functional area activities and gives them a direction. HR policies and practices are designed in light of the organizational mission and strategy. In fact, this is the basic standpoint of SHRM philosophy. Organizational strategy reflects the set of methods to achieve the mission and requires the restructuring of principles and practices in functional areas. The HR policies of a firm should support activities to implement organizational strategy. Selection, recruitment, training and development, performance appraisal, and rewards should facilitate the achievement of the corporate strategy.

Size of the Organization

The size of an organization also determines organizational and HR strategies. Size is determined in terms of various parameters such as sales, revenue, geographical extent of business, or output. The most common indicator of size, however, is the number of employees. HR practices are affected by size. Research studies have pointed towards a significant relationship between organizational size and HRM activities. Large organizations tend to follow more formal and structured HR practices. Bigger firms tend to have more robust and sophisticated HR systems than small- or medium-sized firms. Large organizations tend to be decentralized for effective management, thus ensuring more participation of employees. Company size affects SHRM orientation: the larger a company, the greater the emphasis on SHRM.[24]

Structure of the Organization

The structure of an organization, basically, can be vertical or horizontal. Vertically structured organizations have a strict hierarchy, which reflects centralization. In these organizations, HR policy-making is under the tight control of top management. On the other hand, horizontally structured organizational systems provide more flexibility to employees. There are studies that show the link between organizational structure and HR culture.[26] Decentralized team-based organizations have HR systems that support that kind of a structure. HR activities in such organizations tend to be more flexible and innovation-oriented. Employees who work in a matrix-structured workplace typically have dual reporting relationships, although only one may be the formal supervisor–employee relationship. Employees may utilize different skill sets in more than one area of the business, working cross-functionally to achieve goals. Implementing HR policies in such a system would be different from an organization with traditional organizational structure.

Organizational Culture

The history and traditions of an organization determine how an organization works. Past practices set a precedent to construct current activities and the future. Accordingly, traditions set the basis for design of HRM functions. At the same time, the history, traditions, and past practices of organizations also can be the source of resistance in implementing new strategies or any changes in organizations or functions. Organizational culture is one of the main internal factors affecting HR practices. It is the job of HR specialists to adjust proactively to the culture of the organization.

Philosophy and Priorities of Management

The philosophy and priorities of management are an important source for HRM practices. Shareholder priorities and management agendas affect HR activities. The values of top management about HRM might be as one of the main factors affecting related strategies and policies. Hiring or promotion policies, policies of wage and salary, and training budget all depend on priorities of the management, especially the top management. In addition, the top management might pay attention to efficiency profitability, which guides HR strategies.

Line managers also affect HRM choices through their own functional priorities and agendas, which are aligned with firm strategies. Often issues of power and internal politics may also cast their influence on HR decisions. Internal political dynamics affect HR decision-making. Top management or unit managers might prefer HRM policies that let them gain power. Accordingly, they can reward or promote people who are close to them. Often termination, downsizing, and lay-off decisions are impacted by the interplay of power and politics.

Role of Unions

The role and activities of unions also influence HRM practices of firms. Labour unions seek to bargain with management over the terms and conditions of employment for their members. Organizations that have an active trade union have to consider the demands of unions when they are designing their HR strategies. Often many activities of HRM are determined and structured through negotiations and labour contracts. Unions also put a check on the arbitrariness of management in terms of designing HR policies.

It is thus clear that HR policies do not exist in a vacuum. HR policies and strategies are determined in the light of the larger framework of the environment. Environment includes both external and internal factors. Each of these environmental factors separately or in combination can influence the HRM function of any organization. Changes in the internal and external environmental factors impact HRM choices.

In this context, Richard D'Aveni (1994) introduced the term 'hypercompetition' to indicate the new and radically different scenario in which firms compete.[27] In the traditional business environment, firms focused on building a successful strategy that was translated into a durable competitive position. Hypercompetition, on the other hand, symbolizes a different way of competing where firms need to follow different rules of behaviour and respond to the market needs with dynamic and continually changing strategy. To maximize recruitment and retention and to minimize employee issues, business managers must continually monitor internal and external environmental factors and adjust HR strategy accordingly.

HR Anecdote
The Key to Survival

Every morning in Africa, a gazelle wakes up, it knows it must outrun the fastest lion or it will be killed. Every morning in Africa, a lion wakes up. It knows it must run faster than the slowest gazelle, or it will starve. It doesn't matter whether you're a lion or a gazelle-when the sun comes up, you'd better be running.

This famous quote symbolises the environmental turbulences and the struggle for survival. It shows that no one is safe or immune to the external threats that one encounters every day. As the saying goes, when the sun comes up you'd better be running. It is applicable to everyone—individuals, groups, organizations, societies, and nations. We need to keep persistently pursuing our goals and achieving our dreams or else we lose out and perish. When the sun comes up, we better run.

Source: http://www.businessinsider.com/inspirational-quote-of-the-day-2011-11?IR.

News Grab
Indian economy on fast track

The United Nations World Economic Situation and Prospects (WESP) 2017 report said India's economy is projected to grow by 7.7 per cent in fiscal year 2017 and 7.6 per cent in 2018, benefiting from strong private consumption. It however cautioned that low capacity utilisation and stressed balance sheets of banks and businesses will prevent a strong investment revival in the short term.

The UN report said India has positioned itself as the most dynamic emerging economy among the largest countries and is expected to remain the fastest growing on the back of robust private consumption and significant domestic reforms gradually being implemented by the government.

In India, investment demand is expected to slightly pick up, helped by monetary easing, government efforts towards infrastructure investments and public-private partnerships, and the implementation of domestic reforms such as the introduction of the Goods and Services Tax (GST) Bill. The report added that the GST reform constitutes a 'major change' by establishing a new uniform tax rate. The reform should promote investment in the medium term through lower transaction and logistic costs and efficiency gains. As per industry and government reports, growth slowed down to 7.1 per cent by the second quarter of FY 2018–19. Despite the drop in the GDP growth rate, India still holds the tag of the fastest-growing major economy in the world.

Source: Adapted from *Economic Times,* Indian economy projected to grow by 7.7% in FY 2017: UN Report, 17 January 2017, retrieved from http://economictimes.indiatimes.com/news/economy/indicators/indiaseconomyprojectedtogrowby77infy2017unreport.

CHAPTER SUMMARY

- Business environment may be defined as the total surroundings that have a direct or indirect bearing on the functioning of a business.
- The relationship between business organizations and their environment can be explained through the systems concept.
- A system is a group of interacting, interrelated, or interdependent elements forming a complex whole.
- A business enterprise is a system consisting of various sub-systems, such as departments and divisions. This may also be called the internal environment of an organization.
- The organization is itself part of a larger system—the external environment.
- External environment refers to all the external forces within which an organization operates.
- External environment may be classified as a micro environment or macro environment. A micro environment is the immediate external environment. It includes customers, suppliers, lenders, creditors, and direct intermediaries. A macro environment is the distant external environment. It includes economic, political, legal, social, cultural, and technological environmental factors.
- Strategic HRM policies and programmes function in a complex environment.

- In order to function effectively, HR managers need to pay attention to rapid changes taking place in the organization's environment.
- In the age of hypercompetition, managers must continually monitor internal and external environmental factors and adjust HR strategy accordingly.

EXERCISES AND DISCUSSION QUESTIONS

1. 'The relationship between business organizations and their environment can be explained through the systems concept.' Discuss this statement by identifying components of the system of a business organization.
2. Explain how the micro and macro environments of business impact decision-making in an organization.
3. Taking any organization of your choice as an example:
   i. Identify components of its micro and macro environment
   ii. Assess how these components are likely to affect HR practices in the organization

CASELET

Reliance Jio—The Game Changer?

The curtain is up in India's high-decibel war of the giants as Reliance Industries Ltd (RIL) chairman, Mukesh Ambani, spelled out an aggressive plan for the much-awaited Reliance Jio 4G services at the company's 42nd annual general meeting (AGM) on 1 September 2016. With a bold tariff plan, low-cost mobile phones, and free voice calls for a lifetime, Reliance Jio Infocomm Ltd kicks off a new phase of turbulence in the world's fastest growing telecom market. Some claim the announcement has sparked a virtual bloodbath in the Indian telecom sector and is seen as one of the biggest moments in corporate battles in recent times.

The impending launch of Reliance Jio had been hanging like a Damocles' sword over the other players. The value destruction this venture has unleashed has not spared anyone. The new game is expected to change the playing field for companies in the telecom sector. It will see a realignment of many big players with the small players succumbing before the sheer power of Jio, whose policy of spending its way to market leadership has completely altered the business dynamics of the telecom sector in India. The company is collaborating with nearly all smartphone makers to bundle three months of free data and voice with handsets. Buyers of the bundled devices will be eligible for a SIM card that will allow them to access the Jio network immediately. Presently, the company has over 1.5 million subscribers. Jio's bundling scheme with Samsung has catalysed sales, which grew by 15–20 per cent within one week of the launch. According to a Morgan Stanley research report, Reliance Jio is likely to have 30 million subscribers by the end of the fiscal year with revenue of over $1 billion. The current market leader Bharti Airtel's stock dropped by 9 per cent after Mukesh Ambani's AGM announcement while Idea Cellular Ltd, another important player, lost 7 per cent, indicating how the game was warming up. Jio's entry could also mean the end of the road for marginal players like Aircel, R-Com, Tata DoCoMo, and Telenor. With Jio further looking to improve its network, it is expected that the leading telcos will increase their investments.

For consumers, however, this could be a bonanza, particularly once Airtel and Vodafone also unleash their own competitive tariff plans. Jio will price mobile phone data as low as ₹50 per gigabyte (GB). Two days later, Bharti Airtel slashed 4G and 3G mobile Internet charges by up to 80 per cent to as low as ₹51 per GB in anticipation of the Jio launch. The Jio launch is likely to disrupt the business environment for the telecom players but will benefit the consumers in the process.

The delay in Reliance Jio's launch gave incumbents ample time to tweak their tariffs, and it was feared that that this might limit the former's ability to disrupt the markets. However, the company's entry-level tariffs turned out to be considerably lower than the Street estimates. This came as a surprise as the market was not expecting Jio to aggressively slash prices this way. There has been a significant migration of customers. However, competitors are likely to wait and see how Reliance Jio's services deliver.

It was clear in a week's time that Reliance Jio would offer bundled packs. It now appears that they may have to offer more value for money. Earlier, Jio's launch was expected to be largely disruptive in terms of data services. The fact that the company is offering free unlimited calls right from its ₹149 plan means that the challenge for other players is big. It is important to note that over 70 per cent of the industry's revenues come from voice services.

The saving grace is that in the monthly packs, Reliance Jio has no plans between the entry-level ₹149 offer and the ₹499 offer. Since the average revenue per user for most telcos is much below the ₹499 level, it remains to be seen how many customers would be tempted to upgrade. The return on investment in the telecom sector was already low, in single-digits, even before Reliance Jio's launch. Now, with tariffs set to fall again, and investments set to rise, things are likely to worsen. Reliance Jio's attractive data tariffs may well push Bharti Airtel and Idea to increase their capital expenditures. Despite this, a number of analysts have given 'buy' ratings on stocks of current incumbents.

Analysts feel that this is a surprise as the market was not expecting Jio to aggressively target the low-end market. Reliance Jio launch is definitely set to jolt India's telecom sector. However, some feel that high-end customers may not switch to Jio overnight by abandoning their existing operators. Reliance Jio will ensure that marginal players, such as Aircel, R-Com, Tata DoCoMo, and Telenor, will exit and, thus, the data market will expand significantly. This could benefit Bharti Airtel and Idea Cellular. Bharti Infratel would also emerge as a key beneficiary as data demand would lead to more towers and tenancies.

With its unlimited free voice calls and the promise of arguably the cheapest data services on the network that only supports 4G, the fastest data delivery speed for mobile phones, Jio was bound to start a cost war but faced its first hurdle early on in the race, with charges of frequent call drops over the network. A whopping 80 per cent of Jio's calls have been failing, according to a statement issued by the company within 15 days of its launch. However, it blamed the country's major network providers such as Airtel and Vodafone for this, saying they had not provided enough interconnection points. Reliance Jio has claimed that the issues on its service are not due to natural congestion, but artificial blockage of services. Bharti Airtel, currently the largest network operator in India, claimed that Jio's own network efficiencies were resulting in the large number of call drops and providers had given enough interconnection points to Jio to handle its traffic.

At the Jio launch, Ambani had said that Reliance Industries had deployed the largest 100 per cent voice over long-term evolution (VoLTE) network, which provides crystal clear voice and video quality, instant call connectivity, the least call drops, and a unique ability to use data and voice simultaneously. However, users also felt that they had been denied benefits of superior voice technology as promised.

Alleging that the country's largest telecom operator was abusing its leadership position, Reliance Jio stated that it appears that the quality of service will continue to suffer and Indian customers will be denied the benefits of superior and free voice services as a result of such anti-competitive behaviour. Whatever the scenario, this implies that the actual problem may be much graver—and that not only Reliance, but all network operators may have to work on improving the number and quality of towers in the country. Any anti-competitive move aimed at stifling competition will be against public interest and fair play.

Reliance Jio had grabbed 9.29 per cent subscriber market share by 31 March 2017, according to the subscription data released by the Telecom Regulatory Authority of India. The telecom operator added 58.39 lakh subscribers in March. The same month saw Airtel with the largest chunk of the market share pie at 23.39 per cent, followed by Vodafone at 17.87 per cent. Idea Cellular with 16.70 per cent was a close third. The data also revealed that Jio was also the top in the wireless broadband service provider list, followed by Bharti Airtel, Vodafone, and Idea Services.

Jio after six months of free offers launched Prime membership that gave its subscribers discounts on app usage and data benefits for a year for a one-time recharge of ₹99. It has since rolled out the Dhan Dhana Dhan scheme, which had minimum recharges of around ₹300 for benefits for three months.

As of 20 May 2017, Reliance Jio, which is now the fourth largest telecom operator in the country, continued to drive growth in the mobile telephony segment. It has crossed the 100 million customer mark. Uncertainties, however, still loom for the telecom sector, a recent addition being the anticipated VoLTE feature phone launch by Jio. This can increase the addressable market for Jio substantially.

Incumbents have weathered the storm of Jio's free services fairly well. As Merrill Lynch's analysts say, Jio's impact will not be as large and sudden as in the previous two quarters, since it has finally started charging for its services. However, given the precarious state some of their finances are in, they can barely afford a further worsening of the industry's structure. Going by the mood Jio has been in, it all remains uncertain. It is too premature to make any speculations now but the business environment for the telecom sector in India is not the same any more.[27]

Questions for Discussion

1. How has the business environment altered for telcos after the launch of Reliance Jio?
2. Can the launch of Jio be seen as a sustainable business model given the Indian conditions? Comment.
3. Reliance Jio is being seen as a game changer in the Indian market with disruptive competitive strategies. What kind of HR approach do you think this kind of an organization would need?

NOTES

1. The United Nations, retrieved from www.un.org.
2. C. Bell (1987), Development economics, *New Palgrave: A Dictionary of Economics 1*: 818–825.
3. International Monetary Fund, retrieved from https://www.imf.org; L. Nielsen (2011), *Classifications of countries based on their level of development: How it is done and how it could be done*, report submitted to International Monetary Fund, retrieved from https://www.imf.org/external/pubs/cat/longres.aspx?sk=24628.0, retrieved 21 June 2016.

4. United Nations Development Programme, *Human development report*, retrieved from hdr.undp.org.

5. Organization for Economic Cooperation and Development, retrieved from www.oecd.org.

6. The World Bank, retrieved from www.worldbank.org.

7. Ibid.; T. Khokhar and S. U. Serajuddin (2015), Should we continue to use the term "developing world"? *The Data Blog – The World Bank*, retrieved from http://blogs.worldbank.org/opendata/should-we-continue-use-term-developing-world.

8. In calculating gross national in US dollars, the World Bank uses the *Atlas* conversion factor instead of simple exchange rates. The purpose of the *Atlas* conversion factor is to reduce the impact of exchange rate fluctuations in the cross-country comparison of national incomes. The *Atlas* conversion factor for any year is the average of a country's exchange rate for that year and its exchange rates for the two preceding years, adjusted for the difference between the rate of inflation in the country and international inflation; the objective of the adjustment is to reduce any changes to the exchange rate caused by inflation, retrieved from *www.worldbank.org*.

9. J. M. Keynes (1930), *A treatise on money* (New York, NY: Harcourt, Brace and Company).

10. S. N. *Eisenstadt* (1966), The basic characteristics of modernization, in *Modernization, protest and change*, ed. S. N. Eisenstadt, pp. 1–19 (Eaglewood Cliffs, NJ: Prentice-Hall).

11. *G. A. Almond and* J. *S. Coleman* (1960), *The politics of the developing areas* (Princeton, NJ: Princeton University Press).

12. L. Diamond (2008), *The spirit of democracy: The struggle to build free societies throughout the world* (New York, NY: Henry Holt and Company, LLC).

13. *Encyclopedia Britannica*, retrieved from https://www.britannica.com.

14. UNESCO, retrieved from http://en.unesco.org/.

15. A. Adler (1992), *Understanding human nature* (Oxford, UK: Oneworld Publications).

16. Economist Intelligence Unit, retrieved from www.eiu.com.

17. United Nations Population Fund (2011), *Report on status of elderly in select states of India*, retrieved from http://countryoffice.unfpa.org/india/?publications=5828.

18. Census of India (2011), retrieved from www.censusindia.gov.in.

19. World Economic Forum (2014), *The global gender gap report*, retrieved from reports.weforum.org/global-gender-gap-report-2014/.

20. International Labour Organization, retrieved from www.ilo.org.

21. M. S. Bogdanowicz and E. K. Bailey (2002), The value of knowledge and the values of the new knowledge worker: Generation X in the new economy, *Journal of European Industrial Training* 26(2–4): 125–129, doi:10.1108/03090590210422003.

22. P. F. Drucker (1999), *Management challenges of the 21st century* (New York, NY: Harper Business).

23. G. Hofstede (1984), *Culture's consequences: International differences in work-related values* (Beverly Hills CA: Sage Publications); G. Hofstede (1991), *Cultures and organizations: Software of the mind* (London, UK: McGraw-Hill).

24. See studies by S. E. Jackson, R. S. Schuler, and J. C. Rivero (1989), Organizational characteristics as predictors of personnel practices, *Personnel Psychology 42*: 727–786; M. A. Huselid (1995), The impact of human resource management practices on turnover, productivity, and corporate financial performance, *Academy of Management Journal 38*(3): 635–672; D. E. Terpstra and E. J. Rozell (1993), The relationship of staffing practices to organizational level measures of performance, *Personnel Psychology 46*(1): 27–48.

25. P. Buller (1988), Successful partnerships: HR and strategic planning at eight top firms, *Organisational Dynamics 17*: 27–42; R. B. Othman and Z. Ismail (1996), Strategic HRM: A comparison between selected manufacturing and service firms, *Research and Practice in Human Resource Management 4*(1): 43–65; Jackson et al., Organizational characteristics.

26. R. A. D'Aveni (1994), *Hypercompetition: Managing the dynamics of strategic maneuvering* (New York, NY: The Free Press).

27. With inputs from https://www.jio.com; https://www.livemint.com/Money/vQ05ux9lj6a483J1UVuYZK/Reliance-Jio-sets-the-cat-among-the-pigeons.html, retrieved 5 September 2017; https://indianexpress.com/article/technology/mobile-tabs/reliance-jio-4g-launch-ril-agm-live-3007424/, retrieved 5 September 2017.

CHAPTER 3

Technology and HRM

Chapter Overview

This chapter deals with developing an understanding of how technology affects HRM. It specifically focuses on the trends in the nature of work vis-à-vis the growth of information and communications technology (ICT). It introduces the concept of electronic HR (e-HR) and highlights how various HR sub-systems such as recruitment, selection, training, appraisal, and compensation are getting transformed owing to the impact of IT. It also highlights how traditional organizational structures are giving way to more flexible e-enabled organizational forms.

Learning Objectives

1. To understand the trends in the nature of work due to the influence of technological environment and more specifically due to ICT
2. To comprehend the impact of ICT on HRM sub-systems like staffing, training, appraisal, compensation, and employee relations
3. To comprehend the impact of ICT on HR culture and organizational structure
4. To examine the role that Internet and social media are playing in transforming HRM functions

OPENING STORY

Kumbh Mela Goes Hi-tech

From using artificial intelligence to building the largest temporary city in the world, the 2019 Kumbh Mela at the Indian city of Prayagraj, earlier Allahabad, is believed to be one of the biggest religious congregations. Spread over 3,200 hectares of land with millions of pilgrims taking dip in the holy water of the Ganges River, the Kumbh Mela is equipped with hi-tech facilities and modern gadgets.

Hi-tech huts have been set up for seers and pilgrims. Over 1,000 CCTV cameras and artificial intelligence will be used by the Integrated Command and Control Centre of the police for crowd management. At the same time, they can also monitor anything that is suspicious. The police have acquired hi-tech bikes to handle emergencies. Stalls facilitating pilgrims with virtual reality experience have been set up. Social media is being deployed to keep citizens informed about the festival. Around 4,000 hotspots are being set up across the area for providing high-speed wi-fi. The administration has a fleet of 55 motorbike fire fighting system. A temporary hi-tech hospital with a capacity of 100 beds is brought up at the *mela* ground. In a first, a disease surveillance unit is put in place to keep an eye on the prevalence and pattern of diseases during the event. The government will deploy epidemic intelligence officers who would coordinate with medical units to keep Kumbh disease free. IBM Intelligent Video Analytics is being pressed into service by Indian Railways for crowd control at stations. A mobile app will help disseminate information to train users.

As per the officials, Kumbh Mela is getting such branding for the first time. All this requires massive deployment of skilled and hi-tech personnel who have been trained to enable smooth management of the mega event. Police personnel fire fighters, doctors, paramedic staff, surveillance and IT teams among other staff will help manage the *mela*. The *mela* is an interesting case study for technology and HR integration.

TECHNOLOGICAL ENVIRONMENT

Technology can be defined as the method or technique for converting inputs to outputs in accomplishing a specific task. The terms 'method' and 'technique' include all the knowledge, skills, know-how, processes, and means for accomplishing a task. Technological innovation refers to the increase in knowledge and skills or the discovery of a new or improved means that enhances people's ability to achieve a given task.

Technology is seen in terms of the knowledge of individuals or it can be embedded in machines, computers, devices, and equipment that can be operated by individuals for attaining an objective. Thus, technology can be classified in several ways. For example, blueprints, machinery, equipment, and other capital goods are sometimes referred to as hard technology, while soft technology includes skills, know-how, capabilities, and so on. When a dominantly human-centric technology is used in a process, it is usually referred to as labour-intensive. A highly advanced technology deploying machines and equipment is generally termed capital-intensive.

Technological environment refers to the type of technology in use, technological advancement, automation, balance between capital and labour-intensive technologies, research and development vis-à-vis technology, technological inventions and innovations, demand and supply of technological products, cost of technological products, technology innovation-diffusion cycle, pace of obsolescence of technology, technological collaborations and transfer of technology, use of ICT, technical know-how, and the protection of technology through intellectual property rights (IPR). Technology is the single greatest factor that distinguishes modern economies from primitive ones.

A technological change is an increase in the efficiency of a method or process that results in an increase in output without an increase in input. The telephone is an example of a product that has undergone massive technological changes over the years. Telephones have changed dramatically since Alexander Graham Bell spoke into the first phone in 1876. From the candlestick phone that was separated into two pieces to the rotary dial phones to push button phones to answering machines to cellular phones finally evolving into smart touch screen phones, the telephone has come a long way.

Likewise, the camera is another product that has seen several births and rebirths. It was not until 1885 when George Eastman created the modern photograph film technology that cameras became a product that consumers were proud to own. The first Kodak camera that Eastman created was sold with the film already loaded inside and consumers needed to send the entire unit to the company to get their film developed. The company would then reload the camera with new film and send it back to the consumer so they could take more pictures with it. Later, Eastman created a smaller, handier, and convenient camera, called the Brownie, that could be carried anywhere. The camera further evolved from still pictures to having motion picture capabilities. While many companies were trying to create better technology for their cameras, an entirely new concept in the technology of camera came onto the scene in 1948, which changed the playing field for camera manufacturers. The Polaroid was a unique camera that attracted consumers because of its instant gratification capabilities. People could take a picture with the Polaroid camera and have their photos developed instantly. In recent years, the digital technology spilled over into the camera industry, giving rise to digital cameras. The integration of phones and cameras is perhaps one of the most exciting inventions of recent times. Interestingly, mobile phones with inbuilt cameras have become the most popular devices now. There are now more than 4 billion people worldwide taking pictures with their mobiles.[1] The camera phone is already the most widely used type of camera in history!

Changes in technology have become particularly significant in the post-millennium world. In fact, technology is today a decisive factor. Organizations are required to modify products according to the level of technological knowledge and demands of the target costumer. Technology is having a massive impact all around. Computers and Internet alone had an impact of epic proportions. Developments such as these affect business and human resources.

The varying technological environments of different countries affect the working of business organizations. Changes in the technological environment have had some of the most dramatic effects on businesses. Companies need to constantly scan the technological environment for innovations and technological changes taking place as these are likely to affect its working and operations. It is vital that organizations stay abreast of these changes—not only because this will allow them to incorporate new and innovative ideas into their offerings but also because it will enable them to attain competitive advantage.

TRENDS IN THE NATURE OF WORK

Technology has had a huge impact on how people work, and therefore on the skills and training of today's workers. Some of the significant implications of technology, specifically ICT, for HR practitioners are as follows:

- **More capital-intensive technology** Today, more and more business organizations are adopting capital-intensive technologies. Automation is taking place on a rampant scale. As manufacturers integrate Internet-based customer ordering with just-in-time manufacturing, production and scheduling become more efficient and precise. With the use of technology, productivity has also gone up.

- **Rise of service industry** Owing to increasing automation, manufacturing processes are becoming more integrated and efficient. The net effect is that manufacturers have been squeezing slack and inefficiencies out of production, enabling companies to enhance their productivity.[2] The service industry has emerged as a major employment-generating sector. ICT has emerged as a key industry within the service sector.

- **Occupational shifts** Projections of the growth and decline in certain types of jobs illustrates the economic and employment shifts currently occurring. There is migration of workers from rural to urban areas. People are shifting from tradition jobs to more skilled jobs in manufacturing and service sectors. It is interesting to note that the fastest-growing occupations are related to the service sector. The increase in the technology jobs is due to the rapid increase in the use of IT.

- **Creation of high-tech jobs** Knowledge-intensive high-tech manufacturing in most industries is replacing the blue-collar factory jobs. Today, organizations are spending time keying commands into computerized machines that do work with more precision and exactness, thus avoiding human errors and wastages. This has made production faster, cheaper, better, and more proficient. New product development and innovation is taking place on a much faster plane. All this mandates creation of specialized high-tech jobs.

- **Demand of knowledge work and human capital** Survival in the present transnational economy is conditional on human capabilities. Winning springs from organizational capabilities, skills, knowledge, and competencies of people.[3] Strategist Michael Porter stressed that HR is a key to obtaining competitive advantage.[4] HR managers now list critical thinking/problem-solving and IT application as the two skills most likely to increase in importance over the next few years.[5] In general, today's jobs require more professional education and more skills. Owing to technological developments, skill and educational requirements tend to increase, thereby increasing the demand for intellectual capital.

- **Redesign of work methods and processes:** Work methods, processes, operations, and techniques have changed over time. As technological development takes place, production processes and methods also develop; process flows become more rational, tasks more specific, techniques more capital-intensive, product designs more standardized, and so on. In the present turbulent times, when organizations are constantly enveloped in a digital environment, there is growing realization of deploying technology to gain strategic leverage.[6]

- **Redesign of Jobs** Widespread use of information systems and automation has eliminated the need for many administrative and routine positions. A lot of old jobs have been eliminated or done away with. All this redesign of jobs has changed the traditional concept of work. The era of the 'smart machine' and the skilled professionals who operate such machines will produce conditions in which there is less need for supervision and more demand for flexibility and openness. Companies are experimenting with innovative work practices such as flexitime, flexiplace, and telecommuting, among others.

- **Development of coping mechanisms** Employees' responses to changing technology are different. While some employees are open to technology adaptation and are quick to respond, others may not be so forthcoming in terms of adopting technological changes. Learning new skills is not just a cognitive process but also a physical process since it leads to improved performance.[7] Frequent counselling, coaching, mentoring, and feedback mechanisms have to be put in place in order to enable employees to cope with the pressures of changing technology.
- **Need for training and retraining** Technological change appears to affect individuals differently, as some grow and develop along with new technology while others fall behind. Technological change is also causing skill obsolescence in many professions. Because of the rapidity of change, professionals run a risk of having their skills become obsolete very fast. Companies often try to provide retraining, challenging assignments, attractive rewards, and benefits for technical specialists in all phases of their careers.
- **Retention of employees** Retention of employees is a particular concern for many employers. Since most employees today are knowledge workers, they get job offers more easily. In some industries (for example, retail, customer service, and hospitality), turnover rates of 30–40 per cent are common. Research says that most of the employees leave an organization out of frustration and constant friction with their superiors or other team members.[8] In some cases, low salary, lack of growth prospects, and motivation compel an employee to look for a change.

Technology and HRM have a broad range of influences on each other. Technological influences on HRM are being driven primarily by strong demands from HR professionals for enhancement in speed, effectiveness, and cost containment. The HRM function can meet the challenge of becoming more strategic, flexible, cost-efficient, and customer-oriented by leveraging IT.

IT AND HRM

During the past 10 years or so, new forms of ICT have been launched, most of which have implications for how people construct their identities and how they work. There has been the rapid growth in electronic networking all across the globe. These developments affect communication between individuals, within organizations, and also between individuals and machines. They affect all aspects of society, including work, business, and private life.

A number of implications arise out of this. First, there has been the dramatic reduction in the costs of digital information and communication processing. People are getting accustomed to instant solutions. The world is witnessing the *click-of-the-mouse* phenomenon. IT has brought the world to our doorsteps giving us access to all that we could imagine. Second, there has been the technologically driven 'digital convergence' between communication and computer technology, which has created various forms of communication such as mobile communication, e-mails, video conferencing, and chatting. Third, these technologies render physical space and distance irrelevant. This has radically affected how people work. Today, people are working beyond the borders of time and space.

On account of the implementation of e-enabled technology in organizations, the very nature of the workplace has transformed. Virtual HR or e-HR has emerged due to the growing sophistication of IT and its widespread use in organizations. It is beginning to enable organizations to deliver state-of-the-art HR services more efficiently. The biggest benefit of using IT in HRM is the freeing of HR staff from intermediary and administrative roles involving documentation and arduous record-keeping, thus enabling them to concentrate more on strategic decision-making. IT can help automate a lot of routine tasks such as job application scanning, payroll processing, benefits administration, and other transactional activities, so that HR professionals are free to focus on more strategic matters. HR technology has reduced the response time and enhanced the quality of HR service in the workplace.[9]

Some people term the new phenomenon as the 'consumerization of HR', wherein employees not only demand to use a wide range of devices and systems to change the way they work and communicate, but the entire HR department is changing the way it functioned till now. Today's technology gives HR professionals access to the power of real-time data. Employees, who are the end users of HR services, are increasingly deploying IT capabilities to have access to HR information and services.

What Is E-HR?

In a world becoming more and more comfortable with access to real-time answers, HR has only one way to go—the transformation of systems, processes, and methods towards real-time delivery. This has given shape to e-HR.

In essence, e-HR refers to the use of electronic and web-enabled techniques in the context of human resource of an organization. HR services can now be done remotely and all transactions are now electronic, hence the title e-HR. Electronic means of communication have enabled people to work from anywhere and anytime, thereby transforming the entire framework of people management. HR departments are becoming paperless departments, with documentation and administrative work becoming automated. They are being seen as more efficient and professional than ever before.

This shift from traditional HR function to e-HR has not been a quantum leap for organizations. Instead, HR departments have evolved their e-solutions over a period of growth stages starting from simple one-way information publishing using computers to doing complex HR transactions today with the help of IT[10]:

The impact of IT on HR can be understood from two perspectives:

- *Impact on HR sub-systems*   IT has transformed the way HRM activities such as recruitment, selection, training, pay calculations, and appraisal are performed.
- *Impact on HR culture and structure*   IT has had a significant impact on the nature of organizational structuring, culture, and employee behaviours, resulting in the evolution of new organizational forms.

The next section discusses how IT has impacted HR sub-systems and HR culture.

IMPACT ON HR SUB-SYSTEMS

E-HR has significantly affected the functioning and delivery of HR function. HRM has undergone transformation owing to the impact of new-age technologies.

Integrated human resource information or management systems (HRIS/HRMS) are becoming increasingly common today. HRMS can be used to streamline HR processes and to provide a single source of all associated employee and organizational data. Today's HR software offers increasingly sophisticated functionality, giving companies the opportunity to automate labour-intensive processes and devolve routine transactions to line managers and, in some cases, even to employees themselves. HRMS is the system to acquire, store, manipulate, analyse, interpret, and disseminate relevant information on HR. An HRMS is a systematic procedure for collecting, storing, maintaining, retrieving, and validating the data needed by an organization for its HR activities. HRMS can also provide management with a decision-making tool, rather than merely a robust database.

E-HR solutions are increasingly being harnessed to streamline and automate administrative HR processes and services. HR *intranets* can play a leading role in these changes, providing employees, line managers, and the HR function itself with easy online access to a comprehensive repository of HR information and policy and act as a new channel for employee communications. With Internet and e-mail facilities, employees can access data, exchange information, and carry on business transactions online.

Oracle, Siemens, PeopleSoft, and Adrenalin are some of the leading HRMS solutions providers. They are providing both vertical and horizontal HR solutions. Vertical applications deal with all HR functions in an integrated module. For example, a typical HRMS will include many or all of the following modules:

- Payroll module
- Recruitment, selection, and applicant database module
- Compensation administration module
- Training and staff development module
- Performance management, appraisal, and performance planning

Horizontal applications deal with one specific HR function, for example, staffing.

An HRMS is a computerized system that accomplishes two very important purposes. First, it allows the keeping of personnel data in a form that can be easily accessed and analysed. Second, it allows the use of that data to fulfil the various functions usually associated with an HR department. A major strength of HRMS is that it is comprehensive and can handle information and HR processes for almost every possible organizational function and that it is integrated and accessible through a common computer interface. Integration allows exceedingly sophisticated data management and reporting.

Firms have invested heavily in the implementation of these enterprise or integrated software. HRMS leads to effective and efficient management of HR. Certain companies allow employees to update their information, keep track of their benefits, salaries, and performance appraisal feedback, and access all relevant HR and company related information that can help in speedy decision-making. Companies can today keep computerized skill repository for identifying and developing internal talent, knowledge, and abilities. These e-HR systems also offer various search capabilities, such as those for conducting organization-wide searches related to global staffing as well as extensive report generation options. Executives can access HR information when making strategic or operational decisions. In addition, these systems also allow firms to automate human resource processes and transactions.

With refinements in HRMS taking place, talent analytics and workplace analysis are becoming important concepts. It gives HR a fact-based view of the current workforce, identifying emerging trends so businesses can adapt. Predictive analytics allow for better risk-management decisions. For example, they can identify employees who could benefit from additional training or highlight teams that may be struggling. Analytics also allow recruiters to assess potential employees through real information by basing hiring decisions on facts instead of hunch, and can improve the quality and placement of new hires.

Aided by the capabilities of HRMS, key HR sub-systems have migrated towards real-time delivery. Some of the changes taking place in HR sub-systems are discussed below:

- **Manpower planning**   Manpower planning is a prerequisite to all HRM activities. IT has enabled organizations to carry on manpower planning through use of systems like the enterprise resource planning (ERP) packages. ERP signifies the techniques and concepts employed for integrated management of business from the viewpoint of effective use of management resources, including human resource, to improve the efficiency of the organization. Enterprise software systems have been implemented to integrate the major areas of business such as manufacturing, sales, finance, supply chain management, and human resources. These information systems have enabled companies to gain numerous benefits such as efficiency gains, quicker response times, better inventory control, enhanced coordination, and improved decision-making.

  ERP and such other systems enable organizations to keep employee records, maintain HR master data and sub-data, prepare planning scenarios, do HR accounting, auditing and personnel cost management, lay down staffing schedules and carry on job analysis, and prepare job descriptions and specifications efficiently and effectively. All this data can be made available on a real-time basis so as to help align HR requirements with emerging business needs.

  HRIS facilitates both job analysis and manpower planning. Companies can maintain an updated skill inventory of their employees that can be used for manpower planning, identifying internal sources of labour and making promotion decisions. Employees can match job openings with their skills. Several organizations, such as P&G, AT&T, and American Express, to name a few, post job openings on electronic bulletin boards. Employees interested in the vacancies can apply online. Software then helps them match employee skills with job analysis data to produce a list of prospective employees.

- **Staffing**   The Internet is playing a growing role in the recruitment strategy of many organizations. An increasing number of companies are now providing career information or advertising specific vacancies on their corporate websites. At the same time, there has been a rapid proliferation of specialist recruitment websites offering their services to employers and potential candidates alike. Some companies have now geared up to receive job applications online and are using recruitment management software to streamline their administration. Some are also making use of online filtering of applications and testing facilities. Online technical skills testing are now done remotely on the web before interviewing candidates. Web-based simulation 'games' are used, which electronically simulate the job and assess whether candidates have sufficient skills to do it. Even interviews can be done through video conferencing.

- **Training**   A wide spectrum of training activities are being delivered electronically. Most commonly, courseware use tests, quizzes, and colourful graphics to provide relatively basic process- and knowledge-based training to large and disparate audiences. E-learning may also take the form of the virtual classroom, which can facilitate global knowledge sharing in an interactive environment. Trainers are using computer-based training and video conference discussion sessions which people can attend without leaving their homes. People enjoy the exercises as video games without the fear of losing face at doing the wrong things in public. The main benefits, companies are finding, from delivering training electronically include improved accessibility of training materials; increased flexibility, as training can be delivered anywhere and anytime; better consistency, with all staff receiving the same information at the same level; sustainability of content and learning; and substantial savings in the cost of travel and associated expenses.

- **Performance appraisal and compensation**   Employees now have online access to actual performance data as well as customer and team 360-degree feedback. Managers now have online job descriptions and performance appraisals. Performance management systems (PMSs) help set goals, self-review by employees, and discussions with bosses, counsellors, and mentors. Organizations are also establishing electronically driven compensation and reward systems. In addition, because of advanced software, even the level of benefits given to an employee can now be tied to an employee's performance. With online data, employees can self-monitor their progress and, thus, manage their own performance.

- **Career planning**   Organizations nowadays are establishing customized online learning and growth plans to help employees manage their career and to ensure they are continually challenged and are developing and growing as an employee. Career path planning, competency profiling, career mapping, needs analysis, and career counselling are some of the activities being done online. Organizations maintain systems of tracking career moves and progressions of employees, and this information is made available to employees. Feedback is received from employees on various career-related issues. Counselling sessions can be undertaken online. New career opportunities can be posted online for employee information. HR departments can identify career needs and help design individual career development plans. Organized employee data helps align needs with opportunities in the organization.

- **Employee relation management**   Expert software systems are used to monitor people metrics. Employee relations management (ERM) software by companies such as Siebel

Systems provide a web-based package of programmes to tackle tasks such as communicating with workers, training them, connecting them electronically, helping them collaborate, managing their performance, and sharing information about company performance and finances with employees. Companies are adopting innovative measures to ensure commitment such as posting organization's philosophy and values on computer screen savers.

These software tools act like 'smoke detectors', which warn HR in advance of potential people problems, so that preventive action can be taken. *Pre-exit surveys, what do you like,* and *what do you need more* surveys are used by organizations to warn managers about issues before those become threats or turn into lawsuits. These expert systems give managers instant access to laws, data, past practice, and legal advice.

Looking at the importance of IT in HRM activities, subsequent chapters highlight the role and impact of IT in different HRM functions at relevant places.

Taking the Office to the Clouds

The cloud is one innovation that is changing HR in a big way. Both collection and storage of data have always been a big part of HR's function. Until the cloud happened, data storage meant hard drive space, piles of paper, filing cabinets, and desk drawers. Naturally, this led to inefficiencies, security issues, data loss, and chaotic office spaces.

Today, all of this information can instead be stored in the cloud—documents and other pertinent information can be easily accessed online while data can be collected through simplified forms and automated processes. Employee information, such as forms, documents, personal files, payroll data, performance reviews, and contact information, can be archived and organized in one secure location.

Cloud-based systems have already made a tremendous impact on HR. However, in the future, HR's challenge will include the need for higher levels of interpretation and broader application of the cloud-based systems. Employees can easily log on to a portal where all that information is at their fingertips. One could use the same portal to apply for leave, change personal information, or view appraisal reports. Mobile HR apps make it easy for employees to access this kind of information anywhere and anytime. At the same time, cloud-based mobile platforms allow individuals to access their information more readily than ever before. Because of efficiencies, cost savings, employee expectations, and the power of storage—for HR and organizations as a whole—cloud technology is increasingly getting popular.

IMPACT ON HR CULTURE AND STRUCTURE

A fundamental shift in the economies has taken place—a shift that was less about any specific new technology but more about a new behaviour that is reaching critical mass. Millions of people at home and at work are communicating electronically. IT has led to the proliferation of some striking and overwhelming trends in the working conditions and job life of employees. IT and HR interaction has brought about a new information culture based on the 4-I principle—instantaneity, interactivity, informality, and intangibility, enveloped around the idea of information[11]:

- **Instantaneity**   We belong to a generation that is increasingly getting accustomed to instant solutions. It is synonymous with speed.
- **Interactivity**   IT facilitates people to people connectivity, thereby creating access to an ocean of information that can be shared even over long distances for decision-making purposes.
- **Informality**   IT has removed the barriers of space and time. There are no rigid rules now. IT tends to break and/or weaken the rigid chain of command prevalent in rank-oriented hierarchical organizational setups.
- **Intangibility**   IT is rooted in the concept of a virtual world. We may be working with a colleague whom we may have never met and who may be thousands of miles away.

Figure 3.1 explains the aforementioned 4-I principle.

Figure 3.1   The 4-I Principle

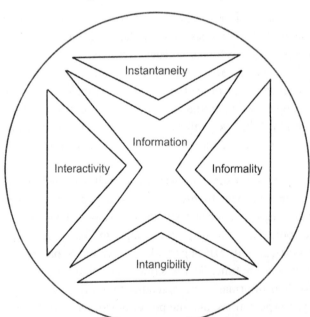

Source: M. N. Khan and F. T. Azmi (2005), Reinventing business organizations: The information culture framework, *Singapore Management Review 27*(2): 26–37.

Davis and Myer called this new phenomenon the *blur effect*.[12] The previously well-defined boundaries, methods, mechanisms, systems, objectives, issues, and opportunities within organizations have all become 'blurred'. Constant improvements in technology are rendering old systems redundant. Technology is having a major impact on the structure and forms of organizations. Not only is the nature of work and management changing, but organizational structures and culture are also changing as a result of advances in IT.

Emerging Organizational Forms

Traditional organizations were structured vertically, that is, they delegated authority in a pyramidal or triangular hierarchical fashion. Power was concentrated primarily at the top while people at the lower levels were assigned the task of implementing top management decisions. This organizational form existed in traditional organizations, emanating mainly from the mass production movement in the United States in the late 19th century.

Frederick Winslow Taylor, in his book *Principles of Scientific Management*, introduced the principles for designing and managing mass production facilities, such as Ford's automobile factory in Michigan.[13] The hierarchical structure was designed to manage highly complex processes, such as automobile assembly, where production could be broken down into a series of simple specialized steps. This centralized hierarchical structure was seen as an effective system for managing a large number of workers. It clearly demarcated people's responsibilities and functional area specialization. Hierarchy infused order and efficiency into the system. However, hierarchical structures tend to centralize power and authority at the highest levels. Bureaucracies slow down decision-making, communication, and action. This is dysfunctional in the present dynamic business environments that require quick action. Hierarchies are rigid structures and lack agility.

Owing to rapid changes in the environment, businesses have been moving away from traditional hierarchies in favour of structures that are more flexible and based on a team approach or network. A number of organizations are becoming decentralized and flat. A flat organization is an organization that has people and positions structured around fewer levels and is more team-based. The information culture warrants reinventing and redefining the organization. Organizations need to change the traditional organizational structure and setup. They need to do away with the typical chain of hierarchy and pave the way for more flexible systems. The information culture has led to important trends in organizational structuring, which also support the notion of SHRM. Some of these new and emerging forms of organizations are virtual organization, hyperarchy organization, velcro organization, and ambidextrous organization.

Virtual Organization

A virtual organization is an organization involving different entities (individuals or enterprises) coming together to work and requiring IT to support their coordination and communication. This new form of organization emerged in the 1990s and is also known as digital organization, network organization, or modular organization.[14] IT is the backbone of a virtual organization.

The term 'virtual organization' is used to describe a network of independent firms that join together, often temporarily, to produce a service or product. The ultimate goal of the virtual organization is to provide innovative, high-quality products, or services instantaneously in response to customer demands. A virtual organization can be considered to be a loose amalgam of technology, expertise, and networks, where people are not bound together by rigid lines of authority and there is blurring of organizational boundaries. Members of the network may include individuals and companies from all across the globe. The concept of virtuality is embedded in the concept of discontinuities.

The notion of discontinuity refers to the increasing flexibility in work, which has gradually altered the very nature of workplace. Emerging technologies have enabled organizational boundaries to become less confining, allowing dramatic changes in the workplace. Present day organizations comprise groups of people having discontinuous work group memberships or physical or temporal locations, often having discontinuous tasks and interacting with a discontinuous set of people working for other companies on a discontinuous set of projects.

The shift to this new organizational structure has been a result of the response to unprecedented changes in the environment. Many organizations are forming strategic relationships in order to compete effectively.[15] Many of these strategic relationships are conceived as a means to increase both the efficiency and effectiveness of those involved in these strategic relationships. Interorganizational relationships have become one of the most frequently used means of entering or expanding in the global marketplace.[16] The virtual organization concept is a specific case of such relationships.

The term 'virtual' is often used to differentiate work environments where individuals are physically or temporally dispersed. The chief feature of this structure is a team-based approach to problem diagnosing and solving. Members of these teams may be located in different countries and could have very different cultural backgrounds, having access to each other via IT. Thus, a virtual organization is a collection of business units in which people and work processes from the business units interact intensively in order to perform work that benefits all. These business linkages enable organizations to more tightly coordinate the transactions and activities across a value chain. The virtual corporation is more permeable than traditional organizational forms. C. K. Prahalad and V. Ramaswamy in their path-breaking work *Co-opting Customer Competence*, published in *Harvard Business Review* in 2000, state that the shift away from formal, defined roles is already occurring in business relationships.[17] Major business discontinuities, such as deregulation, globalization, technological convergence, and the rapid evolution of the Internet have blurred the roles that companies play.

There are several examples of virtual corporations today. When Apple Inc. linked its easy-to-use software with Sony's manufacturing skills in miniaturization, Apple was able to get its product to market quickly and gain a market share in the notebook segment of the personal computer (PC) industry. Apple today works with more than 100 external partners who are connected to a core 'Apple ideology'. Sun Microsystems is considered a successful example of virtual organization comprised of independently operating companies. With numerous 'SunTeams', members operate across time, space, and organizations to address critical business issues. Sun managers identify key customer issues and then form global teams with the critical skills and knowledge needed to address the issue. Meetings may take place via video conference calls.

As the electronic commerce (e-commerce) marketplace continues to grow, more and more consumers prefer the convenience of purchasing goods online. A number of companies have embraced the advantages of combining brick-and-mortar locations and supplemental Internet-based storefronts to meet the needs of the vast majority of consumers.[18] However, some e-commerce giants such as Amazon and Alibaba have become notable players in the market by operating through online presence alone. These can be called truly virtual companies.

William Davidow and Michael Malone, authors of *The Virtual Corporation*, claim that virtual corporations will be central to the new business revolution. Their concept of the virtual corporation brings diverse innovations together into a coherent vision for the 20th century corporation.[19]

Hyperarchy Organization

The term 'hyperarchy' appeared in a work by Philip Evans and Thomas S. Wurster titled 'Strategy and the new economics of information', published in the *Harvard Business Review* in 1997.[20] The article appeared at a time when fundamental shifts in the economics of information were underway—a shift that Evans and Wurster stated was less about any specific new technology than about the fact that a new behaviour was emerging and reaching critical mass. Millions of people at home and at work had started communicating electronically. This was starting to affect workplace behaviour and culture. Although the term 'hyperarchy' appeared way back in 1997, it gained ground much later as technology became even more pervasive.

The idea of hyperarchy has been derived from the hyperlinks of the World Wide Web. The World Wide Web is a hyperarchy. It allows one to move freely from one link to another. It is an agile and responsive information-sharing system. There are no rigidities here. Within a completely flat structure, all information on the Web is available to everybody who has access. On similar lines, a hyperarchy-based organization structure allows freedom, flexibility, access, and close-knit ties. Hyperarchy engenders the formation of a culture where information is freely exchanged. Decentralized decision-making enables more rapid adaptation to the environmental changes

Traditional hierarchies usually constraint communication and create asymmetries in information sharing on account of their overdependence on rigid chains of command and strict compartmentalization. Information moves up and down in gaps in hierarchical pyramids, and each gap results in delay and effort. A hyperarchy, on the other hand, provides employees easy access to one another and to people outside the organization in a rich variety of ways. It paves the way for a fluid, team-based, cross-functional collaborative work arrangement where people are not constrained by strict boundaries, levels, or departments.

Figure 3.2 depicts the differences between a hierarchy and a hyperarchy.

As can be seen from the figure, hyperarchy is a more flexible arrangement of people, not bound by strict and rigid chains of command and scalar reporting relationships typical of a hierarchy, but being woven around the concept of teams and flat structure. Evans and Wurster opine that in the future, more and more knowledge-based productive relationships will be designed around fluid, team-based collaborative communities, either within organizations (for example, deconstructed value chains) or in collaborative alliances with outsiders (for example, deconstructed supply chains).

Figure 3.2 Hierarchy versus Hyperarchy

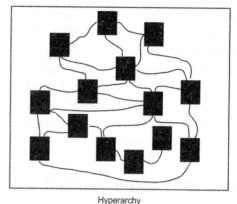

Hierarchy   Hyperarchy

Source: Adapted from P. Evans and T. S. Wurster (1997), Strategy and the new economics of information, *Harvard Business Review*, September–October, pp. 71–82.

A certain degree of hierarchy enables managers to optimally execute their roles and responsibilities by way of unity of command, distribution of power, and clearly delineated tasks and functional control. Using a hierarchical structure establishes clear authority, responsibility, and accountability vis-à-vis work. Firms like General Motors have developed and grown through hierarchy formats. However, hierarchies are limited because such organizations are not agile and cannot handle challenges emanating from environmental turbulences. As a result, advocates of hyperarchy agree that shared coordination within an organization through social networking or a peer-to-peer structure enables creation of a quick-response culture.

The important thing to note is that hyperarchy is not an antithesis to hierarchy. It is an improvement over the traditional form of structuring. Some elements of hierarchy are retained here as well. For instance, even though hyperarchy is based on a flat, team-based structure, it is arranged around positions and levels, though the emphasis on rigid chains is minimal. It is important to note that hierarchies still exist. In fact, organizations need some hierarchy to establish a certain level of order.

Velcro Organization

Large organizations have several units that cater to different businesses or markets. The challenge for organizations is to ensure that the different operating units maintain their distinct focus and yet integrate in such a manner as to achieve world-class standards of performance. Organizations need to continuously and effortlessly combine resources to address new and evolving opportunities that lie across the boundaries of existing business. The answer to this apparent contradiction between unit accountability as well as cross-unit strategic integration is the *velcro organization*.[21]

The concept of a velcro organization draws its analogy from velcro fasteners—a material made with a surface of tiny hooks and a complementary surface of a clinging pile that can be pressed together or pulled apart for easy fastening and unfastening. When the fasteners were invented in 1948 by Swiss engineer George de Mestral, they proved to be so popular that they replaced the earlier types of fasteners and hooks existing in the market. Velcro fasteners were superior in terms of ease, flexibility, and fastening strength. The feature 'easy fastening and unfastening' became the basis for developing the concept of a velcro organization.

As new challenges and opportunities emerge, business models need to be revised. Organizations are constantly required to realign resources—people, machines, infrastructure, and systems. Managers need to create agility like velcro hooks, where resources can be reconfigured seamlessly and with as little effort as possible. Like velcro fasteners, the relationships should be tight when managers are operating, but also capable of being loosened quickly for reassembly, when managers have to work in temporary groups.

A velcro organization provides linking pins between people and units. Large firms have to be organized into small projects that permit managers to support the intense work that goes into being competitive. Cross-functional collaboration between people and resources is common in a velcro organization. It has a tight–loose structure, that is, working together cohesively and easily rearranging in different groups and teams. A set of capabilities must be in place to build a velcro organization. Managers must be aware of the skills and competencies in their company. The work environment has to enshrine values such as flexibility, collaboration, and willingness to accommodate. Building these capabilities takes time and commitment.

Ambidextrous Organization

The concept of an ambidextrous organization became popular through an article in the *Harvard Business Review* by Charles O'Reilly III and Michael Tushman (2004).[22] They explain the idea of an ambidextrous organization through an analogy to the Roman god Janus, who had two sets of eyes—one pair focusing on what lay behind, the other on what lay ahead. Managers and corporate executives should be able to relate to this, they state. Managers must constantly look backwards, attending to the businesses of the past, while also gazing forward, preparing for the innovations required in the future. This requires executives to explore new opportunities even as they work diligently to exploit existing capabilities.

The term 'ambidextrous' literally connotes the ability to use both hands with equal facility. It usually refers to someone who is unusually skillful, adroit, and versatile. Organizational ambidexterity refers to an organization's ability to be efficient in the management of today's business and also be adaptable for coping with tomorrow's changing demand. Business organizations need to be versatile. Organizational ambidexterity refers to the ability of an organization to both explore and exploit—to compete in mature technologies and markets where efficiency and control are needed and to simultaneously compete in new technologies and markets where flexibility and experimentation are required. An example could be the Toyota production system, where employees perform both routine tasks such as automobile assembly (exploitation) but are also expected to continuously change their jobs to become more efficient (exploration).

O'Reilly and Tushman found, through their research, that some companies have actually been quite successful at both exploiting the present and exploring the future. In particular, these companies separate their new, exploratory units from their traditional, exploitative ones—making way for different processes, mechanisms, structures, and cultures. At the same time, they maintain tight links across units for coordination. These separate units are held together by a common strategic intent. In other words, they manage organizational separation through a tightly integrated senior team. They prove that a business does not have to escape its past to renew itself for the future.

To succeed in the long run, organizations need to innovate. O'Reilly and Tushman opine that to compete, companies must continually pursue various types of innovation—incremental, architectural, and discontinuous. *Incremental innovations* refer to small improvements in existing products, processes, and operations that enable companies to operate more efficiently. Google's launch of Gmail is an example of such dedication to incremental innovation. When Gmail was launched, it had limited features. Over time Google released more features and made the service better, faster, and easier to use. Years later, Gmail was taken out of the 'beta' version and finally listed as being 'complete'. *Architectural innovations* involve applying technological or process advances to fundamentally change some element of their business. For instance, using technological capabilities, banks shifted from human tellers to ATMs. *Discontinuous innovations* refer to radical advances, such as digital photography, that profoundly altered the terms for competition, rendering old products obsolete. It is important to note that not only can an established company renew itself through the creation of breakthrough products and processes, but it can do so without destroying or even hampering its traditional business.

The new and emerging organization designs, namely virtual, hyperarchy, velcro, and ambidextrous organizations, are characterized by one unique feature—their amorphous form. They can be seen as having flexible and permeable corporate boundaries, as against rigid traditional structures. Figure 3.3 depicts the evolving organizational forms.

Figure 3.3 Organization Design—Phases of Evolution

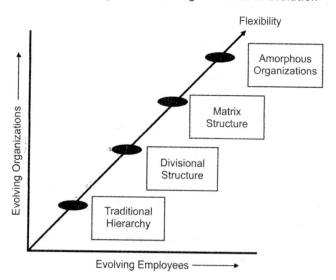

CHALLENGES AND OPPORTUNITIES

Every successful HRMS implementation involves a thorough needs analysis. Organizations should first examine how HRMS will be deployed. In a lot of cases, HRMS comes with a heavy cost—the cost of hardware, software, and installation of the system. Along with it is the cost of training the personnel who will be handling the system. A lot of organizations, therefore, go for horizontal applications before implementing complete e-HR. Recruitment solutions, for instance, can be dramatically effective as stand-alone systems. Organizations can start to see immediate returns from reducing their administrative burdens and recruitment costs. They can be used for testing water before implementing e-HR on a wider scale.

Further, success in the implementation phase relies on the ability of managers to manage change. When e-ventures fail, it is most often organizational issues such as top management shortsightedness and long-standing internal barriers that are the reasons. Bringing about organizational change for effective implementation of e-HR warrants a closer examination of how people will accept the new technology. Another organizational challenge is the creation of performance metrics to assess the value-added contribution of the new e-HR initiative. IT has the potential to lower administrative costs, increase productivity, lower speed response times, improve decision-making, and enhance service delivery. Since implementing e-HR involves huge expenditures, organizations need to have a mechanism in place to measure the paybacks resulting from it.

Creating hyperarchy, velcro, or virtual organization can be very complex and problematic; they fail as often as they succeed. Firms need to ensure that the skills and competencies of partners are complementary, not overlapping. Maintaining a separate identity and at the same time integrating with others is crucial. The boundary-blurring between different units demands effective coordination mechanisms to manage this loose collection of firms. Virtual structures create a loss of control over some operations. This ambiguity requires management to design rewards, benefits, employee development, staffing, and other employee-related issues carefully. New forms of organizations mandate providing training that is critical to team success.

Success requires a more complete makeover. It requires challenging old assumptions and systems. There is a reason why many start-ups have fewer problems in imbibing the information culture than established firms—it is easier to start something new than to change something old.[23] To imbibe opportunities, organizations need to rely on small moves, which are faster and safer than large ones. It is a globally accepted fact that systems and cultures cannot be built overnight—they evolve gradually. Organizations have to adopt a steady and continuous process of innovation and change management.[24] They need to be flexible, but flexibility has to be disciplined. The creation of flexible organizations imposes psychological and emotional traumas on people. There is a limit to an individual's elasticity.

In the present turbulent times when organizations are constantly enveloped in a digital environment, there is a growing realization of the need for deploying technology to gain strategic leverage and create new sets of competencies. IT is not a self-steering projectile. It needs to be shot correctly.

SOCIAL MEDIA AND HR

Social media are computer-mediated tools that allow people to create, share, or exchange information, interests, ideas, pictures, and videos in virtual communities and networks. Social media is the collective of online communication channels dedicated to community-based input, interaction, content sharing, and collaboration. Websites and applications dedicated to discussions, networking, blogging, social curation, and information sharing are among the different types of social media. Facebook, Twitter, LinkedIn, and Instagram are some prominent examples of social media. Social media has emerged as a powerful business and HR tool. Companies are experimenting with various social media tools and leveraging the same to create value for the organization. Business organizations are harnessing the power of social media for effective HRM.

Social media analytics is the practice of gathering data from online networks, blogs, and social media websites and analysing that data to make business decisions. The most common use of social media analytics is to mine customer sentiment to support marketing and customer service activities or mining through social network profiles to identify potential employees. According to a recent Microsoft survey of 9,000 workers across 32 countries, 31 per cent employees would be willing to spend their own money on a new social tool if it made them more efficient at work. This finding is quite interesting as it shows the extent to which employees see the business value of using technology on the job.[25]

Social media is being used most commonly by HR managers for talent acquisition, talent management, and talent retention.

Talent Acquisition

Talent acquisition has been the most obvious area of opportunity within many companies who embrace social media's potential. Social media sites like LinkedIn and Facebook are becoming increasingly important in job searching. If properly executed, it can help in accelerating the entire recruiting process from posting openings to sourcing candidates, reviewing CVs, making an offer, and onboarding. It often results in an efficient recruitment process and value for money.

Companies such as Entelo, Gild, TalentBin and the United Kingdom's *thesocialCV* analyse not just a job candidate's LinkedIn profile, Twitter feed, and Facebook postings but also their activity on specialty sites specific to their professions and other community forums. This approach to recruitment is creating a new technical world order, where job applicants are found and evaluated on the basis of their interests, personality profile, and interactions rather than merely on the basis of selection interview. These companies, at the intersection of data mining and recruiting, have made a business proposition out of locating 'hard to find' talent.

While more than 90 per cent of hiring managers use the professional networking site LinkedIn as a tool to source candidates; in certain industries like IT, more than 50 per cent of hiring managers scan candidates' profiles on Facebook and Twitter. A recent survey found that 43 per cent of job candidates research their prospective employer and read the job description on their mobile devices. And yet, only 20 per cent of Fortune 500 companies have a mobile-optimized career site. The rest of the 80 per cent of companies are missing the fact that tablet and smartphone users expect to see job listings and information in a visual way.[26]

Talent Management

Social media is being used as a tool to integrate employee-centric HR operations, regardless of where employees are in the world or organization hierarchy. Social media is also helping companies deliver robust and real-time training, development, performance feedback, and support. Progressive organizations are dispensing with the annual performance cycle and moving to more real-time feedback and coaching. Social media tools make true 360-degree feedback a reality. For instance, immediate insight and feedback about a team's performance can be gained from their internal and external customers using social media.

A large number of people, especially youngsters, like to play video games, and companies are taking note of this. They are deploying 'games' to a range of processes such as selection, induction training, onboarding, learning, and development. Companies are harnessing the potential of video games to elicit the same level of engagement to problem-solving, solving puzzles, and cracking codes for the purpose of selecting or training, for instance.

The technology research firm Gartner predicts that 40 per cent of global Fortune 1,000 companies will soon use games as the primary method to transform their business processes.[27] Companies are leveraging game mechanics as a tool to drive higher levels of business performance. A number of such games are used in training modules to help develop key skills such as negotiation, communication, time management, change management, and problem-solving. Companies are reporting greater training effectiveness and trainee satisfaction through these modes.

In a recent survey conducted by the Society for Human Resource Management, 45 per cent of HR leaders do not think annual performance reviews are an accurate appraisal for employees' work. Companies are leveraging the social recognition data to continuously collect information on employee performance from peers, teams, and customers. This facilitates an ongoing dialogue rather than a once-a-year review.[28] The software company Adobe relies on *CheckIn*, an informal system of real-time feedback, which has no forms to fill out or submit to HR. Instead, managers are trained in how to leverage the wisdom of people in an employee's social networks to create a holistic view of the employee's performance.

Talent Retention

Social media is being frequently used for employee communication, collaboration, and engagement. It is being used for transparent and effective collaboration with employees, customers, and suppliers. It is helping organizations in networking. Social media can be leveraged for connecting employees to interest groups. Many companies are deploying internal, more secure versions of instant messaging, YouTube, Twitter, and virtual classrooms to collaborate.

Social media has revolutionized how we communicate. Organizations are adopting tools to make it far easier to find experts, collaborate with peers, and learn from colleagues. This form of social learning and collaboration is helping build a sense of community and connection among employees. The consulting firm Accenture has added gaming concept to its social collaboration platform. Accenture studied how people play games, what motivates people to compete while gaming, and what strategies they adopt and then harnessed those principles to weed out negative traits in order to enhance collaboration and networking.

Social media platforms also help in brand building through employees. Innovative companies are mining connections on key social networking sites, maintaining their reputation online, and watching how their own talent is interacting online. They are also leveraging social media to create talent communities that engage passive candidates and promote their brand. Companies such as Ernst & Young and Sodexo are building employer brands on social networks to position themselves as the best place to work and to interact with potential candidates. They are using these networks to build an image and fish talent.[29]

Merits and Risks of Using Social Media

Social media has shown to increase productivity and employee engagement. It can also foster innovation through collaboration. As a result, a lot of organizations using social media technology have claimed several advantages resulting out of it. It is clear that social media tools are transforming the way we work and will continue to do so. Social media is redefining how companies innovate by connecting people and ideas in ways that have previously not been explored. It is changing the way we do business today. However, it is not without internal and external risk.

Social media presents organizations with several risks:

- Employees may start spending too much personal time on social media, thereby impinging on work time.
- Employees inadvertently or deliberately leak privileged information that belongs to the organization.
- Sharing of sensitive personal and private information with others at the workplace may be seen as encroachment upon the right to privacy by individuals.
- Negative publicity about the organization may be carried out by disgruntled employees.
- There is potential for viral growth of negative sentiment either in response to organization policy or about its products or services.
- Misrepresentation of organization's position on public issues may take place.
- There may be damage to company's reputation or desired brand image.

Many companies that use social media struggle to successfully integrate it into their daily business routines. However, as companies begin to realize the true value to be gained by social media adoption, they are giving serious thought to designing a sound social media policy. A positive social media policy with a positive orientation leads to employee engagement. To effectively implement and cultivate the appropriate usage of social media in a multigenerational workforce, it is essential for organizations to develop effective communication plans that allow for ongoing dialogue and feedback. While baby boomers and traditionalists may be more resistant initially to using social media and accepting social media policy, Generation X and Y will almost positively embrace the use of social media. A carefully planned communication strategy needs to be put in place in order to involve employees at all levels in efficacious use of social media. It is critical for HR professionals to understand what these tools are used for and assess the risks and opportunities they may present to an organization.

The rapid evolution of social media raises issues of employees' right to privacy and associated legalities that need to be thoroughly examined. Once leaders are better informed on the nature of social media utilization in their organization, they can prepare a strategy to leverage social media as a tool that aligns with the overall vision, mission, and strategy of the organization. Many leading organizations already have the framework of a policy that governs communications and this framework can provide an excellent foundation to beginners to consider while designing their own social media policy. It is important to have HR and legal teams involved in this discussion to make sure the emerging policies strike an appropriate balance between workplace and personal use while maintaining legal balance.

INTERNET OF THINGS, BIG DATA, AND HR

HR professionals are surrounded with a host of digital technology innovations in every aspect of HR functioning. Internet of Things (IoT) is one such innovation. IoT is an exciting concept, a world where 'billions of things are talking to each other', as technology experts describe it. Simply put, IoT is about connecting any device to the Internet (and/or to each other). This includes everything from cellphones, computers, printers, TVs, washing machines, coffee makers, microwave ovens, watches, wearable devices, and almost anything else one can think of. The IoT is, thus, a giant network of connected 'things' (and people). The relationship will be between people and people, people and things, and things and things.

Broadband Internet is becoming widely available, the cost of connecting is going down, more devices are being created with Wi-Fi capabilities and sensors built into them, technology costs are also decreasing, and smartphone penetration is mind-boggling. All of these things are creating a perfect climate for IoT. It is becoming increasingly clear that all this is a prelude to a vastly connected world. The analyst firm Gartner states that by 2020, there will be over 26 billion connected devices. That is a huge array of connections and networks (some even estimate this number to be much higher).[30]

The IoT rings in possibilities of a 'smart' scenario. So your alarm clock wakes up you at 5 a.m. and then notifies your coffee maker to start brewing coffee for you. The cellphone tells you the most important things to do. Your car could have access to your calendar, knows that you have a meeting, and tells you the best route to take through its global positioning system (GPS). Maybe your office equipment knows when it is running low on supplies and automatically re-orders more. The lights in your home or office have sensors that map activity across the entire floor, tracking motion and automatically switching off when no one is around. The watch you are wearing keeps track of your step count, blood pressure, and sugar levels, giving you health alerts. The reality is that the IoT allows for virtually endless opportunities and connections to take place.

IoT is about data, devices, and connectivity. All this is leading towards the Big Data universe. 'Big Data' is a term that describes the large volume of data—both structured and unstructured—that has the potential to be mined for useful decision-making. IoT generates Big Data on a daily basis, which can be capitalized by business organizations. By feeding all that information into the cloud, anyone with a smart device can access that information, and by running analytics on that data, draw trends and conclusions. For example, a package delivery company used sensors on trucks to monitor speed, directions, braking, and idling, among other things. IoT software helped the company plan more efficient routes, eliminate idling, and schedule truck maintenance in advance.

With the promising capabilities of IoT, a business manager will be able to control various activities in the company—from controlling inventory to managing field service employees. When every tool and device is connected to one centralized system, it becomes much easier to control different aspects of the business. This will improve data analysis and management, and broaden the opportunity to expand business.

The IoT is becoming an increasingly growing topic of interest and discussion. It should not be a surprise that workplaces will benefit greatly from IoT integration and Big Data. It is expected to change the organization of work and workspaces in substantive ways. This is going to impact HR in a number of ways. HR professionals are faced with a host of digital technology innovations in every aspect of HR functioning.

IoT is not just about finding more fascinating data, it is about drawing even more fascinating conclusions with this data lake and using it for decision-making. It is paramount that HR and IT units work together to design strategies so that data is properly managed, and duplicate or inconsistent data is weeded out. With humans at the centre of all these machines and devices and the huge repository of data, it is time for HR to gear up and prepare the workforce for this new wave of technology. IoT will empower people to better manage aspects of their work lives. These developments will enable employees to deliver more in less time. IoT has already entered the workplace and presents several exciting possibilities to the HR domain to engage in new ways and rethink the work environment.

In such an environment, HR departments can gather information about productivity, performance, communication patterns, teamwork, and other HR trends to create a more efficient and work-conducive environment. For instance, IoT-enabled building systems could provide real-time access to the location of employees, the analysis of which could help derive insights on time and motion, workflows, and efficiencies. IoT has great use in factories and manufacturing facilities. IoT sensors placed throughout a factory can determine when machines require maintenance or alert plant managers if temperature or humidity levels are too high for sensitive processes such as painting or mixing ingredients. Sensors can help detect dangers and threats at workplaces. Integrated devices and sensors installed in factories can help raise alarms about any possible danger, such as a machine gone unsecured, a chemical leak, or a fire breaking out. This can help make the plant safer.

IoT is aiding extensively in people analytics. Organizations are taking advantage of this already. IoT technology is fundamentally changing the way people metrics are handled. By gathering data about people and their workplace activities, companies are able to use an ever-widening range of information to help make the business run better. IoT can also give HR the potential to better keep track of routine HR issues such as employee attendance or disturbances on the shop floor. It is expected that IoT will help potentially improve interactions and collaborations among employees.

Perhaps most important to the future of IoT is rethinking the very concept of the workplace itself. IoT helps create flexible workspaces where individuals have the freedom to work without necessarily being confined to a traditional 'office' space. There will be new jobs, new tasks, and new skills required in an IoT world. HR function should develop the capability to deal with Big Data to derive insights that could shape the organization's strategy. This may require training in modern core skills like technical know-how, data mining, data analytics, and predictive thinking.

IoT is not without its challenges. The biggest HR challenge is to connect everything without losing human interaction. It is important to avoid that isolation and humanize technology, using it as a way to get teams together and preserve the human feeling of teamwork, even if they are not physically together. HR managers should also anticipate the disruptions that IoT will bring to their existing teams. IoT integration is likely to cause a strange level of workplace anxiety and inhibition to change. Many of these potential issues can be avoided by training, coaching, and communication. It is important to realize that IoT is more than just devices and computers; it is a complex, constantly evolving ecosystem. Barriers remain before this technology will fundamentally reshape our lives, but the direction is clear.

Dramatic advances are happening as IT begins to transform our lives in profound ways and envelops us in its distinctive culture. Much of this progress is real-time, with changes coming down the pike at quickening speed. As technology's potency and ubiquity have increased, so too has its strategic value. The intrinsic power of IT can be used to gain a competitive edge through the digitization of business models. IT is not a silver bullet. However, if it is aimed correctly, it can be an important competitive weapon.

HR Anecdote

A computer geek was swept away in a sea and kept shouting f1, f1 but no one really came to him and he drowned. (For general information, f1 = help)

Technology has pervaded our lives so much that we have almost become its slaves. As in the case above, we often forget our normal ways in our race for being technologically ahead.

The technology we use changes the way we work and live and the way we work and live changes the technology in use. This hand-in–glove interaction is called coevolution. Take the example of the invention of the spinning frame during the industrial revolution of the 18th century. The spinning frame made possible large-scale cloth production and created the need for factories. This made the spinning wheel evolve into giant machines.

We are seeing a similar coevolution between information technology and our lives now. The two major applications for PCs that transformed work were the word processor and the spreadsheet. With these tools, one could create documents and do calculations. Consequently, the focus shifted to not just creating documents but sharing them. The Internet with its communication and sharing facilities became widespread.

YouTube started in 2005 (Me at the zoo – YouTube—*https://www.youtube.com/watch?v=jNQXAC9IVRw* is the link of the first video uploaded to the site) as a video sharing website. Now that it's easy to share videos, more and more companies are utilizing its power of information dissemination into their HR programmes. Videos help share information in a more compact and digestible way. This evolutionary chain continues—from documents to images to videos to virtual reality and what next.

Source: Adapted from The co-evolution of technology and organising, retrieved from http://www.anecdote.com/2009/05/the-co-evolution-technology-organising/.

News Grab
The world belongs to HR data experts

HR departments around the world will experience profound shifts during the next few years, and it's all being driven by a single factor data. It will change the way organizations recruit and manage their staff. The potential benefits for those who get it right are massive. With the knowledge, HR must be able to show credible data relating to factors such as productivity, engagement, and performance.

Data-driven recruitment and management
Rather than using job descriptions, HR departments will increasingly focus their recruitment activity on staff profiles. These profiles will be based on high-performing people already within the organization. A new data-driven approach will be taken for staff management too. Rather than promoting people on personal intuition or pressure from managers, decisions will be based on data gathered about their actual performance.

Predictive analytics
In order to really utilize their employees' best skills, businesses will look at their workers' behavior more closely. Cloud-based systems will take talent and succession-planning data, to help predict and make intelligent next-role recommendations and connect employees with mentors to help prepare them for that particular role. Predictive analytics not only leads to the source of the breakdown, but also provides forward-looking insights that illustrate how an issue or employee may evolve.

Chief human resource officers (CHROs) will recognize that modern, intuitive application user interfaces and consumer friendly applications matter more than ever in the year ahead. Many CHROs are looking for ways to create quality experiences that will delight instead of frustrate employees. Digital solutions are the gateway to collecting and analysing quality data. So, through the information gleaned from the digital HCM software, businesses will be able to determine how to best align talent strategies to business objectives and remain a top competitor in the workplace. Through embracing the opportunities of data and analytics, the HR department of 2017 and beyond will become an even more vital resource for successful organizations.

Source: Adapted from *Economic Times*, The year 2017 belongs to HR data experts, 24 January 2017, retrieved from https://economictimes.indiatimes.com/small-biz/hr-leadership/people/the-year-2017-belongs-to-hr-data-experts/articleshow/56699830.cms.

CHAPTER SUMMARY

- Changes in technology have become particularly significant in the post-millennium world.
- New forms of ICT have emerged, most of which have implications for how people construct their identities and how they work.
- On account of the implementation of e-enabled technology in organizations, the very nature of the workplace has transformed.
- E-HR refers to the use of electronic and web-enabled techniques in the context of HR of an organization.
- IT has transformed the way HRM activities like recruitment, selection, training, pay calculations, and appraisal are performed.
- IT and HR interaction has brought about a new information culture based on the 4-I principle: instantaneity, interactivity, informality, and intangibility.
- Some of these new and emerging forms of organization, owing to IT, are virtual organization, hyperarchy organization, velcro organization, and ambidextrous organization.
- Social media has emerged as a powerful business and HR tool. Social media is being used most commonly by HR managers for talent acquisition, talent management, and talent retention.
- HR function is getting significantly impacted by the new wave of IoT and Big Data.

EXERCISES AND DISCUSSION QUESTIONS

1. What do you understand by e-HR? Explain how key HR systems have transformed to support e-HR.
2. Discuss how IT has impacted the nature of organizational structure and culture, resulting in the evolution of new organizational forms.
3. 'Social media has emerged as a powerful business and HR tool'. Write a note to explain this statement. Give examples to support your argument.
4. Using the example of any organization:
   i. Identify areas where IT is being used extensively in HRM
   ii. Show whether IT has impacted its culture and structure
   iii. Try talking to a senior HR manager of the organization to know whether this transformation has led to any positive outcomes

CASELET

Circular Organization at Harley-Davidson Motor Company

The biggest takeaway in a circle organization is that ... positive change will happen as long as you don' try to force it your way. If you lead participative change, it will work.

— **Richard F. Teerlink**, Former CEO, Harley-Davidson Motor Company

Background Note

In 1903, Harley-Davidson (H-D) was established at Milwaukee in the United States by William S. Harley (William) and Arthur Davidson (Arthur). They manufactured their first motorcycle in a 10 × 15 feet wooden shed with a hand-written sign on the door that read 'Harley-Davidson Motorcycle Company'. On 17 September 1907, the name 'Harley-Davidson Motor Company' was incorporated. In 1908, H-D sold the first motorcycle for police duty to the Detroit Police Department in Michigan in the United States. In 1917, during the First World War, there was an increased demand for the US motorcycles overseas. This increase in demand made H-D a leader in innovative engineering by the 1920s.

HR Initiatives

H-D implemented the Accenture human capital development framework (HCDF) to encourage greater employee participation and collaboration. This initiative was undertaken in order to bring about improvements in its HR functions, and thereby attain improved performance. One major intervention that H-D adopted to encourage greater employee participation and collaboration was the circle organization.

The rationale behind creating such circles was to come out of the chain of control leadership style of management and foster teamwork among the employees. H-D took these initiatives after the company's new management realized that in order to survive in a highly competitive market in the long run, it was essential to make the company a continuous learning and improving organization where there was free and open communication between all levels of the employees. Each and every employee, it felt, should be able to comprehend their roles in the company and the consequence of their roles to the company.

The purpose was to move from a triangular organization to a circular arrangement—one that could promote creation of self-directed teams. Creating such a circular organization had two important outcomes—first, it helped build a close-knit flexible team structure that transcended the boundaries of hierarchy and, second, it helped identify future leaders by enabling managers to work with people from different units and departments.

The circle organization is depicted as three interlocking circles that define 'the interdependent core processes' of an organization; these are surrounded by a larger circle that represents all stakeholders. In H-D's case, the circle groups depict those who 'create demand', 'produce product', and 'provide support'. In the centre, where all intersect, stands the leadership and strategy council (LSC), a small, innovative entity that identifies the business issues affecting the entire organization (for example, strategic plans, HR policies, and operating budgets) and coordinates cross-functional interdependent activities. A circle organization can increase organizational flexibility, become more customer-centric, and deflate internal hierarchies.

The 'musts' for employee involvement at H-D were:

- Management, with the help of its words and actions, must reveal that continuous improvement of quality and efficiency is a way of life, and not merely another programme.
- Management must be firmly committed to people-building philosophy, which implied the belief that employees are thinking, rational human beings and, hence, should be encouraged to develop and grow.

- Management must be strictly committed to the employee involvement programme and should display that commitment to cultivate mutual trust between the employees and the management.
- Employees should be comprehensively trained in problem-solving and methods of quality control.

Though H-D showed some progress on the human capital infrastructure and human capital strategy front, it still has a long way to go. Even with a sound vision and strong employee buy-in, a circle organization cannot simply power ahead. There are some employees who were slower on adapting to the new form and some who thought it was a lot of interdependency of roles. There was an increase in employee turnover during the transformation period. It was tough to bring about the change from a comfortable system to one that demanded lot of flexibility and discomfort. That is why the important thing to understand is that it is an evolutionary, incremental process. However, overall, people started to understand how this process was intended to make their life a lot more meaningful in the workplace. The Chairman says, 'People think business is hard and tough. They've forgotten that the world is a bunch of communities.'[31]

Questions for Discussion

1. Discuss the unique features of organizational design at Harley-Davidson.
2. Identify the problems faced by the company and suggest precautionary measures for such an organizational form.

NOTES

1. Retrieved from http://wearesocial.com/uk/special-reports/digital-social-mobile-worldwide-2015. Retrieved 15 September 2016.
2. G. Dessler (2013), *Human resource management* (Upper Saddle River, NJ: Pearson Education).
3. D. Ulrich (1997), *Human resource champions* (Boston, MA: Harvard Business School Press).
4. M. E. Porter (1991), Towards a dynamic theory of strategy, *Strategic Management Journal 12*(8): 95–117.
5. Dessler, *Human resource management*.
6. D. Kenny and J. F. Marshall (2000), Contextual marketing: The real business on the Internet, *Harvard Business Review 78*(6): 119–125.
7. I. Beardwell and L. Holden (1998), *Human resource management* (New Delhi, India: Macmillan India Limited).
8. R. W. Griffeth, P. W. Hom, and S. Gaertner (2000), A meta-analysis of antecedents and correlates of employee turnover: Update, moderator test, and research implications for the next millennium, *Journal of Management 26*(3): 463–488.
9. K. Isaacson and S. Peacey (2012), *Human resource and social media*, report by KPMG. Retreived from https://www.kpmg.at/fileadmin/KPMG/Publikationen/Broschueren_und_Studien/Human_ Resources_and_Social_Media.pdf.
10. K. McCormick (2003), The rise and rise of E-HR, *Monster HR*, 11 June.
11. M. N. Khan and F. T. Azmi (2005), Reinventing business organizations: The information culture framework, *Singapore Management Review 27*(2): 26–37.

12. C. Meyer and S. Davis (1998), *Blur: The speed of change in the connected economy* (New York, NY: Perseus Publishing).

13. F. W. Taylor (1947), *The principle of scientific management* (New York, NY: Dover Publications).

14. J. Black and S. Edwards (2000), Emergence of virtual or network organizations: Fad or feature, *Journal of Organizational Change Management 13*(6): 567–576.

15. R. Grenier and G. Metes (1995), *Going virtual: Moving your organization into the 21st century* (Upper Saddle River, NJ: Prentice Hall).

16. R. Varadarajin and M. Cunningham (1995), Strategic alliances: A synthesis of conceptual foundations, *Journal of Academy of Marketing Science 23*(4): 282–296.

17. C. K. Prahlad and V. Ramaswamy (2000, January–February), Co-opting customer competence, *Harvard Business Review 78*: 79–87.

18. R. Bradt (1998), *Virtual organizations: A simple taxonomy*, Infothink. Retreived from http://www.infothink.com/resources/ virtual org summary.html.

19. W. II. Davidow and M. S. Malone (1993), *The virtual corporation* (New York, NY: Harper Business).

20. P. Evans and T. S. Wurster (1997, September–October), Strategy and the new economics of information, *Harvard Business Review 75*: 71–82.

21. J. L. Bower (2003, November/December), Building the Velcro Organization: Creating value through integration and maintaining organization-wide efficiency, *Ivey Business Journal 68*(2): 1–10; Prahlad and Ramaswamy, Co-opting customer competence, 79–87.

22. C. O'Reilly, III and M. Tushman (2004), The ambidextrous organization, *Harvard Business Review 82*(4): 74–83.

23. Prahlad and Ramaswamy, Co-opting customer competence, 79–87.

24. D. Farrell (2003), The real new economy, *Harvard Business Review 81*: 104–112.

25. Retrieved from http//news.microsoft.com/download/presskits/enterprisesocial/.../ESCResearchSumPPT.pdf.

26. Retrieved from https://www.glassdoor.com/employers/popular-topics/hr-stats.htm.

27. Retrieved from www.forbes.com/sites/jeannemeister/2014/01/06/2014-the-year-social-hr-matters.

28. SHRM/Globoforce Employee Recognition Survey 2013, retrieved from www.globoforce.com (Press Releases Archive).

29. Retrieved from http://www.livemint.com/Leisure/3lcJnntrIsZo4jTMDVGMXJ/Newage-hiring.html.

30. J. Morgan (2014), A simple explanation of the internet of things, retrieved from https://www.forbes.com/sites/jacobmorgan/2014/05/13/simple-explanation-internet-things-that-anyone-can-understand/#626aaf2b1d09.

31. With inputs from https://www.harley-davidson.com.

Strategy Formulation

Part I

THE FRAMEWORK OF STRATEGIC HUMAN RESOURCE MANAGEMENT
Chapter 1: Concept of Strategic Human Resource Management

Part II

CONTEXT OF SHRM
Chapter 2: Environment of SHRM
Chapter 3: Technology and HRM

Part III

STRATEGY FORMULATION
Chapter 4: Strategy Formulation and HRM
Chapter 5: Work Flow Analysis and Strategic Job Analysis

Part IV

STRATEGY IMPLEMENTATION
Chapter 6: Strategic Human Resource Planning and Staffing
Chapter 7: Strategic Training and Development
Chapter 8: Performance Management and Compensation
Chapter 9: Employee Relations, Engagement, and Termination

Part V

STRATEGY EVALUATION
Chapter 10: Strategic HR Evaluation

CHAPTER 4

Strategy Formulation and HRM

Chapter Overview

This chapter focuses on strategy formulation in human resource management (HRM). The chapter delves with the role of human resource (HR) function in the strategic management process and vice versa. It highlights the importance of human resources to strategy. It also discusses the various approaches to integration of strategic planning and HRM and the factors affecting integration. The typology of HR systems in light of strategic issues is also discussed.

Learning Objectives

1. To understand the role of HR function in the strategic management process and the role of strategy in HR function
2. To develop an understanding about the intrinsic importance of human resources to strategy
3. To comprehend the various approaches to integration of strategic planning and HRM and the factors affecting integration

OPENING STORY

Rethinking the Role of HR

The increasing emphasis on strategic HR and the need for HR departments to add value got even more evident when the call for change in the HR function was seen on the cover of July–August 2015 issue of the *Harvard Business Review* (*HBR*). With its subtitle *It's Time to Blow Up HR and Build Something New. Here's How,* the verdict was clear. However, this is not the first time that *HBR* has emphasized the need for HR function to reinvent. In fact, the pioneering work of Dave Ulrich that highlighted the changing roles of HR professionals, 'A new mandate for human resources', was published in the January–February issue of *HBR* in 1998. In his path-breaking article, Ulrich begins by asking 'Should we do away with HR?' He then goes on to opine,

> In recent years, a number of people have been debating that question. The debate arises out of serious and widespread doubts about HR's contribution to organizational performance.... There is good reason for HR's beleaguered reputation. It is often ineffective, incompetent, and costly; in a phrase, it is value sapping. Indeed, if HR were to remain configured as it is today in many companies, I would have to answer the question above with a resounding

'Yes—abolish the thing!' But the truth is HR has never been more necessary. The competitive forces that managers face today and will continue to confront in the future demand organizational excellence. The efforts to achieve such excellence—through a focus on learning, quality, teamwork, and reengineering—are driven by the way organizations get things done and how they treat their people. Those are fundamental HR issues. To state it plainly: achieving organizational excellence must be the work of HR.

Ulrich then goes on to describe a multifaceted approach to delivering HR services that meets the needs of both employees and employers, and positions HR as a significant contributor to organizational success. Ulrich's model of HR roles discussed therein serves today as a valuable framework for understanding the complex set of activities that HR professionals carry out, from operational to strategic jobs, keeping in mind both people and processes to gain competitive advantage.

Seventeen years later, the July–August 2015 issue emphasizes on 'Rethinking HR'. The title *It's Time to Blow Up HR* only reiterates how the HR mandate is still left to go a long way. Adi Ignatius, the editor, states that 'the month's spotlight advocates rethinking HR from top to bottom. It's not that we don't like HR; it's just that we believe it can be improved'.

Marc Effron and Miriam Ort, in their digital article published on *HBR*'s website, however, disagree with the premise that HR needs to be completely overthrown. They opine that it is much easier to propose dramatic reinvention and trendy new practices than it is to execute the fundamentals of great HR. While change in the HR function is overdue, the function will not be deemed successful until it can flawlessly do one thing—improve business results by increasing the company's talent quality and depth. Getting to that outcome is simpler and easier than it might appear.

In order to add significant value to a business, HR must be able to support and enable the execution of strategy through building organizational capability. The great advantage that HR has in this area is that, ultimately, all strategy is executed by people—people who need to be supported, trained, and equipped to fulfil the strategic vision. This is the real role of HR. HR has plenty of room to improve, and this is a moment of enormous opportunity.

Sources: D. Ulrich (1998), A new mandate for human resources, *Harvard Business Review*, 76(January–February): 124–134; A. Ignatius (2015), Rethinking HR (Editorial), *Harvard Business Review*, July–August; M. Effron, and M. Ort (2015), The unsexy fundamentals of great HR, *Harvard Business Review*, 19 August. retrieved from https://hbr.org/2015/08/the-unsexy-fundamentals-of-great-hr, retrieved 5 September 2016.

STRATEGIC MANAGEMENT PROCESS

The strategic management process involves defining an organization's strategy. It is a process by which managers make a choice of a set of strategies for the organization that will enable its goals. Strategic management is a continuous process that appraises the business and industries in which the organization is involved, appraises its competitors, fixes goals to meet all the present and future competitors, and then reassesses each strategy.

A strategic management process typically involves the following five steps:

1. **Laying down Strategic Intent**   The first thing organizations do is define their strategic intent. It refers to defining the intention or purpose of why the organization is existing. It

involves clearly articulating the organizational vision and mission. Organizations also lay down their goals and objectives on the basis of the overarching vision and mission.

2. **Environmental Scanning**   Environmental scanning refers to a process of collecting, scrutinizing, and providing information for strategic purposes. The purpose is to identify both the strengths and weaknesses of the organization as well as any threats and opportunities that may arise along the path.

3. **Strategy Formulation**   Strategy formulation is the process of deciding the best course of action for accomplishing organizational objectives. Strategy formulation involves determining how the goals will be attained. After conducting a thorough environment scanning, managers formulate strategies at different levels in an organization, namely corporate, business, and functional strategies.

4. **Strategy Implementation**   Strategy implementation implies making the strategy work as intended or putting the organization's chosen strategy into action. Strategy implementation includes designing the organization's structure, distributing resources, developing a decision-making process, and managing human resources.

5. **Strategy Evaluation**   Strategy evaluation is the final step of the strategy management process. Strategy evaluation and control actions include performance measurements, consistent review of internal and external issues, and making corrective actions when necessary. Evaluation makes sure that the organizational strategy as well as its implementation help in attaining the organizational objectives.

The above is a more formal, rational, analytical, and outcome-oriented strategic management process. This traditional approach to strategic management assumes that strategy formulation and implementation are separate functions. Top management of the company formulates a comprehensive strategy, which is then implemented by lower-level staff.[1] A command-and-control or top-down mentality pervades the organization. The logic of the formal analytical view of strategic planning rests on an 'ends–ways–means' model. This rational decision-making is concerned with the content or 'what' of strategy and has nothing to say about how to achieve it.[2]

As an alternative to the 'rational-outcome' view, other writers have drawn attention towards the rationality of the 'process', that is, how outcomes are actually achieved. According to this stream, formulation and implementation merge into a fluid process of learning through which creative strategies evolve in an emergent fashion.[3] Strategic decision-making in a learning organization takes shape in an entrepreneurial fashion, that is, bottom-up. The learning approach is based on a means–ways–ends sequence. A company begins by investing in its capabilities and then it encourages its managers to exploit ways to achieve its ends.[4]

As already discussed in Chapter 1, two divergent approaches to SHRM can be identified based on the above two approaches to strategic management[5]:

- **Instrumental approach**   This approach draws upon the rational-outcome model to view HRM as something that is driven by corporate strategy.
- **Humanistic approach**   This approach utilizes the process theory to emphasize the reciprocal relationship between strategic management and HRM.

Although the two types of strategic management processes differ, their use is not mutually exclusive, as companies often tend to employ both approaches. It is probably more useful to think of strategic management as a balance between rational-outcome and emergent approaches.

IMPORTANCE OF HUMAN RESOURCES TO STRATEGY

Over the years, HRM has become increasingly important to general management, largely as a result of its role in providing competitive advantage. This is in contrast to traditional emphasis on transferable resources, such as technology, equipment, or machines that can be purchased by competitors. Increasingly, it is being recognized that competitive advantage can be obtained through human resource competencies, which is inimitable, unlike technology or equipment.

Apart from its role in providing competitive advantage through a quality workforce, the necessity of controlling direct and indirect labour costs has also elevated the role of HRM. General managers have gained greater awareness of the impact of inefficient use of human resources. Managers have realized the cost of underutilized workers, lack of trust, resistance to change, poor employee relations, and lack of motivation and dissatisfaction resulting from job. Interestingly, greater attention is being paid by senior managers towards proper utilization of human resources through better HR practices and culture.

It is interesting to note that, with the emergence of SHRM philosophy, the role of HR managers has elevated from being strategy implementers to strategy formulators. It is understood that improved HRM can play a key role in the organization's competitive strategy and in the development of distinctive competencies. Not surprisingly, HRM is becoming integrated into the strategic management process. As HRM becomes a more important component of a company's competitive strategy, general management has an incentive to ensure alignment and consistency between corporate strategy and HR strategy.

HR is gaining importance in the strategic management process. The rationale is that HR practices that are aligned with future strategic needs produce superior organizational performance.[6] Strategic thinkers need to understand the importance of having the right kind of people in order to lead the organization towards attainment of its goals. Thus, a coherent HR strategy must be developed and linked to the organization's overall strategy.

Realizing the fact that people are the most important asset, Hindustan Unilever Limited (HUL), a subsidiary of Unilever and one of India's largest fast-moving consumer goods company, has leveraged the capabilities of people to drive business success. It had the distinction of being a 'dream employer' and 'employer of choice' in the recent past, according to leading ranking agencies. The company maintains that sustainability is central to its way of doing business and its brands too try to integrate the concept of sustainability. The performance of employees is considered essential for the growth of the company. It, therefore, tries to build a work culture that is focused on winning, wherein every employee is encouraged to fully develop. HR professionals play a lead role in helping to attract, develop, and retain the right talent so as to deliver outstanding business performance.

INTEGRATION OF STRATEGY AND HRM

The integration of business strategy and HR strategy is particularly important for success in the long run. Furthermore, with the recognition of the potential contributions of HR, senior managers have taken on greater responsibilities for these planning efforts. Integration of strategic planning and HR planning is gaining currency. It is an activity that demands integration of the skills and knowledge of the human resource for attaining strategic goals.

Various approaches to this integration can be visualized depending on the degree of fit between HR and organizational strategy. There are two predominant approaches to HRM and strategy integration.[7] One group of authors talk about the reactive role of HRM, viewing organizational strategy as the driving force determining HRM strategies, that is, derived from an instrumental approach to SHRM.[8] A second group of authors have suggested that HR should play a more central and proactive role by becoming involved in the strategy formulation phase, that is, derived from a humanistic approach to SHRM.[9]

Torrington and Hall have talked of five such possible types of integration[10]:

- *Approach A* There is no relationship at all between organizational and HR strategies in the organization. This is a typical picture that existed several years ago and still exists today in several small and traditional organizations.
- *Approach B* There is a growing recognition of the importance of employees, and HR strategy is designed to fit the organization's strategy.
- *Approach C* It takes the relationship one step further, as it recognizes the need for a reciprocal relationship between strategy and HRM. Strategy may not always be feasible and alternative possibilities need to be reviewed.
- *Approach D* It shows a much closer involvement between organizational and HR strategies. It considers HR as the key to competitive advantage. Organizational and HR strategies are developed together in an integrated way.
- *Approach E* It offers an alternative form, different from integration, which places HR strategy in the prime position. The argument is that if people are the key to competitive advantage, then there is a need to build on people's strengths.

Other authors have also identified various types of linkages. Lengnick-Hall and Lengnick-Hall have proposed a reciprocal linkage between competitive strategy and HR strategy.[11] Golden and Ramanujam have identified four stages in the evolution of HR–strategy linkages almost along the lines of Torrington and Hall.[12] These are administrative linkage, one-way linkage, two-way linkage, and integrative linkage. The last stage goes beyond the reciprocal relationship to an equal involvement of the HR function in the development of strategic business plans and HR strategies. Dyer distinguishes four types of linkages between HRM and the strategy formulation process: parallel, inclusion, participation, and review.[13] Baird and Meshoulam state that the stage of development in HRM should match the stage of development of the parent organization.[14] Strategic integration is appropriate only after the HRM function has progressed through earlier forms of development.

The strategy and HR planning linkage is affected by a number of influences, including environmental factors. Some of these factors are size of the organization (large versus small), age of the organization (new versus experienced), sector (manufacturing versus service), level of technology (capital versus labour intensive), ownership status (public versus private concerns), life-cycle stage (growth versus maturity), and unionization (high versus low).[15] The stage of growth and age of the organization also affect integration due to learning and maturation effects.[16] The current situation of markets, whether declining, stable, or growing, as well as industry characteristics impact integration. Service companies show higher level of strategic HR perspective.[17] Changing demands of the industry and skill requirements also have the potential to affect the degree of integration between strategic planning and HR planning.[18]

Firm-level factors, such as having a progressive organizational philosophy, values, and a strong culture are also positively related to integration. Personal factors, such as HR manager's capability, top management's support, and employee competence also impact the views that an organization has towards integration. Where senior management gives credence to the HR department as a pivotal function, there are more chances of integration. Likewise, HR managers' credibility and business acumen impact how much influence they are able to exercise in the strategy formulation process. The HR function often fails to play a major role in the organization's strategy formulation process because of the planning inadequacies of HR executives. HR executives need to inculcate planning skills, including knowledge of planning methodologies and techniques; business acumen and understanding; change management skills; information management skills; and a knack for crunching numbers and statistics—often very important for planners and strategists.

STRATEGY FORMULATION AND PLANNING

Strategy deals with providing direction, coordination, and a decisional framework. The strategy formulation process emphasizes purposeful activity through a logical formulation of goals, examination of alternatives, and delineation of plans prior to actions. The process of strategic planning involves generation of alternative strategies for achieving the organizational objectives.

Most organizations, until a few years ago, viewed the HRM function as having an implementation role, and it has been less common to find companies using unique HR capabilities as a primary input in strategy formulation. However, recently companies have started relying on HR capabilities in the strategy formulation process. HRM can play an important role in the strategic planning process. For example, an organization may think of expanding in a new country. HRM would be expected to provide feedback on the talent acquisition and staffing implications. It may examine the competencies, capabilities, and strengths needed for the new strategy.

In a large number of organizations today, HR managers are directly part of the strategic planning process. Senior HR managers are part of executive committees making the final decisions on these planning proposals. Very often, HR directors guide policy decisions by participating in strategy formulation at the level of board of directors. HR executives play an important role in each stage of the strategy formulation process. For instance, HR executives can play an important role in determining the strategic intent. They provide critical information about the existing and required capabilities that will aid in the achievement of objectives. They also play an important role in environmental scanning and analysis. HRM is in a unique position to supply competitive intelligence that may be useful in strategy formulation. For example, HR managers can provide information on competitors' skills and competencies. HR executives provide vital information that may help in better assessment of strengths, weaknesses, opportunities, and threats. If the HR department maintains a robust HRMS, it may identify critical weaknesses in its capabilities and skills.

Just as the concept of strategy and strategic planning is important, so is the concept of HR strategy. The SHRM perspective involves a two-way process. HR managers participate in the strategy formulation process and HR inputs serve as a vital ingredient in evaluating strategic alternatives. At the same time, HR strategy is extremely important as it lays down an action plan for managing human competencies, which are the backbone of the success of any organization. Senior managers are expected to participate in the process of determining HR strategies. HR strategy focuses on the alignment of the organization's HR practices, policies, and programmes with corporate and strategic business unit plans.

It is important to make a distinction here—that the HRM strategic planning is different from HR planning. The HRM strategic plan lays down the HR strategy and objectives in the same way as the organizational strategic plan discussed earlier. It is the major objective of the HR function that the organization wants to achieve. On the other hand, HR planning, sometimes also called manpower planning, consists of the detailed plan regarding demand and supply of people to ensure that the strategic plan is achieved. The HR plan deals with manpower planning to ensure that there are right people with the right competencies at the right place.

HR strategy is an elaborate and systematic plan of action developed by the HR department. The HRM strategic plan can be seen as a larger objective that the organization wants to achieve, and the HR plan as the specific activities carried out to implement this strategic plan. In other words, the HR strategic plan may include long-term goals, while the HR plan may include short-term objectives that are tied to the overall strategic plan.

An HRM strategic plan cannot be written alone. The plan should involve everyone in the organization. For example, as the plan develops, the HR manager should meet with various people in departments and find out what skills the best employees have. In addition, the HR manager will likely want to meet with the financial department and executives who do the budgeting, so that they can determine HR needs and recruit the right number of people at the right time. In addition, once the HR department determines what is needed, communicating a plan can gain positive feedback that ensures the plan is aligned with the business objectives.

TYPOLOGY OF INTEGRATED HR SYSTEMS

A typology of strategic HR systems indicates how HR activities vary in their contributions to corporate strategy. Integration of HR strategies varies according to strategic archetypes. Various typologies of strategic HR systems have been proposed by scholars. Three such frameworks deserve mention here.

Porter's Competitive Strategies

Michael Porter's framework provides a good basis for understanding competitive strategies at the business level. Porter's framework specifies three business strategies for competition: (*a*) cost leadership as the low-cost product or service provider, (*b*) differentiation, such as by superior quality or service, and (*c*) focus or niche strategies that concentrate on a narrow area of differentiation. Such business competitive strategies are important to HR strategy formulation because different HR practices are consistent with different competitive strategies. If a firm has adopted a cost leadership strategy, then it should have HR practices consistent with this strategy. With cost leadership, a firm would probably not have a compensation system that offers extensive perks for executives, nor would it pursue a practice of wage leadership. Innovation and quality strategies require employee commitment, while cost leadership strategies can only be achieved through employee participation in cost-cutting.

Miles and Snow's Typology

Raymond Miles and Charles Snow have developed combinations of HR practices suited for different firm strategies, which is by far the most popular typology.[19] Miles and Snow observed four basic types of strategic behaviour and organizational characteristics (*a*) defenders (low-cost producers), (*b*) prospectors (product differentiators and innovators), (*c*) analysers (imitators of successful prospectors and focused operations), and (*d*) reactors (companies with dysfunctional strategies).

Defenders operate in a narrow domain and protect it aggressively. The basic strategy of defenders is to 'build' or 'make' human resources. The role of HR may be limited to file maintenance or record keeping, having only an administrative linkage. Prospectors are virtually the opposite of defenders. They continually search for new products or markets. Prospectors need a decentralized market-based design with employee participation. Prospectors require that the HR department be proactive and involved in strategic decisions. Prospectors typically 'buy' in talent. Analysers are a hybrid of defenders and prospectors. Analysers are expected to have greater HR–strategy integration in order to design HR practices to strike a balance between the two strategies. Analysers report higher levels of integration. Reactors lack a consistent strategy. Table 1.3 (given in Chapter 1) depicts this typology.

Sonnenfeld and Pieperl's Typology

Systematic differences in utilization of HR practices may be explained by a typology of HR systems developed by Jeffrey Sonnenfeld and Maury Peiperl.[20] Companies in this typology are classified as clubs, baseball teams, academies, and fortresses.

Club

Companies in the club category compete through efficiency in controlling costs, maintaining quality, and providing customer service. Their HR policies emphasize development and training, as employees are hired mostly at the entry level, talent is developed, and higher-level vacancies are filled by promotions. In terms of 'make' or 'buy', these companies 'make' their own higher-level employees.

These organizations rely more on internal sources of labour and promote group-based performance and promotion criteria. They have a unique HR planning system.

- *Manpower Planning*   Early career hiring, mainly entry level recruitment, and little hiring at the top levels in the organization
- *Career/Succession Planning*   Formal training programmes, well-defined career paths and career ladders, and mainly seniority-based promotion
- *Termination Planning*   Low turnover and primarily natural termination (for example, through retirement)

Baseball Team

Companies in this category pursue an innovation strategy. Organizational culture that fosters risk-taking, cooperation, and creativity is valued. Accordingly, companies pursuing an innovation strategy invest in training their employees. There is a 'buy' approach to talent. Nonetheless, there also may be development through rapid assignment changes. Appraisal is result-based and promotions take place on the basis of merit.

These organizations also rely extensively on external sources of labour. They promote individual-based performance and promotion criteria. These are highly competitive organizations in the rising sectors of the economy.

- *Manpower Planning*   Hiring at all levels and career stages, infusing fresh blood in the organization, competitive hiring, and tapping bigger labour market
- *Career/Succession Planning*   Focus on individual development programmes, individual recognition, and some merit-based promotion
- *Termination Planning*   High turnover and frequent terminations (for example, lay-offs and retrenchment)

Academy

Academies are somewhat of a hybrid in that they are both product innovators and competitors. They attempt to exploit niches in the marketplace. These companies both 'make' and 'buy' human resources. There are extensive career paths within the companies. Performance appraisal tends to emphasize process. Personnel policies are to some extent consistent with their companies' overall strategies.

These organizations also rely on internal sources of labour. However, they promote individual performance and promotion criteria.

- *Manpower Planning*   Mainly internal sources of labour, early career hiring, mainly entry level recruitment, and little hiring at the top levels in the organization

- *Career/Succession Planning*   Extensive training and development, well-defined career paths and career ladders, individual recognition, and merit-based promotion
- *Termination Planning*   Low turnover and primarily natural termination (for example, through retirement)

Fortress

Companies in this category are in highly competitive markets and are at the mercy of their environments. Because companies in this category are essentially reactive, there are few systematic strategic implications.

These organizations rely extensively on external sources of labour. They promote group-based performance and promotion criteria.

- *Manpower Planning*   Hiring at all levels and career stages, infusing fresh blood in the organization, and tapping bigger labour markets
- *Career/Succession Planning*   Little formal training and development programmes, and little succession planning
- *Termination Planning*   High turnover and frequent terminations (for example, lay-offs and retrenchment)

Figure 4.1 depicts the typology.

Figure 4.1   Organizational and HR Planning Typology

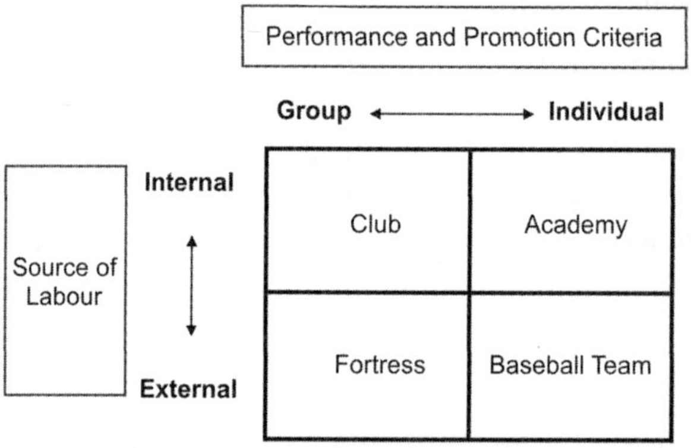

Source: Adapted from J. Sonnenfeld and M. Peiperl (1988), Staffing policy as a strategic response: A typology of career systems, *Academy of Management Review 13*(4): 588–600.

In a growing number of organizations, human resource is now viewed as a source of competitive advantage. There is greater recognition that distinctive competencies are obtained through highly developed employee skills. Strategist Michael Porter has stated that HRM is a key to obtaining competitive advantage. All this necessitates a closer linkage between HRM and the strategic management process of the firm.

HR Anecdote

One of the first steps to accomplishing great things in life is to cease dwelling on the negative things. Individuals and organizations need to carefully assess their strengths and capabilities.

Alice and the Mad Hatter in Wonderland had a conversation that illustrates this:

Alice: Where I come from, people study what they are not good at in order to be able to do what they are good at.

Mad Hatter: We only go around in circles in Wonderland, but we always end up where we started. Would you mind explaining yourself?

Alice: Well, grown-ups tell us to find out what we did wrong, and never do it again

Mad Hatter: That's odd! It seems to me that in order to find out about something, you have to study it. And when you study it, you should become better at it. Why should you want to become better at something and then never do it again? But please continue.

Alice: Nobody ever tells us to study the right things we do. We're only supposed to learn from the wrong things. But we are permitted to study the right things other people do. And sometimes we're even told to copy them.

Mad Hatter: That's cheating!

Alice: You're quite right, Mr. Hatter. I do live in a topsy-turvy world. It seems like I have to do something wrong first, in order to learn from what not to do. And then, by not doing what I'm not supposed to do, perhaps I'll be right. But I'd rather be right the first time, wouldn't you?

In reality, organizations cannot always be right the first time. We all learn from mistakes. Plans may not work the way they were envisaged to. However, one must keep refining. Strategic HR planning and integration is a difficult exercise. It necessitates ensuring adequate human resource competencies to meet the strategic goals of the organization. It also requires remaining flexible so that the organization can manage change if the future is different than anticipated. Otherwise, we will end up going around in circles, as the Mad Hatter said, and will always end up where we started.

News Grab
HR is a strategic partner to business: Survey

A recent survey on HR transformation in the IT sector in India, conducted by Randstad Technologies unveiled interesting findings regarding business-aligned HR. While 56% of the HR leaders said that their department was aligned with their organization's vision and strategy, 29% thought that they own a place at the table and are accorded the status of 'strategic partners'.

36% of the HR leaders felt that excessive focus on transactional activities and limited bandwidth were the major reasons of HR not being aligned with business. 28% of the survey respondents mentioned that alignment of people plan with business requirement should be the main focus area, followed by short, medium and long term business planning. 18% believe that employee engagement is also a key factor to succeed in this. For HR to play the role of an effective business partner in any organization, they need to have a thorough understanding of the core business areas, feel 22% of the HR leaders who participated in the survey.

A majority of the respondents agreed that talent analytics will play a critical role in sourcing and retaining talent in the next 5-10 years, followed by flexible working options to attract increasingly mobile talent and increasing automation that will shift the talent needed in an organization to highly skilled roles.

Source: Economic Times, HR is a strategic partner to business: Survey, 27 September 2016, retrieved from http://economictimes.indiatimes.com/small-biz/hr-leadership/hr-is-a-strategic-partner-to-business-survey/articleshow/54545659.cms.

CHAPTER SUMMARY

- The strategic management process involves defining an organization's strategy.
- HRM has become increasingly important to general management, largely as a result of its role in providing competitive advantage.
- The integration of business strategy and HR strategy and planning is particularly important for success in the long run.
- There are two predominant approaches to HRM and strategy integration, namely reactive and proactive.
- The strategy and HR planning linkage is affected by a number of influences such as the size and age of the organization, sector, and life-cycle stage of the organization, among others.
- HR executives play an important role in each stage of the strategy formulation process.
- HR managers participate in the strategy formulation process, and HR inputs serve as a vital ingredient is evaluating strategic alternatives.
- Senior managers are expected to participate in the process of determining HR strategies.
- Various typologies of strategic HR planning systems have been proposed by scholars linking HR planning systems with strategy types.

EXERCISES AND DISCUSSION QUESTIONS

1. Identify the predominant approaches to HRM and strategy integration.
2. Discuss the various typologies of strategic HR planning systems and identify their features.
3. Choose a large-sized organization and collect data on:
   i. The profile of its top management team and board of directors. Are HR executives part of this team?

ii. The nature of its strategy formulation process. Do HR executives play any role in this process?

CASELET

Strategic HR Integration at The Walt Disney Company

You can design and create, and build the most wonderful place in the world. But it takes people to make the dream a reality.

—Walt Disney

With its corporate headquarters located in California, The Walt Disney Company is one of the largest media and entertainment companies in the world. Founded on 16 October 1923 by brothers Walt and Roy Disney as a small animation studio, the company today boasts of having one of the largest Hollywood studios and owns theme parks and several television networks. It currently has over 150,000 employees working over 40 countries to make the company a success.

From small beginnings as a cartoon studio, the company continues to provide quality entertainment around the world. The company strives to create an optimal employee experience while meeting its business needs. Its human resource is key to its strategic advantage. The company is committed to developing an inclusive and employee-friendly workplace. Disney's values focus on the human element of their business—not only their guests, consumers, and audiences, but also their employees and cast and crew members.

The company has a conscious process of linking HRM with strategic goals and objectives in order to improve business performance and foster innovation. Issues such as the recruitment of staff, development, succession planning, and retention are accommodated in HR plans. The company's priority is to strategize on how they are managing their human resources in the current global environment. This requires adapting HR plans to meet the strategic goal of global expansion and excellence. Integrating and aligning different teams and departments is a key part of this strategy.

At Disney, managing cross-cultural adaptability is an important HR imperative. HR policies are aimed at supporting and building the desired organizational culture. The company has a unique ability to harness the imagination in a way that inspires others, improves lives across the world, and brings hope and smiles to everyone. Together as one team, employees embrace the values that make the company an extraordinary place to work. The hallmarks of this culture are commitment to a tradition of innovation and focus on quality and a high standard of excellence.

These values live in everything that is done. They create a unified mission that all the people believe in and work towards. The company considers its employees and cast members as the most valuable part of the organization. The motto is simple—everyone is important. It is based on the idea put up succinctly in the acronym RAVE that stands for 'Respect, Appreciate, and Value Everyone'.

The company offers a comprehensive total rewards package that helps one to get rewarded for the results they deliver. The rewards of working at Disney include an attractive salary, incentive and special recognition programmes, employee stock option plans (ESOPs), retirement and financial benefits, complimentary theme park admissions, transport assistance, and so on. The health and wellness benefits include various medical benefits, Disney Health Pursuits Wellness Resources, employee assistance programme (EAP), dental and vision care, dependent day care, insurance, time-offs, paid holidays, and vacations. Their world-class training programmes are customizable to suit individual's goals. The Walt Disney Company promotes a learning environment that encourages everyone, no matter what their role, to increase their engagement and assist them in reaching their goals.

Contribution of HRM strategy in achieving objectives

At Disney, employees are aware of the fact that innovation is their primary mandate. The company has adopted the phrase 'Dream as a team', which works really well in achieving its business objectives. The company has regular brainstorming sessions among employees where new and innovative ideas are developed for future growth of the business. Strategic decision-making, thus, is not done by the top echelons. It flows from below. And this is what makes Disney a truly participative organization.

'Innovative', 'creative', and 'profitable' are the key words of their mission statement. Employees are clear and aware of their roles and how they can contribute to the strategic objectives. They employees are made well equipped with the technical, professional, and managerial skills needed for making that contribution.

HR planning is done to ensure that it has the right personnel, who are capable of completing those tasks that help the organization to reach its objectives. Development of new theme parks and animation studios makes manpower forecasting and planning a very vital function. Attracting and retaining the right people who will help foster innovation, creativity, and profitability is an essential part of the HR plan.

The Walt Disney Company incorporates best-in-class business standards as well as strong HR practices. Disney's workplace policies and practices include commitment to non-discrimination and freedom from workplace harassment. Considering the varied cultural contexts in which Disney operates, training and socializing employees to be more receptive of the cultural nuances is very important.

Disney's future

In today's business context, the right approach and management of the company's employees can greatly affect its overall performance. A strategic approach to managing its HR is vital to its growth. Aligning HR strategy with business strategy and operational strategy is key to their future growth. A sound and efficient HR plan will contribute to achieving the organizational objectives in an effective manner. At Disney, strategically aligned culture and HRM policies play a vital role.

Despite its innovative people-related initiatives, the company has faced several HR problems. There have been serious industrial relations (IR) issues from time to time relating to formation of unions, which the company has been discouraging. Disney also has been grappling with a high employee turnover rate. Further, increases in costs of pension and postretirement benefits have inflated the HR budget for Disney.

Having a diverse workforce is critical to the business. The Walt Disney Company seeks to work towards an inclusive environment that fosters diversity, creativity, innovation, and camaraderie. However, there have been problems in handling this culturally diverse workforce. There have been instances of ethnic conflicts in the company. Some employees have refused to participate in certain entertainment programmes because they felt it contradicted their cultural or religious beliefs. There were also issues related to the hiring of expatriates since the locals felt that the foreign hires were taking away their jobs. A top-level manager says, 'Our people make our films great, and we strive to build a culture that feeds and respects their spirit.' The challenge is how to sustain that spirit.[21]

Questions for Discussion

1. What are the key aspects of Disney's HR plans that drive its success? Discuss how HR is a vital input to the strategic decision-making process.
2. What are the impending concerns for the company and how can it cope up with the challenges discussed in the end?

NOTES

1. H. I. Ansoff (1965), *Corporate strategy* (New York, NY: McGraw Hill).
2. L. Mayne, O. Tregaskis, and C. Brewster (1996), A comparative analysis of the link between flexibility and HRM strategy, *Employee Relations 18*(3): 5–24.
3. H. Mintzberg (1990), Strategy formation: Schools of thought, in *Perspectives on strategic management*, ed. J. W. Fredrickson, pp. 105–236 (New York, NY: Harper Business); J. B. Quinn (1989), Retrospective commentary, *Sloan Management Review 30*(4): 55–60.
4. For the debates in strategic management between Ansoff and Mintzberg and between Porter and Prahlad on planning versus learning as the basis for strategy formulation and implementation, see Ansoff, *Corporate strategy*; H. I. Ansoff (1991), Critique of Henry Mintzberg's The Design School, *Strategic Management Journal 12*: 449–461; H. Mintzberg (1987), Crafting strategy, *Harvard Business Review 65*: 66–75; H. Mintzberg (1990), The design school, reconsidering the basic premises of strategic management, *Strategic Management Journal 11*: 171–195; Mintzberg, Strategy formation, 105–236; H. Mintzberg (1991), Learning and planning: Reply to Igor Ansoff, *Strategic Management Journal 12*(6): 463–466; G. Hamel and C. K. Prahalad (1989), Strategic intent, *Harvard Business Review 67*(3): 63–76; G. Hamel and C. K. Prahalad (1993), Strategy as stretch and leverage, *Harvard Business Review 71*(2): 75–84; M. E. Porter (1985), *Competitive advantage: Creating and sustaining superior performance* (New York, NY: The. Free Press); M. E. Porter (1991), Towards a dynamic theory of strategy, *Strategic Management Journal 12*(S): 95–117.
5. D. Goss (1995), *Principles of human resource management* (London, UK: Routledge).
6. B. E. Becker and B. Gerhart (1996), The impact of human resource management on organizational performance: Progress and prospects, *Academy of Management Journal 39*(4): 779–801; M. A. Huselid (1995), The impact of human resource management practices on turnover, productivity, and corporate financial performance, *Academy of Management Journal 38*(3), 635–672.
7. K. Golden and V. Ramanujam (1985), Between a dream and a nightmare: On the integration of the human resource management and strategic business planning processes, *Human Resource Management 24*: 429–452.

8. S. J. Smith (1982), New work life estimates reflect changing profile of labor force, *Monthly Labor Review 105*(3): 15–20; J. W. Walker (1980), *Human resource planning* (New York, NY: McGraw-Hill).

9. Authors who have suggested a more proactive role for HR include L. Dyer (1983), Bringing human resources into the strategy formulation process, *Human Resource Management 22*: 257–271; L. Dyer (1984), Studying HR strategy: An approach and agenda, *Industrial Relations 23*(2): 159–169; L. Dyer (1985), Strategic human resource management and planning, in *Research and practice in personnel and human resource management*, Vol. 3, pp. 1–30 (Greenwich, CT: JAI Press); C. A. Lengnick-Hall and M. L. Lengnick-Hall (1988), Strategic human resource management: A review of the literature and a proposed typology, *Academy of Management Review 13*(3): 454–470.

10. D. Torrington and L. Hall (1995), *Personnel management: HRM in action* (London, UK: Prentice Hall); D. Torrington and L. Hall (1996), Chasing the rainbow: How seeking status through strategy misses the point for the personnel function, *Employee Relations 18*(6): 81–97.

11. Lengnick-Hall and Lengnick-Hall, Strategic human resource management, 454–470.

12. Golden and Ramanujam, Between a dream and a nightmare, 429–452.

13. Dyer, Strategic human resource management and planning, 1–30.

14. L. Baird and I. Meshoulam (1988), Managing the two fits of strategic human resource management, *Academy of Management Review 13*(1): 116–128.

15. Y. Cohen and J. Pfeffer (1986), Organisational hiring standards, *Administrative Science Quarterly 31*(1): 1–24; M. Easterby-Smith, D. Maihia, and L. Yuan (1995), How culture sensitive is HRM? A comparative analysis of practice in Chinese and UK companies, *International Journal of Human Resource Management 6*(1): 31–59; J. J. Lawler, H. Jain, C. S. Venkata Ratnam, and V. Atmiyanandana (1995), Human resource management in developing economies: A comparison of India and Thailand, *International Journal of Human Resource Management 6*(2): 319–346; S. A. Snell (1992), Control theory in strategic human resource management: The mediating effect of administrative information, *The Academy of Management Journal 35*(2): 292–327.

16. For instance, see J. T. Delaney and M. A. Huselid (1996), The impact of HRM practices on perceptions of organizational performance, *Academy of Management Journal 39*(4): 949–969; Huselid, The impact of human resource management, 635–672; S. E. Jackson, R. Schuler, and J. C. Rivero (1989), Organizational characteristics as predictors of personnel practices, *Personnel Psychology 42*(4): 727–786.

17. A. O. Ozcelik and F. Aydýnlý (2006), Strategic role of HRM in Turkey: A three-country comparative analysis, *Journal of European Industrial Training 30*(4): 310–327.

18. K. W. Green, W. H. Cindy, D. Whitten, and B. Medlin (2006), The impact of strategic human resource management on firm performance and HR professionals' work attitude and work performance, *International Journal of Human Resource Management 17*(4): 559–579.

19. R. E. Miles and C. C. Snow (1984), Designing strategic human resource systems, *Organizational Dynamics 13*(1): 36–52.

20. J. Sonnenfeld and M. Peiperl (1988), Staffing policy as a strategic response: A typology of career systems, *Academy of Management Review 13*(4): 588–600.

21. With inputs from https://www.thewaltdisneycompany.com; https://www.shrm.org/resourcesandtools/hr-topics/employee-relations/pages/disney-employee-engagement.aspx.

CHAPTER 5

Workflow Analysis and Strategic Job Analysis

Chapter Overview

This chapter focuses on discussing the concepts of workflow analysis and job analysis. It discusses the significance, purpose, and steps involved in workflow and job analysis. Furthermore, it carries out a discussion on the shift in concept and practice from traditional job analysis to strategic job analysis. Themes such as dejobbing, strategic job modelling (SJM), and competency mapping are discussed in the light of strategic job analysis.

Learning Objectives

1. To get familiarized with the concepts of workflow analysis and job analysis
2. To develop an understanding of the need, significance, purpose, and outcomes of workflow analysis and job analysis
3. To understand the rationale of why and how traditional job analysis has evolved into strategic job analysis
4. To understand concepts such as dejobbing, SJM, and competency mapping in the light of strategic job analysis

OPENING STORY

The Future of Work

The world of work is undergoing a major process of change. There are several forces transforming it, from the onward march of technology and the impact of climate change to the changing character of production and employment, to name a few. In order to understand and to respond effectively to these new challenges, the International Labour Organization (ILO) has launched a 'Future of Work' initiative. The ILO understands the need to respond effectively to the world of work and ongoing changes in order to be able to advance its mandate for social justice.

The Future of Work initiative is the centrepiece of the ILO's activities to mark its centenary in 2019.

Future of Work initiative timelines

2016: A broad framework is needed to give the Future of Work initiative the necessary structure and focus for concrete results to be obtained. In 2016, all ILO member states are invited to undertake national 'Future of Work' dialogues structured around four 'centenary conversations':

- Work and society
- Decent jobs for all
- The organization of work and production
- The governance of work

2017–2018: In 2017, a high-level Global Commission on the Future of Work will be established. Its purpose will be to examine the output from the national dialogues and other input it may consider necessary. The commission will publish a report and recommendations in the course of 2018.

2019: In the first half of 2019, all member states will be invited to organize events to mark the ILO's centenary and to discuss the commission's report. The culmination of the 'Future of Work' initiative will be the 2019 International Labour Conference, with the possible adoption of a Centenary Declaration.

ILO's initiative highlights the growing concern with the fast-changing work landscape. The types of skills that employers need are changing all the time. Employees are under pressure to continually learn and adapt to evolving and emerging industries. Managing this transition is an important challenge, as is preparing for the future of work.

Source: https://www.ilo.org/global/topics/future-of-work/lang--en/index.htm.

FUTURE OF WORK AND TALENT MANAGEMENT

This is the first chapter of the section of the book that encapsulates the basic crux of human resource management (HRM). The next few chapters will focus on discussing the human resource (HR) process flow, which includes a discussion of HR activities such as workflow analysis, job analysis, staffing (recruitment, selection, and placement), training, performance appraisal, career development, and compensation. It is important at this point to clarify that this book is on strategic HRM (SHRM) and not HRM *per se*. The focus of this book is to enable the reader to understand the strategic aspects of HRM. Traditional text books on HRM deal with a discussion of the concepts, theories, and frameworks related to the different activities in the HR flow. The current book, however, delves into the long-term strategic dimensions of these HR activities.

Typically, HRM flow involves a series of activities:

1. **Workforce and Job Analysis**   Determining what tasks and activities need to be done and by whom
2. **Human Resource Planning**   Forecasting and planning manpower requirements
3. **Recruitment**   Attracting applicants who match a certain job criteria
4. **Selection**   Shortlisting candidates who are the nearest match in terms qualifications, expertise, and potential for a certain job
5. **Placement**   Deciding upon the final candidate who gets the job and giving them placement offers

6. **Training and Development** Designing programmes for skills and abilities upgradation
7. **Performance Management** Evaluating employee performance to train, motivate, and reward workers
8. **Compensation and Reward** Determining salaries and wages for employees and dispensing with rewards
9. **Industrial Relations** Maintaining healthy relations with employees and resolving disputes
10. **Employee Termination** Developing awareness of legal provisions and ensuring rightful termination of employment

The traditional view takes a linear approach to carrying out these activities. Often, these activities were carried out as separate sub-functions. Thus, in a lot of organizations, HRM activities appeared to be discrete and often disjointed. SHRM entails that HR activities are to be viewed as interrelated and not disconnected. As discussed in Chapter 1, an important principle of SHRM is internal fit. It refers to the integration between various HRM sub-functions or sub-systems, such as staffing, compensation, and training. HR activities have to be consistent with each other. Thus, employers today often view all these activities as part of an integrated talent management process.

Talent management can be defined as an integrated process of planning, acquiring, developing, managing, and rewarding employees. Talent management can be seen in terms of a set of integrated HR processes designed to attract, develop, motivate, and retain productive employees. The goal of talent management is to create a high-performance, sustainable organization.

Having a talent management perspective requires that the various HR activities (such as recruiting, selecting, training, appraisal, and compensation) are parts of a single interrelated process. For example, having employees with the right skills at the right place starts from planning right to recruiting the right way to selecting the right applicants, and subsequently giving the right kind of training, and so on. This perspective to managing talent supports the notion of SHRM.

Unprecedented patterns of forces are radically reshaping the world of work. These shifts are redistributing power, wealth, competition, and opportunity around the globe. Businesses across the world are beginning to understand that in order to attract and retain employees, they need to redefine work. Figure 5.1 highlights what the future of work looks like.

It is important to reflect that the expected change is not surprising. However, what is unique is the pervasive nature of the change and its accelerating pace. Disruptive innovations are creating new business models and destroying old ones. New technologies are having a huge impact on how people work, communicate, and collaborate. As workforces become more diverse and work becomes more flexible, traditional career models may soon be a thing of the past. Organizations and individuals will have to be prepared to undergo new learning cycles and adapt themselves to these new challenges, not only to survive but also to succeed. There will be a major shift away from the thinking that we stay in one profession and have one job for decades. The future of work is going to redefine how talent is acquired, managed, and retained. This will vastly impact how jobs are designed.

Talent management begins with understanding what jobs are needed and the human traits and competencies needed in order to do those jobs effectively. *Workflow analysis* and *job analysis* can be seen as two important starting points in the larger domain of talent management.

Figure 5.1　Workforce of the Future—The Competing Forces Shaping 2030

The Possible Worlds of Work in 2030	Expected Nature of Business	Expected Nature of Work and Workforce
The Red World	Innovation and ideas rule	Innovation and collaboration are valued. Workforce is nimble and agile
The Blue World	Corporate is king: Size and influence would matter	It's a world of exceptional talent and high performance
The Green World	Companies care and are socially responsible	Workplaces reflect values and a strong social conscience
The Yellow World	Humans come first	Humanness is valued and work brings people together like communities

Sources: Adapted from PwC (2017), *Workforce of the future: The competing forces shaping 2030*, study in China, Germany, India, UK and the US that highlights four possible scenarios of work in 2030; retrieved from https://www.pwc.com/gx/en/services/people-organisation/publications/workforce-of-the-future/workforce-of-the-future--the-red-world-in-2030.html.

WORKFLOW ANALYSIS

Workflow analysis is a study of the way work (inputs, activities, and outputs) moves through an organization. It is a detailed study of the flow of work from job to job in a work process.

Workflow analysis involves defining work and then dividing it into jobs.

- Work: Effort directed towards producing or accomplishing results
- Job: A grouping of tasks, duties, and responsibilities that constitutes the total work of an employee

Workflow design refers to the flow of activities and tasks that need to be carried out in an organization to realize its goals and objectives. Workflow analysis is the process of identifying and determining the tasks necessary for the production of a good or service, prior to allocating and assigning these tasks to a particular job category or person. Only after a thorough understanding of workflow design can a manager make informed decisions regarding how to design tasks and activities that will be performed by people in that workflow. It is important to conduct this type of analysis on a regular basis to ensure that inconsistencies and inefficiencies in tasks can be identified and new tasks can be designed to attain the changing organizational goals and requirements.

Workflow analysis is extremely useful because it provides information to managers to understand all the tasks required to carry out a process as well as the skills necessary to perform those tasks. Organizations benefit from a workflow because it ensures that goals are accomplished through optimal utilization of resources. This, in turn, enhances efficiency and productivity.

A workflow consists of an orchestrated and repeatable pattern of activity through a systematic arrangement of resources into processes that transform inputs into outputs. It can be depicted as a sequence of tasks and activities necessary to be performed in an organization in order to get the end product. To put it simply, a workflow is a process that a company deploys to get things done. By understanding each step, workflow analysis can help in determining inefficiencies within a specific department or across the entire organization.

For instance, a work output for an automobile company could be a car. Input or raw materials for the assembly of automobiles include various parts (steering wheels, tyres, door panels, and so on), human skills, and equipment. Human skills refer to the worker's knowledge, skills, abilities, and efforts necessary to perform the tasks. Equipment could be the technology, machinery, facilities, and systems necessary to transform the raw materials into the final product. Process will involve converting input into the final product, for example, a car.

Just like every organization has a workflow defined in terms of input, process, and output, every department also has its own workflow. Different departments or units within an organization may have different workflows depending on their objectives. For example, the operations department will be concerned with such activities as acquiring raw materials, maintaining the right level of inventory, designing process layout, and transforming inputs into final products. Likewise, the accounting department will have its own processes through which it keeps track of bills that need to be paid, invoices that need to be sent, receivables to be collected, and payments that have to be made. A clear definition of this workflow helps every department or unit identify its own activities, processes, and deliverables.

Figure 5.2A illustrates a simple workflow of an organization. Figure 5.2B shows the related workflow of an HR department.

In order to succeed, a business needs to be flexible and it needs to evolve by keeping up with the changes occurring outside. Often, multiple functional teams or members of different departments and units must work together to complete an organizational goal. This situation is called workflow interdependency and is a common feature with organizations today. For example, a marketing team and a finance team may need to work together to create an advertising budget. A clear workflow analysis plan may be needed in such interdependency situations to determine the ideal methods of communication and resource sharing.

Figure 5.2A Workflow of an Organization

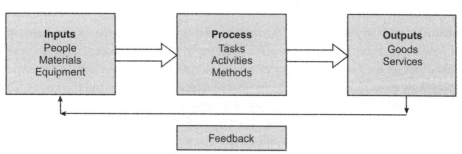

Figure 5.2B   Workflow of HR Department

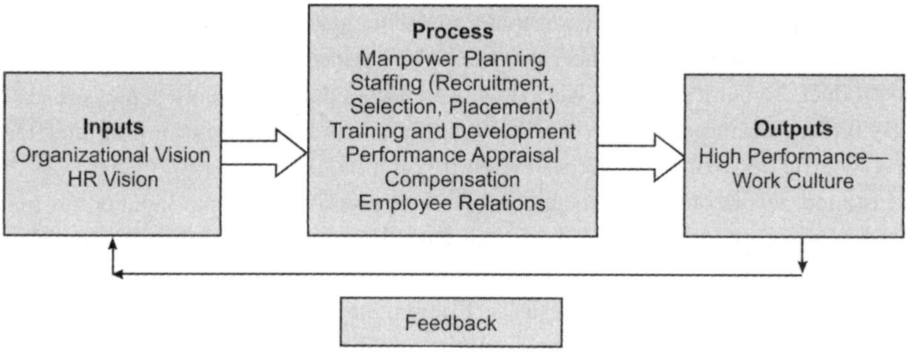

Workflow analysis can also be seen as a cross-sectional examination of the way the organization is structured. The goal of workflow analysis is to figure out what activities need to be done in order to attain the organizational objectives, how and by whom those activities will be done, and whether certain tasks need to be eliminated. This streamlines the efforts of the workforce. The goal of organizational structuring is to establish work responsibility based on workflow analysis, allocate authority to carry out tasks, and determine who will report to whom.

Steps in Workflow Analysis

Conducting a workflow analysis is not a simple thing to do. It requires careful scrutiny and understanding of business situations. Different businesses will require different orientations to workflow analysis. However, a typical workflow analysis will involve some basic steps, which are listed below:

1. **Understanding business goals and strategies**   Workflow analysis will usually begin with the process of understanding the goals and strategies of the company. This provides a good starting point to work from. The goals lend a direction to what needs to be done and strategies provide an answer to how it is to be done.
2. **Identify inputs, process, and outputs**   It is important to clearly identify and delineate how the business activity combines human, physical, and financial resources to create goods and services. This will help explain the role of the input–process–output cycle in overall business activity.
3. **Identify unit-wise tasks**   Next, the analyst needs to understand the requirements in terms of how every department or unit will contribute to the input–process–output cycle in the light of the goals. This gives them an even clearer look at how business is run day-to-day. Everything from human resources and manufacturing to finance and marketing is looked at closely, right down to how every task is processed.
4. **Documenting time, resources, and effort needed**   The next step will involve listing and documenting how much time and effort is needed for each task, as well as how much it will cost a business to accomplish these tasks. The workflow business analyst will be able to

see which activities are needed and which ones are actually doing more harm than good or have become obsolete and could be improved.

5. **Prepare a final workflow** After spending the necessary time getting to know the tasks of the company from the lowest level to the highest level within an organization, a workflow analyst will finally be able to put together a comprehensive plan that will recommend the best steps the company should take to attain its results most efficiently and productively.

JOB DESIGN, JOB REDESIGN, AND JOB ANALYSIS

The terms 'job design', 'job redesign', and 'job analysis' have overlapping meanings and are often used interchangeably. There is a subtle but important distinction between these terms.

Job design refers to organizing tasks, duties, and responsibilities into a productive unit of work. It involves the content of jobs and the effect of jobs on employees. Identifying the components of a given job is an integral part of job design. Job design can influence performance and job satisfaction. Because people are more satisfied with certain job configurations than with others, it is important to be able to identify what makes a 'good' job.

A model that shows how to make jobs more motivating is the Job Characteristics Model, developed by Richard Hackman and Greg Oldham.[1] This model describes jobs in terms of five characteristics:

1. **Skill variety** The extent to which a job requires a variety of skills to carry out the tasks involved
2. **Task identity** The degree to which a job requires completing a 'whole' piece of work from beginning to end (for example, building an entire component or resolving a customer's complaint)
3. **Task significance** The extent to which the job has an important impact on the lives of other people
4. **Autonomy** The degree to which the job allows an individual to make decisions about the way the work will be carried out
5. **Feedback** The extent to which a person receives clear information about performance effectiveness from the work itself

According to the Job Characteristics Model, the more of each of these characteristics a job has, the more motivating the job will be. The model predicts that a person with such a job will be more satisfied and will produce more and better work.

Individual responses to jobs vary. A job may be motivating to one person but not to someone else. A job that gives little latitude may not satisfy an individual's need to be creative or innovative. Therefore, managers are realizing that understanding the characteristics of jobs requires a much broader perspective than it did in the past. Maintaining a proper person–job fit is a simple but important concept that involves matching the characteristics of people with the characteristics of jobs. Successfully and continuously reshaping people is not always an easy thing to do. **Job redesign** is, thus, done to ensure better person–job fit, so that the job is interesting for the job holder. Job redesign is a strategy followed by many Indian companies, such as Wipro, Infosys, Mahindra & Mahindra, and Max India, in order to keep pace with changing environmental demands.

The traditional concept of specialized jobs and division of labour infuses efficiency but also breeds boredom and monotony. Several scholars have emphasized the dehumanizing aspect of pigeonholing workers into repetitive, tedious jobs. Job redesign is an effort where job responsibilities and tasks are reviewed, and possibly re-allocated among staff, to improve output and reduce monotony. Three common ways or methods to redesign an employee's job are job enrichment, job enlargement, and job rotation.

Job enlargement means assigning workers additional activities at the same level. Job enlargement is a job redesign strategy that increases only the tasks of a particular job. While job enlargement is limited in that it does not provide the additional responsibilities or authority that job enrichment does, it is useful in reducing some of the monotony associated with doing the same thing day in and day out. *Job enrichment* means redesigning jobs in a way that increases the opportunities for the worker to experience feelings of responsibility, achievement, growth, and recognition. *Job rotation* means systematically moving workers from one job to another. It assigns workers to an alternate job on a temporary basis. It provides employees with an opportunity to learn new things and thereby reduces boredom and slackness. These practices aim at increasing responsibility or autonomy, providing meaningful work experience, and enhancing skill variety.[2]

Several companies use job enrichment and enlargement as a continued strategy for job redesign. For example, Indian subsidiaries of MNCs such as Coca-Cola, Nike, Intel, and Microsoft frequently enrich and enlarge jobs. At LG, it has worked as an effective retention tool for talent. While the attrition level at LG is around 8 per cent, management claims there have been negligible drop-outs among the employees whose jobs have been enlarged or enriched. At Philips India, there is focus on job redesign, including job enlargement and job enrichment, on a continuous basis. Several government bodies in India, such as the Income Tax Department and the Ministry of Culture, have also introduced job enrichment and enlargement.

Another concept that merits discussion at this point is business process reengineering (BPR). It is a fundamental rethinking and radical redesign of business processes to achieve dramatic improvements in critical measures of performance such as cost, quality, service, and speed. BPR advocates that enterprises go back to the basics and re-examine their very roots. It involves redesigning business processes, usually by combining steps, so that small multi-tasking teams do the jobs formerly done by a sequence of departments. Reengineering also required delegating more authority to the teams, who now did their jobs with less supervision.

Job analysis, unlike job design or job redesign, focuses on analysing existing jobs to gather information for other activities such as recruitment, selection, training, appraisal, and compensation. Job design focuses on designing new jobs that are required in an organization. Thus, job design has a more proactive orientation towards creating a job, whereas job analysis has a passive, information-gathering orientation. Job redesign, on the other hand, focuses on redesigning existing jobs to make them more efficient and motivating.

UNDERSTANDING JOB ANALYSIS

Job analysis refers to the determination of the tasks that comprise the job as well as the skills, knowledge, and abilities required of the worker for successful performance. Job analysis is the procedure through which we determine the duties of the positions and the characteristics of the people to hire for them. Job analysis has been called the building block of everything that the personnel department does.

Job analysis collects and analyses information related to various aspects of jobs. It is performed on ongoing jobs only to identify the job content and the skill requirement to perform specific tasks in a given job. It involves a formal study of jobs, which is essential in determining the duties and the nature of the jobs in the organization.

Job analysis information is useful to managers in various ways. Managers must have detailed information about all the jobs in their work group to understand the workflow process. Managers need to understand the job requirements to make intelligent hiring decisions. Since a manager is responsible for ensuring that each individual is performing his or her job efficiently and effectively, he must clearly understand the tasks required in every job.

Job analysis is a primary tool to collect job-related data. Any job vacancy cannot be filled until and unless the organization has job analysis data. It is necessary to define these accurately in order to place the right person at the right place and at the right time. This helps both the employer and employee understand what exactly needs to be delivered and how. Job analysis entails three important components: *job content*, *job context*, and *job requirements*.

Job Content

It contains information about various job activities included in a specific job. It is a detailed account of actions that an employee needs to perform. The following information about job content needs to be collected:

- Duties and responsibilities of an employee
- Specific tasks and activities
- Tools and equipment to be used while performing a specific job
- Desired output level and deliverables
- Type of training required

Job Context

Job context refers to the situation or condition under which an employee performs a particular job. The information collected will include:

- Working conditions
- Whom to report and whom to supervise
- Physical and mental demands
- Risks and hazards involved

Job Requirements

These include basic but specific requirements that make a candidate eligible for a particular job. The collected data includes:

- Educational qualifications
- Skills and knowledge
- Abilities and aptitude
- Experience and exposure
- Personality attributes and traits

Two important outcomes of job analysis are **job description** and **job specification**. Job description includes information related to job content and job context, whereas job specification involves detailing the job requirements.

Job Description

A job description is an organized, factual statement of the duties and responsibilities of a specific job. It is a list of the tasks, duties, and responsibilities that the job entails. Job description includes basic job-related data that is useful to advertise a specific job and attract the right pool of potential candidates. The main purpose of job description is to collect job-related data in order to hire for a particular job. It helps in attracting, targeting, recruiting, and selecting the right candidate for the right job.

Typical Items in a Job Description

- Job title
- Organizational location of the job
- Supervision to be given and received
- Duties to be performed
- Materials, tools, machinery, and equipment needed
- Designation of the immediate superiors and subordinates
- Salary levels, including pay, allowances, bonus, incentive wage, method of payment, hours of work, shift, breaks, and so on
- Conditions of work, namely location, time, speed of work, and health hazards
- Training and development facilities
- Definition of unusual terms involved in the job

Job Specification

Also known as employee specifications, a job specification is a written statement of the minimum required employee qualifications that represent the possession of minimum acceptable human qualities by the prospective employee to perform a job. It is a list of the knowledge, skills, abilities, and other characteristics (KSAOs) that an individual must have to perform the job. It includes educational qualifications, specific qualities, experience, skills required to perform a job, roles involved in a job, and other unusual sensory demands. It also includes general health, mental health, intelligence, aptitude, judgement, emotional ability, adaptability, flexibility, values and ethics, manners and creativity, and so on.

Typical Items in a Job Specification

- Educational qualifications, including degree, diploma, certification, or licence
- Knowledge required to perform a job successfully
- Personal ability, including aptitude, reasoning, manipulative abilities, handling sudden and unexpected situations, problem-solving ability, mathematical abilities, and so on
- Specific skills, such as communication skills, IT skills, operational skills, motor skills, processing skills, and so on
- Personal characteristics, such as the ability to adapt to different environment, work ethic, eagerness to learn and understand things, and so on
- Prior experience and exposure in similar work or industry

Both job description and job specification are essential parts of job analysis information. Writing them clearly and accurately helps organizations and workers cope with many challenges while on board.

Figure 5.3 presents a sample job description and job specification used typically in organizations.

Figure 5.3 Example of Job Description and Job Specification

Position: Manager HR
Reports to: Senior Manager HR
General Description: To aid senior manager HR in recruitment, training, payroll, HR database, salary calculations, and other HR administrative work.

Duties and Responsibilities
- Carrying out recruitment process
- Providing advice to managers on grievance, attendance, and disciplinary issues
- Briefing new managers on the policies and procedures of an organization
- Ensuring the maintenance of all payroll data by HR administrators
- Reviewing and revising HR policies in compliance with changing or new legislation
- Maintaining and updating policy manuals, employee handbooks, and related documentation
- Conducting new employee orientation programmes and other educational and training programmes
- Receiving employee complaints and acting accordingly to resolve them

Skills and Specifications
- Problem-solving skills

- Articulate communicator and ability to interpret written and statistical data
- High standard of attention to detail
- Solid commitment to employee service
- Ability to convey difficult and challenging information to managers

Education and Qualification
- Bachelor's degree in Human Resource, Business Administration, or related field.
- Master's degree in Business Administration from an accredited institution.

Experience
1–3 years in recruitment or HR administration

Job analysis data is used for various HR activities, such as HR planning, staffing, training and development, performance management, and compensation. It serves as the basis for all HR activities.

Figure 5.4 depicts the uses of job analysis data.

Figure 5.4 Uses of Job Analysis

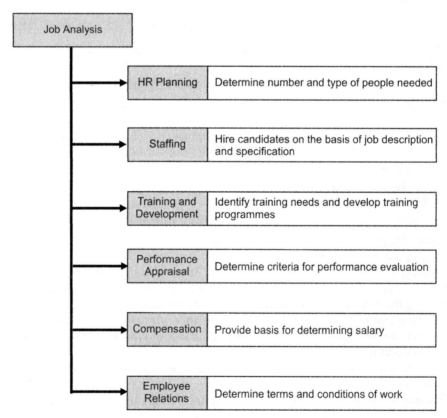

Conducting Job Analysis

Typically, a job analysis involves the following steps:

- **STEP 1: Determine why job analysis is being done** The first step is to understand why job analysis information is needed. This will help decide what type of data to collect. Some data collection techniques, such as interviewing the employee, are good for writing job descriptions. Other quantitative techniques, such as the position analysis questionnaire commonly used in many organizations, provide ratings for each job and, hence, help to compare jobs for job evaluation and compensation purposes.
- **STEP 2: Select relevant positions** It is important to select which positions to focus on for the job analysis. For instance, it is unnecessary and irrelevant to analyse the jobs of 50 assembly line workers when a smaller sample of 10 jobs will do.
- **STEP 3: Review relevant secondary information** In order to generate job analysis information, relevant information about a job may be gathered from background or secondary data. Organization charts show the organization-wide division of work, and where the job fits in the overall organization. A process chart shows the flow of inputs to and outputs from a job (for example, a quality control personnel is expected to review components from suppliers, check components going to the plant, and provide information regarding the component's quality to the managers).
- **STEP 4: Analyse the job** In brief, analysing the job involves collecting data from participants and stakeholders (deploying the methods discussed in the next section), identifying the areas of responsibility, and segregating the duties and tasks that the job entails. The information collected from secondary sources may be verified with the employee performing the job, the immediate supervisor of the incumbent, and other relevant people and stakeholders. This will help confirm that the information is factually correct and complete.
- **STEP 5: Develop job description and job specification** Once job analysis is done, job description and job specification may be developed in a comprehensive manner.

Job analysis information may be collected from various sources. In general, it will be useful for the manager to go to the job incumbents to get the most accurate information about what is actually required to be done on the job. Managers can ask others familiar with the job, such as the supervisor, to supplement the information received from the incumbents. Team members may also be an important source to generate information about roles and responsibilities entailed in a job. More recently, especially with the growth of the service sector, even clients and customers may give valuable information about a particular job holder and his role.[2]

STRATEGIC JOB ANALYSIS

Although we tend to view jobs as static and stable, in fact, jobs tend to change and evolve over time. It is important that the job analysis process must detect changes in the nature of jobs. Traditional HR thinkers consider job analysis as a static, one-time activity. In reality, jobs are continuously changing. Thus, job descriptions and job specifications often become irrelevant with time. The following criticism of traditional job analysis is often pointed out:

- In a fast-changing environment, by the time job descriptions are written, they are out of date. Job analysis is timed, while jobs are changing.
- Job analysis is a by-product of the mass production approach, with emphasis on job specialization and division of labour. Some feel it is an anachronism left over from the days of rigid bureaucracies with pyramid hierarchies.
- Job descriptions strictly enforce a job mentality and inhibit out-of-box thinking.
- Job analysis is usually independent rather than focusing on interdependence of jobs. In the present times, there is focus on team work and group action. Thus, having an isolated view of jobs does not help.
- Job analysis is usually not progressive and does not clarify how the incumbent can grow in the job.
- Some people feel that job analysis is often done by HR administrative staff who may know little about the technical aspects of each job.

One major problem with traditional job analysis and job descriptions is that it perpetrates what is known as the Parkinson's law syndrome. Parkinson's law is based on the adage that 'work expands so as to fill the time available for its completion'. Articulated by Cyril Northcote Parkinson, as part of the first sentence of a humorous essay published in *The Economist* in 1955 and then reprinted in the book *Parkinson's Law: The Pursuit of Progress*, the law suggests that work (and especially paper work) is elastic in its demands on time, thus making people spend a lot of time in completing it. This is what Parkinson's law says—we expand our work so as to complete it in the maximum available time.

In traditional hierarchical organizations, Parkinson's syndrome at work is a common phenomenon. It was observed by Professor Parkinson that even a series of simple tasks increased in complexity to fill up the time allotted to it. That mentality is reflected in the fact that managers often reward workers for hours spent rather than results produced. People using static job descriptions may 'appear' to be working most of the time, yet the output may still be low.[3]

Strategic job analysis has brought about a shift in focus from:

- **Narrow functional roles to generalist orientation**   Strategic job analysis mandates that the focus should shift from a narrow, technical, and specialist mindset to a broader, more generalist orientation for job holders.
- **Specialization to multi-skilling**   The traditional concept of division of labour involves specialization in individual tasks so that the workers become highly proficient in their area. The focus has now shifted to multi-skilling, which is a labour utilization strategy where workers possess a range of skills appropriate for more than one work process and are used flexibly on several tasks and projects.
- **Job descriptions to job fluidity**   Jobs are becoming more and more dynamic in keeping with the requirements of the changing external environment. Traditional way of defining jobs through static job descriptions is gradually paving way for dynamic and 'fluid' job

demands and responsibilities. People no longer take cues from a job description. Signals come from the changing demands of the environment.

- **Jobs to profiles**   Jobs are statically defined duties, whereas job profiles list multiple competencies, traits, knowledge, and experience that employees must be able to exhibit in a multi-skilled world. The present competitive world demands shift in focus from doing jobs to developing profiles.
- **Tasks to roles**   The above changes have necessitated that organizations and employees lay more emphasis on performing certain roles rather than carrying out activities and tasks. Individuals are required not just to complete tasks but adopt different roles at different times.
- **Skills to attitudes**   Another important change taking place in organizations is that employee attitudes are becoming more important than employee skills. An attitude is generally defined as the way a person responds to his or her environment. Having the right attitude and predisposition in a continuously changing environment sometimes takes precedence over having a certain skill.
- **Intelligence quotient to emotional quotient**   Intelligence quotient (IQ) is a measure of one's ability to think and reason. Emotional quotient (EQ) or emotional intelligence (EI), on the other hand, is the ability of individuals to recognize and understand emotions and to use emotional information to guide thinking, behaviour, and decision-making. Research has shown that EQ is more directly linked to productivity and performance than IQ in the present organizational settings.[4]
- **Technical skills to conceptual and human skills**   Henry Mintzberg theorized that managers are required to possess certain skills and competencies that allow them to play their roles effectively and efficiently. He talked about three important skills, namely technical, conceptual, and human skills, necessary for managers. Technical skills refer to the ability to utilize tools, techniques, and procedures that are specific to a particular field. Human skills enable them to understand and get along with other people while getting the most out of them. Conceptual skills enable managers to think of the abstract, examine different situations, and see beyond the present in order to recognize new opportunities and threats. Today, conceptual and human skills are increasingly becoming more important than technical skills.
- **Duties to personal contributions**   It is an accepted fact that the growth of every organization depends on the dedication, hard work, creativity, and ability of each and every employee. In a fast-paced economy, making personal contributions is valued more than carrying out duties and tasks.
- **Present incumbency to future opportunities**   Organizations are focusing more on future employability of their employees in various assignments within the organization rather than just having the skill to perform present jobs. The importance given to concepts such as multi-skilling, multi-tasking, and job rotation reiterates the fact that future growth and employability of employees is paramount.

Table 5.1 shows the differences between traditional job analysis and strategic job analysis.

Table 5.1   Traditional versus Strategic Job Analysis

Traditional Job Analysis	Strategic Job Analysis
Focus on what is required to be done	Focus on outputs to be achieved
Look at the job from an inside-out approach	Look at the job from an outside-in approach
Written by administrative HR department	Written in consultation with stakeholders
Clearly defines duties and tasks	Describes broad responsibilities only
Access to job descriptions by incumbent only	Access to all job descriptions by all
Individualistic in nature	Reflects the interdependence of the job
Reviewed when a job becomes vacant	Reviewed regularly for updates

STRATEGIC JOB ANALYSIS AND DEJOBBING

The traditional concept of job is getting redefined. Under precarious settings of the new age, laying down specified duties and tasks can be fatal. 'Jobs' are best suited for static and stable environments, not for the workplace of today. In this context, the term 'dejobbing' has been used by William Bridges.[5] The need for responsiveness has blurred the conventional meaning of job. In the new set-up, jobs change each day in keeping with the external changes. In times of rapid change, employees have to see themselves as providing solutions, rather than as 'doing my job'.

With dejobbing, workers are paid not for their ability to work for fixed hours but rather for their performance. Employees are given the flexibility and freedom to innovate and experiment. Dejobbed organizations prepare their employees not for today's jobs but for tomorrow's roles.

The level of dejobbing varies with the stage of growth of an organization. In start-up companies, 'job-hazyness' is a common phenomenon. Since start-ups are in their formative stages, jobs *per se* have not crystallized as yet. People just do whatever needs doing. These organizations symbolize a natural form of dejobbing. However, when start-ups grow and expand, jobs begin to firm up. This gives rise to concrete job descriptions. As organizations further grow and competition intensifies, managers may realize the need for handling unplanned work demands and challenges. This phenomenon necessitates the need to dejob the organization. Thus, in high-growth stages of the organization, dejobbing may become a prerequisite.

Various internal and external factors support the concept of dejobbing. Some of the external factors supporting dejobbing are rapid product and technological change demanding faster response times, increasing global competition, need for deregulation and decentralization, demographic changes (such as changing workforce profile and competencies) that necessitate creating flexible workplaces, and rise of a service economy that has prompted the creation of dynamic and agile business organizations. All these trends require shifting from static to dynamic jobs. The various internal factors that support the concept of dejobbing are: creation of flatter organizations with less reporting structures, creation of networked and boundaryless organizations with interlinked units and departments, focus on nimble work teams and cross-functional collaboration, and the need for continuous reengineering requiring redesigning of jobs to meet changing market needs.

Dejobbing is seen as a trend that will go hand in hand with the concept of strategic job analysis. Organizations delving on the path to dejobbing need to inculcate a learning mindset. The role of leaders is critical in setting the necessary conditions for the organization to develop learning capability. Since individuals exhibit diversity in their behaviours and disposition, executives will have to delineate carefully crafted strategies for employees while propelling the organization on the path of dejobbing. It requires putting in place a workable and customized coping strategy while dejobbing.

It is important to note that dejobbing is a phenomenon that is more prevalent in high-growth sectors and industries. For instance, in high-tech industries, it is a common practice for employees to work in cross-functional project teams and shift from project to project. However, in many industries that use lower-skilled workers, traditional jobs may still continue to exist. Clearly, the two different types of jobs—the lower-skilled operational jobs and the high-tech jobs—require different approaches. Many of the typical processes associated with conducting a traditional job analysis and writing job descriptions and job specifications are still relevant with the lower-skilled, task-based, routine type of jobs. However, for fast-moving organizations in industries at the technological edge, a traditional job description is now becoming an obsolete concept. Employees in these 'virtual jobs' must be able to function without job descriptions and without the traditional guidelines.

COMPETENCY PROFILING AND STRATEGIC JOB MODELLING

Apart from the concept of dejobbing, two other related concepts that need some discussion in the light of the concept of strategic job analysis are competency profiling and SJM.

Competency Profiling

A job is traditionally a set of closely related activities carried out for pay, but as discussed earlier, the concept of job is changing. Modern-day organizations are instituting management practices such as autonomous work teams, multi-skilling, organic structures, and flexible work arrangements. Under such circumstances, relying on a list of conventional job duties can be counterproductive. The concept of strategic job analysis, thus, necessitates that job descriptions should become flexible and futuristic. Consequently, the focus has shifted from defining tasks and duties to creating competency profiles.

Job profiles or *competency profiles* list the competencies, traits, knowledge, and experience that employees in multi-skilled job contexts must be able to exhibit to meet multiple job demands. Talent management can effectively take place through these competency profiles. The aim of writing job profiles is to create detailed descriptions of what is required for exceptional performance in a given role or job, in terms of required competencies (know-how, behaviours, and abilities); personal attributes (traits and personality); knowledge (technical and/or professional); and experience (educational and work achievements). Each job's profile then becomes the anchor for designing HR activities for the job.

Competency profiling or competency mapping is a process of identifying key competencies for an organization or a job and incorporating them throughout the various processes (for example, job analysis, recruitment, and training). A competency-based job description provides the factors for assessment during the performance evaluation. These competencies serve as basis for training needs identification.

The competency framework serves as the bedrock for all HR applications. Competency mapping can play a significant role in recruiting and retaining people as it gives a more accurate analysis of the job requirements and links it to the candidate's capability. It helps in designing suitable selection tests that traditional job descriptions do not. It provides scope for designing development tools and methods for enhancing employee skills.

Employers often use competency-based job analysis to create such profiles. Competency-based job analysis means describing the job in terms of measurable, observable, and behavioural competencies (knowledge, skills, and/or behaviours) that an employee doing that job must exhibit. Traditional job analysis is job-centric (What tasks are to be done in this job?). On the other hand, competency-based analysis is employee-centric (What competencies employees must have to do multi-skilled jobs?). Defining competencies and writing them is similar in most respects to traditional job analysis. However, the approach is different. Instead of compiling a list of job duties, one needs to understand what competencies are required and how those competencies will be developed in order to effectively multi-task.

Example of Competency Mapping

Figures 5.5A and 5.5B show a sample competency map for an HR manager.

As can be seen in Figure 5.5A, for the function, performance and rewards, the competencies at different levels are:

- *Foundational level*   Payroll preparation, database maintenance, dispensing with rewards, preparing paychecks, and so on
- *Intermediate level*   Records and information management, structuring benefits, packages, supervising level 1, and so on
- *Advanced level*   Laying down compensation policy, environment scanning for industry benchmarking, drawing guidelines for compensation, supervising level 2, and so on

Figure 5.5B shows the descriptions of each skill. These descriptions of the entire competency set may be maintained using human resource information system (HRIS). For example, for oral communication, the incumbent can click on the row to enable detailed descriptors for that skill. It may include speaking abilities, listening abilities, language and fluency, speech effectiveness, and so on.

Selection tests will focus on capturing basic skills in each area. Each skill will be evaluated during 360-degree appraisal and points given on a scale. The average of points will show the overall performance on that skill. Compensation calculations will be done based on points. Training will be provided to bridge the gaps in each skill level. Each column serves as a standard to earn raises and incentives. Each colour code serves as a basis for promotion to the next block/level. Once all blocks have been sufficiently attained, the incumbent gets promoted to the intermediate level.

Figure 5.5A   Competency Mapping of HR Manager's Job

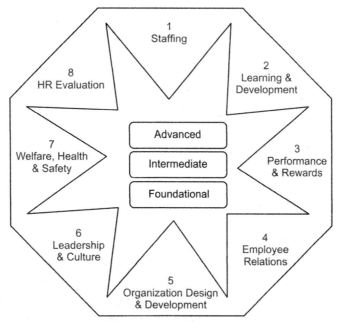

3-Level of Competencies for 8 Broad Competency Domains
Level 3: Advanced (Higher-level competencies)
Level 2: Intermediate (Mid-level competencies)
Level 1: Foundational (Early career-level competencies)

Figure 5.5B   Competency Levels for HR Manager's Job

Skills at Foundational Level

1 Oral communication

2 Written communication

3 Understanding instructions

4 Documentation and record-keeping abilities

5 Interpersonal skills

6 Self-management

7 Time management

8 Presentation and behaviour

Skills at Intermediate Level

9 Goal achievement

10 Teamwork

11 Personal accountability

12 Persuasion skills

13 Customer responsiveness

14 Diplomacy and tact

Skills at Advanced Level

15 Problem-solving ability

16 Resilience

17 Conflict management

18 Negotiation

19 Conceptual thinking

20 Planning and organizing

21 Creativity

Strategic Job Modelling

A similar concept to competency mapping is SJM. SJM aims at understanding the ultimate objective of the organization and then drawing it into work requirements.

In the book *Strategic Job Modeling: Working at the Core of Integrated Human Resources*, Jeffery S. Schippman calls job modelling an upgraded approach to job analysis. According to the author, traditional job analysis procedures are too short-sighted to meet the strategic and future-oriented needs of today's organizations. SJM is about a 'next-generation' job analysis method that involves translating business strategies into work performance and competency requirements.[6]

The purpose of SJM is to develop a trajectory of work competencies that are expected from an incumbent in a particular 'job'. This differs from a traditional job analysis approach that details only the present duties. SJM takes into account two set of competencies:

- Can-do competencies: present skills
- Will-do competencies: future skills

So, while conventional job analysis provides a past-tense description of something static, SJM provides a future-tense description of something dynamic and changing. The concept of SJM and competency profiling are closely linked to dejobbing.

Example of SJM

British Petroleum (BP) realized the need for a more efficient, faster-acting organization. To help accomplish this, they felt they had to shift employees from a job duties oriented that's-not-my-job attitude to one that motivated them to obtain the skills required to accomplish their broader responsibilities.

BP replaced job descriptions with a skills matrix. BP created skills matrices for each job or job family (such as drilling managers). The skills matrix is presented in Figure 5.6.

Figure 5.6 Skill Matrix at BP

H	H	H	H	H	H	H
G	G	G	G	G	G	G
F	F	F	F	F	F	F
E	E	E	E	E	E	E
D	D	D	D	D	D	D
C	C	C	C	C	C	C
B	B	B	B	B	B	B
A	A	A	A	A	A	A
Technical Expertise	Business Awareness	Communication and Interpersonal	Decision Making and Initiative	Leadership and Guidance	Planning and organizational Ability	Problem Solving

Source: Adapted from G. Dessler (2013), *Human resource management* (New Jersey: Pearson Education).

Notes:

- A, B, C, and so on, are descriptors for each level of the skill, for example, in technical expertise (A) might read: basic knowledge of handling machine while (H) might read: conducts and supervises complex tasks requiring advanced knowledge of a range of skills.
- Dark boxes indicate minimum level of skill required in each category for the position.

As shown in Figure 5.6, each matrix lists the types of skills required to do that job (such as technical expertise) and the minimum level of each skill required for that job or job family. This matrix focuses on skills and behaviours rather than individual jobs. Each skills matrix describes steps in the career ladder, from the lowest to the highest, along a vertical axis. The horizontal axis describes the skills and competencies that are required for each step. Talent management in this BP unit now involves recruiting, hiring, training, appraising, and rewarding employees based on the competencies they need to perform their ever-changing jobs, with the overall aim of creating a more flexible organization. The skills matrix for each position is maintained using HRMS.

Skills matrices differ significantly from job descriptions; they specify roles and levels of performance rather than jobs in a box. Through this system, managers know what to expect of their employees and employees know what the organization expects of them. Skills matrix is futuristic because it talks of skill development in terms of future requirements.[7]

Survival in the present demanding world is conditional. With technological developments taking place at lightning speed, individuals who do not keep pace will be left behind. To survive in the dejobbed world, mastery of technology is a prerequisite. Employees need to have a broad range of skills that spill across functional rigidities. Mastering multiple skills that include cross-functional and cross-cultural abilities increases one's employability. Making oneself indispensable for the organization is the only way to survival.

Today's challenging world demands strategic thinking and adaptability and a self-branding mindset. Self-branding involves looking at oneself as a winning brand. We need to develop a plan to create a valuable asset out of ourselves. In the present times, everyone is a contingent worker since every person's employment is contingent on making contributions to their organization.

HR Anecdote

An old master instructed an unhappy apprentice to put a handful of salt in a glass of water and then drink it. 'How does it taste?' the Master asked. 'Awful,' spat the young apprentice.

The Master chuckled and then asked the young man to take another handful of salt and put it in the lake. The two walked in silence to the nearby lake and when the young man swirled his handful of salt into the lake, the old man said, 'Now drink from the lake.' As the water dripped down the young man's chin, the Master asked, 'How does it taste?' 'Good!' remarked the apprentice. 'Do you taste the salt?' asked the Master. 'No, said the young man.

The Master sat beside this troubled young man, took his hands, and said, 'The pain and troubles of life is like pure salt; no more, no less, exactly the same. But the amount we taste depends on the container we put it into. So when you are in pain and have troubles, the only thing you can do is to enlarge your sense of things..... Stop being a glass. Become a lake!'

This story has implications for our work. At the workplace, we face numerous problems and challenges. A narrow approach to work makes our problems seem like the salt in the glass. To handle these everyday challenges better, we need to 'enlarge our sense of things'. We need to 'become a lake'. We need to move away from narrow concepts of work to broader horizons of work competencies.

Source: Retrieved and adapted from: http://www.ezsoftech.com/stories/mis20.asp#change.

News Grab
Companies introducing creative concepts in naming key roles

Corporate India is tossing out old, stodgy nomenclatures in favour of more creative, personalised designations. At one company for instance, the CEO is called the 'chief pusher', quite simply because he pushes and nudges employees into delivering the goods. The organization also has a chief listening officer (HR head) and chief enabler (technology head) and also a chief dreamer (strategist). Training head's designation was renamed as 'chief capability officer'.

Companies like Aegis believe in preventing any dilution of ethics. They created the post of a 'chief ethics officer', whose job is to keep a check on any kind of fraudulent behaviour. Sapient Corporation believes in recognising individuals, rather than a collective mass of people. It has banned the use of words like 'employees', 'workforce', and 'head'. 'We are not resources or tools but assets for the company,' says Vice President, People Success. His job definition: Help people in the company succeed.

People in their late 20s and 30s do get excited by them. In some cases, they help attract people for jobs in the company. People in organizations like those above prefer the 'quirkier' titles they now have. They feel that these new designations are not about informality; they are created so that one can identify with the philosophy and culture of the firm. In most organizations that work on similar lines, executives want their titles to resonate their approach to work instead of seniority. It breaks down hierarchies.

Hierarchy is gradually crumbling in India and work areas are flatter, where everyone is in self-actualisation mode. In most cases, though, the choice of designation is reserved for those who have proved themselves. The rest of the employees can stick to well-worn labels. The core content of the 'glamourised' role does not change.

The Bangalore-based IT services firm Mind Tree created the role of an 'Agile Evangelist', a post headed by chief architect, for product engineering and IT services. The role involves promoting agile adoption across all businesses of MindTree. The objective is to make the customers successful by leveraging the benefits of agile methodologies and delivering high-quality software in a timely manner.

Philips in India has two kinds of designations for its employees. One is an email signature, like that of an 'architect' or a 'programmer' similar to the employee's counterparts the world over, and the other is reserved for visiting cards, keeping in mind the importance of designations in countries like India.

Source: Retrieved and adapted from https://economictimes.indiatimes.com/jobs/companies-introducing-creative-concepts-in-naming-key-roles/articleshow/12644995.cms.

CHAPTER SUMMARY

- Talent management can be defined as an integrated process of planning, acquiring, developing, managing, and rewarding employees.
- Workflow analysis and job analysis can be seen as two important starting points in the larger domain of talent management.
- A workflow consists of an orchestrated and repeatable pattern of activity through a systematic arrangement of resources into processes that transform inputs into outputs.
- Job analysis refers to the determination of the tasks that comprise the job as well as the skills, knowledge, and abilities required of the worker for successful performance.
- Two important outcomes of job analysis are job description and job specification.
- Traditional HR thinkers consider job analysis as a static, one-time activity. In reality, jobs are continuously changing, thereby necessitating a shift towards strategic job analysis.
- The need for responsiveness has blurred the conventional meaning of job. In the new set-up, jobs change each day, in keeping with the external changes. This is called dejobbing.
- Competency mapping is the process of identifying key competencies for a job and incorporating them throughout the various processes (for example, job analysis, recruitment, and training).
- SJM is about a 'next-generation' job analysis method that involves translating business strategies into a trajectory of competency requirements.

EXERCISES AND DISCUSSION QUESTIONS

1. Discuss the reasons for shift from traditional job analysis to strategic job analysis. Is strategic job analysis the future of work?

2. Explain the concept of dejobbing. Giving examples, show how competency profiling and SJM support this new notion of dejobbing in modern-day organizations.
3. Examine a sample job from a company of your choice.
    i. Highlight the nature of the job, and its job description and specification.
    ii. Is the job profile traditional/static or dynamic? Point out elements of the job in support of your answer.
    iii. Collect information on the key industry trends and competitive challenges for the job in question and identify critical competencies for the future. Try to construct a competency profile for the job.

CASELET

Job Remodelling at Tata Motors

Tata Motors is the world's fourth-largest bus and truck manufacturer and India's largest automobile company. Through subsidiaries and associate companies, Tata Motors has operations in the UK, South Korea, Thailand, Spain, South Africa, and Indonesia. Among them is Jaguar Land Rover, the business comprising two iconic British brands. The company, formerly known as Tata Engineering and Locomotive Company, began manufacturing commercial vehicles in 1954, with a 15-year collaboration agreement with Daimler Benz of Germany.

Tata Motors has aspirations for a future that will be more global and more competitive, where customer expectations will be quite different from previous years. In late 2010, as part of its vision for transformation, Tata Motors articulated a human capital strategy that sets a future road map for the company's HR agenda. The HR agenda had near- and long-term goals. How to manage costs, productivity, and talent were considered to be the near-term HR challenges. The long-term agenda was to create an HR culture concomitant with the new strategic imperatives of the company. This agenda was supposed to act as a mantra for a turnaround of sorts for the company.

Tata Motors underwent a comprehensive organizational transformation. It started with the new vision and mission document, which allowed people to see a clear link between what they are doing and what the company aimed to achieve. A lot of HR processes and systems were revisited towards this end. The company reframed its vision and mission and defined the kind of culture it needed to create, given the new challenges. Building that culture was easier said than done because it meant that all HR sub-systems had to be reoriented to be in line with the new culture. Culture reinvention along the 'Aces' path (accountability, customer focus, excellence, and speed) was seen as an HR priority as it comprised a huge change management component.

The New HR Roadmap

It started with an extensive process mapping exercise to benchmark and align the HR processes with global best practices. As part of this, a key focus area was managing talent and leadership. It started with the thought that a company's success eventually depends on talent across all levels, with the right skills, the right engagement, and the right kind of diversity. At Tata Motors, employees are seen as the most important asset. It was reaffirmed that the company had erroneously believed that human asset management is part of the HR function's agenda. The new strategy suggested that while human capital strategy is enabled and facilitated by the HR function, it is actually owned by leadership and management across levels. It was, thus, thought that the so-called gap between line managers and HR must end. That led to the shift from an HR function strategy to a strategic human capital strategy.

A major part of this transformation and the new HR agenda was the move to redesign jobs at Tata Motors. The HR strategy was to respond to the changing needs of the entire ecosystem. Towards this end, the company adopted several steps that focused on redesigned job descriptions. For instance, the company created a small team from the in-house group of HR professionals to work on the HR agenda for dealers and to look at the entire HR life cycle of the people who actually touch the end customer. Jobs were remodelled to ensure greater connect with dealers and customers.

As a part of this job remodelling initiative, it was decided that the company would concentrate on offering different assignments, enabling competency-building and behavioural training, taking people out of their comfort zone, and so on. This would be coupled with the leadership development project, which is about identifying potential leaders at every level through education coaching, and mentoring. The focus was on skill and capability building of the workforce.

Implementation of a 'Fast Track Selection Scheme', which is a system for identifying potential talent and offering them opportunities for growth within the organization, was part of this initiative. Further, the company's 'Talent Management Scheme', which includes the identification of high performers and high potentials, was geared to provide them with challenging assignments for faster development. The company's 'Pact' (performance and coaching tool) initiative was anchored in the philosophy that managers must move away from thinking of themselves as bosses to thinking of themselves as coaches. A significant part of the change in performance measurement, talent management, and assessment criteria was about using hardwired HR processes to support what is really a soft cultural transition. Introduction of performance rating based salary review and quality-linked variable payment was another initiative to boost competency-building.

There were some obvious challenges, such as the availability of skills. It was felt that the auto industry is not necessarily the first choice of many potential employees; how the company positions itself as a sector of choice was a challenge. The challenge was clear—the old image of the auto sector as a manufacturing business had to change; it must promote itself as a consumer-oriented sector at par with new-age industries that offered prospective employees dynamic jobs and career growth.

Quantitatively, the company has single-digit attrition, which was not so bad. It was felt that most of the attrition happens in the first five years, when employees are keen to switch jobs and try out new things. It was felt that younger employees are uncomfortable with hierarchies and static job descriptions. The new competency framework for designing jobs was expected to offset this by providing a more vibrant career environment, one that is built around levels of competencies and not levels in organizational hierarchy.

The Path Not So Smooth

Continuing with its HR innovations and job remodelling agenda, in 2017 Tata Motors carried out its largest-ever HR overhaul that was never seen in its 72-year history. Ruffling several feathers, the company shrunk designations from a whopping 140 to just 5. All the levels were rolled into a new simplified structure. While announcing the flat structure, the company decided that instead of the specific designations, employees will be known simply by their function or responsibility, for instance, 'sales—medium and heavy commercial vehicles', and those heading a team will simply be called 'head' followed by the function, across its plants and offices.

The earlier structure was a very tall hierarchy. Now, it was designed to become flat. This was part of its organizational restructuring exercise that was expected to transform the organization into a much leaner company with a flat hierarchical structure. Tata Motors initiated a no-designation policy in its bid to create a hierarchy-free culture in the company that would undo any old notion of designations and job descriptions. This was done to achieve a global mindset, through a strong and continued focus on operational excellence and multi-skilling.

The decision to knock off designations and replace them with the specific functions of employees was intended to make competency-building more robust. By removing hierarchical barriers, it was also widely believed that performance would be enhanced and employees would be motivated to build skills in multiple related domains. The company's aim was to become a lean and agile organization by empowering its employees with clear accountability, functional leadership, faster and effective decision-making, and improved customer focus.

However, soon the company's strategy to move to a flat structure turned flat. It was felt that some people were finding it difficult to represent their roles during their external, social interactions. There were operational challenges in communicating outside—to the government, customers, and vendors. It soon became pretty clear that not everyone was happy with the move and for a senior employee who wore his designation on his sleeve, the abrupt scaling down was quite disheartening. In the Indian context, hierarchy is a big thing even though it may not be such a big deal in the West. There were people working for more than 25 years and suddenly their designations were at par with someone who had just joined. Obviously, they felt it was very unfair. People found it very difficult to accept this kind of a radical transformation. To deal with this, Tata Motors introduced a new salary structure that promised to reward its best performers handsomely but even this could not help much. It also posed a challenge for those who would join Tata Motors from other companies, as doing so could mean sacrificing the current superior designation and accepting a lower designation band.

Thus, the company had to bring back some of the designations. Although the non-hierarchical, simple five-level structure remains the same, the company had to get some simplified and standardized designations back into place. It was realized that cultural change is a gradual journey and may require some time to sensitize the workforce to accept a job overhaul as massive as this.

Despite hiccups, the above initiatives have indeed helped the company bring in unprecedented 'outside in' thinking to HR. The new HR policies today are benchmarked with the best in the world. Historically, a variety of practices were deployed at various Tata Motors locations; the company is now creating a single Tata Motors way. It has harmonized and upscaled HR in the company. Many HR initiatives of Tata Motors have been adopted by other companies of Tata group as well. The company was awarded the 'HR Innovation of the Year' award by the Asia Pacific Excellence Award in 2017.

Tata Motors claims that despite periods of tough calls, there is very little attrition as compared to the industry. The company website sates, 'We are trying to create a more contemporary organization that appeals to employees from any country, culture, or industry;

a world-class destination for best-in-class talent.' The company was recently named in one survey as the 'best company to work for' in the auto and manufacturing segment. The challenge is how to keep this alive.[8]

Questions for Discussion

1. What were the changes in job design brought out at Tata Motors? How were these changes aligned with the strategic mandate?
2. What challenges did the company face in its effort to create a flat, hierarchy-less job structure? Is cultural change a gradual journey? Discuss.

NOTES

1. Job characteristics theory is a popular theory of work design. It provides a set of implementing principles for enriching jobs in organizational settings. Job Characteristics Theory is firmly entrenched within the work design literature and has become one of the most cited in the organizational behaviour field. See J. R. Hackman and G. R. Oldham (1980), *Work redesign* (Reading, MA: Addison-Wesley); J. R. Hackman and G. R. Oldham (2005), How job characteristics theory happened, in *The Oxford handbook of management theory: The process of theory development*, ed. K. G. Smith and M. A. Hitt, pp. 151–170 (Oxford, UK: Oxford University Press).
2. R. A. Noe, B. A. Gerhart, J. R. Hollenbeck, and P. M. Wright (2014), *Human resource management: Gaining a competitive advantage* (New York, NY: McGraw-Hill Education).
3. C. N. Parkinson (1955), Parkinson's law, *The Economist*, London, 19 November; C. N. Parkinson (1957), *Parkinson's law and other studies in administration* (Boston, MA: Houghton Mifflin Company).
4. D. Goleman (2009), *Emotional intelligence* (New Delhi, India: Bloomsbury Publishing India).
5. W. Bridges (1994), *Jobshift: How to prosper in a workplace without jobs* (Reading MA: Addison-Wesley).
6. J. S. Schippmann (2013), *Strategic job modeling: Working at the core of integrated human resources* (Mahwah, NJ: Psychology Press).
7. G. Dessler (2013), *Human resource management* (Upper Saddle River, NJ: Pearson Education).
8. With inputs from https://www.thewaltdisneycompany.com; https://economictimes.indiatimes.com/industry/tata-motors-scraps-designations-to-create-a-flatter-organisation-boost-creativity/articleshow/59060469.cms; https://www.thehindubusinessline.com/companies/flat-response-tata-motors-brings-back-designations/article9791248.ece.

Strategy Implementation

Part I

THE FRAMEWORK OF STRATEGIC HUMAN RESOURCE MANAGEMENT
Chapter 1: Concept of Strategic Human Resource Management

Part II

CONTEXT OF SHRM
Chapter 2: Environment of SHRM
Chapter 3: Technology and HRM

Part III

STRATEGY FORMULATION
Chapter 4: Strategy Formulation and HRM
Chapter 5: Work Flow Analysis and Strategic Job Analysis

Part IV

STRATEGY IMPLEMENTATION
Chapter 6: Strategic Human Resource Planning and Staffing
Chapter 7: Strategic Training and Development
Chapter 8: Performance Management and Compensation
Chapter 9: Employee Relations, Engagement, and Termination

Part V

STRATEGY EVALUATION
Chapter 10: Strategic HR Evaluation

Strategic Human Resource Planning and Staffing

Chapter Overview

Job analysis identifies the duties and human requirements for each of the company's jobs. The next logical step is to decide which of these jobs need to be filled and how to fill them. This entails carrying out human resource planning (HRP). It involves linking business strategies to future manpower needs, forecasting labour demand and supply, and laying down the human resource (HR) plan to meet the labour needs. Thereafter, staffing is carried out, which typically involves recruitment, selection, and placement. This chapter deals with all these issues.

Learning Objectives

1. To understand the concept of strategic human resource planning
2. To identify the steps involved in strategic human resource planning
3. To understand the process of staffing involving recruitment, selection, and placement
4. To develop an understanding of strategic staffing issues

OPENING STORY

Strategic Manpower Planning in Indian Armed Forces

Human Resource Development is an essential command function and, in this context, it needs to be understood that the soldier of tomorrow has to be an innovator who can combine imagination and knowledge with action.

—Indian Army Doctrine (2004)

Some time back, the Ministry of Defence, India, indicated that the Indian Armed Forces were short of 9,845 officers at the level of majors/lieutenant colonels and equivalent ranks. These figures indicate that the army was short of 7,899 officers, followed by the navy with 1,499 officers and air force with 357 officers. Several questions arise: Why is there a shortage of officers? Why are there impediments to lateral induction of service personnel into the armed forces? How can the services provide better promotion avenues or reduce its alarming suicide rates? All these issues directly or indirectly concern the realm of 'strategic manpower planning'.

Manpower needs of the armed forces are more complex than that of the corporate world. The requirement of the armed forces to commit soldiers to extreme conditions necessitates a deep understanding and knowledge of human capital management. Human capital development in the armed forces is an extremely vital issue because the strength of the organization has always been its manpower. It has been aptly said that platforms and organizations do not defend the country, people do; units and formations do not sacrifice and take risks for the nation, people do! In reality, the manpower aspect is often relegated to the rear echelon and is disassociated from the overall strategic planning. As the country marches towards economic prosperity, there is a need to concurrently focus on consolidating its armed forces into an extremely cohesive, optimally equipped, modern, and operationally ready force capable of meeting challenges.

HR Dimension in Perspective Planning

Given its size, diversity, and complexities, the challenges that confront the armed forces, when it comes to the management of its human resource element, is a gigantic one. Higher defence planning for the armed forces is a complex iterative process involving a large number of agencies. National Security Strategy (NSS) is the starting point for the process of formulation of the Long Term Integrated Perspective Plan (LTIPP), of which strategic manpower plan is a component. The most important document that would provide the basic guidelines for the formulation of the LTIPP is the Strategic Defence Planning Guidance (SDPG), which articulates the contingencies that the armed forces may be called upon to respond to in a 15-year time horizon. The contingencies would be prioritized and fund availability duly earmarked for the same time span. The SDPG would be the key input for formulating the defence capability strategy, which would enumerate each type of capability required for each type of contingency. Thereafter, it would establish the gap in these capabilities and prioritize the bridging of such gaps. The next stage would be the Defence Capability Plan (DCP), which is the government plan for investment in equipment for the development of future capabilities in the Indian Armed Forces. This plan would list the capability required with an associated time frame along with options for achieving those capabilities. This would facilitate the formulation of a meaningful and achievable LTIPP. The DCP would be reviewed annually to cater to the changing strategic environment.

The LTIPP would flow out of the DCP and would essentially list out programmes and projects required to be taken up to achieve the capabilities listed therein. The three services would prepare their respective long-term perspective plans after examining the force levels, force structures, and requirements in terms of human capabilities. Acquisition of manpower will flow out of the LTIPP. All this is a very complex process and involves identifying the capability needs of the armed forces.

The LTIPP contains a number of components, such as research and development and infrastructure development plan, equipment procurement plan, and strategic manpower plan. The infrastructure development plan primarily aims at keeping the existing forces suitably equipped. The force structure development plan includes restructuring the forces through additional military platforms and systems and through restructuring of units, formations, and establishments. Strategic manpower plan aims at projecting qualitative and quantitative requirement of manpower, forecast the availability of manpower, and subsequently the annual intake plan.

Army's Existing Manpower Planning

Owing to the constraints of a developing economy and given the Indian strategic culture, the Indian army at present is not carrying out strategic manpower planning based on the capability-based model described above because LTIPP formulation does not follow the mandated top-down process. The maintenance of 'forces in being' or accretions is worked out on a stand-alone basis and forms part of the five year defence plans. An assessment at a tri-service level is not carried out to ascertain whether *Capability A* is more desirable than *Capability B*. Such analyses were at one time a mandate of the defence plan but were not implemented properly. It is only when the armed forces adopt capability-based manpower planning models can it become more efficient and strong.

Sources: Adapted from

http://www.claws.in/1329/strategic-manpower-planning-in-the-armed-forces-vikram-taneja.html.
http://www.indiandefencereview.com/spotlights/army-management-of-human-capital-i/.

STRATEGIC HUMAN RESOURCES PLANNING (SHRP)

Workforce planning or personnel planning is the process of deciding what positions the firm will have to fill and how to fill them. A number of terminologies coexist in this context. *Manpower Planning* (MP) deals with assessing the demand and supply of people. *Human Resource Planning* (HRP) is different from MP because it emphasizes the arrangement of staff in light of the organization's long-term requirements. MP is more of a traditional, short-term, and ad-hoc approach to filling vacancies. HRP is a long-term approach to meeting skill requirements.

A key goal of HRP is to get the right number of people with the right skills, experience, and competencies in the right jobs at the right time and at the right cost to meet long-term needs. HRP is the process by which management ensures that it has the right people, who are capable of completing tasks that help the organization reach its objectives.

HRP is a bit different from the broader concept of strategic human resource planning (SHRP). Many companies plan their human resources in a 'band-aid fashion', which involves reacting to short-term forces, rather than being proactive. There is no linkage to business imperatives. This kind of HRP is deficient. SHRP, on the other hand, links people management to the organization's strategic plan. It deals with the linkage between strategic business planning and HRP. SHRP is done by HR managers in association with strategic managers. In basic terms, planning within HR should be done strategically, since longer term thinking is required to effectively manage human resources over time. In fact, in the present context, if one considers the complexity of any HRP, it seems obvious that the process has to be strategic in nature. Hence, HRP and SHRP may be interpreted as the same for practical purposes.

SHRP plays a vital role in the achievement of an organization's overall strategic objectives. A comprehensive HRP will also support other strategic objectives undertaken by the marketing, financial, operational, and technology departments. In essence, SHRP should aim to capture 'the people element' of what an organization is hoping to achieve in the long term, ensuring that it has the right people with the right mix of skills and behaviours.

Applying a talent management perspective to workforce planning requires being proactive. Specifically, it requires paying continuous attention to workforce planning issues. Managers call this newer, continuous workforce planning approach predictive workforce monitoring. For instance, Intel Corporation conducts semi-annual organization capability assessments. The staffing department works with the organization's business heads twice a year to assess both immediate as well as future workforce needs.[1]

SHRP PROCESS

This process focuses on aligning the HR plan to support the accomplishment of the company's mission, vision, goals, and strategies. People are the primary source of competitive advantage. Successful companies integrate and align HRP to the organization's strategic plan. In order to link HRP to overall business planning or strategic planning, the following steps need to be followed.

Aligning HR Vision with Company Vision

The first step to SHRP would involve ensuring the alignment of the HR vision with the organization's vision. This will then become the starting point of all HRP. As the pace and magnitude of change in the environment increases, the approach to SHRP changes substantially. First, the planning process is more agile; changes in plans are much more frequent and are often driven by external changes rather than made on a predetermined time schedule. Second, the planning process is more proactive. Successful organizations no longer simply respond to changes in their environment, but they proactively shape their environmental forces. Third, the planning process is no longer exclusively top-down; input into the process comes from different organizational levels. This creates more employee ownership of the plan. It capitalizes on the fact that often the most valuable business intelligence can come from employees who are at the bottom of the hierarchy.

Environmental Scanning

A key component of HRP is understanding the workforce needs and planning for projected shortages and surpluses in specific occupations and skill sets. A good HRP process requires internal and external environmental scanning.

- **Internal Scan** This requires identifying factors internal to the organization that may affect HR capacity to meet organizational goals. For instance, what are the key internal forces affecting the organization's operations (cultural issues, technology requirements, budget issues, expectation of employees, skill requirements, collective agreements, trade union demands, and so on)? What knowledge, skills, abilities, and capabilities does the organization have? How has the organization changed its organizational strategy? How is this likely to impact manpower requirements?

- **External Scan**   In order to do HRP, one needs to have a sense of the current external environment and anticipate things that may happen in the future in the labour market place. External scan requires questions such as what are the key external forces affecting the organization's operations (for example, economic and market changes, political exigencies, sociocultural issues, demographics, and technological developments)? How might the external environment differ in the future? What implications will this have for the organization?

Developing Forecast through Workforce Analysis

Workforce analysis involves identifying current and anticipated future supply of labour and skills (supply analysis), identifying what one will need in the future in terms of skills and competencies (demand analysis), and then identifying the gaps between the supply and demand (gap analysis).

Demand Analysis

The demand for human resource is a derived or secondary demand. It depends on the primary demand for a firm's goods and services. An organization's staffing needs, thus, depend on external environmental and market conditions as well as its corporate strategy. Forecasting workforce demand, therefore, starts with estimating the demand for one's final products or services. The planning process may also involve developing contingency staffing plans to address the potential changes in demand.

The basic process of forecasting personnel needs in many organizations starts with forecasting revenues first. Then, they estimate the size of the staff required to support this volume. However, managers must also consider other strategic factors, such as projected turnover, decisions to expand, enter new markets or upgrade (or downgrade) products or services, productivity targets, and availability of financial resources.

Demand estimation of the number and type of skills required can be done by carrying out an extensive jobs and skills audit.

Jobs and Skills Audit

A jobs and skills audit is an examination of existing jobs and skills in the organization. The key concerns are examining the number and type of present jobs and the anticipated changes in organizational strategies and their implications for skill requirements. Organizations need to carry out a jobs and skills audit for each unit or division. It is important at this stage to develop decision rules (fill rates) for positions to be filled. It involves estimating when positions are likely to become vacant and how they will be filled, whether internally or externally.

There are several simple tools for projecting personnel needs. *Trend analysis* is a very common tool. It means studying variations in an organization's employment levels over the last few years.

Another simple approach, *ratio analysis*, involves making forecasts based on the historical ratio between some causal factor (such as sales volume) and the number of employees required (such as number of salespeople). A *scatter plot* shows graphically how two variables such as revenues and staffing levels are related. If they are, then while forecasting revenues, one can also estimate the personnel needs. HR planners also use a mathematical process known as *Markov analysis* (or transition analysis) to forecast the availability of internal job candidates. Markov analysis involves creating a matrix that shows the probabilities of movements of employees in a chain of command. It shows a possible career chart for each employee and how they are likely to move up from position to position. An estimation of the time required for these movements will give an understanding of the need to fill different positions.

Whichever forecasting tool one uses, managerial judgement should play a big role. Often, HR planners will have to rely on insights and judgements more than any tool. Environmental dynamics keep changing and so does the approach for planning HR needs. Typically, textbooks on HRM discuss in detail the use of these tools. The current book focuses more on the strategic aspects of HR functions.

Supply Analysis

After estimating the demand for manpower, the next step is to estimate the likely supply of candidates. Supply of candidates may be both from internal or external sources. It is reasonable to start analysing the supply of internal candidates first.

Internal Supply Assessment

The main task in estimating the internal supply is determining whether current employees are qualified and suitable for the projected openings. Organizations maintain databases to track organizational capabilities inventory and to determine employees' knowledge, skills, and abilities (KSAs). The critical information needed in order to tap internal sources of capabilities are:

- Employee demographics (qualifications, skills, know-how, experiences, and so on)
- Training imparted to employees
- Employee career progression (promotions, transfers, and moves)
- Individual job performance data
- Workforce trends—such as eligibility for retirement and separation rate

Data on employee skills can be maintained using a manual system or through computerized inventories in the form of human resources management system (HRMS).

Manual system

Traditionally, organizations have maintained data on skill sets using organizational charts and replacement charts. An *organizational chart* is a diagrammatic depiction of the structure of an organization and shows the different jobs or positions with their relationships and relative ranks.

An organizational chart helps see different positions and the promotion channels open so as to determine possible movements and vacancies leading to an understanding of demand and supply of candidates. A *personnel inventory and development record form* compiles qualifications information on each employee. The information includes education, skills, trainings received, courses untaken, career and development interests, and past assignments and positions. *Personnel replacement charts* show the present performance report and promotability for each position's potential replacement.

Computerized skills inventories

Maintaining a comprehensive skill inventory using HRMS, as discussed in an earlier chapter, helps keep track of the set of available competencies in a more organized manner. HRMS maintains real-time data on employee skills, performance records, qualifications, and promotion paths.

External Supply Assessment

Organizations may often look towards external sources of labour in order to fill vacancies and get the required talent on board. The external supply will depend on many things such as:

- Net migration for an area
- Individuals entering and leaving the workforce, schools, and colleges
- Changing workforce composition and patterns
- Economic forecasts
- Technological developments and shifts
- Government regulations and pressures

Gap Analysis

The next step involves laying out the gaps in demand and supply. Gap analysis requires comparing supply with demand analysis to determine future shortages and excess in the number of employees needed, types of occupations, and competencies. It necessitates developing an action plan to match the projected supply and demand. Workforce planning should logically culminate in a workforce action plan.

Formulate HR Plans

Developing an action plan to match the projected labour supply and labour demand is the next logical step in HRP. Based on the internal and external scan, HR managers may lay down the HR plans in accordance with the major human resource priorities and the strategies that will achieve the desired outcome. This lays down the employer's projected workforce demand–supply gaps as well as staffing plans in order to fill the required positions. The HR plan should identify the number and types of positions to be filled, ratio of internal and external sources to be tapped for these positions, time involved in filling the positions, training required in placing the people, and promotion programmes to be effected. This will also entail working out the resources in terms of advertising costs, recruiter fees, travel and interview expenses, promotion budget, relocation costs, and so on.

Vertical and Horizontal Integration

HRP needs to be linked to larger business plans. HRP is not an end unto itself, and neither is HR management an end in itself. The function is meant to support and enable the company to attain its business goals and, hence, it needs to be linked to and driven by those business or strategic goals. This is called vertical integration. Second, it is important to remember that the whole process of HRP is to serve the stakeholders and 'customers' of the HR department. This means that the planning process must actively involve all stakeholders—functional area heads, managers, executives, and line employees. The planning process must be concomitant with plans of other functional areas, such as marketing, operations, or finance. This is called horizontal integration. HR plans must be vertically and horizontally integrated.

Monitoring, Evaluating, and Reporting

Monitoring, evaluating, and reporting the results of HRP helps to attain all-round integration and competitive advantage. It involves assessing and sustaining organizational competence and performance. As with any planning endeavour, the outcomes of the implementation of an HR plan should be measurable. With many personnel functions, there are good, already available metrics (such as employee turnover or churn and frequency of grievance), but it is also good to try to assess the effects of the implementation of an HR plan on the achievement of the organization's business goals. To establish an effective SHRP process, practitioners should consult all stakeholders on the nature of the strategy. Since SHRP involves the collection and use of personnel data, an HRMS helps in carrying out the task more efficiently.

SHRP is not just about MP. It includes other components as well. Apart from the core issues of HRP discussed earlier, a comprehensive SHRP process includes career planning, succession planning, and termination planning.

Strategic issues related to career planning, succession planning, and termination planning are discussed in detail in later chapters.

STRATEGIC STAFFING

The HR function of staffing involves manning the organization through proper and effective selection of personnel. Staffing is the process of matching appropriate people with jobs. Staffing entails using HRP information to determine the number and kind of candidates needed by the organization and then locating those who have the potential. Staffing function is the most important managerial act along with planning, organizing, directing, and controlling. Staffing is a continuous activity. This is because staffing function continues throughout the life of an organization due to terminations, transfers, and promotions that take place.

Staffing primarily involves three activities:

- **Recruitment** The process of searching for prospective employees and stimulating them to apply for jobs
- **Selection** The process of testing and analysing qualifications and characteristics of applicants to establish their suitability for jobs
- **Placement** The process of giving a job offer to selected candidates, assigning rank and responsibility, and inducting newly hired candidates

The next section focuses on recruitment, selection, and placement in detail.

STRATEGIC RECRUITMENT

Recruitment or hiring refers to the process of attracting suitable candidates for jobs within an organization. It is a process of searching for prospective employees and stimulating and encouraging them to apply for jobs in an organization.[2] Recruitment is a linkage activity bringing together those with jobs and those seeking jobs. In simple words, the term 'recruitment' refers to discovering the source from where potential employees may be selected. Recruitment is concerned with reaching out, attracting, and ensuring a supply of qualified personnel.

The traditional philosophy of recruiting has been to get as many people to apply for a job as possible. This approach of recruiting is called the 'flypaper' philosophy. It focuses on attracting as many candidates as possible.[3] A general weakness of the traditional recruitment process or the flypaper philosophy is that some recruiters spend time using search and recruiting tools that do not lead to the right candidates. Generating a huge number of applications is not always useful. What is more important is to generate a pool of applications from the right target market and then being able to filter out the most suitable candidate. Thus, the 'quality' of candidates is more important than 'quantity'. When the objective is to attract people who are more likely to stay longer, the 'matching' philosophy of recruitment may be more efficient.[4] This calls for strategic recruiting.

Strategic recruiting refers to:

- Recruitment activities to be designed to match corporate strategies
- Recruitment activities to be designed with a long-term perspective
- Recruitment activities to help match candidates with jobs
- Recruitment activities to help create a responsive and dynamic organization

Strategic recruitment follows the *3L* principle: *lowest cost*, *least time*, and *likeliest candidates*. Strategic recruitment would refer to adopting recruitment policies, sources, methods, and techniques to attract the 'right' people and 'right' set of competencies, for the 'right' positions in the organization. There is empirical evidence of the importance of a strategic alignment between recruitment and corporate strategies.[5]

Sources of Recruitment

There are two sources of recruitment, namely internal sources and external sources. Internal sources tap candidates from within the organization, while external sources refer to looking outside the organization for identifying talent. This section discusses the different internal and external sources of recruitment to understand how they can be attuned to meet the strategic requirements of an organization.

Internal Sources of Recruitment

It is believed that most often the best employees can be found within the organization. When a higher post is given to a deserving employee, it motivates the other employees of the organization to work hard. The most common internal sources of recruitment are promotions, job postings, transfers, and job rotation.

Promotions

Promotions are the most important source of internally filling vacancies. Promotions refer to shifting people to positions carrying more prestige, higher responsibilities, and more pay. Promotions motivate employees to improve their performance so that they can rise higher. To achieve this, the promotion programme should be comprehensive and linked to strategic goals. At Federal Express, for instance, open positions are filled, whenever possible, by qualified candidates from within the existing workforce.

Promotion from within is aided first by careful employee selection. It is important that the employee selection process should be such that it fetches candidates who have the potential to be promoted at later stages. This is what the talent management perspective also states. Delta Airlines, for instance, is known for long-term promotion perspective. The company website states, 'We hire for the future.' The employment process favours applicants who have the potential for future promotions. That explains how senior-level managers climbed the ranks at Delta from an entry-level position to become heads of their respective departments.

Effective promotion from within depends on internally consistent HR policies. It requires putting in place a comprehensive training and development framework. It also requires career-oriented appraisals and taking care of developmental needs through a formal career plan. Thus, organizations need to have a comprehensive mechanism to train people in order to take the right promotion decisions. Finally, it requires a coordinated and centralized system for accessing employee records. Planned strategic recruitment, thus, helps not only to fill short-term vacancies but also to meet future needs.

Job Postings

Organizations often make effective use of skills inventories for identifying internal applicants for job vacancies. It is difficult, however, for HR managers to be aware of all current employees who might be interested in the vacancy. To help with this problem, they use an approach called job posting and bidding. Job postings refer to posting job vacancies on notice boards, electronic bulletin boards, and so on, and also listing its attributes like required qualifications, experience, and so on. In the past, job posting was done through the use of bulletin boards and company publications for advertising job openings. Today, however, job posting is done through more innovative recruiting techniques using online media.

American Express' career management system includes a simple job posting programme. Openings in this organization are posted on a worldwide electronic system accessible to employees. Computer software allows the employees to match the available job with their skills and experience. It then highlights where gaps exist so the employees know what is necessary if they wish to be competitive for a given job. Federal Express has a job posting/career coordination system called the Job Change Applicant Tracking System (JCATS). Announcements of new job openings take place via this electronic system. When properly implemented, job postings can substantially improve the quality of placements.

Transfers and Lateral Moves

Many times, positions are also filled through transfers of employees to new departments, units, plants, or subsidiaries (in case of MNCs) in the same organization. Often transfers are used for filling vacancies that the company wants to retain with its existing employees. This may happen when the company wants an existing experienced employee to take up a particular position in another department or unit.

In any organization, promotion avenues are limited. The number of available jobs decreases higher up in the organizational chart. This may call for horizontal or lateral promotions. The strategic role of lateral promotions is better understood in light of flatter organizations nowadays. Since in flat organizations the scope for vertical or upward movement is limited, employees start experiencing career plateaus. A career plateau is the point in time in a professional's career where the possibility of a vertical promotion is low. The position of the employee becomes stagnant with repetitive work and responsibilities. Thus, employees are given lateral or horizontal promotions.

In case of lateral moves, employees are transferred to new positions that may be visually at the same level in the organizational hierarchy chart but are experientially different, hence giving the employee a sense of accomplishment. The employee's job responsibilities, status, and authority may change, thus giving the employee new opportunities and a chance to learn new skills. Transfers and lateral moves serve a strategic purpose and can be used to the benefit of the organization as well as the employee. IBM has a suite of software tools that not only maps out the sideways moves employees might need to make to get from point A to point B in their careers but also links them to people in those jobs or business units for information.

Job Rotation

Job rotation refers to moving people from position to position in the same organization to enhance employee skill, knowledge, and experience. It prepares people for change by multiskilling them. It helps in creating a more responsive organization. Just like transfers, job rotation to new positions is also accompanied by job enlargement and job enrichment.

While promotions are upward movements and transfers are lateral movements, job rotation can be seen as a circular/elliptical movement. Deloitte has popularized the notion, both in-house and with clients, of a 'career lattice' rather than a 'career ladder'—a metaphor for the often sideways or diagonally up-or-down directions in which careers move today. Lateral moves and rotations impart that agility and help create future-ready strategic competencies at the workplace by letting people develop a myriad of skills in different areas. Job rotations are a good, though often a temporary, way of filling vacancies.

External Sources of Recruitment

All organizations have to use external sources for recruitment to higher positions when existing employees are not suitable. When expansions are undertaken, there is an even greater need to tap external sources.

Walk-ins or Unsolicited Applications

The most common and least expensive approach for hiring candidates is walk-ins or unsolicited applications. Many good candidates can be found in this pool. While direct applications are particularly effective in filling entry-level and unskilled positions, some organizations compile excellent pools of potential employees from direct applications even for skilled positions. Direct applications can provide a pool of potential employees to meet future needs. These can be good sources of leads.

The reputation of the company has a great deal to do with the usefulness and size of the pool of unsolicited applicants and résumés. Organizations such as Coca-Cola, Google, Microsoft, GE, and IBM receive thousands of unsolicited applications every year. Not only do unsolicited résumés reduce the cost of recruiting, they also increase the probability of hiring the very best employees. Nowadays, it is common for companies to collect résumés through their websites, seen as a virtual walk-in, and pool them for future. Software is used to match job specifications with résumé information.

Employee Referrals

Before going outside to recruit, many organizations ask present employees to refer friends or relatives for a position. A growing number of companies are aggressively promoting referrals. They have formal systems of employee referral for occupations with great demand. Some organizations even offer 'finder's fee' for a successful referral. Referral bonuses range from a gamut of money and trips to time-offs to merchandize coupons and credits. Microsoft is presently offering referral incentives to its employees for Internet experts. Some companies in the service sector train their employees to recruit new employees from among the firm's customers.

When used wisely, referrals can be a powerful recruiting technique. They help get a person who is supposed to have been acquainted with the job and the organization by the referring employee, thus enabling better acclimatization of the new employee. Current employees will usually provide accurate information about the job applicants they are referring since they are putting their own reputation at stake.

The big advantage is that referrals tend to generate more applicants, more hires, and a higher yield ratio of hires to applicants.[6] A recent survey by the Society for Human Resource Management found that employee referrals continue to be employers' top source of hires, delivering more than 30 per cent of all hires. It also stated that 69 per cent of the surveyed companies said employee referral programmes were more cost-effective than other recruiting practices.[7]

Advertising

A common method for recruiting is advertising. Recruitment advertising includes all communications used by an organization to attract talent to work within it. Advertising can range from a simple classified advertisement to an elaborate media campaign. The associated tasks may be undertaken by in-house staff or delegated to advertising agencies or specialists. The latter is especially likely with large companies, which have big advertising budgets and high stakes.

Recruitment advertising should effectively address two issues: the choice of advertising medium and the design of the advertisement.

Choice of media

Common media for advertising are newspapers, magazines, periodicals, professional journals, TV, radio, outdoor advertising (such as billboards, subways, buses, and trains), telephone, and now the Internet. The choice of the medium depends on the positions for which one is recruiting. For example, local or vernacular newspapers may be a good source for semi-skilled/manual, blue-collar, shop-floor, or lower-level administrative positions. On the other hand, while recruiting for specialized skills and higher positions, one may go for national newspapers, professional publications, or the Internet.

The important thing is to target a suitable media that will help reach out to the right prospective candidates. For highly specific and specialized jobs, employers can advertise in trade and professional journals such as publications of industry bodies and associations—for example, NASSCOM (the industry association of the Indian IT and BPM sector); the Federation of Indian Chambers of Commerce and Industry (FICCI), which is an association of business organizations in India; and the National HRD Network. While the majority of advertising is still in newspapers, many organizations are now going beyond the typical newspaper advertisements. Internet advertising is becoming increasingly popular now.

Creating advertisement

Creating recruitment advertisement is a crucial activity for organizations. The content and design of the advertisement are the most important things. Job applicants view advertisements that have detailed information as more attractive and credible.

Advertisers must use the right message and right media. It is important for employers to be visible and convey the 'right' message to build equity in the minds of the talent pool and the public at large. It must include a detailed job description. Ideally, an advertisement also should provide information on the job's human requirements for potential applicants to gauge if the job is a good fit with their personalities.

Recruitment advertising has come a long way—from being modest and monotonous to being bold and beautiful. For most companies, it is an opportunity for brand building. The advertisement must represent the values of the company. For example, IBM's popular tagline 'Are you ready to build a smarter planet?' was deployed in its recruitment advertisements too. Infosys was perhaps the first to drive this trend in India when it rewrote employer and corporate branding through recruitment advertising. These advertisements hope to retain employees as much as they do to attract.

Some recent trends in recruitment advertising that are being witnessed are as follows:

- *AIDA Principle of Advertising*   AIDA principle of advertising, so often used in brand advertisements, has also been adopted in recruitment advertisements. AIDA implies the following:
  - **Attention:** Catch attention (for example, use of colour, bold letters, and open spaces)
  - **Interest:** Create interest (for example, 'this ad is for you' and 'are you an achiever?')
  - **Desire:** Kindle desire (for example, 'go places', 'join the leaders', and 'be a winner').
  - **Action:** Inspire action (for example, 'call now' and 'apply now').
  The purpose of the advertisement is to attract, evoke interest, and desire and then prompt action from prospective candidates by applying for the job.
- *Use of Employees in Advertisements*   Instead of the traditional testimonials, more companies are spotlighting employees, talking about their skills, jobs, and accomplishments. IBM showcased its work culture in its recruitment advertisements through its employees. The famous recruitment campaigns of Infosys with the taglines 'the *ahead of the curve* face of new India' or 'the *let's erase boundaries* face of new India' too highlighted the accomplishments of its employees.
- *Promotion of Intangible Benefits*   In cases where a job is highly attractive and, thus, does not need promoting, employers have turned to emphasizing certain intangible benefits of the company, such as opportunities for advancement, employment security, creative freedom, and entrepreneurial opportunities. Lockheed Missile & Space Company has run a series of advertisements that promote company benefits. Convergys highlighted 'not just a better job but a better life' in its advertisements in India.
- *Point-of-Purchase Recruitment*   A growing number of service companies are recruiting using point-of-purchase advertisements. For example, Pizza Hut places recruiting coupons on its take-out boxes. Featuring a drawing of a large lead pencil, the ad suggests, 'If you want a good job, get the lead out'. The coupon provides a mini résumé form for prospective applicants who do not have résumés. Quik Wok, a Chinese food take-out chain, uses bag stuffers that picture a fortune cookie and proclaim, 'Not everyone will have the good fortune to work at Quik Wok.' They carry descriptions of job opportunities. The success of point-of-purchase ads has eliminated the use of classified advertisements in many companies. Users have found the strategy to be a low-cost, highly efficient, and flexible form of recruiting.

Figure 6.1 compares a typical traditional classified advertisement with a more recent innovative advertisement.

Figure 6.1 Change in Recruitment Advertisements

An old advertisement   A recent advertisement

A CEMENT GIANT REQUIRES
MANAGERS (LAW AFFAIRS)
(For Satna, Jabalpur & Varanasi)
Law Graduates / PG with 10–15 years experience in MP/UP/Bihar, having excellent computerized drafting & communication skills (Hindi / English) required as under :-

Satna & Jabalpur	Exposure of Civil, Criminal & Labour cases including Writs desirable.
Varanasi	Exposure of Consumer Protection and Negotiable Instruments cases desirable.

Remuneration & designation will be commensurate with the competency. Resume with photograph may be sent to:
POST BOX NO.12, HPO JABALPUR-482 001 (M.P.)

We're looking for computer engineers who like to solve difficult problems. Call us on this number now:
$x = 24$, $y = 30$
Phone = $044.(y^2 - x).(y^2 - 10^2) \times 10$.

Source: Retrieved from http://timesofindia.com.

An increasing number of companies are replacing the traditional classified advertisements with creative, clever, and eye-catching advertisements. These advertisements are essentially a company's résumé designed to send a unique message about the company. Many of these so-called advertorials are used for display at information kiosks, participation in job fairs, distribution of materials at campus visits, and media coverage of the company that doubles as advertising.

Contract Recruiting

Companies in fast-growing industries are seeking the expertise of a relatively new type of external specialist, the contract recruiter. The recruiter screens résumés, conducts telephone and in-person interviews, coordinates campus recruiting, prepares and executes formal offers, and performs any number of contractual recruiting responsibilities. These specialists are becoming popular because they can provide several benefits to client companies. Some contract recruiters develop expertise in certain employment fields (such as web designing or advertising). Companies can benefit from the specialists' contacts and highly focused capabilities. Now online recruitment agencies are becoming increasingly popular (for example, Monster and Naukri.com). They are discussed under the section on Internet-based recruiting.

Employment Agencies

Employment agencies or employment exchanges are used by many companies for identifying potential workers. There are two types of employment agencies: public agencies operated by the government and privately owned agencies. Public agencies are government funded agencies that provide free placement services. In the United States, the Department of Labor supports these agencies through grants and other assistance, such as a nationwide computerized job bank. In India, the National Employment Service operated by the Directorate General of Employment and Training, Ministry of Labour, runs over 950 employment exchanges all over the country. It publishes a weekly bulletin named *Employment News* that features vacancies.

Many specialized public agencies place people who are in special categories, such as those who are disabled. In India, the Office of the Chief Commissioner for Persons with Disabilities under the Ministry of Social Justice and Empowerment is mandated to take steps to safeguard the rights of persons with disabilities. It was set up as part of the Persons with Disabilities (Equal Opportunities, Protection of Rights and Full Participation) Act, 1995. The Act basically enlists facilities that people with different types of disabilities are entitled to.

Government agencies are quite popular for seeking candidates for blue-collar or lower-level positions, usually at the local level. Private employment agencies are important sources to target applicants for white-collar and managerial personnel. Private agencies charge either the employee or the employer for a placement or referral. The major functions of these agencies are to increase the pool of possible applicants and to do preliminary screening. To get the best out of this, companies must give the agency an accurate and complete job description and ensure that the screening process is carefully planned. Organizations may supplement the agency's screening through its own verification process.

Executive Search Firms or Headhunters

Executive recruiters (also known as *headhunters*) are special employment agencies that companies source to seek out executives and management talent. Executive search firms are generally used for higher-level managerial recruitments, although many are now also providing solutions for middle- or entry-level managerial positions.

Many recruiting firms now specialize in 'targeted' recruiting for many jobs. Companies like Head Hunters India, Michael Page India, and DHR International are actively involved in headhunting. Executive search firms are relying on technology and becoming more specialized. They maintain Internet-based databases of specialized personnel for specific jobs or specific industries. They also have strong networks and liaisons with industry people. They help companies find the right talent and also screen the applicant pool. The fees for search firms can be high, but they help save the company the hassle of fetching the right candidates. A variant of executive search firms is the on-demand recruiting services (ODRS) that provide short-term specialized recruiting assistance to support specific projects.

Special Events Recruiting

When the supply of employees available is not large or when the organization is new or not well known, organizations use special events to attract potential employees. To attract professionals, organizations may have hospitality suites at professional meetings. Executives also make speeches at association meetings or schools to get the organization's image across. Companies may make their presence at seminars, conferences, and meets or other academic, cultural, and social events to tap talent. Sometimes recruiters or firms sponsor a meeting or event at which they may have a kiosk or booth to publicize jobs available. It appeals to job seekers who wish to locate in a particular area and those wanting to minimize travel and interview time.

Job Fairs

A job fair, also referred commonly as a career fair or career expo, is a unique model where job seekers can meet, interact, and interview with several top employers under one roof that serves as a dual advantage. It is an event in which employers and recruiters give information to potential employees. These job fairs often offer networking programmes, résumé reviews, and workshops for job seekers.

Job fairs have several benefits for recruiters. One of the benefits of participating in job fairs is that they give companies access to large pools of qualified candidates. For instance, many colleges and universities hold career fairs for their students. The events give employers the chance to recruit employees who are educated in specific subject areas. A job fair allows companies to connect with a large pool of potential employees without having to advertise. While companies may have to pay a fee to participate in a job fair, they can save time and money by allowing recruiters to zero in on exceptional candidates quickly. Career fairs also give companies the opportunity to hire college freshers as summer interns, forming relationships that may result in long-term employment in the future.

The TimesJobs.com multi-industry job fair is held regularly across metropolitan cities in India. Now online job fairs are becoming common. This is discussed under the section on Internet-based recruiting.

Temping and Leasing Agencies

Employers increasingly supplement their permanent workforces by hiring contingent or temporary workers, often through temporary help employment agencies. Temping refers to hiring workers for a specified duration or on a project basis, rather than recruiting them on a permanent basis. Though contract labour in factories has always existed, the proliferation of white collar temporary workers in India is relatively new. Temp agencies provide a cost-efficient way for companies to conduct business without having to hire a full-time staff.

Employers can hire temp workers either through direct hires or through temporary staff agencies. Direct hiring involves simply hiring workers and placing them on the job. The employer usually pays these people directly, as it does to all its employees, but classifies them separately, as casual, seasonal, or temporary employees, and often offers fewer benefits. The other approach is to have a temping agency supply the employees. Here, the agency handles all the recruiting, screening, and payroll for the temps. In this case, a temp works with a client company, but is on the payroll of a third-party staffing company. The temping basically operates on two revenue models. The temping agency mainly receives a percentage of salary or it may get a fixed fee for every employee placed.

A concept often used along with temping is that of employee leasing. Employee leasing is a contractual arrangement in which a firm (called the leasing firm) transfers its employees to another firm (called the subscriber firm) for carrying out the latter's activities on payment of a fee. Workers are officially employed by the leasing firm, often called professional employer organization (PEO), which is responsible for overseeing all HR-related functions, but workers work for another company. Employee leasing companies offer a plethora of staffing solutions ranging from providing temporary staffing, onsite management of the leased workforce at the client facility to responsibility for the supervision of the leased employees. The IT industry is the biggest client of employee leasing firms.

The difference between temping and leasing is very subtle. A temporary agency contracts with businesses to provide workers on contingent basis. Employee leasing firms supply companies with an entire workforce for extended amounts of time, rather than on day-to-day basis. The leasing firm takes over all HR functions for the workers. However, most companies offering these solutions operate in both the spheres, hence blurring the distinction.

Currently India has around 1.3 million temps, which puts it among the top five countries using such workers, according to a report by the Indian Staffing Federation (ISF), an apex body of temp staffing firms in the country. The temporary staffing industry is expected to grow from 1.3 million to 9 million and represent 10 per cent of the organized workforce in the country by 2025. Around 80 per cent of this workforce is below the age of 30.[8]

Increasingly, in India, companies are using the services of staffing firms such as TeamLease, Ikya, and Manpower, most of which have sprung up in the last decade. Virtual Technology Leasing (VTL), TeamLease, Mafoi, and Manpower Inc. are the big players in the employee leasing space—all having operations in India.

A related concept in this context is that of body shopping. Body shopping is the practice of consultancy firms recruiting IT workers in order to contract their services on short-term basis. Body shopping originated in the IT sector in 1996–1999, when there was a huge demand for people with technology skills, to prevent systems being affected by the Y2K bug. Most specialist Y2K consulting companies operating in the United States and Europe outsourced their manpower requirements to technology companies in India. Their consultants either worked on-shore or off-shore, generating huge profit margins and, thus, making body shopping a lucrative alternative.[9] Many of these Indian IT companies were criticized for merely farming out professionals to overseas companies. The term was often used to indicate the 'selling' of individuals to clients to simply fill a position rather than long-term engagement. It often involved shifting employees from company to company, involving low wages, minimal benefits, and no job security.

Campus Recruiting

One major source of recruits for professional and managerial positions is the college campus. In college recruiting, the organization sends an employee, usually called a recruiter, to a campus to interview and screen candidates. Coinciding with the visit, brochures and other literature about the organization are often distributed. It may involve conducting a pre-placement talk or a seminar where executives talk about various facets of the organization. College recruiting is an important source for recruiting management trainees and professional and technical employees.

The campus recruiter can conduct a test or interview or carry out group discussions and team exercises to identify prospective employees. As with other forms of recruiting, organizations are becoming more creative and strategic in their use of college recruiting. The recruiting process should commence long before there are any visits to the campus. Another good strategy is to set up long-term associations with a few universities. For example, Monsanto has an informal tie-up with a few select institutes for its engineering jobs through regular internship programmes. GE hires 800 to 1,000 students each year from about 40 schools and uses teams of employees and interns to build GE's brand at each school. Similarly, IBM has a specialized recruiting staff who focus on improving the results of IBM's on-campus recruiting efforts. Citibank hires professors to lecture in the company's training programmes. Some companies are identifying a number of students in their junior year and focusing efforts on these select recruits. These actions are designed to enhance the professors' knowledge of the company, which it is hoped will be communicated to students. Companies are also giving extra care to designing recruitment brochures, individualized publications, and personalized invitation letters. They are mindful of the impact that these things have on their future campus recruiting efforts. Companies also need to measure the efficacy of the recruitment process in terms of how many offers they make, how many are accepted, and what is the retention rate of these hires.

Summer Internships

Another approach to recruiting and getting specialized work done that has been tried by organizations is to hire students as interns during their summer trainings. An internship can also mean real work experience for the student, a possible future job, a chance to use one's talents in a realistic environment, and in some cases, earning course credit hours. They allow organizations to get specific projects done, expose themselves to talented potential employees, and provide trial-run employment to determine if they want to hire some of these trainees full-time.

Internships can be a win-win situation for the intern as well as the organization. For students, it may mean being able to hone business skills. Employers can train them as potential employees. Companies such as Accenture and IBM actually begin identifying talented students in their senior year in high school. Their hope is to develop a lasting relationship with these talented young people.

Boomerang Employees

Boomerangs—also commonly referred as 'rehires' and 'retreads'—are all names given to employees who are rehired by their ex-employers. They are the alumni, or former employees, who return to an organization. Keeping in view the prevalent job scenario, organizations have started welcoming back employees who have left them on a good note and had proved to be good performers in the past. In this case, rehiring an old employee is a good strategy.

The trend of boomerang hiring is catching up fast in the corporate world. A few years ago, hiring the ex-employees of an organization was not an acceptable practice. Today it is not so. Rehiring an employee is beneficial because of the high costs involved in recruiting and training new employees. It takes time for the new employee to adapt and adjust to the organizational culture, understand work, and start delivering results, whereas the former employee is already familiar with the culture, procedures, and practices of the company. Boomerangs often come back with a renewed sense of commitment and loyalty, and bring new experiences and perspectives, sometimes even better skills and knowledge.

Organizations are also starting alumni clubs for their ex-employees. The notion was pioneered by McKinsey, a management consultant. McKinsey has a huge online database of former consultants. They are given access to a website that posts job vacancies. Alumni at Procter & Gamble and Microsoft have set up their own networks. In India, the BPO industry, which is facing the hard truth of high attrition rates and retention problems, has adopted the policy of boomerang hiring. A leading name in the BPO industry, 24/7 Customer has a policy for boomerang hiring. In the IT space in India, Wipro is considered a pioneer in boomerang hiring.

Hiring former employees may have several risks. In some cases, the job responsibilities and the required skill set itself changes over the course of time, making it difficult for the boomerang to adjust again. Many employees tend to bring back the baggage of bad experiences with them. Despite problems, often boomerangs are found to be the best fit for a job.

Talent Poaching

The terms 'employee poaching', 'talent poaching', or 'talent raiding' can be defined as an act of enticing key employees to move from one firm to a competitor. Often considered unethical, it remains in practice. Talent poaching has emerged as the biggest HR challenge for enterprises, both big and small, across all industry verticals. The worst hit have been the manpower-centric software and outsourcing firms, and more recently the aviation sector, with state-run airlines losing their crews to private airlines. Retail and IT industries have also been an active hunting ground for poachers.

Pepsi was one of the first companies to take Coca-Cola to court for employee poaching, after it hired several of its employees. Similarly, Jet Airways sued one of its pilots for joining Sahara, a rival airline, within a few months of completing aircraft training. In both cases, the courts refused to restrain the employees from joining a competitor of their former employer on the grounds that this would be a curtailment of the right of the employees to improve their employment prospects. The courts also ruled that any restraint that operates beyond employment is legally unenforceable (Section 27 of the Indian Contract Act). In both of these cases, there was no agreement between the competitors that they would abstain from hiring each other's employees for a specific period of time. Some companies have a non-poaching or non-solicitation agreement with the competitors. A non-compete clause, which is a contract between an employee and employer, is also often used to prevent poaching. This usually means the employee cannot work for the company's competitors or start his or her own competing business for a specific duration of time.

Internet-based Sources

For most employers today, Internet-based recruiting is by far the most popular recruiting source. Web-based recruitment helps companies promote their jobs and their company through the use of recruitment videos and online video advertisements. The different Internet-based sources for recruiting are as follows:

Company Website

Most employers nowadays recruit through their own websites. It gives job seekers a one-click solution for finding jobs. Organizations are becoming increasingly sophisticated in designing their recruitment websites. Companies such as HSBC or Starbucks are leading the way and have segmented their careers website into microsites. A corporate recruitment website can serve as the useful and cost-effective strategy for recruitment. Websites should be interactive, easy to navigate, and help people find relevant information. Many organizations cite the experiences of current employees or post videos that can help candidates to get a real feel for the culture of an organization. Providing clear instructions helps candidates understand what the process involves.

Online Recruiting Portals

Online job portals help posting vacancies with their job description and specification on the portal and also searching for suitable résumés posted on the website corresponding to the openings in the organization. Job portals also have a feature where 'passive' job seekers can submit their résumés for consideration in future. Résumé scanning is one major benefit provided by the job portals for the client organizations. Online recruitment websites help organizations to automate the recruitment process and save their time and costs. Jobs can be posted on the website almost immediately, and the process is also cheaper. The CareerBuilder.com, the largest US online employment website, has launched an application for iPhones that offers a unique way to search nearly 2 million jobs on its site. The National Career Service Portal is the job portal of the Ministry of Labour and Employment, Government of India. Job seekers can avail the benefits of this portal by registering themselves. The platform provides information on over 3,000 career options from over 53 key sectors. One can find career counsellors and information about local employment services too.

Social Networking Sites

Recruiting for professionals and managers is shifting from online job boards to popular social networking sites such as Facebook, Twitter, and LinkedIn. Organizations often also announce openings on these sites. Companies can search for candidates, post job advertisements, join groups, post vacancies, and promote themselves. Video sharing sites such as YouTube help companies to post recruitment-related videos. The popularity of social media helps companies get their recruiting message in front of the right people at the right time. Recruiters often browse through social media posts and discussion forums to identify potential candidates. Some companies post employee testimonials on social networking sites as a way to attract applicants. A recent study found that social network profiles of job applicants were surprisingly good predictors of how well they might fit into an organization.[10] Social media analytics tools help track prospective applicants, mine their social media profiles, and generate relevant information. A large number of companies, such as Infosys, Cipla, and Microsoft India, are increasingly using the power of social media for talent acquisition.

Mobile Recruiting

The explosion of smartphones has created a massive audience of potential job seekers to address. Mobile recruiting is the act of finding job candidates through the use of mobile career pages. Recruiting technology vendors and corporate recruiters are constantly developing new ways to reach out to the mobile user, with the hope of increased engagement and further visibility. While mobile devices are more convenient for job seekers and passive candidates, most companies do not currently have mobile-optimized websites. A recent statistic suggests that only 8 per cent of the Fortune 100 companies have mobile-optimized career sites.[11] It is believed that if a company's career site is not mobile-friendly, it is missing out on a lot of potential candidates. Companies need to take into account the fact that 40 per cent candidates often abandon a non-mobile-optimized application process.[12] Some employers use text messaging to build an applicant pool. Popular mobile phone chatting applications such as WhatsApp are also being used for this purpose. Mobile recruiting promises to be the most important trend since social networking.

Virtual Job Fairs

At a virtual job fair, recruiters can post vacancies, screen candidates, collect curriculum vitae (CVs) or résumés, and build a pool of qualified candidates. Online visitors can view openings, listen to presentations, leave résumés, participate in live chats, and get contact information from recruiters. Recruiters are available for chat, videoconferencing sessions, or online interviews during a certain time slot. It leverages the global reach of the Internet to eliminate the constraints of physical or temporal boundaries while searching for candidates. Though sometimes challenging to manage in times of higher unemployment, some experts claim recruiting costs have been reduced by 80 per cent using these methods. Timesjobs.com hosts virtual job fairs where one can find the perfect job from the comfort of one's home.

The Internet has transformed the way companies recruit employees. Technology lets companies be more creative about the media they use. For example, Electronic Arts (EA), a video game publisher, uses its products to help solicit applicants. EA includes information about its internship programme on the back of its video game manuals. EA has developed a database of more than 200,000 potential job candidates. It uses tracking software to identify potential applicants with specific skills and to facilitate ongoing e-mail communications with everyone in its database.

Internet recruiting brings forth several advantages. HR professionals can increase the talent pool by advertising job openings virtually everywhere in the world. Companies can save expenses and administrative time by using the Internet. HR personnel can easily scan through digital applications and résumés using tracking software. The advantage of using the Internet and social media is that recruiters can conveniently pull up an applicant's 'online personality', without meeting an applicant face-to–face, saving a lot of time and money.

Internet hiring has its limitations too. It is often difficult to design résumés and post them in the required format. Many respondents have expressed concerns about the privacy of information. Often poor graphics and slow Internet speed make it difficult to use websites or upload CVs. With a large number of small- and medium-sized companies swarming to the Internet, the legitimacy and authenticity of the recruiters is also questionable. Often HR professionals misinterpret an applicant's personality due to incomplete or misleading information on social networking sites. Despite many limitations, Internet-based recruitment is gaining popularity. However, many feel that even the best Internet strategy cannot replace newspaper advertisements. Hence, Internet recruiting should be supplemented with traditional recruiting efforts as well.

Internal versus External Recruitment

There are several major advantages to internal recruiting. First, organizations typically have better knowledge of internal applicants' skills. Internal candidates would require less orientation and training. They are already acclimatized with the functioning of the organization. When employees get promotions, it enhances their motivation and commitment. This translates to lower turnover rates and higher productivity.[13] Another advantage is that internal source is more cost-effective. HCL Technologies has a comprehensive internal recruiting policy that helps foster stability and continuity in the managerial ranks of the company.

There are disadvantages to internal recruiting as well. Hiring from within can sometimes backfire. Employees start expecting promotions as their legitimate right. When promotions are not granted, it leads to disgruntlement. This phenomenon was seen in the case of Air India where dissatisfied employees went on strike after being denied promotions. Sometimes organizations may not have employees with the right competencies and yet it may promote people because the organizational policy so ordains (as in the case of many public sector undertakings [PSUs] in India, where promotion is given by virtue of seniority). Inbreeding is another potential drawback. The approach simply promulgates old ways of doing things. Creative problem-solving can be hindered by lack of new blood. Another drawback is that internal recruiting promotes *unit raiding*, where divisions may compete for the same people. Another possible disadvantage is that internal politics may impede fair promotion. Sometimes managers get rid of a troublesome employee by evaluating that employee so positively that the employee would be more likely to get an opportunity in another department or unit. In numerous organizations, inter-departmental promotions or transfers have long been considered hidden forms of punishment for errant employees—a neat, confrontation-free way to settle scores, at times. This is just the opposite of unit raiding.

A related phenomenon is explained by the *Peter Principle*, a concept in management theory formulated by Laurence J. Peter.[14] According to the Peter Principle, very often promotion is based on the candidate's performance in their current role, rather than on abilities relevant to the intended role. This eventually results in them being promoted to their highest level of competence and potentially then to a role in which they are not competent, referred to as their 'level of incompetence'. For example, an excellent engineer may be a poor manager because he might not have the necessary interpersonal skills to lead a team. This phenomenon is more common in hierarchy-oriented systems. To overcome these limitations, internal recruiting programmes must be strategically integrated with other HR functions.

On the other hand, external recruiting can facilitate the introduction of new ideas and thinking into corporate decision-making. However, external recruiting can be very costly. New personnel typically take longer to learn the workings of the organization and require investment in onboarding and training.

One way in which recruiting can be more strongly linked with strategy is to focus on those sources providing the most desirable employees. For example, studies have shown that those making recruiting contact with the company through newspaper advertisements and college placement offices had lower retention rates than those responding to professional journal or convention advertisements or contacting the company of their own volition. Employees who responded to newspaper advertisements also had higher absenteeism rates. Further, those recruited through college placement offices had the lowest levels of job satisfaction.[15] Unfortunately, as with most of the research in this area, it is difficult to generalize from such results.

Another strategic recruiting issue is the extent to which the company should rely on internal or external recruiting, or a mix of the two. Some well-managed companies hire externally only at the entry level and fill all higher-level positions from within the firm. Examples of such companies include Merck, 3M, and IBM.

In the beginning of the chapter, we discussed that strategic recruitment follows the *3L* principle: *lowest cost*, *least time*, and *likeliest candidates*. It refers to adopting recruitment strategies that attract the 'right' people and 'right' set of competencies, for the 'right' positions in the organization. The process should be carried out involving lowest possible time and money and be able to fetch the right candidates. Table 6.1 presents an assessment of different recruitment sources on the *3L* principle.

Organizing how you recruit is an important decision. The HR manager has to work with functional managers to understand what a position really entails and what key aspects to look for in a candidate. Godrej Consumer Products has put in place a successful strategically linked internal recruiting programme called the 100 Leaders Programme. The programme helps build leadership and functional capabilities and develop a pool of engaged leaders with global skills and mindsets. It has identified over 100 members with the potential to lead various functions of the organization. Over a period of time, this is expected to fuel the company's succession management programme in line with its growth plans.

Table 6.1 Recruitment Sources and 3L Principle

Source	Low Cost	Less Time	Likely Candidate
Promotions/Transfers/Job postings	✓	✓	✓ (if based on merit accompanied by a sound training and appraisal system)
Walk-ins	✓	✓	✓ (for entry-level positions)
Referrals	✓	✓	✓ (since employee reputation is at stake)
Advertisements	✗	✗	✓ (if targeted properly as per AIDA)
Contract recruiting/employment agencies/headhunting	✗	✗	✓ (for highly specialized jobs)
Campus recruiting	✗	✗	✓ (if prerecruitment work is done)
Summer interns	✓	✗	✓ (if careful grooming is done)
Leasing/Body shopping	✗	✓	✓ (for highly specialized jobs)
Special events/fairs	✗	✗	Maybe (since visits are voluntary)
Boomerang employees	✓	✗	✓ (candidate has multiple experiences and is familiar with the company)
Poaching	✗	✗	✓ (candidate has experience of rival)

Note: ✓ indicates that the source usually supports this principle. ✗ indicates it may not.

STRATEGIC RECRUITMENT AND REALISTIC JOB PREVIEW

In the context of the matching philosophy of strategic recruitment, the process of realistic recruitment is recommended. An important component of realistic recruiting is Realistic Job Preview (RJP). RJP refers to giving a realistic preview of the job to applicants during recruitment to provide them with information on both positive and negative aspects of the job.

RJPs are presentations of relevant, balanced, and unbiased information about the organization, the job, and work conditions. Most traditional recruitment efforts focus solely on the positive aspects of the job, often overoptimistically describing the conditions of employment. This has been called the flypaper approach because its goal is to attract as many candidates as possible. The flypaper approach is less desirable because it is unbalanced.

RJPs provide realistic information on characteristics of the job to applicants so they can evaluate the compatibility of the job with their own work preferences. The prospective employee is better informed about what the organization will provide them (in terms of pay, hours, culture, and so on) and also what will be expected from them (late hours, stress, degree of physical risk, and so on). RJPs can result in a self-selection process for people most likely to have difficulty on the job. It allows candidates to withdraw from the process voluntarily if the job does not meet their standards or career goals. Employees who join are better able to cope because of more realistic expectations about the job. It is said that RJPs 'vaccinate' applicants by lowering their unrealistic expectations. RJPs also convey honesty on the part of the organization.

For instance, applicants for bank teller jobs at Sun Bank are told that they will spend most of the workday on their feet, that customers may be rude and demanding, that some work periods will be particularly stressful, and that tellers will be expected to work on Saturdays. When the New York City Administration for Children's Services was having problems with employee retention, it began using these ads: 'Wanted: men and women willing to walk into strange buildings in dangerous neighborhoods, and be screamed at by unhinged individuals.' Many companies doing international work provide extensive RJPs for potential expatriates and their families. Bechtel, the giant construction company, provides a 60-minute video of life in Saudi Arabia that applicants view before they make a commitment for an assignment. Realism reduces applicants, but improves employee retention.

Table 6.2 shows the difference between traditional job preview and RJP.

Table 6.2 Traditional Preview and Realistic Job Preview

Traditional Preview	Realistic Job Preview
Initial job expectations too high	Realistic job expectations
Job is viewed as attractive	Job is viewed as challenging
High number of applicants	Reasonable applicants
Work experience dissatisfying	Work experience satisfying
High attrition rate at a later stage	Low attrition rate

RJPs can be developed using job analysis information. The critical incident technique is particularly effective here. This can be incorporated in job postings and recruitment advertisements. There are several ways to provide realistic job previews:

- Information provided by recruiters and interviewers
- Videos and audios
- Online or physical job samples
- Short tests administered on candidates to share information on the company
- Representative visual depictions of the work environment
- On-site visit
- Organization-specific literature

RJPs can be used as an inoculation against disappointment with the realities of a job. Candidates selected after RJPs match better with the organization, thus supporting the notion of strategic recruitment. Research shows lower rates of employee turnover for employees recruited with RJPs, particularly for more complex jobs, and higher levels of job satisfaction and performance. This is evidence of a gradually increasing trend towards use of RJPs for successful employee hiring.

STRATEGIC SELECTION

Selection is the process of testing and analysing qualifications and characteristics of applicants to establish their suitability for jobs. It involves selecting on the basis of an appropriate set of knowledge, skills, and abilities (KSAs) of applicants. Job analysis can provide the basis for identifying appropriate KSAs. Once an organization has decided upon a set of selection criteria, a technique for assessing each of these must be chosen.

Strategic selection is an attempt to get a 'fit' between what the applicant can do and what the organization needs. The purpose is to ensure a fit between the applicant's abilities and the organization's requirements. Estimates are that hiring an inappropriate employee costs an employer three–five times that employee's salary.

Strategic selection implies:

- Selection activities to be designed to match corporate strategies
- Selection activities to be designed with a long-term perspective
- Selection activities to help create a responsive and dynamic organization
- Selection activities to follow the RVU principle: Reliability, Validity, and Utility

Strategic selection helps avoid select and reject errors (pick and drop errors): A select error refers to selecting candidates who later perform poorly on the job. Reject error refers to rejecting candidates who would have performed well on the job. There is an opportunity cost in the failure to select the right employee, and that cost is that the right candidates, if rejected, will go somewhere else. There is an important saying, 'If you don't hire the right one, your competitor will.' Thus, it is important that organizations should make efforts to select the right people, keeping the strategic requirements in mind.

The main aim of strategic selection is to achieve person–job fit. *Person–job fit* refers to matching the competencies that are central to performing the job with the prospective employee's KSAs. However, a candidate might be right for a job but wrong for the organization. Thus, while person–job fit is usually the main consideration in selection, employers should care about *person–organization fit* as well.

Reliability, Validity, and Utility (RVU)

At the heart of an effective selection system is knowledge of what constitutes appropriate job performance. Once this is known, employee characteristics required to achieve that performance can be determined. A selection criterion is a characteristic that a person must have to do the job successfully. To test whether an employee possesses those traits identified as selection criterion, it is crucial to identify predictors as measurable indicators of selection criteria.

The information gathered about an applicant should be focused on finding predictors that will help meet the criteria. Predictors can take many forms, but they should be job-relevant, valid, and reliable. Any selection tool used (for example, a test) should be able to identify the predictor. Using invalid predictors can result in selecting the 'wrong' candidate and rejecting the 'right' one. In order to ensure this, the organization must be certain that the selection mechanisms have reliability, validity, and utility.

It is now important to understand the concepts of reliability, validity, and utility in more detail.

Reliability

The main goal of selection is to make accurate predictions about people. If these decisions are going to be correct, the techniques used for making them must yield reliable information. Reliability refers to how stable or repeatable a measurement is over a variety of testing conditions.

The reliability of a selection tool can be judged in a variety of ways:

- *Test–retest reliability*   In practice, one common way to assess reliability is to correlate the scores of applicants given the same test on two different occasions.
- *Alternative-form reliability*   This is determined by correlating scores from two alternate forms of the same test. Most standardized academic achievement tests, such as the SAT and the GMAT, have numerous forms, all of which are assumed to be reliable. An applicant's score should not vary much according to which form of the test he or she happens to take.
- *Inter-rater reliability*   When a measuring tool relies on the judgements of people (such as in an employment interview), reliability is often determined by using inter-rater reliability. This refers to the extent to which two or more interviewers' assessments are consistent with each other.

Because measuring reliability generally involves comparing two measures that assess the same thing, it is typical to judge a test's reliability in terms of a *reliability coefficient*. This basically shows the degree to which the two measures (for example, test score on one day and test score on another day) are correlated. Many things may cause a test to be unreliable. These include physical conditions (noise, physical surroundings, place, and so on), differences in the test taker (physiological state, health, psychological state, mood, and so on), and differences in the person administering the test (behaviour, administration technique used, and so on). Thus, to control for these extraneous variables, it is important to ensure that testing conditions should also be the same.

Validity

For a selection tool to be useful, it is not sufficient for it to be repeatable or stable. Both legally and organizationally, the measures that it yields must also be valid. Validity addresses the questions of what a test measures and how well it has measured it. In selection, the primary concern is whether the assessment technique results in accurate predictions about the future success or failure of an applicant.

The following are brief descriptions of three types of validity that the HR specialist should be familiar with:

- *Content validity*   The degree to which a selection method measures the KSA to perform the job is called content validity. A test has content validity if it reflects an actual sample of the work done on the job in question. A content validity study begins with a comprehensive job analysis to identify what is done on a job and what KSAs are used. A test is devised to determine if individuals have the necessary KSAs. An example of a content-validity test is a typing test for a secretarial position. Such a test can roughly replicate conditions on the job. The applicant can be given a typical sample of actual work under 'normal' working conditions. Similarly, an arithmetic test for a retail cashier should contain problems that typically would be faced by cashiers on the job. If the content of the typing test is actually representative of the work that is done on the job, then the test is said to be content-valid.

- *Construct validity*   A construct is a trait that is not typically observable. For example, we cannot see leadership, we can only assume that it exists from the behaviour someone displays. A test, therefore, has construct validity when it actually measures unobservable traits. When selection procedures involve the use of tests to measure more abstract job behaviours, such as leadership style or personality, construct validity, rather than content validity, is more appropriate. Because a hypothetical construct is used as a predictor in establishing this type of validity, personality tests and tests that measure other such constructs are more likely to be used.

- *Criterion-related validity*   The extent to which a selection technique can accurately predict one or more important elements of job performance is referred to as criterion-related validity. This is the most important form of validity. Scores on a test are correlated with measures of actual on-the-job performance. The test is called a *predictor*; the performance score is referred to as a *criterion*. The validation process demonstrates that a significant statistical relationship exists between a predictor and a criterion measure of successful performance on a job. A predictor is any piece of information that can be used to screen applicants. Predictors include information from application blanks (education level, experience, and so on); reference checks; scores on tests; data from interest and personality inventories; and interviewer ratings. Criterion measures are any measures of work behaviour, job products, or outcomes that have value to an employer. Criteria relevant to personnel selection may include measures such as quality or quantity of output, supervisory ratings, sales, positive customer review, production rates, error rates, and absences.

  If the predictors satisfactorily predict criterion, they are valid. The degree of relation is described by a *correlation coefficient*, which is an index number giving the relationship between a predictor and a criterion variable. These coefficients can range from −1 to +1. A correlation coefficient of +.90 indicates that the test is a good predictor, whereas a +.02 correlation coefficient indicates that the test is a very poor predictor.

  There are two different approaches to criterion-related validity.

  - **Predictive Validity**   This involves testing correlation between test scores of applicants and their performance scores when some time interval has passed after they are hired. Here, the test is administered to applicants before they are hired. Then, these applicants are hired using only existing selection techniques, not the results of the new tests one is developing. After they have been on the job for some time, one would measure their performance and compare it to their earlier tests. One can then determine whether their performance on the test could have been used to predict their subsequent job performance. The steps in a predictive-validity study for a given test are:
    i. Administer the test to a large sample of applicants.
    ii. Select individuals for the job. It is actually preferable if the test whose validity is being measured is not used in the hiring decisions.

    iii. Wait for an appropriate amount of time and then collect measures of job performance.

    iv. Assess the strength of the predictor–criterion relationship by calculating a correlation coefficient.

- **Concurrent Validity**   Testing correlation between test scores and performance scores of current employees. The steps in concurrent validation are:
  - i. Administer the tests to present employees performing the job.
  - ii. At approximately the same time, collect performance measures for these employees.
  - iii. Correlate the test scores with the performance measures.

The usual way to determine whether there is a significant relationship between scores (the predictor) and performance (the criterion) is to determine the statistical relationship between (*a*) scores on the test and (*b*) performance through *correlation analysis,* which shows the degree of statistical relationship. If the test is significantly related to performance, it has concurrent validity. It can be considered for future use with applicants in the selection process.

Concurrent validity represents an at-the-same-time approach, while predictive validity represents an at-a-future-time approach. Predictive validity is an important form of criterion-related validity, but the employer must wait until it can obtain meaningful measures of job performance for the people who were hired. The biggest advantage of concurrent validation is that it can be conducted relatively quickly. Therefore, it is usually less expensive than predictive validation. Another advantage is that data on performance are readily available. The disadvantage is that the current employees may not be representative of new applicants. Current employees have already received on-the-job training and have been screened by the existing selection techniques. If experience is important in job performance, such validation will be biased in favour of applicants with experience. A drawback of the criterion-related validity approach is that employees who have not performed satisfactorily are probably no longer with the firm, while extremely good employees may have been promoted or may have left the organization for better jobs. Nowadays, there are specialized research agencies to help design a reliable and valid selection process, keeping in mind the pitfalls and limitations.

Utility

Utility refers to the overall usefulness of a personnel selection procedure. The concept encompasses both the accuracy and the importance of personnel decisions. Moreover, utility implies a concern with costs. These costs relate to setting up and implementing personnel selection procedures as well as costs associated with errors in the decisions made. Utility, thus, refers to the economic gains derived from using a particular selection method. It focuses on cost–benefit analysis of a particular selection mechanism. There are several metrics used in determining the utility of a selection mechanism (these measurement aspects are discussed in detail in the last chapter).

    To summarize, for a selection tool to be useful, it must be reliable, valid, and have utility. Maintaining RVU at all stages of the selection process is important.

THE SELECTION MECHANISM

Carrying out selection involves working out two important administrative issues: (*a*) constituting the selection team and assigning responsibility and (*b*) designing the selection process.

The Selection Team

The selection function in any organization may be concerned with various activities such as receiving applications, scanning them, administering tests, conducting interviews, carrying out background checks, making selection decisions, giving offers, and placing new employees. In many organizations, selection often was and still is carried out in a rather unplanned manner. By no means can such a process be called strategic. Often the HR administrative staff alone may not have all the requisite knowledge of what is required in different jobs in different departments.

To avoid these problems, a lot of organizations have a team to carry out the process. The team may comprise staff from the HR department as well as managers from the unit concerned. Sometimes, HR staff may do the initial screening of the candidates, while the unit managers or supervisors make the final selection. The typical responsibilities of the HR unit may involve screening applications, conducting preliminary screening interview, helping design selection tests, administering the test, conducting interviews, obtaining background information, conducting reference checks, and referring candidates to managers for final selection. Once the final selection is done, the HR unit will have to carry out the administrative task of announcing results, giving offer letters, and arranging for their induction. The departmental managers who are part of this team are responsible for helping to determine the criteria and predictors for the position for which the selection has to be done. They also provide inputs in designing the selection test. Their main role is interviewing candidates and making final selection decisions in collaboration with HR specialists.

In some organizations, selection duties may be centralized into a specialized unit called employment office or placement cells. Carrying out selection is easier because issues can be resolved by one central unit. It is easier for the applicant to have only one place in which to apply for a job and do a follow-up. Furthermore, selection costs may be cut by avoiding the duplication of effort. In addition, these units typically have a legal expert to ensure legal compliance and handle any anomalies in the selection process.

Nowadays, considering the time and expense that go in the selection process, more and more organizations have outsourced the process. In that case, external recruiters conduct the process keeping the organization's requirements in mind. They collaborate with the HR team or concerned managers in the organization while carrying out the process.

The Selection Process

Most organizations follow more or less similar steps to select applicants for jobs. Variations on this basic process depend on the type of organization, sector, or industry, nature of jobs to be filled, number of people to be selected, and pressure of outside forces such as legal factors, political situations, pressure groups, or unions. This process can take place in a day or over a much longer period of time.

We will now discuss the stages in the selection process in detail. Simultaneously, we will also discuss how each of the stages may be designed to make them more reliable and valid so as to support the concept of strategic selection.

Stage 1: Initial Screening

Initial screening may contain several steps. It can be broken down into two broad steps: screening of application forms and preliminary interview.

Screening of Application Forms

Applicants apply for a job using letters, CV, application forms, or a combination of these. Before detailed selection can take place, it is necessary to screen the applications using some initial criteria.

Application blanks or forms, as these are typically referred to, vary in length and sophistication for different jobs. Application blanks ask for detailed information to determine whether the individual is qualified for the position. They provide interviewers with a profile of the applicant that can be used in the interview. Technically, a CV can be treated by an employer as an application form. However, since CVs contain only information that the applicants want to present, some employers require that all who submit résumés complete an application form as well. This will help ensure that information is available about all applicants using uniform criteria.

The two primary purposes of the application form are to eliminate applicants failing to meet minimum qualifying requirements, and for the remaining applicants to formulate a hypothesis about their personality and motivation to be explored at the interview. Application blanks can be a useful initial screening tool for jobs that require some type of professional certification (for example, a UGC-NET certificate for teaching positions in Indian universities). This makes the selection process far more efficient by reducing the number of applicants that need to be interviewed.

Preliminary Interview and Job Preview

In addition to screening candidates, the selection process has a brand-building dimension too. Many employers also use it as an opportunity to create a good image in the minds of applicants during the first interface. This touch point must be handled by staff who are respectful, polite, tactful, and able to offer assistance in a friendly manner. This stage is used for giving a realistic preview of the job to applicants. It is important that details about the organization and the job must be presented honestly and clearly. It helps candidates self-screen themselves, resulting in better placement, thereby reducing future turnover.

In some cases, an initial screening interview is done to see if the applicant is likely to match the positions available. Since there are minimum standards for certain jobs, candidates may undergo this initial screening to see their basic eligibility and fit for the job. Nowadays, software is used to scan résumés or application blanks using keywords.

RVU vis-à-vis Application Blanks

Application blanks, if carefully designed, can serve as a reliable and valid tool. A potentially useful supplement to the traditional application blank is the biographical information blank (BIB). A BIB usually contains many more items than a typical application blank and asks for information related to a much wider array of attitudes and experiences. BIB items are based on an assumption that these prior behaviours and experiences will be strongly related to an applicant's future behaviour. For example, a common BIB item asks applicants to list their favourite subjects in high school. This assumes that people who preferred English will perform differently on a given job from people who preferred science or maths. Whether such an item should be included on a BIB, however, depends on its ability to differentiate the performance of good and poor workers on the job in question. For example, a recent research study found that BIB items can predict relevant Big Five personality constructs and general mental ability.

Another variation to the traditional application blank is the weighted application blank (WAB), an application form that is designed to be scored more systematically and is more like the BIB. A job analysis is used to determine the KSAs needed for the job, and an application form is developed to include items related to the selection criteria. To develop the scoring system for a WAB, high and low performers who currently work for the company are compared on a variety of characteristics (for example, education and years of experience) that were known at the time they applied for a job. Weights are assigned to the degree of difference on each characteristic. The weights are then totalled for each applicant, and the one with the highest score is the preferred choice.

To develop a WAB, it is necessary to develop questions that differentiate between satisfactory- and poor-performing employees and that can be asked legally. On the positive side, WABs enable an employer to evaluate and compare applicants' responses numerically to a valid, job-related set of predictors. One difficulty is that the time and effort required to develop such a form is high. For many small organizations and for low-skilled jobs that do not require lot of information, the cost of developing a WAB can be too high and, hence, it may not be too high on utility. Moreover, the form must be updated frequently to ensure that the factors previously identified are still valid predictors of job success.

To further enhance the RVU of an application blank, the following guidelines can be used:

- *Access quantifiable factors*   Check factual data from the application form against the minimum acceptable requirements set out, such as age, qualification, and experience.
- *Check for validity/consistency*   Skilled selectors develop a feel about good applicants based on the consistency of the data contained in their application forms. Are there any time gaps in education and if so what happened during this period? Does the career record contain a series of jobs running consecutively or are there periods unaccounted for? Checking the form in this way for ambiguous information and following this up at the interview stage helps make valid selection decisions.

- **Ensure valid information is obtained** BIBs may be designed to capture relevant information depending on the nature of job. For example, for an HR position, questions related to soft skills, communication, and interpersonal relationships may be asked.

The information received on application forms may not always be accurate. In an attempt to prevent inaccuracies, many application forms carry a statement of veracity that the applicant is required to sign.

It is important that the data requested on application forms must be job related so as to make better assessment of the applicant. Care must be taken that the application blank does not directly or indirectly violate laws related to employment discrimination. In some countries, it is not permitted to ask questions related to gender, race, height, weight, marital status, and number of dependents. Thus, application blanks have to be carefully conceptualized and designed. CVs and application blanks also serve as basic employee records for applicants who are hired. They can be used for research on the effectiveness of the selection process later on, a vital requirement of the strategic selection process.

Stage 2: Selection Tests

Most organizations nowadays use tests to screen applicants. Tests can be of great benefit in the selection process when properly used and administered. Individuals trained in testing mechanism should be involved in designing and conducting a test. Various kinds of tests can be used, focusing on specific job-related aptitudes or skills. These include tests of intelligence, aptitude, ability, or interest. Some of the most common types of tests are:

Performance Simulation Tests

These tests are aimed to find out if the applicant can do the job successfully by actually making him do it. They have become very popular these days. They sufficiently well meet the requirements of the job relatedness as compared to the written tests. The two of the known performance simulation tests are:

i. *Work sampling* It is an effort to create a miniature replica of a job. Applicants demonstrate that they possess the necessary skills by actually doing the tasks. By carefully devising work samples based on job analysis, the KSAs needed for each job can easily be evaluated. Studies have almost consistently demonstrated that the validity of work samples is superior to aptitude and personality tests. Examples of such tests include programming tests for computer programmers, driving tests for delivery personnel, typing or word-processing tests for clerical persons, and preparing a balance sheet for an accountant. Standard trade tests have been developed for electricians, machinists, and a host of other trades.

ii. *Assessment centres* In assessment centres, line executives, supervisors, and/or qualified psychologists evaluate candidates as they go through two to four days of exercises that simulate real problems that the candidates are likely to encounter on the job. Based on the requirement that the actual job incumbent has to meet, activities might include interviews, in-basket problem-solving exercises, group discussions, and business games. The evidence on the effectiveness of assessment centres is extremely impressive.

Cognitive Ability Tests

This group includes tests of general reasoning ability, intelligence, and specific mental abilities. Some of the common cognitive ability tests are:

i. *Intelligence tests* These test the intelligence quotient of applicants. Common intelligence tests are *Binet Simon test* (one of the first intelligence tests focusing on comprehension and reasoning), *Thurstone test* (specialized types of intelligence tests for reasoning, word fluency, verbal comprehension, and arithmetical ability), or *Wechsler Bellevue Intelligence Scale* (utilizes multiple factors, such as digit span, comprehension, vocabulary, picture arrangement, and object assembly).

ii. *Aptitude tests* These tests measure whether an individual has the capacity or latent ability to learn a given job if given adequate training. Specific aptitudes that are usually tested are mechanical, clerical, musical, and academic aptitudes, dexterity (finger and hand), and hand–eye coordination, and so on. Some of the tests under this category are MATRIX (Management Trial Exercise designed by Proctor and Gamble), CAT (Clerical Aptitude Test to assess vocabulary, spelling, arithmetical ability, and so on, and SAT (Scholastic Aptitude Test to assess verbal and arithmetic abilities.

iii. *Mental ability tests* These tests measure reasoning capabilities. Some of the abilities tested include spatial orientation, comprehension and retention span, and general and conceptual reasoning. The General Aptitude Test Battery (GATB) is a widely used test of this type.

Psychological Tests

Psychological tests are regarded by some as having almost magical properties but can easily be misused and misinterpreted by untrained people. Psychological tests have a time limit but questions asked become progressively difficult. These tests are a most sophisticated tool for measuring human characteristics, and are, therefore, extensively used in selection decisions. Various psychological tests are described below:

i. *Interest tests* These tests are designed to find out the interest of an applicant in the job he has applied for. Two of the most widely used tests are:
   - *Strong vocational interest blank*, in which the applicant is asked whether he likes, dislikes, or is indifferent to many examples of school subjects, occupations, amusements, peculiarities of people, and particular activities.
   - *Kuder preference record*, in which a questionnaire tests the interest in mechanical, scientific, social service, artistic, literary, or musical abilities.

ii. *Personality test* The importance of personality to job success cannot be denied. Personality tests invoke from the candidates a response that helps understand their mental make-up and behaviour. Some of the common personality tests are:

- *Trait tests*   Psychologists agree that personality is composed of traits or characteristics that can be used to differentiate people. Traits can help in employee selection, matching people to jobs, and in guiding career decisions. The most widely accepted frameworks for mapping traits are *Myers-Briggs Type Inventory* and the *Big Five* personality traits. These are personality assessment instruments. They use questions to ask people how they behave in particular situations and identify traits/characteristics to classify people into different personality types. The Big Five is considered a useful predictor of success and job performance. The Big Five talks of five traits—emotional stability, extroversion, agreeableness, openness, and conscientiousness. Conscientiousness has been found to be most frequently related to job success across most occupations.[16] Other traits are shown to be relevant for different types of jobs.

- *Thematic apperception test (TAT)*   This is one of the most popular projective tests in which the candidate is shown a series of pictures and asked to write a story for each of the pictures. The psychologist analyses the story in terms of length, vocabulary, bizarre ideas, plot, mood, and so on. He then tries to generate a general personality description, such as the candidate's needs, pressure upon him, defence, and ego activities.

- *Rorschach ink-blot test*   In this test, the candidate is asked to organize unstructured ink blots into meaningful concepts. The resulting projections are analysed in terms of use of colour and shades, use of part or whole of a blot, seeing of movement, definiteness of forms, and so on. An integrated picture of the candidate's personality is then formulated.

- *Miner sentence completion test*   In this test, candidates' thinking and imagination capabilities are tested by asking candidates to complete a sentence such as, 'I want to work for this company because ------ .'

iii. *Emotion test*   This requires testing for a person's emotional make-up

- *Emotional Intelligence*   The ability to perceive, control, and evaluate emotions. Many experts now feel that EQ is a better predictor of success than traditional IQ tests. A sample question could be: 'In my group, I am generally aware of how each person feels about the other people.' Responses may be taken on a five-point Likert-type scale, ranging from *strongly agree* to *strongly disagree.*

- *Emotional Literacy*   Emotional literacy is the ability to use emotions and emotional situations with efficacy. To be emotionally literate is to be able to handle emotions in a way that improves your personal power. People with high emotional literacy are good negotiators. A sample question could be: 'I adjust my behaviour depending on who I am interacting with.'

iv. *Perception tests*   To test a candidate's perceptual abilities, eye for detail, and keen observation. There are several types of perception tests:
  - *Vision test/observation test*
  - *Speech perception test*
  - *Colour test*
  - *Hazard perception test*
  - *Attribution test*
  - *Values and ethics test*

RVU vis-à-vis Tests

Tests should follow the RVU principle. Management must ensure that the test used is job related. Performance simulation tests are very high on validity since they actually simulate a job-like situation but are costly. Tests on intellectual, spatial, mechanical, perceptual, and motor abilities have shown to be moderately valid predictors for many semi-skilled and unskilled operative jobs in industrial organizations. Intelligence tests are reasonably good predictors for supervisory positions. Psychological tests are used as an easy option in the decision-making process with managers becoming over-dependent on the test results. Personality tests are also valid but it will be unwise to use personality tests as a general criterion for screening out 'undesirable' applicants, since the same personality characteristic that leads to failure in one job might lead to success in another.

The following steps can be followed to make tests more effective:

1. **Analyse the job**   Undertake an objective job analysis to find out job description and specification for the job or position for which selection has to be done. The purpose is to identify the traits and skills required for good performance in that job. This will later help in determining which candidate should be selected.

2. **Find out success predictors and success criteria**
   - Success predictors are the human traits and skills necessary for success in a job.
   - Success criteria are the standards set for success in a particular job. These could be production-related (such as quantity and quality), personnel data (such as absenteeism and length of service), or judgements (such as supervisor's feedback).

     For example, for an assembler's job, the predictors could be manual dexterity or patience, whereas the criteria could be factors such as quantity produced per hour or rejects per hour. Several tests should be used as a 'test battery' that can measure a variety of possible predictors.

3. **Ensure reliability**   For a particular job, tests chosen should be reliable. The choice is usually based on experience, previous research, or judgement. To make tests reliable, they can be administered on existing employees to check test–retest reliability, alternative-form reliability, and inter-rater reliability. This has been discussed earlier in the chapter.

4. **Ensure validity**   Two popularly ways to validate a test is through *Predictive Validity* and *Concurrent Validity*. Predictive validation is a dependable way to validate a test. Predictive validity is determined over a period of time. It is determined using the scores on a test obtained from a sample of applicants for a job and correlating it at a later time with their on-the-job performance measures.

   Concurrent validity is also used to determine whether a selection test can predict job performance. In concurrent validation, a test is administered to present employees. The test scores are then correlated with the actual performance measures of these employees. If there is a correlation, it shows the test has concurrent validity.

   The steps to determining predictive and concurrent validity are discussed in the beginning of this chapter.

5. **Ensure utility**   This involves doing a cost–benefit analysis of the test to ensure that the testing mechanisms developed have utility for the organization. The metrics used for assessing the utility of a selection mechanism will be discussed in a later chapter on strategic evaluation.

6. **Cross-validation and Revalidation**   Before putting the test into use, one may want to check it by cross-validating, that is, by again performing steps 3 and 4 on a new sample of employees. An organization should revalidate the test periodically so as to keep it relevant. Tests are not infallible. Thus, tests should be supplemented with interviews and background checks. Further, the test must be validated in one's own organization, with the assistance of a qualified psychologist. The fact that the same tests have been proven valid in similar organizations is not sufficient. Performance on tests may vary depending on the place and time of test, moods, family issues, physical condition, and such other factors. Administering tests in settings that are comfortable and similar for all applicants helps get the best results.

Stage 3: Selection Interview

Typically, the next stage after conducting a test is selection interview. The purpose of a selection interview is to determine whether a candidate is good enough for the position based on direct interaction. Interviews can be categorized as structured or unstructured and past or future oriented.

An *unstructured interview* has no predetermined script or protocol. Questions are not prepared in advance; there is no attempt to guarantee that applicants are asked the same questions. Typically, the interviewer does not have a scoring protocol either. A specific type of unstructured interview is the nondirective interview. It uses general questions to know about the applicant. The interviewer then picks up on an idea in the applicant's response to shape the next question. When used by some highly skilled interviewers, the unstructured interview may lead to useful insights about an applicant. Difficulties with such interviews arise in keeping it job-related and obtaining comparable data on various applicants. In *structured interview*, the interviewer has a standardized list of questions to ask of all applicants. These questions are usually generated with the aid of a job analysis in order to identify specific types of information. Standardization of questions helps lower the possibility of biases. Substantial research indicates that structured interviews will generally be more reliable and valid than unstructured interviews.

The second dimension along which interviews can vary is whether they focus on past behaviour or on hypothesized future behaviour. The first, the *behavioural description interview* (BDI), asks applicants to relate actual incidents from their past that are relevant to the job for which they are applying. BDIs are based on the assumption that the past is the best predictor of the future. An example would be: 'Thinking back to your last job, tell me about a time when you resolved a conflict with a customer.' They use the critical incident technique. In the *situational interview*, questions encourage applicants to respond to hypothetical situations they might encounter on the job. For example, 'If one of your customers complained about bad service, how would you react?' Responses to these hypothetical questions are then scored according to their appropriateness for the job. The *stress interview* is a special type of interview designed to create anxiety and put pressure on the applicant to see how the person responds. In a stress interview, the interviewer assumes an extremely aggressive posture. It may intimidate the job candidate and, thus, it needs to be used with caution.

Interviews are designed to probe into areas that cannot be addressed by the application form or tests. These areas usually consist of assessing candidates' motivation, ability to work under stress, interpersonal skills, and ability to 'fit in' in the organization. These qualities have demonstrated relevance for performance in managerial positions. However, its use in identifying 'good performance' for most lower-level jobs appears questionable. In any case, the interview is the most widely used selection device that organizations rely on to differentiate candidates.

RVU vis-à-vis Interviews

The topic of interviews has generated numerous studies covering topics such as verbal–non-verbal behaviour, personality characteristics, impression management, interviewer–interviewee similarity, and pre-interview impressions.

Interviews may lose their relevance if the following biases prevail:

- Stereotyping: categorizing groups and making generalized assumptions about them
- Halo or horn effect: thinking very high or very low of someone because of one positive or one negative characteristic respectively
- Preconceived notions: evaluating someone on the basis of purely preconceived impression about him/her
- Bias: prejudiced evaluation by discrimination on the basis of religion, caste, sex, colour, race, and so on
- Self attribution: evaluating people favourably if they appear similar in characteristics as the interviewer
- Spill-over effect: assessment of a person's characteristics on the basis of his past performance or impression
- Contrast effects: evaluation of a person's characteristics in comparisons with other people recently encountered

The questioning techniques that an interviewer uses can significantly affect the type and quality of the information obtained. Certain kinds of questions should be avoided. For instance, it is best to avoid questions that rarely produce a true answer, such as: 'Do you get along with your coworkers?' This question is almost inevitably going to be answered positively. Leading question—one to which the answer is obvious from the way that the question is asked—should also be avoided. For example, 'You are a good team worker?' No one is likely to say no to this. Questions already answered on the application blank should be probed, not asked again. Further, all questions asked should be directly related to the job for which the interviewee has applied.

Just like asking good questions is an art, so is listening. A good interviewer is also a good listener. It is important to have an understanding, friendly, and neutral demeanour. Interviewers who are good listeners make applicants comfortable. They also interpret responses better, leading to better selection decisions.

The following steps are recommended to improve the reliability, validity, and usefulness of interviews:

- Plan the interview for a well-conducted in-depth selection process
- Review the application form for completeness and accuracy
- Structure the interview to some extent so that it follows a set procedure
- Have detailed information about the job for which the candidates are interviewed
- Standardize the evaluation form to avoid biases and have inter-rater reliability
- Provide training to interviewers to better conduct and interpret the interview
- Having knowledge of pseudo-sciences, for example, physiognomy—study of face and non-verbal expressions—can provide valuable help to interviewers
- Use a panel rather than one interviewer for more objective assessment
- Focus on a diverse range of questions so as to get a broad view of the applicant's skills.
- Match content of interview with job outcomes expected
- Base interview questions on objective job analysis and job requirements
- Reduce biases, errors, and personal notions affecting the interview process

Stage 4: Background Checks

Some organizations use different tests to check the genuineness of the candidate before finally inducting them. These may include:

- *Polygraph tests*   Polygraph or 'lie detector test' is an attempt to reduce dishonesty among employees. The polygraph is a mechanical device that measures a person's physical response, heart rate, and breathing rate when speaking to detect lies. The use of polygraph is ordinarily justified by an organization on the basis of trying to obtain the best 'whole person'. Many countries have, however, prohibited polygraph use for employment screening except for employment in critical sectors such as security, defence, arms, and nuclear power.

  Since polygraph testing is often not acceptable, a growing number of firms use what are called the 'honesty' tests. Individuals are asked questions such as: 'Would you tell your boss if you knew your coworker was misusing office equipment?' Concerns about the validity of honesty tests exist. Yet they are valid as general screening instruments and cannot be used as stand-alone tests.
- *Reference checks*   Sometimes organizations may check the background of individuals through reference checks from past employers, teachers, and people who are acquainted with the candidate. Telephoning a reference or getting a testimonial from teachers or past employers are common ways to do this.
- *Physical examination*   The physical fitness of the candidate may be tested through medical check-ups that may include general fitness tests, vision tests, aural ability test, drug tests, and so on.

Stage 5: Selection Decision

The final decision will rest on how many candidates have to be inducted. Making the right decision depends on management judgement; the evidence must be assessed and the best match made of person to specification, while taking into account the present and future demands of the job.

If an employer chooses to use only one predictor (for example, a test) to select who will be hired, the decision is straightforward. If the test is valid and encompasses a major dimension of a job, and the applicant does well on the test, he or she can be hired. This is the *single predictor* approach. Selection accuracy depends on how valid that single predictor is in predicting performance. However, if more than one predictor is being used, they must be combined in the most rational ways. Having too many predictors may actually harm the quality of selection decisions. It is important to ensure that only predictors that genuinely distinguish between successful and unsuccessful employees are used. Table 6.3 shows comparative RVU of common selection tools.

Table 6.3 RVU of Common Selection Tools

Method	Reliability	Validity	Cost
Application nlank	High	Low	Low
BIB/WAB	High	High	Moderate
Reference letters	Moderate	Low	Low
Job samples	High	High	High
Assessment centres	Moderate	High	High
Cognitive ability test	Moderate	Moderate	Moderate
Psychological tests	Moderate	High	Moderate
Interviews	Low	Moderate	Moderate
Background checks	Moderate	High	High

Recruitment and selection are vital functions of HR in an organization. The slightest mistake will lead to a *square peg in round hole*. In the long run, these people would be a liability to their organization. The role of HR manager is very crucial in selecting and recruiting the right kind of people who can be an asset for the company. Instead of following a blind elimination process, focus should be on selecting people based on the skills and competencies required for the job.

PLACEMENT AND INDUCTION

The last stage of staffing, after recruitment and selection, is placement or induction. Placement refers to assigning rank and responsibility to an individual and identifying him with a particular job. Induction refers to the introduction of a person to the job and the organization. The purpose is to make the employee feel at home and develop a sense of pride in the organization and commitment to the job. The induction process is also envisaged to indoctrinate, orient, acclimatize, and acculture the person to the job and the organization.

Thus, while placement is a process of assigning a specific job to each of the selected candidates, induction is the process of receiving and welcoming an employee and giving him basic information to settle down and start work. However, both activities take place almost simultaneously and they comprise part of the company's onboarding programme.

The basic thrust of induction training or onboarding training, during the first one or few weeks after a person joins service in the organization, is to introduce the person to the people with whom he will work and make the person aware of the company policies, work culture, working conditions and requirements, duties and responsibilities, and other workplace issues. The purpose is also to help the newcomer overcome his apprehensions vis-à-vis the new environment and to build employee confidence. There is also a need to develop in the newcomer a sense of belongingness and loyalty and to enable him to integrate with the organization.

While the HR staff may provide general orientation relating to the organization, the immediate supervisor should take the responsibility for specific orientation relating to the job and work-unit members. The follow-up of orientation is to be coordinated by both the HR department and the supervisor. Proper induction would enable the employee to get off to a good start and to develop his overall effectiveness on the job and enhance his potential.

Placement and induction typically involve the following: (*a*) intimation of selection decision and extension of offer letter, (*b*) reporting and joining formalities by the candidate, (*c*) taking over charge and responsibilities—initial briefing sessions, and (*d*) induction and socializing.

The Socialization Process

The socialization process is the process that helps new employees adapt to the organization's culture. It is the process by which new employees become acclimated to the culture of a new workplace.

There are three stages in socialization:

- **Pre-arrival Stage**   This is the period of learning in the socialization process that occurs before a new employee joins the organization. The selection process is used in most organizations to inform perspective employees about the organization as whole. RJPs serve the critical purpose of informing candidates about the different aspects of the organization. The information gained during recruitment and selection helps gain knowledge about the company.

- **Encounter Stage**   Upon entry into the organization after being selected, new members enter the encounter stage. This is the stage in the socialization process in which a new employee sees what the organization is really like and confronts the possibility that expectations and reality may diverge. Where expectation and reality differ, new employees must undergo socialization that will detach them from their previous wrong assumption and replace these with the organization's values.

- **Metamorphosis Stage**   This is the stage in the socialization process in which a new employee changes and adjusts to the organization. This may mean going through several changes—in perception, working styles, attitudes, behaviours, and value systems. Hence, it is termed as the metamorphosis stage. Metamorphosis is complete when new members have become comfortable with the organization and have internalized the norms of the organization.

The purpose of induction is to acclimatize the candidate about the company. This can be done by the supervisor, colleagues, team members, and so on. Some companies assign companions or 'buddies' to new entrants. These buddies usually become friends and acquaint the employee about the company. Socialization can also be done by assigning role models, mentoring, or through understudy assignments. New entrants are provided with company literature and reading material for understanding the work and corporate culture. Onboarding sites and internal social networking platforms are important elements of the overall staffing strategy of many companies. Induction programmes should be structured to some extent to ensure that each employee receives the information they require when they start work.

HR Anecdote
Shakespeare and HR

Former Dean of Northwestern University's Kellogg School of Management, Professor Dipak Jain explains why Shakespeare's insights into human nature hold enduring value for HR managers:

William Shakespeare, in his writing, has touched every aspect of the human being, and by studying his works, business leaders can reap valuable insights. Shakespeare in his art created a microcosm of the universe. Shakespeare teaches us about leadership and loyalty, about honour and duty, the merits of forgiveness, and the great value of community.

The character of Hamlet provides insights helpful for modern managers. Hamlet reveals how doubts can paralyze. Today, we might state that the character displayed an inability to act in an environment where informational uncertainty was a critical component. Leaders can fail by putting themselves before others, by inaction or rash action, or by an inability to distinguish false counsel from true. This last instance occurs in *Othello*, with Othello failing to see the manipulations of his adviser, Iago, who plots the destruction of those around him, including Othello. The lesson offered by this play for today's leaders is to seek wise and diverse advice. The stories in the plays *Henry IV* and *Henry V* as well as *Julius Caesar* chronicle a leader's journey—with vivid experiences of how human nature influenced this journey. The story of jealousy and betrayal in Julius Caeser shows how unpredictable human beings are. Caesar's iconic last words 'et tu, Brute?' speak volumes about the complexity of human relationships.

These lessons depict myriad human shades. This indicates that people may not be what they appear to be. Selecting the right people is, thus, a gargantuan exercise requiring a lot of insight into human behaviour.

Source: Retrieved and adapted from http://www.kellogg.northwestern.edu/news_articles/2005/dean_on_shakespeare.aspx.

News Grab
Hiring talent a challenge in 2018: Survey

Talent acquisition is understood to be challenging for recruiters in India in 2018, according to the 'State of Talent Acquisition in India' survey, by talent assessment and skill measurement company Mettl. The respondents spanned sectors such as pharmaceuticals/healthcare, IT/ITeS, retail, manufacturing and BFSI from companies including Siemens, IBM, McCann, Wingify, Apollo Munich, Microsoft, Cipla, Infosys and TCS.

The report took into account the challenges for recruiters in a rapidly changing digital, economic, demographic and social landscape. The pace of technological changes is expected to continue to create demand for new skill sets and job roles, and that organizations realize the need to have a develop a blended approach to talent management and recruitment. Attracting talent will be a top priority and organizations must create systems and routines to give employees the learning opportunities they seek.

The survey based on responses from more than 1,860 HR and business leaders across India, shows that 87.6% organizations had an increased hiring budget in 2018, up from 67.8% the previous year. Further, 76.3% of organisations expected to have an increased recruitment volume in 2018 compared to 64.5% last year. 36.17% respondents said they would use social media to source talent. Other sources that companies will look at include job fairs and campus placement (23.83%), talent sourcing firms (18.64%), internal referrals (13.36%) and talent pipelining (9%).

Source: Adapted from *Economic Times*, Hiring talent a challenge for companies in 2018: Survey, 15 January 2018, retrieved from https://economictimes.indiatimes.com/jobs/hiring-talent-a-challenge-for-companies-in-2018-survey/printarticle/62514447.cms.

CHAPTER SUMMARY

- SHRP links strategic business planning and HRP.
- HRP needs to be linked to the larger business plans as well as the plans of other functional areas such as marketing, operations, and finance.
- Apart from the core issue of MP, SHRP process also includes career planning, succession planning, and termination planning.
- Staffing primarily involves three activities: recruitment, selection, and placement. Strategic staffing involves designing these activities to match corporate strategies.
- Strategic recruitment is based on the 3L principle: lowest cost, least time, and likeliest candidates.
- There are two sources of recruitment, namely internal and external sources. Organizations need to strike the best balance between the two sources so as to attract the 'right' people and 'right' set of competencies for 'right' positions.
- RJP involves giving a realistic preview of the job to applicants during recruitment to provide them with information on both positive and negative aspects of the job.
- Strategic selection involves designing a selection mechanism that has RVU.

- The last stage of staffing is placement or induction. Placement refers to assigning rank and responsibility to an individual. Induction refers to the introduction of a person to the job and the organization.

EXERCISES AND DISCUSSION QUESTIONS

1. Discuss the concept of strategic human resource planning (SHRP). Explain how it is different from manpower planning (MP).
2. What is strategic staffing? Discuss the principles of strategic recruitment and selection.
3. Choose a company from the Fortune 500 list:
   i. Visit the company's website and discuss how the website is being used for hiring activities.
   ii. Try to search relevant information to show how the company is using the power of Internet (for example, social media platforms, virtual job fairs, and online recruiting portals) for carrying out staffing.

CASELET

Mirakle Couriers: Driving Social Change

The story of Mirakle Couriers is extremely awe inspiring. Keen to explore and make a mark in the social sphere, Dhruv Lakra, a management graduate from Oxford University, returned to his native country, India. He established a courier company that is unique in itself. His company is run by people with hearing impairment!

Dhruv realized that there are hardly any employment opportunities for deaf and mute people. One day, when he was taking a courier delivery, he realized that he did not even exchange a single word with the delivery boy. It was then that he decided to set up a courier company employing only the hearing impaired since employees do not really need to communicate much with customers. This was the birth of Mirakle Couriers.

It is important to understand Dhruv Lakra's venture against the sociocultural background of India. Dhruv has set out to challenge the very mindset that disabled people cannot be integrated into the mainstream of the economy. People with disabilities face many challenges in less developed countries. Lack of education and their own inhibitions prevent them from getting jobs. Further, the negative perceptions about disabled people make things worse for them. For deaf people in particular, circumstances have always been very harsh. Being deaf is an invisible disability as there are no obvious physical attributes.

Mirakle's initial challenge was to gain a foothold in a fast-expanding industry. There are big players in the courier industry in India with extensive distribution networks that comprise branches, warehouses, IT infrastructure, and human resources across various cities. For Mirakle, the challenge to stand up against this kind of competition was indeed tough. However, Dhruv was determined to set up a profitable company. The intention was to provide opportunities to the deaf and mute, but not be dependent on anyone for resources. The company website clearly states: *We are not a charity but a social business. Our business model is based on creating a service-driven profitable enterprise that employs the deaf.*

Staffing Challenges

Initially, the key challenge was to staff the organization. It was difficult hiring people. He realized that people with disabilities often have low self-expectations and self-esteem about their own potential to work. In India, disabled people have been over-dependant on their families for even small tasks. As a result, many of them are not even trained in basic life skills such as personal hygiene, dressing and grooming, using public transport, travelling, and observing personal safety.

After some research, Dhruv discovered that there were certain voluntary groups for deaf and mute people in the city of Mumbai, where he was planning to set up his enterprise. Through their help, he managed to get a few boys on board. He then got in touch with a few societies and NGOs working with the hearing-impaired and recruited a few people who were willing to work. He also approached schools for the hearing impaired to recruit staff. As business expanded, the need for hiring and training naturally increased. However, as Mirakle's reputation grew, potential candidates started landing up at its office looking for a job. The company hires young deaf men and women from the underprivileged sections and then trains them.

Onboarding the hired staff was the next challenge. The deaf and mute face peculiar communication problems that make it extremely difficult to train them. Due to lack of education, many of them could not read or understand even simple sentences. Dhruv himself learnt the Indian Sign Language (ISL) to communicate and train his team. Initially, he accompanied the delivery boys to deliver letters so as to train them and acquaint them with the places and localities in Mumbai. They had to be shown their way around the town. They had to be taught some essential *do's and don'ts* such as using simple sign language that general people could understand. They were trained in basic etiquette of delivering courier packages and 'interacting' with the customers, most of whom may not realize that they are actually deaf and mute. To overcome many of these problems, the company designed distinct orange colour T-shirts with the words Mirakle Courier written on it. The purpose was to make them visible. Delivery boys were asked to carry identity cards.

After joining Mirakle, employees are placed and assigned roles based on their capabilities. Most of the boys are in delivery and field jobs while girls are mainly in back office operations. Dhruv is CEO but he himself delivered letters initially. He is a leader, manager, mentor, and guide. Likewise, others too are ready to take on multiple responsibilities when needed. Everyone works together like a great team. The company conducts reading and writing workshops on a regular basis. The back office girls, who had never used a computer before, were trained to proficiently scan and process delivery reports using computers.

Of late, technology is also being used for communication and operational efficiency. Most communication is done via mobile text messaging, emails, and messaging apps such as WhatsApp which are easy to use for the hearing impaired. To help boys locate places, Google maps are also being used now. All the employees have now been provided with access to ATMs by the State Bank of India without telephonic confirmation.

The initial months were challenging due to the training required and the need to overcome mindsets and scepticism. It was not easy convincing clients to give business to his firm. People were reluctant as they were scared that the company did not have adequate capabilities to handle courier and that their documents or parcels would get lost. However, as clients noticed the dedication and sincerity, the business started to grow and the company broke even in the first year of operations.

Mirakle has won several awards, including the Hellen Keller Award in 2009 for being the 'Role model supporter of employment opportunities for disabled people'. In 2010, they were bestowed with the National Award for the Empowerment of Persons with Disabilities by the Government of India. It has been a difficult ride for Mirakle. The employees of Mirakle Couriers feel that they have 'come a long way'. They state that earlier they were either jobless or were employed in low-paying jobs. Working at Mirakle has made them self-sufficient, given them a sense of respect, fulfilment, and dignity. Mirakle is a small company but with big dreams.[17]

Questions for Discussion

1. Discuss the hiring, onboarding, and initial training issues faced by Mirakle. How was the company able to resolve these?
2. What are the challenges that Mirakle is likely to face in the future, keeping in mind the sociocultural fabric of the country? Suggest some innovative ways to keep the operations viable and scalable.

NOTES

1. G. Dessler (2013), *Human resource management* (Upper Saddle River, NJ: Pearson Education).
2. E. B. Flippo (1980), *Personnel management* (New York, NY: McGraw-Hill Education).
3. *Fortune*, World's most admired companies (2018), retrieved from http://fortune.com/worlds-most-admired-companies.
4. See, for instance, J. Sonnenfeld and M. Peiperl (1988), Staffing policy as a strategic response: A. typology of career systems, *Academy of Management Review 13*(4): 588–600; D. E. Terpstra and E. J. Rozell (1993), The relationship of staffing practices to organizational level measures of performance, *Personnel Psychology 46*: 27–48.
5. Terpstra and Rozell, The relationship of staffing practices, 27–48.
6. Dessler, *Human resource management.*
7. Retrieved from https://www.shrm.org/resourcesandtools/hr-topics/talent-acquisition/pages/employee-referrals-remains-top-source-hires.aspx.
8. Retrieved from www.indianstaffingfederation.org/wp.../05/Flexi-Staffing-in-Govt.-Public-Sector.pdf.
9. X. Biao (2006), *Global 'body shopping': An Indian labor system in the information technology industry* (Princeton, NJ: Princeton University Press).
10. D. H. Kluemper, P. A. Rosen, and K. W. Mossholder (2012), Social networking websites, personality ratings, and the organizational context: More than meets the eye? *Journal of Applied Social Psychology 42*(5): 1143–1172.
11. J. Mathew (2012), Recruitment 5.0: The future of recruiting- the final chapter, retrieved from https://www.ere.net/recruitment-5-0-the-future-of-recruiting-the-final-chapter.
12. H. Gurion (2013), 5 mobile myths that could mortally wound your recruiting efforts, *VentureBeat*, retrieved from https://venturebeat.com/2013/02/19/5-mobile-myths-that-could-mortally-wound-your-recruiting-efforts.
13. See, for instance, B. S. Billingsley and L. H. Cross (1992), Predictors of commitment, job satisfaction, and intent to stay in teaching: A comparison of general and special educators, *Journal of Special*

Education 25(4): 453–472; K. N. Gaertner and S. D. Nollen (1989), Career experiences, perceptions of employment practice and psychological commitment to the organization, *Human Relations 42*: 975–991

14. L. J. Peter and R. Hull (1969), *The Peter Principle* (New York, NY: William Morrow & Co Inc.).

15. H. J. Bernardin and J. E. Russell (1993), *Human resource management: An experiential approach* (New York, NY: McGraw-Hill).

16. S. P. Robbins and T. Judge (2013), *Organizational behaviour*, 15th ed. (Boston, MA: Pearson).

17. With inputs from http://www.miraklecouriers.com/.

CHAPTER 7

Strategic Training and Development

Chapter Overview

This chapter focuses on the meaning and concept of strategic training and development. It discusses the concepts of organizational learning and unlearning as broad themes of strategic training and development. It highlights how learning and unlearning take place and the strategic issues concerning the two concepts. Further, it delves into a discussion on career planning and development as well as succession planning.

Learning Objectives

1. To get familiarized with the concept of strategic training and development in contrast with the traditional concept
2. To understand the frameworks of organizational learning and unlearning and how they support the broad idea of strategic training and development
3. To develop an understanding of the concepts and strategies related to career planning and development as well as succession planning

OPENING STORY

Barbie Doll's Journey

She is close to 60 years old now, but continues to set new fashion trends, expressing the dreams of young girls. She is Barbie, the most popular fashion doll. Barbie was considered an icon of American culture. She is regarded as a role model who inspired young girls to become independent and self-reliant. Sales of Barbie merchandise are more than $1 billion annually. Mattel, the makers of Barbie, claims that approximately three Barbie dolls are sold every second. The doll was marketed as a 'Teen-age Fashion Model'. Barbie dolls have appeared in various avatars—doctor, pilot, singer, artist, and much more. Barbie collectibles come out with a great line of dolls from around the world.

Emerging Markets and India

Mattel has been known for creating dolls that are culturally unique. However, with all the Western Barbies abounding, Asians seem to take the back seat in Barbie's world. Barbie did not start seeing Pacific Island until the release of the 'Hawaiian Barbie' in 1978 and 'Oriental Barbie' for Asians in 1981. These Barbies were exact replicas of the original with some variations in skin, hair, and eye colour.

The 1990s saw the introduction of Barbies for the Indian market under the 'expressions of India' series. Barbies have their dresses recreated to depict women in traditional Indian dresses. The Soni Punjabi Barbie doll, a beautiful bride, is dressed in a *salwar-kameez* typical to north India. Sundari Gujarati Barbie is a doll that sparkles with the extravagant tradition of Gujarat. Roopvati Rajasthani Barbie doll, in all its finesse, is a symbol of the glorious tradition and magnificence of Rajasthan. Wedding Fantasy Barbie brings alive the beauty and grandeur that mark the joyous celebration of a traditional Indian wedding.

Initially, these Indian versions picked up well, but later their sales started to dwindle. Barbie had always been seen as an icon of Western culture, and that is what Indian girls wanted. Much to the surprise of the makers, girls preferred to buy a more Western version of Barbie than an ethnic one. The company had to take back many of these unsold Barbies and reintroduce the original version. This was a big lesson to learn—a localization strategy may not always work well.

Recently, Barbie's presence has been said to be a negative influence in the life of young girls. Many people claim that young girls may see the doll as their role model, leading to issues with body image and gender role. Because of its stereotyped image of being only glamorous, Barbie is sometimes used as a term for a girl who is 'dumb'. Barbie's height and exaggerated hourglass figure drew criticism for not being proportionate and 'normal'. If scaled into real life proportions, she would be unable to stand on her feet. The enormous range of accessories give rise to the accusation that Barbie encourages young girls to focus on shallow trivia. In fact, Saudi Arabia outlawed the sale of Barbie dolls at one time for not conforming to its culture.

All these were serious learnings for Barbie. With a shaky market, the biggest challenge was to retain the interest of young girls. With young girls shifting to video games, computers, and gadgets, the number of those playing with dolls was decreasing. In addition, Barbie faced stiff competition from 'Disney Princess' or 'Frozen' range of dolls. All this sent the company into serious rethinking and unlearning of many of its past strategies. There was a need to innovate and at the same time change the stereotype image of Barbie as 'just' a fashion doll.

FROM TRAINING TO LEARNING

Wide-sweeping changes are taking place in the business environment, which are constantly throwing new challenges towards business organizations. Even well-established companies are finding it difficult to deliver consistent results. Today, organizations are expected to emphasize quality, continuous improvement, flexibility, adaptability, and innovation. This calls for not just extensive training in task skills but a completely new work orientation. There is an urgent need to rethink ways of skilling people. This requires strategic integration of training and development with the organization's philosophy.

Training refers to planned programmes designed to improve performance and to bring about measurable changes in knowledge, skills, attitude, and social behaviour of employees for doing a particular job. Integrating training with strategy requires identifying employee behaviours and competencies the firm will require to execute its strategy.

Strategic training and development involves:

- Integrating training and development with corporate strategies
- Building long-term competencies
- Encouraging a continuous and ongoing approach to acquiring new knowledge
- Building a dynamic organization through multi-skilling
- Shifting the focus from traditional *training to learning*

Traditionally training has been an individual-oriented, task-based exercise to impart technical and functional area knowledge in order to solve problems. Hence, it was reactive and prescriptive. The focus on 'learning' seeks to emphasize the proactive measure of acquiring and sharing knowledge. The purpose is to develop effective role behaviours and not just task-specific skills. While the emphasis in the first is on training, that of the second is on overall development. While training is imposed by the organization, learning has to be an individual-driven strategy.

This shift in emphasis from the traditional training perspective to learning can be visualized as given in Table 7.1.

Table 7.1 Training versus Learning

Training (Traditional Approach)	Learning (Strategic Approach)
Focus on training	Focus on learning
Task-based	Role-based
Skill acquisition	Personality development
Instilling technical expertise	Instilling business acumen
Reactive	Proactive
Prescriptive	Diagnostic
Limited management attention	Management priority
Problem-solving approach	Opportunity-seeking approach
Count hours of involvement	Measure impact on performance
Individual-oriented	Group-oriented
One-time programme	Ongoing process

It is important to remember that while training is a time-bound programme, learning is ongoing. Organizations today need to shift from a training model to a learning model.

ORGANIZATIONAL LEARNING

The terms 'learning organization' and 'organizational learning' are very similar in that they connect to each other, but differ in that one involves the *action* of learning in an organization and the other involves the *process* of gaining that learning in the organization. Peter Senge (1990) in his book *The Fifth Discipline* describes a learning organization as a place where people continually expand their capacity to create the results that they desire, where there is consideration for collective aspiration and where people are continuously learning how to learn together.[1] Collaboration is seen as the essence of what distinguishes organizational learning from individual learning. Organizational learning is defined as the phenomenon of improving actions through collaborative knowledge and understanding.[2] On the other hand, a 'learning organization' is a term used for a firm that purposefully creates structures and strategies to enhance learning.[3] A learning organization facilitates the learning of all its members and continuously transforms itself. Organizational learning is actually the '*activity* and *process* by which organizations eventually reach the ideal of a learning organization'.[4]

Learning is the basis for developing an organization's core competence. Business organizations need to constantly rejuvenate themselves for enduring success. Learning is now seen as a crucial tool for attaining competitive advantage. It augments the ability to adapt to a rapidly changing environment. Learning has several benefits. For *individuals*, learning helps develop problem-solving and decisional abilities, enhances self-development, and helps provide a sense of accomplishment through enhanced knowledge. It improves performance and helps build morale and confidence. For *groups*, learning helps in improved interaction, builds cohesiveness, provides a climate for cooperation, and encourages sharing of ideas through team spirit. For the *organization*, learning helps in improving productivity and performance, increases financial returns, reduces costs and wastages, helps in making informed decisions, and leads to attainment of goals.

THE LEARNING FRAMEWORK

Learning is not a one-shot programme; it is an ongoing process. It calls for developing a comprehensive learning framework that incorporates the learning philosophy and strategy. There is need for a continuous learning orientation on the part of organizational members. Figure 7.1 illustrates the concept of the *learning iceberg* that summarizes this.

Figure 7.1   The Learning Iceberg

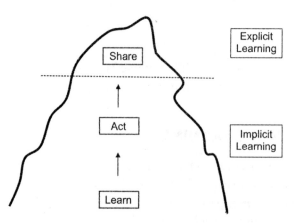

The concept of *learning iceberg* is based on the *learn–act–share* perspective. The learning concept is visualized as an iceberg that is hidden beneath water with only the tip visible. The implicit components of learning iceberg are *learn* and *act*, whereas *share* is the explicit dimension symbolized by the tip of the iceberg.

- *Learn*   This forms the base of the iceberg. It refers to the subtle and gradual acquisition of new skills, capabilities, and know-how on an ongoing basis. In a learning organization, individuals are motivated to acquire learning on a regular basis, thereby leading to incremental change in one's knowledge and competencies.
- *Act*   Once new learning has been acquired, it needs to manifest itself in actual day-to-day working behaviours. Thus, new skills, capabilities, and know-how must start getting utilized in the organization in the form of improved methods, processes, and decisions.
- *Share*   Organizational members need to pass on new learning to others, leading to synergies and desirable outcomes. Knowledge is meaningful only when it is shared. Thus, learning has to be shared.

While *learn* and *act* may take place on an individual basis, sharing of knowledge calls for a collective give and take. Hence, while learn and act are implicit, sharing is the explicit part of the learning iceberg.

LEARNING AND KNOWLEDGE MANAGEMENT

Knowledge management is the process of capturing, developing, sharing, and effectively using organizational knowledge. Knowledge management is the systematic management of an organization's knowledge assets for the purpose of creating value. It consists of the processes, strategies, and systems that are directed towards storage, sharing, and preservation of knowledge.

Knowledge management implies a strong tie with learning as it involves the management of knowledge that is useful and creates value for the organization. Both are inextricably linked. The eventual success of the *learn–act–share* strategy depends on how effectively information is codified and stored. Knowledge management plays an important role in organizational learning, helping in identifying, documenting, and making available the knowledge of individuals or teams, as well as providing the basis for systematic knowledge sharing. Knowledge management helps understand the value of new knowledge created and helps store this knowledge and makes it readily available for people at the right time.

The idea of archiving knowledge deserves mention here. Knowledge can be stored in personal, organizational, and external archives.[5] The personal archives refer to stored information in the possession of individual members. This information faces loss with the departure of its possessor from the organization. The organizational archives refer to stored information in the possession of the organization. Finally, the external archives refer to stored information in the possession of external entities who make it available through contractual agreements. In general, all information is subject to loss unless it has been stored in the archives. The eventual success of the *learn–act–share* strategy depends on how effectively information is codified and stored.

As discussed, all learning and knowledge needs to be stored in some form. Knowledge management, thus, helps in sustained learning. Often within organizations, processes and best-practice examples are not documented and are simply lost when people decide to move on. At one point of time, NASA realized that 50 per cent of its workforce were going to retire within a short period of time and unless they came up with a viable solution, years of experience and knowledge would be lost. Efforts to retain at least some knowledge were integrated into a new knowledge debrief. This 'debrief' is now regularly conducted through asking employees to complete job manuals, write case studies, tell stories, give best practice examples, and share their preferred knowledge resources. This helps store information in a way that is most meaningful for remaining employees. The process adds to the learning curve of newer staff and ensures that valuable expertise is hard-wired into the corporate memory. Successful companies such as Honda, Toyota, GE, and American Express have devised mechanisms to share and store learning for long-term success.

THE ADDIE MODEL

The analysis–design–develop–implement–evaluate (ADDIE) training model has been used by training experts for years.[6] It remains relevant even today. It can be applied to the broader concept of learning. What is needed is orienting the traditional ADDIE approach to suit the strategic imperatives of an organization.

The ADDIE model entails:

- *Analysing* the training need
- *Designing* the training strategy and programme
- *Developing* the training content
- *Implementing* the training programme
- *Evaluating* the effectiveness of training

We shall discuss each step in detail and see how it can be applied to the larger domain of learning.

Learning Needs Analysis

The training needs analysis involves addressing the organization's training needs. It is the process that helps discover the training and development needs of people so that they can carry out their job effectively and efficiently. Training needs analysis is the first stage in the training process and involves a procedure to determine what type of training will address a current problem that has been identified.

A major shortcoming in the traditional training needs analysis procedure was that it identified training as a short-term, ad-hoc solution to handle an existing problem. Thus, the focus was on identifying training needs as a reactive, remedial, and prescriptive solution to existing problems. Organizations are facing great pressure to change these days—to facilitate and encourage overall development—beyond traditional training. This has engendered the need to think not just in terms of current needs analysis but also future long-term needs analysis. Needs analysis, therefore, should involve assessing both *current/short-term* training needs as well as *strategic/long-term* learning needs.

Current training needs analysis aims to improve current performance, training new employees or those whose performance is deficient. The main task here is to determine what the job entails and how to improve performance in carrying out the tasks of each job. Managers use task analysis to identify new employees' training needs and performance analysis to identify existing employees' training needs. Task analysis uses job description and job specification data in order to identify the tasks required to be done in a job so as to train the employee in carrying out the tasks more efficiently and effectively. Performance analysis refers to analysing performance appraisal reports of employees to identify performance loopholes and uncover training needs. There are various ways to identify performance gaps. Job-related performance data (for example, productivity, absenteeism, wastages, product quality, downtime, damages, error rate, and customer complaints) can be used to determine performance gaps.

Strategic learning needs analysis focuses on identifying the know-how that employees will need in order to become employable for future jobs. Strategic plans require that the organization will have to meet new training needs. Strategic learning needs analysis is tied to succession planning. It means identifying the kind of training and development that employees need to fill key positions in the long term. For strategic training needs analysis, managers take help of competency profiling. As discussed in a previous chapter, the competency profile consolidates a precise overview of the competencies (knowledge, skills, and behaviours) someone would need to do a job well. The employer can then formulate training programmes aimed at developing these future competencies.

Creating a learning organization requires placing emphasis on not just current training needs but also long-term strategic competency building. Competency profiling helps in identifying the competencies needed in the future in order to attain the long-term competency needs of the organization.

Designing the Learning Strategy

After conducting needs analysis, the next task is designing the overall learning strategy. It means planning the overall learning approach including its objectives and delivery methods. During this stage, the organization designs the long-term *learn–act–share* strategy. The typical steps in designing a learning strategy are:

- Setting objectives: Learning objectives should specify in measurable terms what the employee should be able to accomplish through the learning initiatives. It needs to identify the learning goals and objectives.
- Designing a learning approach: The broad learning agenda needs to be broken down into specific action plans. Managers address several issues during the design stage, such as designing training and development methodologies (lectures, computer-based learning, and so on) and choosing trainers (in-house or hired from outside). They also decide how

to organize the various training modules and components, develop an overall plan for implementing the programme, and lay down training schedules and timelines.

- Laying down a training budget: This will involve assessing training costs. Typical costs include direct costs (the cost of hiring trainers, developing training content, and acquiring training material) and indirect costs (time involved in training and opportunity cost of training, for example, when employees undergo training, they miss out on their work).

The learning strategy should include details of how to set a learning environment that motivates employees to learn and to share what they learn.

Developing the Content

Developing the programme means actually creating the training content and materials, developing the training method (for example, lab training and computer-based training [CBT]) and arranging training equipment and materials needed (such as books, reading material, trainer's resources, and computers). There is a vast array of online and offline content from which to choose and create the training content. This may include trainer's manuals, guides, self-help books, instructional reading material, videos, and other related stuff. Some organizations create their own training content, some may develop it based on information available online and offline, while some may actually hire external trainers to develop specialized content.

Implementing Learning Strategy

Once the approach is conceptualized, it is time to implement it as part of a continuous learning strategy. This mandates laying down the ways and methods whereby learning will be imparted. There are two ways of imparting learning, namely on-the-job and off-the-job.

On-the-job Methods

Under these methods, employees learn through observing peers or managers performing the job and trying to imitate their behaviour. These methods do not cost much and are less disruptive as employees are always on the job. The trainee is learning while doing. Some of the commonly used methods are:

1. **Coaching** A coach is a trainer or consultant who identifies the employee's strengths and weaknesses and provides counsel as to how to capitalize on those strengths and overcome the weaknesses. Coaching is a one-to-one approach. It helps in quickly identifying the weak areas and tries to focus on them. It also offers the benefit of transferring theory learning to practice.

2. **Mentoring** Mentoring is also one-to-one interaction like coaching. It is used for managerial employees. The focus in mentoring is on the development of right attitudes. Mentoring is always done by a senior person.

3. **Job Rotation** Job rotation is another on-the-job learning technique. It involves an employee moving from job to job at planned intervals in order to learn multiple skills. It is the process

of training employees by rotating them through a series of related jobs. Rotation not only makes a person well acquainted with different jobs, but it also alleviates boredom. Rotation is mainly used for managerial level employees.

4. **Job Instructional Technique (JIT)**   Many jobs consist of a sequence of steps. JIT is a step-by-step, structured, and systematic on-the-job training method in which a trainer (*a*) prepares a trainee with an overview of the job, (*b*) demonstrates the task or the skill to the trainee, (*c*) allows the trainee to show the demonstration on his or her own, and (*d*) follows up to provide feedback and help. The trainees are presented with some learning material to understand their job. It helps to deliver step-by-step instruction and keep track of when the learner has learned. Self-help on-the-job learning is also quite common nowadays due to the use of computers. Employees can read from manuals and computer-based material or videos while actually working and learning through trial and error.

5. **Programmed Learning**   A similar idea to JIT is programmed learning. Whether the medium is a textbook, PC, or the Internet, programmed learning is a step-by-step, self-learning on-the-job that consists of three parts:

   i. Presenting questions, facts, issues, or problems to the learner
   ii. Allowing the person to respond to these issues
   iii. Providing feedback on the responses, with instructions on how and what to do
   Programmed learning facilitates learning by letting employees learn at their own pace, get immediate feedback, and reduce their risk of error. Computerized *intelligent tutoring systems* take programmed learning one step further. These systems track the methods and approaches of each learner and then adjust the instructional sequence to the trainee's unique needs.

6. **Apprenticeship**   Apprenticeship is a system of training a new generation of practitioners of a skill. This method of training is in vogue in those trades, crafts, and technical fields in which a long period is required for gaining proficiency. The trainees serve as apprentices to experts for long periods. They have to work in direct association with and also under the direct supervision of their supervisors. The object of such training is to make the trainees all-round craftsmen. It is an expensive method of training. The apprentices are paid remuneration according to the apprenticeship agreements.

7. **Understudy**   In this method, a superior gives training to a subordinate as his understudy, such as an assistant to a manager. The subordinate learns through experience and observation by participating in handling day-to-day problems. Basic purpose is to prepare subordinate for assuming the full responsibilities and duties.

8. **Action learning**   Action learning programmes involve analysing and solving problems and learning in the process. It usually involves teams and assigning them real-world business problems that extend beyond their usual areas of expertise. Teams explore through the problems, brainstorm, collaborate, and try to solve the problem. They are aided by experts through coaching and feedback. The focus is to increase employees' learning capacity while responding to a real world challenge usually in a cross-departmental team. Reflection is an important part of the experience. Groups are empowered and trusted with the necessary resources to take on the issue, and as a result, can present the organization with suggestions on better procedures.

Designing an on-the-job training strategy requires a thorough understanding of how learning will be acquired. It is important to place the learner as close to the normal working environment as possible so as to enable the creation of an on-the-job experience. On-the-job learning takes place gradually through trial and error. As soon as the learner demonstrates ability to do the job, he may be allowed some free hand to apply learning in real operations. A follow-up mechanism needs to be put up to ensure that learning has actually taken place.

Although managers cannot manage informal learning completely, they can ensure that it occurs. Sun Microsystems implemented an informal online learning tool called *Sun Learning exchange*. This has evolved into a platform containing more than 5,000 informal learning ideas addressing varied topics from sales to technical support. Employees share their ideas and look up for one while working to aid them in their work.

Off-the-job Methods

Off-the-job learning methods involve conducting training or learning programmes separately from the job environment. Common methods include:

1. **Lectures and Conferences**   Lectures and conferences are the traditional method of instruction. Most training programmes start with lectures and conferences. Numerous companies and universities offer classroom-type management development seminars and conferences. The Advanced Management Program of Harvard's Graduate School of Business Administration is one example. In India, several leading institutes such as the IIMs regularly conduct Management Development Programmes (MDPs) for managers and executives.

   Many firms, particularly big ones, establish in-house development centres, training institutes, or even corporate universities. A corporate university is any educational entity that is basically setup by the parent organization to foster learning. Corporate universities are a growing trend nowadays. Learning imparted through such centres ensures the alignment of learning with corporate strategic goals. A number of companies, such as IBM, Walt Disney, Boeing, and Motorola, have their own such institutes. For instance, Apple University is a training facility of Apple Inc., located in Cupertino, California. It was designed to instruct personnel employed by Apple in the various aspects of Apple's technology and culture. Similarly, the Hamburger University is a training facility of McDonald's. It was designed to instruct personnel employed by McDonald's in the various aspects of restaurant management. More than 80,000 restaurant managers and owners/operators have graduated from this facility. In India, Infosys Global Education Centre, Azim Premji University, and Future Innoversity (Future Group) are some such examples.

2. **Vestibule Training**   Vestibule training is a term for near-the-job training, as it offers access to something new in the form of learning. In vestibule training, the workers are trained in a prototype environment on specific jobs in a special part of the plant. An attempt is made to create working conditions similar to the actual workshop conditions. After training workers in such conditions, the trained workers may be put on similar jobs in the actual workshop. This enables the workers to gain learning in the best methods to work and to get rid of initial nervousness. It may also be used as a preliminary to on-the-job training. It prevents trainees from committing mistakes when working on the actual machines.

3. **Simulation Exercises**   Simulation is any artificial environment exactly similar to the actual situation. There are several basic simulation techniques used for imparting training:

   i. **Management Games**   Management games enable trainees to learn by making realistic decisions in hypothetical or simulated situations. Properly designed games help to ingrain thinking habits, analytical, logical, and reasoning capabilities, importance of team work, time management, to make decisions lacking complete information, communication, and leadership capabilities. Use of management games can encourage novel, innovative mechanisms for coping with stress. These games help learners develop their problem-solving skills and leadership skills, and foster cooperation and teamwork.

   ii. **Case Study**   Case studies are trainee-centred activities based on topics that demonstrate theoretical concepts in an applied setting. The case study method presents a learner with a written description of an organizational problem. The person then analyses the case, diagnoses the problem, and presents his or her findings and solutions in a discussion with other learners. A case study allows the application of theoretical concepts to be demonstrated, encourages active learning, and provides an opportunity for the development of key skills, such as communication, group working, and problem solving.

   iii. **In-basket Exercise**   In-basket exercise, also known as in-tray training, consists of a set of business papers that may include e-mail, SMSs, reports, memos, and other items. Now the trainer is asked to prioritize the decisions to be made immediately and the ones that can be delayed.

   iv. **Role Playing**   In a role play, each trainee takes the role of a person affected by an issue and studies the impact of the issues on human life and/or the effects of human activities on the existing situation from the perspective of that person. In particular, role playing presents a trainee with a valuable opportunity to learn not just the course content, but other perspectives on it. The steps involved in role playing include defining objectives, choosing context and roles, introducing the exercise, trainee preparation/ research, role-play, concluding discussion, and assessment.

   v. **Behaviour Modelling**   Behaviour modelling involves showing trainees the right (or model) way of doing something, letting trainees practice that way, and giving feedback on their performance. Behaviour modelling training is a highly regarded psychology-based training intervention. Trainees are made to watch live or video examples showing models behaving effectively in a problem situation. Next, the trainees are given roles to play in a similar simulated situation and are asked to practice the effective behaviours demonstrated by the models.

4. **Sensitivity Training**   Sensitivity training is also known as laboratory or T-group training. This training is about making people understand about themselves and others reasonably, which is done by developing in them social sensitivity and behavioural flexibility. It is the ability of an individual to sense what others feel and think from their own point of view. It reveals information about his or her own personal qualities, concerns, emotional issues, and things that he or she has in common with other members. A group's trainer refrains from

acting as a group leader attempting instead to clarify the group processes using incidents as examples. The group behaviour is the goal as well as the process.

5. **Transactional Analysis**   It provides trainees with a realistic and useful method for analysing and understanding the behaviour of others. In every social interaction, there is a motivation provided by one person and a reaction to that motivation given by another person. This motivation–reaction relationship between two persons is known as a transaction. Transactional analysis can be done by the ego (system of feelings accompanied by a related set of behaviour states of an individual).

As discussed above, while some methods are common for lower-level or technical staff, many other learning methods work well for managerial employees. Training is usually a term deployed in the context of technical staff, while management development is used for managerial staff. It is not always easy to tell where training leaves off and management development begins. As an employee rises up higher in the corporate ladder, the focus shifts from training to development.

E-learning

E-learning has become an important part of society today, comprising an extensive array of digitization approaches, components, and delivery methods to impart learning. Educational technology includes numerous types of media that deliver text, audio, images, animation, and streaming video, and includes computer-based learning, as well as local intranet/extranet and web-based learning. Information and communication systems underlie e-learning processes.

Various terminologies are used for e-learning, such as multimedia learning, technology-enhanced learning (TEL), computer-based instruction (CBI), computer-based training (CBT), computer-assisted instruction or computer-aided instruction (CAI), Internet-based training (IBT), flexible or distributed learning, web-based training (WBT), online education, virtual learning, and digital education. Training technology has largely progressed from using simple audio-visual aids to leveraging the power of Internet to deliver interactive and flexible learning solutions. E-learning can occur in or out of the classroom. It is not a substitute for traditional learning but can be used along with it. It can be both on-the-job or off-the-job learning.

E-learning methods can be classified into two major categories:

Synchronous Learning

Synchronous means 'at the same time'. Synchronous communication between two people requires them to be present at a given time. It involves interaction of participants with an instructor via the web in real time. For example, in virtual class rooms, participants interact with each other and instructors through instant messaging, chat, audio and video conferencing, and so on, and all the sessions can be recorded and played back. It offers the advantage of continuous monitoring and possibilities of global collaboration among learners. Examples of synchronous learning are chat and instant messenger, video and audio conferencing, live webcasting, application sharing, and whiteboard and virtual classrooms.

Asynchronous Learning

Asynchronous means 'not at the same time'. A self-help course is an example of asynchronous learning because online learning takes place at any time. E-mail or discussion forums are examples of asynchronous communication tools. In such cases, trainees ideally complete the course at their own pace, without live interaction with the instructor. Thus, there is flexibility of access to training content. It facilitates interaction among participants through message boards, bulletin boards, and discussion forums. Examples of asynchronous learning are audio-visual aids, e-mail, discussion forums, Wikis/blogs, CBT, WBT, computer simulations, and game-based learning.

Most organizations prefer to use an amalgamation of synchronous and asynchronous learning methods. Electronic performance support systems (EPSS) are computerized tools and displays that automate training processes.

Various types of e-learning mechanisms commonly used today are:

Self-study   Nowadays, this is the most common method, which uses Wiki, blog, and any computer-based reading material to impart learning to employees. This also allows learners to resolve their queries and doubts.

Video/audio aids   This is the second most common method to train learners. Audio-visual aids such as DVDs, videos, films, and PowerPoint presentations are quite popular. It is used when there is a need to show certain processes or events, such as a visual tour of a factory or when there is a need to illustrate some sequences, such as teaching machine operation.

Computer-based training   CBT refers to training methods that use interactive computer-based systems to increase knowledge or skills. E-courses may be made available to learners in the form of a CD or a module that can be run on the learner's system. This works very well for learners who are more motivated to learn new skills and attain professional excellence. Because of their interactive features, CBT is becoming increasingly interactive.

Interactive multimedia training   Interactive multimedia training integrates the use of text, video, graphics, photos, animation, and sound to produce a complex training environment with which the trainee interacts. It combines both the synchronous and the asynchronous ways of learning. More and more employers are moving from textbook and classroom-based learning to interactive learning.

Virtual reality training or simulation   This form of training takes realism a step further, by putting trainees into a simulated environment. The virtual reality puts the trainee in an artificial three-dimensional (3D) environment that simulates events and situations that might be experienced on the job. Sensory devices transmit how the trainee is responding to the computer. The trainee sees, feels, and hears what is going on, assisted by special goggles and auditory and sensory devices. Simulation e-learning is highly interactive and relies heavily on 3D graphics, videos, and audio. In general, interactive and simulated technologies reduce learning time by an average of 50 per cent. Other advantages include instructional consistency, increased retention, and enhanced trainee motivation owing to interactivity and quick response timing.

Internet-based training   Many companies today provide standardized learning environments to their employees worldwide via the Internet. Employers can have a learning portal that offers employees online access to training content. Video conferencing is a popular mechanism for training geographically dispersed employees. Podcasting is another common medium. A podcast is a digital medium consisting of an episodic series of audio, video, or PDF files subscribed to and downloaded through web syndication or streamed online to a device. Conventional web-based learning tends to be limited to online learning, such as reading PowerPoint presentations, participating in instant message chat rooms, and taking online exams. The virtual classroom takes online learning to a new level. A virtual classroom uses special collaboration software to enable multiple remote learners, using their PCs or laptops, to participate in live discussions, communicate, and learn.

Mobile learning   Mobile learning means delivering learning content on mobile devices, such as cell phones, laptops, and iPads, wherever and whenever the learner has the time and desire to access it. The easy availability and affordability of mobile devices has created the scope for mobile-enabled learning. The capabilities of smart phones, including disk space, Internet connectivity, and multimedia functionalities have enabled the creation of training content that is mobile compatible. Employers use mobile learning to deliver training content on various business aspects.

Social media learning   The impact of social media is very strong and it can be utilized for corporate learning as well. Organizations are realizing the true power of social learning and encouraging their employees to interact more among themselves for sharing learning. Employees collaborate and network on social platforms to discuss problems, issues, and experiences. Networking through sites such as Facebook and LinkedIn, posting and viewing videos on Youtube, and sharing blogs are some popular tools for enhanced learning. Social collaboration platforms are also built within the organization's intranet so that the learners do not have to discuss on public platforms and learning emerges from mutual collaboration.

Game-based learning   Games are considered to be fun by all, but they can be a powerful medium of experiential learning as well. Nowadays, many organizations focus on a new mode of learning called 'gamification', which helps them to increase employee productivity and knowledge by motivating them to learn through game-based courses. Such courses focus on creating engagement and motivation for the learners to learn the things while they play. Computerized management games enable trainees to learn by making realistic decisions in simulated situations.

Choosing the right e-learning methods totally depends on the need analysis of the organization. Knowing the benefits of choosing the right e-learning methods can not only make the development process more streamlined and productive but it will also provide a better e-learning experience. The need to teach large numbers of employees remotely in a big company or to enable learners to study at their leisure often makes e-learning much more convenient and efficient. In practice, many employers opt for blended learning. Here, the trainees make use of several delivery methods, such as class lectures, manuals, and self-guided instructions, along with Internet- and web-based learning.

As organizations change the way learning is delivered, employees now see learning as a daily development and not a one-time event. Smaller and more frequent opportunities for desktop and mobile micro-learning have replaced week-long training programmes. With interactive virtual classrooms, video and gamification, it can be fun and engaging. With all these new tools, employers can now create a culture of learning in their workplace and a digital experience that is integrated and collaborative.

Evaluating Learning

An important component of the overall learning approach is evaluating the efficacy of the learning strategy. With increasing emphasis on measuring results, it is crucial that the manager evaluate the learning strategy and programmes. It is important to measure the participant's reactions, level of satisfaction, and to what extent their behaviour or performance has changed as a result of training. It is also important to measure the effectiveness of training in terms of costs and benefit. A careful comparison of the training programmes' costs and benefits can enable the HR team to compute the programmes' return on investment.

The chapter on strategic evaluation discusses these measurement aspects in detail.

THE EMPLOYEE LEARNING MATRIX

In the past, workplace learning was designed to be one-size-fits-all, and at many organizations, it still is. However, learning should be based on employees' specific needs. People learn in different ways. The more personalized a learning experience is, the more engaging it is. Learning requires both ability and willingness to learn. In terms of *ability*, the learner needs to have some basic skills, education, and knowledge base. In terms of willingness, they need to have the necessary motivation and drive to learn. It is rare that learners will exhibit uniformity in terms of ability and willingness to learn. People, thus, differ in their approach to learning. In creating a learning environment, managers, therefore, have to address several issues.

The Employee Learning Strategy Matrix shown in Figure 7.2 classifies employees into four types depending on high or low ability to learn and high or low willingness to learn. The four quadrants show what traits these different types of employees exhibit and what learning approach is needed for them.

Figure 7.2 Employee Learning Strategy Matrix

Low Ability ⟷ High Ability	
Doers	Achievers
Strivers	Idlers

High Willingness ↑ — Low Willingness ↓

The four categories of employees according to the matrix are:

- **High ability-High willingness:** *Achievers*

  These are individuals who have both high levels of ability as well as willingness to learn. They are the star employees chiefly responsible for maximizing organizational performance. They are eager and quick learners and, hence, investments made in them are almost always recouped in the form of greater returns. They need to be developed as leaders and trend-setters vis-à-vis learning strategy. They are often upheld as champions, ambassadors, and change agents who motivate others to learn. They are also potential candidates for future succession planning.

- **High ability-Low willingness:** *Idlers*

  They are those who have the capability but are reluctant to put in efforts to learn. They are usually complacent about things. These are typically 'Type B' people who are happy with the status-quo. They prefer to work less and often idle away. If given the right incentives, challenges, and necessary motivation, they too can be geared up to learn and seek new knowledge.

- **Low ability-High willingness:** *Doers*

  These are individuals who fall short of required ability but have the desire and urge to learn. They have the potential to improve. Mostly they suffer from either dearth of skill or lack of confidence. Doers require careful and empathetic counselling to encourage them to enhance their competencies through learning. They can be harnessed well as they are eager learners.

- **Low ability-Low willingness:** *Strivers*

  These are individuals who have neither ability nor desire to learn. They are laggards and a cost to the company. They are usually wrong people in wrong places. All along they have to strive for survival in the organization. Either they need to be channelized in the right direction or the management may start reconsidering their continuity and existence in the organization.

In today's competitive environment, the traditional HR practice of allocating resources across the board is no longer viable. Thus, companies try to focus more on their 'mission-critical' employees or star employees who are critical to the companies' future growth. For example, high potential employees at Johnson & Johnson's special *LeAD* leadership development programme receive advice and regular assessments from coaches. They are given special guidance in developing new products or markets.

Learners need to be motivated to learn something new. It is important to kindle a desire to learn. With the emphasis shifting from training to learning, more and more organizations are trying to create a learning environment that provides lifelong learning to reduce skill obsolescence and enhance employability. It means providing employees with continuing learning experiences to not just learn new skills but also expand their mental horizons.

In multinational corporations (MNCs), diversity training and sensitization is also an important component of the learning strategy. Diversity sensitization aims to improve cross-cultural sensitivity, with the goal of fostering more harmonious working relationships among the employees. Team training is another important focus area. Cross-functional training and multi-skilling is a common practice nowadays in big companies. Team training includes building interpersonal skills such as in listening, collaborating, and cooperating. Some organizations also use outdoor adventures or trips to build team spirit and camaraderie.

UNLEARNING AND RELEARNING

Just like learning is an important concept, so is unlearning. Most business organizations tend to work with a particular mindset. This sometimes becomes detrimental to their success. In order to comprehend the lurking business challenges, business organizations need to come out of the mindset of yesteryears. It is essential to forget the managerial outlook of the past in order to keep pace with the ever-metamorphosing nature of a business environment. This requires organizational unlearning.

Unlearning is a planned and deliberate effort to come out of a particular style of functioning that is no longer viable. Unlearning does not imply complete severing of ties with the past. In fact, the past does provide a very valuable frame of reference. Rather, unlearning implies doing away with obsolete and stereotyped methods, processes, techniques, and know-how.

There is a difference between forgetting and unlearning. Forgetting can be categorized into two major forms—*planned* and *unplanned*. Planned forgetting is an active, deliberate, and intentional act where old data, information, and knowledge is consciously done away with. Unplanned forgetting is passive and often accidental, whereby organizations may lose vital data, information, or knowledge not actually intended to lose. Organizational forgetting may lead to consequences that may be either *positive* or *negative*. Thus, while forgetting may sometimes be good, in many cases, it may be disastrous too. On the basis of the type of forgetting activity and its consequences, a typology of organizational forgetting can be presented.[7]

This typology visualizes four forms of organizational forgetting, as shown in Figure 7.3.

Figure 7.3 The Forgetting Matrix

	Planned ←——————→ Unplanned	
Positive ↑ ↓ Negative	Unlearning	Decay
	Sabotage	Negligence

Source: F. T. Azmi (2009), Mapping the learn-unlearn-relearn model: Imperatives for strategic management, *European Business Review 20*(3): 240–259.

- **Negligence** This in unplanned loss of company data, information, knowledge, skill, or methods due to dereliction or carelessness. Employee negligence may lead to loss of information. It may also happen if knowledge is not coded and stored systematically. It has negative consequences for the organization, more so if vital information is lost.

- **Sabotage** This is wilful and deliberate destruction of valuable data, information, or knowledge. Often such a phenomenon may be the result of a negative behaviour of employees or outsiders. Emerging cyber crimes such as hacking and data diddling, to name a few, are some of the common examples of information sabotage.
- **Decay** This refers to the phenomenon of natural loss of old skills or knowledge due to the continuous organizational life cycle. As organizations evolve and grow, there is a natural tendency to forget certain information and skills of the past that are no longer required. As skills and knowledge become obsolete, people tend to gradually forget them. This is actually good for the organization.
- **Unlearning** Unlearning involves a conscious effort to weed out knowledge that has become dysfunctional. It requires a planned and deliberate strategy to do away with obsolete knowledge. It is different from decay as it involves a consciously designed strategy to systematically do away with past learning.

While negligence and sabotage have negative consequences, decay and unlearning have positive implications. However, since decay is an unplanned approach to forgetting, it may sometimes result in loss of valuable information. For example, the economic analysis of Lockheed's production records over a 14-year period shows only 60 per cent of the company's experience is retained from one year to the next. Furthermore, according to the popular press, organizational forgetting at NASA has caused numerous preventable accidents and losses worth hundreds of millions of dollars.

Therefore, business organizations cannot afford to have an unplanned approach to forgetting. The focus has to be on organizational forgetting that is planned, deliberate, and systematic, thereby leading to positive consequences for the organization. Organizational unlearning is, therefore, the most desirable form of forgetting.

Apart from learning and unlearning, the third prerequisite to success is relearning. Organizations need to learn, then unlearn, and relearn. The process of unlearning thereafter needs to be followed by the process of relearning. Relearning will foster organizational replenishment with new set of skills and competencies.

Relearning is based on a continuous process of organizational renewal—where traditional and archaic systems are replenished. It is an established fact that change or transition involves assimilation of new skills; hence, the need for relearning. Since every transition is about some relearning, organizations need to have a conscious strategy of managing transitions through a continuous and seamless process of relearning. This can be ingrained in the organizational culture where people consciously acquire new skills and knowledge and relearn. Organizations that do not make a concerted effort to relearn will find lost in old knowledge at a high cost.

CAREER PLANNING AND DEVELOPMENT

Career development plays an important role in engaging and retaining employees. A comprehensive career development policy helps boost employee engagement and increases retention. *Career* refers to the occupational positions a person holds over the years. *Career development* is a series of activities (training, development, and promotion) that contribute to a person's career success and fulfilment. *Career planning* is the deliberate process of identifying an employee's skills, interests, knowledge, and other characteristics; setting career-related goals; and establishing action plans to attain those goals. *Career management* is a process of enabling employees to better understand and develop their career skills and interests and to use these skills and interests most effectively both within the company and after they leave the firm.

Career planning and development requires a more comprehensive strategy than training. It necessitates honing capabilities that go beyond those required by the current job. Development efforts concentrate on how to prepare employees for future jobs in the company. A planned system of development for all employees can help expand the overall level of capabilities in an organization.

Career Management Systems

Organizations deploy various kinds of career management tools. Some of the career development tools commonly used by modern-day organizations are:

Career centres   A career centre is a place (offline or online) that provides employees with access to career development material. Employers create libraries containing books and reading material that help employees enhance their learning and make themselves eligible for career options. These career centres have experienced coaches to guide employees to develop their own career maps. They help employees crystallize their career goals and achieve them. In addition to career development training and follow-up support, these centres provide various career assessment and planning tools.

Career planning workshops   A career planning workshop is a planned learning event in which participants are expected to be actively involved, undertake career planning exercises, and participate in career skills practice sessions. A typical workshop includes self-assessment exercises, assessment of important occupational trends, goal-setting, and planning. Career workshops use vocational guidance tools to help employees identify career gaps, related skills, and their development needs.

Career-oriented appraisals   Performance appraisals should not only tell someone how he or she has done. They must also provide a basis to link the employee's performance, career interests, and developmental needs into a coherent career plan. An effective performance appraisal provides an opportunity to discuss and link the employee's performance, career interests, and developmental needs into a coherent career plan. The main aim is to help the manager and employee translate the employee's performance appraisal into tangible development plans and goals.

Career mapping   Career maps or career paths provide employees with a clear roadmap that outlines what it takes to get from their current position to where they want to be. A career map is a visual, codified approach to career management. Career maps display alternative routes to growth in an organization. Many organizations today allow individuals to build their own career paths with the help of their mentors. Through computer networks, workers and managers alike have access to all the career maps within an organization.

Coaching and mentorship programmes   Many organizations have in place a formal coaching and mentorship programme for career development. Coaching focuses on educating, instructing, and training subordinates. Mentoring means advising, counselling, and guiding. Coaching usually focuses on daily tasks, such as routine operations, productivity, waste, quality, accidents, repairs, and customer complaints. Mentoring focuses on relatively hard-to-grasp longer-term issues and often touches on the person's psychology, such as motives, needs, aptitudes, and behaviours. Coaches and mentors help employees identify their development needs and obtain the training, professional development, and networking opportunities that they require to satisfy those needs.

For the employee, career planning means matching individual strengths and weaknesses with occupational opportunities and threats. For example, a person with a strong social orientation might be attracted to careers that entail interpersonal skills and social interactions. The employer's task is to gauge whether the job is a good fit with the candidate's skills and interests. Career-oriented appraisals help not just to appraise the employee but also to match the person's strengths and weaknesses with a feasible career path. A competent supervisor or manager can help the employee stay on the right career track by providing clear career development plans.

PROMOTIONS AND SUCCESSION PLANNING

Career planning decisions go hand-in-hand with promotion decisions. Employees always welcome promotions as they usually accompany better pay and more prestige and satisfaction. It leads to higher job satisfaction and organizational commitment.[8] For employers, promotions can provide opportunities to reward exceptional performances and to fill positions with competent employees. It also helps develop the needed HR capabilities for future challenges.

Many firms have informal promotion processes. They may or may not post open positions, and key managers may use their own criteria to make decisions. On the other hand, some organizations set formalized promotion programmes. Employees receive a formal promotion policy describing the criteria by which the firm awards promotions. These organizations may have career maps or paths for each employee. They have a system of posting open positions and their requirements for all employees. They usually maintain employee qualification databanks and use HRIS to determine vacancies and availability of manpower.

Promotion decisions have a bearing for a firm's succession planning. Succession planning is the process by which companies and businesses ensure that there is an orderly and planned transfer of powers, responsibilities, and authority as employees get promoted or leave the company. In terms of process, succession planning involves identifying positions and roles where vacancies are anticipated, and identifying how the company will fill those positions. If we think of human resource planning as ensuring that the right people and right skills are available so the company can meet its strategic and long-term goals, then it is clear that succession planning is an important part of this process. Not only does succession planning lead to timely filling of key positions—it also provides motivation and incentive for employees and helps foster a culture of internal promotion, development, and career opportunities

Promotion Decisions: Seniority versus Merit

Probably the most important decision is whether to base promotion on seniority or merit, or maybe a combination of the two. Most employers use prior performance as a guide and assume that exemplary past performance predicts fairly well that the person will do well on the new job. Merit-based promotions require not just performance appraisal but potential appraisal too. Organizations use tests or assessment centres to evaluate aptitude and competence of employees and to identify those with future potential. Other criteria could be education and experience, performance ratings from multiple sources, personnel record (such as absenteeism, discipline, and rewards), and systematic evaluation of needed traits and behaviours.

Vertical and Horizontal Promotions

Promotions are not necessarily upwards. Lateral or horizontal promotions are becoming increasingly common nowadays, especially in flat organizations. For instance, moving a production employee to HR to develop his or her soft skills is an example of horizontal promotion. Lateral promotions are different from transfers. A transfer is a move from one job to another, usually with no change in salary or grade. Employers may transfer a worker to vacate a position where he or she is no longer needed in order to fill one where he or she is needed. Lateral promotions give employees a chance for another assignment accompanied by more status, prestige, job enrichment, or perhaps, personal growth. Employees seek lateral promotions for personal enrichment, more interesting jobs, greater convenience, better hours, and location of work.

Career Plateaus

Career plateau is the point in time in one's career, where the possibility of a vertical promotion is low. Many people experience this situation at one point during their career of becoming 'stuck' with little or no movement up the career ladder, either for professional or personal reasons. The position of the employee becomes stagnant, with repetitive work and bleak chances of growth. There are different kinds of career plateaus:

- **Structural Plateau**   This is a phase when one has progressed to a point where the organizational structure prevents him or her from moving up due to non-availability of vacancies in higher grades.
- **Content Plateau**   This occurs when one has mastered the job and there is no longer a sense of challenge in the current position.
- **Learning Plateau**   When one has ceased growing and searching for learning opportunities to develop competencies, being unable to respond to changes or keep up with technological changes.
- **Life Plateau**   This is the stage when one experiences a loss of identity, direction, meaning, or self-esteem, or when one undergoes doubt in life. In many ways, this is the most serious plateau since it often affects one's health and mental state, thereby having a strong bearing on work performance.

Plateaus are sometimes a consequence of a lack of organizational growth or change. They may also occur because of the rigid pyramidal organizational structures. Another cause of plateaus is related to developmental programmes. Employees who are left out of developmental programmes are often relegated to dead-end career paths and become victims of career plateaus. Often personal inertia or lack of drive in employees, weak employability, and lack of requisite skills may be the reasons behind career plateaus. Career plateaus tend to have a serious detrimental impact on job satisfaction and performance.

Employee development initiatives have to be linked to strategic plans and not designed as standalone HR programmes. Strategically designed developmental plans, challenging assignments, job enrichment and enlargement, job rotation, and lateral promotions are some of the ways to help reduce plateaus. The stress associated with career plateaus may be reduced by managerial interventions such as providing recognition and appreciation. Jobs have to be made more meaningful and engaging. It is important to help employees manage stress and frustration, restructure their views of success, rationalize expectations, and look for more innovative ways to contribute to the organization.

Dual Career Paths

Technical and professional workers, such as engineers and scientists, present a special challenge for organizations. Most of these people like the idea of the responsibility and opportunity associated with advancement, but they do not want to leave the technical field at which they excel. The dual career ladder attempts to solve this problem. Under such an arrangement, a person can advance up either the management ladder or a corresponding ladder on the technical/professional side.

Dual career paths have been used at IBM for years. They are most common in technology-driven industries, such as pharmaceuticals, chemicals, computers, and electronics. Many organizations have created a dual career ladder to reward talented technical people who do not want to move into management. Different tracks, each with attractive job titles and pay opportunities, are provided. The exploration division of British Petroleum (BP) creates two parallel career paths, one for managers and another for engineers. At BP, engineers can move up to non-supervisory but senior positions. These jobs carry similar financial rewards as those for management positions at that level.

Implementing a satisfactory promotion process is not a smooth sail for organizations. Biases, favouritism, and inaccurate appraisals can undermine the effectiveness of the process. In some organizations, promotions sometimes take the form of more challenging and not necessarily higher or better-paid positions. Furthermore, in flat organizations, opportunities for upwards promotion are often limited and there is a dilemma of how to plan out a satisfying promotion strategy.

Companies succeeding with succession planning tie in the process to business strategy. High-performing companies identify talent that can be further developed for future leadership roles. For example, a person targeted to fill an anticipated vacancy from within may be encouraged to take relevant university courses or attend seminars for the skill building act so as to prepare the organization for succession planning.

Companies are today witnessing 'career transitions'. The career ladder in a number of organizations is getting altered. Positions are getting replaced by computers. Many firms have sharpened their focus on core competencies, reducing the need for certain types of workers. Project-based work is growing, making careers a series of projects, not steps upward. Small businesses, start-up companies, and new ventures have shifted the focus away from career ladders of big companies towards new career opportunities. There are massive shifts in traditional career theories and assumptions.

Further, organization-centred career planning is giving way to individual-centred career planning. The organization-centred career planning focuses on jobs and career paths that provide for the progression of people. These paths are designed keeping in mind organizational priorities. Individual-centred career planning focuses on individuals' careers rather than organizational needs. It is done by employees themselves. Such analyses might consider situations both inside and outside the organization that could expand a person's career.

The 'new career' is one in which the individual—and not the organization—manages his or her own development. Many organizations are promoting this self-reliance as the basis for development, encouraging employees to focus on creating employability in the uncertain future. The imperative is to connect employees' personal career aspirations with organizational needs and strategies. Otherwise, the investment that an organization makes in developing employees and succession planning will go in vain.

HR Anecdote

Act I: Long time ago, there was a tortoise and a hare who decided to have a race. The hare sprinted ahead briskly for some time. Realizing that he was far ahead, he decided to rest under a tree and fell asleep. The tortoise, crawling at a steady pace, eventually won the race. **Moral: *Slow and steady wins the race*.**

Act II: The hare realized that he was over confident and took things too easily. He had learnt his lesson. He decided to have a rematch with the tortoise. This time, the hare ran with all his might and didn't stop until he crossed the finish line. **Moral: *In the present times, fast and consistent will outshine*.**

Act III: This time, it was the tortoise that did the soul searching and learnt an important lesson. He realized there is no way he will beat the hare, except on a different course. They started the race and the hare was taken by surprise when they reached a river. The tortoise strolled slowly, dived into the river, swam across it and won. **Moral: *Know your strengths and take on competitors in areas of your core competency*.**

Act IV: The hare and the tortoise realized that they have different strengths. They decided to race again, but as a team. As the race started, the hare carried the tortoise when on land and the tortoise carried the hare on the river. **Moral: *It's good to be individually brilliant but we are stronger as a team*.**

In an age when the environment changes at lightning speed, we have to learn from our mistakes and improve.

Source: Retrieved and adapted from https://www.speakingtree.in/blog/hare-tortoise-story-a-new-meaning.

News Grab
Training Practices in Indian Companies: Survey

A survey by the Institution of Engineering and Technology (IET) shows that nearly two-thirds (65%) of mid-size companies choose to impart soft-skill training over technical training to new employees. In comparison, only a quarter of large-sized companies focus on soft skill development, and the remaining 75% prefer imparting technical skill. The survey covered over 120 large- and mid-sized companies across seven cities.

The survey shows that both large- and mid-sized companies provide some form of training to employees. Overall, 35% of the companies surveyed said that offline methods of training are preferred as they ensure employee attendance and are taken more seriously. The study brings to the fore some challenges in the current training landscape. With automation, AI and blockchain leading the business paradigms, upskilling isn't a one-time activity. The key skill that would help organizations excel is the 'ability to unlearn and relearn'.

Employers need to personalize the training module according to the needs of the employees and industry. 20% of large-sized companies felt training was the most important tool to keep abreast with industry innovations, while 23% of the respondents agreed that training is essential to gain insights for better product development.

With regards to engaging with external agencies to impart training, all large corporates said they have in-house training departments and 29% have tie-ups with external agencies. In the case of mid-sized organizations, only 5% were found to have tie-ups with external training agencies and most of them had HR departments managing the training requirements of the company.

Source: Adapted from B. Sarkar (2018), 65% of mid-size companies opt for soft skill training: Survey, *Economic Times*, 3 July, retrieved from economictimes.indiatimes.com/articleshow/64834815.cms?utm_source=contentofinterest&utm_medium=text&utm_campaign=cppst.

CHAPTER SUMMARY

- Strategic training and development involve integrating training and development with corporate strategies.
- It entails shifting the focus from traditional training to learning.
- Learning is not a one-shot programme, but it is an ongoing process.
- The concept of learning iceberg is based on the learn–act–share perspective.
- The ADDIE training model can be applied to the broader concept of learning.
- E-learning comprises an extensive array of digitization approaches to impart learning.
- Learning requires both ability and willingness to learn. The more personalized a learning experience is, the more engaging it is.
- Unlearning is a planned and deliberate effort to come out of a particular style of functioning that is no longer viable.
- Career development plays an important role in engaging and retaining employees.
- Succession planning is the process by which companies ensure that there is an orderly and planned transfer of powers, responsibilities, and authority.

EXERCISES AND DISCUSSION QUESTIONS

1. Discuss the difference between training and learning. Why is a learning orientation important in today's competitive scenario?
2. Discuss the various modes of e-learning. Is learning today a blended mechanism?
3. Examine the training and development practices in an organization of your choice and comment on the following:
   i. Whether the approach is traditional or strategic in nature.
   ii. The different components of the ADDIE model of imparting learning evident in the organization.

CASELET

How Toyota Learns to Excel

Toyota is known for reliability, quality, and durability. It is the pioneer of modern production techniques and an epitome of operational excellence. Even if its reputation has taken a beating in the last few years because of some product recalls and quality issues, Toyota's standing as the benchmark of an excellent production mechanism is undeniable.

Behind Toyota's secrets to building an exceptional production system, called the Toyota Production System (TPS), is the strength of its highly capable people. However, Toyota's journey to creating this immaculate system was not without hiccups. When people were required to come out of their comfort zones and become multiskilled, the company encountered resistance. This was a big lesson. The architects of the system learned that embarking onto a new system needs time and patience. Above all, it takes persistence and willingness to deal with individual peculiarities and challenges of each person.

The first requirement of TPS was to make people ready for change. They needed people to learn how to think innovatively to deal with failures. That mandated unlearning a lot of things. When Taiichi Ohno, the chief architect of TPS discovered the importance of learning, he sought a method that would support his needs. He found such a tool in the job instruction (JI) method taught by the American occupation forces after World War II. It has been the primary teaching tool for Toyota ever since. Today, the learning capabilities of Toyota employees are a hallmark.

Toyota likes to start with people who possess the capability to become exceptional employees. Toyota selects employees who have the *willingness and ability to learn*. People are carefully selected to join Toyota based on their potential and a judgement that there is a fit with the job and with Toyota's culture. They must have basic problem-solving capabilities and be willing to work as part of a team. People develop specific capabilities after they are hired at Toyota through careful training and development. Toyota's unique learning culture helps mould the individual to fit the needs of the organization as well as support the interests of the individual. It is this mutuality of purpose that leads to satisfied and successful employees.

Toyota is considered as a truly learning organization. Toyota's learning organization is based on the following ideas:

1. Ask 'why' when faced with problems: The emphasis is on identifying the root cause of problems and taking corrective measures.

2. Japanese concepts of *hansei* (relentless reflection) and *kaizen* (continuous improvement): This concept is about reflecting on mistakes and devising ways to improve.
3. Integrate goals: This is Toyota's process of cascading objectives from the top of the company down to the work group level. Toyota realized that the key to organizational learning is to align objectives of all of its employees towards common goals. Each level develops objectives to support the overarching organizational goals.

The basic philosophy at Toyota is to develop gradually (*heijunka*) but continuously through learning. Everything in production undergoes careful scrutiny and quality check. As cars roll out the assembly lines, they go through a final inspection station. If the staff spots even a simple defect, such as chipped off paint, they do not just quietly fix the problem by merely touching up the paint. They try to explore systemic or procedural deficiencies that may have contributed to the problem, asking a series of 'whys' that may actually help uncover more serious and deeper troubles within the process.

The genius of Toyota lies in another Japanese expression *jojo*. It has gradually and steadily institutionalized common sense principles for waste reduction through years of learning. Toyota's success derives from balancing the role of people in a culture that expects and values continuous improvements. Toyota encourages employee empowerment in order to encourage the desired behaviour. The underlying value system of Toyota's culture does that. It has an innovative incentive system to encourage people to develop capabilities and excel.

Toyota's success as a learning organization is not an overnight story. It has taken years of consistent efforts for Toyota to achieve this. Senior managers at the company feel that it took Toyota more than a decade to build an organization that even comes close to the concept of a learning organization. Companies that have tried to emulate Toyota's success mantra have realized that it is not just about management tools but about putting in place a culture that values individuals.

Toyota has HR issues similar to those of other companies, such as attendance problems, resistance to change, dwindling motivation levels, and even reluctance to accept the TPS philosophy. What allows Toyota to be successful in spite of these challenges is the efforts and interest in drawing out the best of the employee's abilities and initiating customized training and learning solutions. Perhaps Toyota has recognized the reality of human behaviour and individual differences, and it has created systems that actually take advantage of those differences. Toyota succeeds as a learning organization because it has relentlessly pursued its passion to excel.

Toyota India

Toyota Kirloskar Motor Pvt. Ltd (TKM) was established in India in 1997. It is a subsidiary of Toyota in a joint venture with the Kirloskar Group of India (Kirloskar being a minority owner) for the manufacture and sales of Toyota cars in India. It is currently the 4th largest car maker in India. The company aims to play a major role in the development of the automotive industry and the creation of employment opportunities, with a business philosophy of 'Putting Customer First' and adopting sustainable business practices.

On 16 March 2014, TKM temporarily suspended production at two of its assembly plants in Bidadi, Karnataka, whose production capacity was 310,000 units annually and had an employee strength of 6,400. There was some disagreement between the labour union and management over the issue of wages. This led to deliberate stoppages of the production line by certain employees and abusing and threatening of supervisors, thereby disrupting production. The company announced on 21 March 2014 to lift the lockout at the plants subject to the acceptance of a service condition that required the employees to sign an undertaking of good conduct. On 22 April 2014, employees called off the strike after 36 days of standoff and resumed full operations.

Despite these industrial relations issues, the company has been able to make steady progress. The philosophy of mutual trust and respect is at the core. Employees are considered the most valuable asset. The company's fundamental DNA—the Toyota Way—enables the company to transcend language and nationality. The two supporting pillars are constant improvement and putting people first. Employee suggestions are taken seriously and implemented to improve the working environment. The company's operational excellence is based on the tools and methods developed by the parent company under the TPS, emphasizing superlative quality and minimal wastage. It adopts the same learning philosophy in India as the parent company. The website reads: 'With a spirit to constantly learn, teach, improve, and innovate, all our stake holders and families will collaborate to help make India a better place'.[9]

Questions for Discussion

1. What are the key aspects of Toyota's production system? Discuss the role of learning in making TPS a success.
2. Toyota has HR issues similar to those of other companies. Despite this, how does Toyota succeed in making a near steady progress globally as well as in India?

NOTES

1. P. Senge (1990), *The fifth discipline: The art and practice of learning organization* (London: Century Business).
2. C. Argyris and D. A. Schon (1996), *Organizational learning II: Theory, method, and practice* (Reading, MA: Addison-Wesley Publishing Company).
3. C. Fiol and M. Lyles (1985), Organizational learning, *Academy of Management Review 10*(4): 803–813.
4. M. K. Smith (2001), The learning organization, *The Encyclopedia of Informal Education*, retrieved from http://www.infed.org/biblio/learning-organization.htm.
5. K. W. Trinh (2005), Organizational memory: Conceptual framework and empirical operation, retrieved from http://www.faculty.haas.berkeley.edu/wakeman/CCC/Trinh.doc.
6. G. Dessler (2013), *Human resource management* (Upper Saddle River, NJ: Pearson Education).
7. F. T. Azmi (2008), Mapping the learn-unlearn-relearn model: Imperatives for strategic management, *European Business Review 20*(3): 240–259.
8. See, for instance, P. P. Carson, K. D. Carson, R. W. Griffeth, and R. P. Steel (1994), Promotion and employee turnover: Critique, meta-analysis, and implication, *Journal of Business and Psychology 8*: 455–466; G. M. Sharma and F. T. Azmi (2014), Relationship between retention factors, organisational commitment and actual turnover: An empirical study of Indian B-Schools, *IIMS Journal of Management Science 5*(2): 126–145.
9. With inputs from https://www.toyota-global.com; L. K. Jeffrey (2004), The Toyota Way: 14 *Management Principles from the World's Greatest Manufacturer* (New York: McGraw-Hill).

CHAPTER 8

Performance Management and Compensation

Chapter Overview

This chapter discusses the concept of performance appraisal and performance management. The limitations of the traditional appraisal process are identified. It focuses on the need to move from performance appraisal to performance management. Further, the concepts of compensation and rewards are discussed. The difference between traditional compensation and strategic compensation is highlighted. Various types of strategic compensation systems are examined. Issues related to compensation of top-level executives are also discussed.

Learning Objectives

1. To understand the concept and process of performance appraisal
2. To appreciate the need to move from performance appraisal to performance management
3. To understand the differences between traditional compensation and strategic compensation
4. To get familiarized with various types of strategic compensation systems

OPENING STORY

Evolving Performance Management Paradigm

Although performance management is a new concept, its origin can be traced back to many ancient civilizations and religious scriptures.

The Pre-historic Times

There is evidence that suggest that the first cave dwellers were handling issues of HR performance. The ancient Paleolithic men focused on selection of leaders, skill development, and so on.

The Ancient Egyptian Philosophy

Egyptians developed well-defined hierarchies with job descriptions. They deployed several time-saving performance management techniques, showing an understanding of what later evolved as time and motion study.

The Babylonian Philosophy

The famous leader Hammurabi prepared the first code of law and emphasized on learning and performance management.

The Chinese Philosophy

In ancient China, principles of people management were well developed. Confucius, the ancient Chinese thinker, focused on fair dealings vis-à-vis people and the role of a good leader in guiding people's performance.

Ancient Indian Philosophy

Indian scriptures are replete with ideas related to managing people. Valmiki, in his epic *Ramayana*, observed that high performers must get recognition. The *Bhagavad-Gita* recommends self-management, transformational leadership, and motivation for enhancing performance. Chanakya talked about incentive for performance in his treatise *Artha-Shastra*.

The Hebrew Philosophy

Hebrew history gives examples of leadership and performance management. Moses, the great leader, served as one of best examples of a participative human resource approach.

The Roman Philosophy

The Romans made use of many modern-day concepts like job descriptions, hierarchy with scalar chains of command, restructuring to enhance performance.

Biblical Philosophy

The Bible asks employers to be benevolent and value justice and equality. A manager must be honest so that workers reciprocate with hard work and higher performance.

Islamic Philosophy

The holy book Quran is a complete guide for life and provides numerous principles for ethical people management. The Quran and *Hadith* provide guidelines for fair selection, education and training, promotion, participative decision-making, and rewards for performance.

PERFORMANCE APPRAISAL

Performance appraisal is the process of evaluating how well employees perform their jobs compared to a set of standards. One important purpose of carrying out appraisals is to measure performance for the purpose of rewarding employees in the form of benefits, incentives, increments, or promotions. Under performance-oriented systems, employees receive raises based on how well they perform their jobs. Similarly, promotion or demotion decisions may be based on performance appraisal. Other administrative uses of performance appraisal could be in decisions related to transfers, layoffs, and termination.

The second important purpose of carrying out performance appraisal is development of employees. The emphasis is on measuring performance gaps and identifying training needs in order to design suitable training and development strategies. Performance appraisal can be a primary source of information for earmarking future developmental needs. When supervisors identify the weaknesses, strengths, potentials, and training needs of employees through performance appraisal, they can work out development plans for employees. Appraisals should also facilitate career planning. They provide a picture of employees' progression in order to aid future succession planning decisions.

Performance Appraisal Process

Performance appraisal typically involves a 3-step process: (*a*) setting work standards and targets, (*b*) assessing the employee's actual performance against those standards, and (*c*) preparing an appraisal report to identify shortcomings in performance.

Setting work standards and targets

Each job has specific job criteria or job performance dimensions that identify the elements most important in that job. Ideally, what to appraise will be obvious from an employee's job description. Individuals' performance on job criteria should be measured, compared against standards, and then the results must be communicated to each employee. Jobs almost always have more than one job criterion or dimension. Some criteria might have more importance than others. Weights are assigned on the basis of the relative importance of several job criteria in one job. For instance, in most universities, a college professor's teaching might be more important than research or service. When measuring performance, it is important that relevant criteria be used. Generally, criteria are relevant when they focus on the most important aspects of employees' jobs.

Performance standards define the expected levels of performance and are 'benchmarks', 'goals', or 'targets'. Performance standards define what satisfactory job performance is. It is important to establish standards before the work is performed, so that all involved will understand the level of accomplishment expected.

Assessing performance

Once targets and standards have been set, the next step is actual appraisal. Performance appraisal is the process of evaluating how well employees perform their jobs when compared to a set of standards. The typical questions to be addressed here are who will appraise, when to appraise, what to appraise, and how to appraise.

Who appraises

The human resource (HR) unit typically designs and maintains the appraisal system. The HR department serves a policy-making and advisory role. They prepare formal reports and documents and use reports for training, compensation, and other activities. Generally, HR provides advice on the appraisal tool to use, but leave final decisions on procedures to operating division head. The manager or supervisor does the actual appraising of the employee, using the procedures developed by the HR unit. Traditional rating of employees by supervisors is based on the assumption that the immediate supervisor is the person most qualified to evaluate the employee's performance. The supervisor is usually in the best position to observe and evaluate his or her subordinate's performance. Managers may offer input on how the final system will work.

When to appraise

A regular time interval is a feature of systematic appraisals that distinguishes them from informal appraisals. The appraisal period may vary for different types of employees. Appraisals typically are conducted once or twice a year, six-monthly, or annually. Probationers or new employees, or those who are new and in a trial period, are usually evaluated more frequently—weekly or monthly—until they complete their probation period. While annual appraisal is common in conventional industry sectors, some high-growth companies in high-tech industries carry out frequent appraisals—six months instead of a year—so that employees receive more frequent training and incentives.

What to appraise

The basic and critical questions in designing the actual appraisal tool are what performance dimensions to measure. Performance measures typically used are both objective and subjective. Objective measures can be directly quantified—for example, the number of units produced. Subjective measures are more judgemental and more difficult to measure directly—an employee's communication skills.

Typically speaking, the data that managers receive on how well employees are performing their jobs can be of three different types. *Trait-based* criteria identify a character trait such as conscientiousness, initiative, and creativity that may be needed for a specific job. Traits tend to be subjective and, therefore, slightly ambiguous, leading to the view that performance evaluations based on traits are too vague to be used for crucial organizational decisions such as promotions or terminations. *Behaviour-based* criteria focus on specific behaviours that lead to job success. For a sales professional, the behaviour 'effective negotiation skills' can be used as a criterion of performance. Behavioural aspects are difficult to measure and are subjective, such as trait-based criteria. *Results-based* information considers what the employee has done or accomplished in terms of specific end-results. For jobs in which measurement of output or productivity is easy, a results-based approach works very well. It is more objective and realistic. However, it overemphasizes objective, quantitative, and measureable criteria and the equally important but qualitative dimensions of the job may be ignored.

Keeping in mind different criteria and their limitations, a combination of criteria are sometimes used by managers for appraising employees.

How to appraise

In terms of how to measure performance, one can use one or more of various tools or methods mentioned below:

Category Rating Methods

The simplest methods for appraising performance are category rating methods, which require a manager to mark an employee's level of performance on a specific form divided into categories of performance. The common category rating methods are:

- **Graphic Rating Scale**   A graphic rating scale lists traits or performance dimensions (such as manual dexterity or interpersonal skills) and a range of performance values as in a five-point Likert-type scale (such as *unsatisfactory* to *outstanding*) for each dimension. It allows the rater or supervisor to tick a descriptor that best defines the subordinate's performance for each trait. The rater then totals the assigned ratings for the traits.
- **Checklist**   The checklist is composed of a list of statements or words. Raters check statements most representative of the traits and performance of employees. The checklist can be modified so that varying weights are assigned to the statements or words. The results can then be quantified.

Comparative Methods

Comparative methods require that managers or supervisors directly compare the performance of their employees with each other. These include:

- **Ranking**   This method involves ranking and listing all employees from highest to lowest in performance by comparing them on a common criterion or parameter.
- **Paired comparison**   The paired comparison method involves comparing an employee with other. For every trait, the rater compares each employee with the other employees. Then,

for each trait, the rater may indicate who the better employee in the pair is. This method is common in organizations that rely heavily on groups or teams.

- **Forced distribution**   Forced ranking or forced distribution is a technique for distributing ratings on a curve. With this method, raters place predetermined percentages of employees into several performance categories. With the forced distribution method, the ratings of employees' performance are distributed along a bell-shaped curve. This is similar to the grading scheme introduced in most schools and colleges nowadays.

Narrative Methods

The narrative method requires managers to provide written appraisal reports. These reports describe an employee's actions, behaviour, and performance rather than ranking them.

- **Critical incident technique**   In the critical incident method, the manager keeps a written record of both highly favourable and unfavourable actions in an employee's performance. When a 'critical incident' involving an employee occurs, the manager writes it down. Compiling incidents are useful as they provide examples of both good and poor performance.
- **Essay**   The essay or free-form appraisal method requires the manager to write a short essay describing each employee's performance. The rater usually is given a few general headings, like strengths and weaknesses, under which to categorize comments. The intent is to allow the rater more flexibility than other methods do.
- **Field review**   The field review has as much to do with who does the evaluation as the method used. This approach can include the HR department as a reviewer or a completely independent reviewer outside the organization. In the field review, the outside reviewer becomes an active partner in the rating process. The reviewer's rating is examined by the supervisor for needed changes.

Behavioural Methods

Under behavioural rating approaches, job incumbents are evaluated according to their performance on a set of job behaviours. Some of the common behavioural approaches are:

- **Behaviourally anchored rating scale (BARS)**   A BARS is an appraisal tool that anchors a numerical rating scale with specific illustrative examples of good or poor performance. BARS match descriptions of possible behaviours with the employee's most commonly exhibited behaviours. It involves identifying critical incidents or behaviours expected in a job, developing performance dimensions, such as negotiation skills, placing the critical incidents on a scale to rate behaviours. It is considered more effective than the other appraisal tools.
- **Behavioural observation scales (BOS)**   BOS are a variation of the BARS approach in that they add graphic rating scales to the observable behaviours that are developed from

critical incidents as in BARS. BOS are used to count the number of times certain behaviours are exhibited.

- **Behavioural expectation scales (BES)**   BES show order of behaviours on a continuum to define outstanding, average, and unacceptable performance.

Behavioural rating approaches require defining the behaviour associated with each level of performance. They are considered superior to other rating approaches in inter-rater reliability or in reducing leniency or halo errors. The greatest contribution of these approaches may be through their role as a feedback mechanism.

Management by Objectives (MBO)

One very popular performance appraisal technique is management by objectives (MBO). The technique was first championed by management expert Peter Drucker and became commonly used in the 1960s.[1] MBO generally refers to a comprehensive and formal organization-wide goal setting and appraisal programme. MBO is a management practice that aims to increase organizational performance by aligning goals and subordinate objectives throughout the organization.

In MBO, managers and employees work together to set goals with the intent of helping employees to achieve continuous improvement through an ongoing process of goal setting, feedback, and correction. The objectives that each manager sets are derived from the overall goals and objectives of the organization. As a result of their input, employees are much more likely to be motivated to accomplish their goals and to be responsive to criticism that arises from subsequent objective measurements of performance. Rewards are based on goal achievement.

There is no one best appraisal method. Category rating methods are easy to develop, but they usually do not contribute to measure strategic accomplishments. Comparative approaches help reduce several biases and errors, but they do a poor job of linking performance to organizational goals. The narrative methods provide detailed and informative descriptions, but suffer from subjectivity issues. MBOs are believed to be a practice that relies heavily on goals. Individual appraisal may often fail to take into account environmental factors that hinder goal achievement, such as lack of resources. The behavioural rating techniques and MBO are considered more future-oriented and modern as compared to the previously discussed techniques.

Preparing Appraisal Report

Once appraisals have been completed, it is important to communicate it to employees so that they have a clear understanding of how they have been assessed through what is called as the appraisal report. The appraisal feedback interview enables the employee and supervisor to have a discussion related to performance. The purpose of the interview is to let the employee and manager work together to identify performance gaps, training needs, and future goals. The process should emphasize counselling and development. A genuine feedback mechanism can help clear up misunderstandings.

WEAKNESSES OF PERFORMANCE APPRAISAL SYSTEM

The traditional performance appraisal approach suffers from several limitations:

- **Periodic assessment**   Traditional appraisal involves a periodic assessment of an employee's performance that lacks continuity.
- **Single person top-down assessment**   In many firms, the assessment is done by a single manager—usually the immediate supervisor or boss. This affects the genuineness and reliability of the process.
- **Poorly trained managers**   In a lot of organizations, managers are not adequately trained to conduct appraisals effectively.
- **Not reliable or valid**   Most companies do not regularly demonstrate with metrics that the process is consistent and that it accurately assesses valid performance. Inter-rater reliability is generally very low between managers. Often there are inconsistent ratings. This happens due to faulty form designs that lack reliability and validity.
- **Central tendency, leniency, and strictness errors**   A manager may develop a rating pattern that is leaning on one side. Some supervisors stick to the middle when filling in rating scales. Appraisers who rate all employees within a narrow range (usually, the middle or average) commit a *central tendency error*. Sometimes in order to avoid conflicts and gain popularity and likeability, managers often rate employees higher than they deserve. This is called as *leniency error*. The *strictness error* occurs when a manager assesses employees strictly or 'harshly' and rates employees low in scores.
- **Not tied to performance improvement**   The purpose of performance appraisal is to provide the organization with an assessment of employee strengths and opportunities for improvement and development purposes. Unfortunately, few companies do this.
- **Focus on weaknesses**   Most performance appraisal systems focus on weak performers. There is significantly less focus on top performers, and, thus, there is no system to capture their best practices and then to share them with others.
- **Confidentiality of assessments**   In many organizations, appraisal reports are kept secret. An overemphasis on privacy concerns might allow managers to favour certain employees, to discriminate, and to be extremely subjective. This also compromises the sanctity of the appraisal process.

These limitations make traditional performance appraisals merely an exercise in paperwork and documentation without much utility.

PERFORMANCE APPRAISAL TO PERFORMANCE MANAGEMENT

The terms 'performance appraisal' and 'performance management' are sometimes used synonymously, but they are different. Performance appraisal typically involves managers rating the performance of their subordinates. Performance management is a comprehensive, continuous, and flexible approach to the management of performance of teams and individuals involving dialogue between those concerned.

In many organizations, appraisal is not tied to the larger strategic goals. In too many organizations, getting a merit raise, bonus, or promotion is completely disconnected from an employee's performance appraisal scores. Often, appraisal is disconnected with training and development, rewards, promotions, or future manpower planning. Performance appraisal should enable self-assessment. If an employee wishes to self-assess his or her performance midstream in order to improve, the processes should facilitate this. Appraisal should be a two-way communication. However, in reality, employees often have no input into the factors that they are assessed on, how often they are assessed, and what type of feedback they can receive.

Performance appraisal takes place as a one-time activity. Aligning the employee's efforts with strategic goals should be a continuous process. An organization cannot afford to continue with mistakes for the sake of implementing a periodic appraisal process. Similarly, when someone does something well, rewards should come immediately, not six months or one year later. Strategic integration of appraisals requires a regular and continuous cycle of appraisal–feedback–development. Periodic assessments only heighten anxiety levels and make employees improve performance only when they know the appraisal period is close. This is because 'recency effects' lead to higher rankings by their bosses. This actually mars the spirit of the entire process.

Recognizing this, many employers today take a more continuous approach to the performance appraisal cycle. For example, at Toyota Motors, supervisors do not fill out forms and appraise employees. Instead, teams of employees monitor their own results, even posting individual daily performance metrics. They continuously align those results with the work team's standards and with strategic needs. Team members who need training receive it immediately. This is performance management in action.

These differences are shown in Table 8.1.

Table 8.1 Performance Appraisal versus Performance Management

Performance Appraisal	*Performance Management*
Not linked to strategic goals	Linked to strategic goals
Top-down assessment	360-degree assessment
Annual appraisal	Continuous review
Use of ratings	Ratings less common
Monolithic system	Flexible process involving dialogue
Focus on quantified objectives	Focus on behaviours as well as objectives
Often not linked to pay	Linked to pay and development
Bureaucratic - complex paperwork	Minimum documentation, use of IT
Confidential reports	Feedback and counselling
Owned by the HR department	Owned by managers

A number of companies are moving from performance appraisal to performance management. Performance management is a goal-oriented and continuous way to appraise and manage employees' performance. It is a continuous process of identifying, measuring, and developing the performance of individuals and teams and aligning their performance with the organization's goals. The difference between performance management and performance appraisal is subtle but distinct. Many companies claim to have put in place a performance management process, but what they have in reality is the traditional performance appraisal. Continuous feedback and strategically linked performance criteria are the two important distinguishing characteristics of performance management.

Figure 8.1 shows how the concept of 'time' varies between performance appraisal and performance management systems.

Figure 8.1   Performance Appraisal versus Performance Management: Timelines

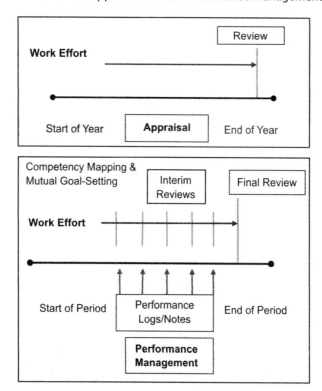

A performance measurement system that is strategically linked helps assess the degree to which the behaviour of employees at all organizational levels are congruent with organizational strategies and contributes to the attainment of strategic goals. Performance management is about providing support as well as direction. This is an inclusive and collaborative process. Evidence suggests that participative goal-setting produces higher performance.[2] The focus is on changing behaviour rather than doing tedious paperwork involving appraisal, with no concrete long-term results. Managing performance is about coaching, guiding, appraising, motivating, and rewarding employees to help unleash potential and improve organizational performance.

Some of the features of strategically linked performance management are:

- There is strategic linkage of performance targets with goals
- Strategic performance management relies on consensus and cooperation
- It relies on setting specific and measurable goals
- It encourages self-management of individual performance
- It requires a management style that is open and encourages two-way communication
- It provides a clear framework for growth

Performance evaluations can be successful only when employees understand the dimensions of performance on which they will be evaluated, know that they are being evaluated on relevant aspects of their jobs, view the evaluation process as valid, and see reward as fair. Feedback loops enable employees to develop an understanding of roles and expectations.

360-degree Appraisal

One of the problems with traditional performance appraisals in which only superiors evaluate their subordinates is that performance is evaluated from only one perspective. Due to the limitations of traditional top-down performance evaluation approaches, 360-degree feedback systems have been adopted by most leading companies such as Shell Oil, Exxon, IBM, GE, and AT&T.

The German Military first began gathering feedback from multiple sources in order to evaluate performance during World War II.[3] One of the earliest recorded uses of surveys to gather information about employees from multiple sources occurred in the 1950s at Esso Research and Engineering Company.[4] From there, the idea of 360-degree feedback gained momentum. However, it gained popularity only recently.

360-degree feedback or multi-source feedback is an appraisal or performance assessment tool that incorporates feedback from all who observe and are affected by the performance of a candidate. 360-degree appraisal has five integral components:

1. **Self-appraisal**   Self-appraisal gives a chance to the employee to look at his/her strengths, weaknesses, and achievements, and judge his/her own performance.
2. **Appraisal by senior**   The manager's perception of an employee's performance is still an important part of the evaluation process. It gives a chance to judge employees on parameters such as communication and motivating abilities, superior's ability to delegate the work, and leadership qualities.
3. **Appraisal by subordinate**   It is the concept of having supervisors and managers rated by juniors or subordinates. It is analogous to the type of rating used in colleges and universities, where students evaluate the performance of professors. This type of rating makes managers more responsive to employees.
4. **Peer or team appraisal**   The use of peer groups as raters is beneficial for organizations that rely heavily on teams. Peer ratings are especially useful when supervisors do not have the opportunity to observe each employee's performance, but other work group members do. The feedback given by peers can help to find employees' abilities to work in a team, and for cooperation and sensitivity towards others.

Participative management approaches such as quality circles (QCs) and total quality management (TQM) emphasize teamwork. Here, individual performance appraisal is seen as part of team performance. Team appraisal is done and any deficiencies in performance of members are collectively discussed.

5. **Outsider appraisal** Rating also may be done by outsiders. The customers or clients of an organization are obvious sources for outside appraisals. For salespeople and other service personnel, customers may be a good source of feedback. For people in purchase departments, reviews from suppliers or vendors may help.

Figure 8.2 illustrates the concept of 360-degree appraisal.

Figure 8.2   360-Degree Appraisal

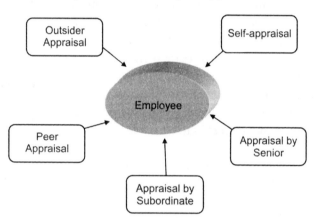

The purpose of 360-degree feedback is to capture all of the differing evaluations that bear on the individual employee's different roles. Multi-rater feedback steadily increased in popularity due to the use of the Internet in conducting web-based surveys.[5] In recent years, Internet-based services are being used with a growing menu of features such as graphic interface, multiple commands, comparative analysis, and aggregate reporting.

Advantages and Disadvantages of 360-degree Appraisal

360-degree appraisal is a powerful developmental tool. Since it involves a comprehensive and all-round feedback, it helps strengthen employee self-development. In addition, because the ratings in 360-degree feedback systems can be anonymous, a much more honest evaluation is possible. It helps improve the credibility of the performance appraisal mechanism.

The 360-degree feedback system is better suited to many of today's organizations, which are decreasing their reliance on centralized control and hierarchical decision-making. 360-degree appraisal also increases the responsibilities of employees towards customers. Most big organizations today that focus on employee development use the 360-degree tool to enable employees to map their career path based on feedback. It is also used for making administrative decisions, such as pay or promotion. Usually, this tool is used for employees at the middle and senior levels. The complexity of their roles enables the organization to generate sufficient data from all stakeholders for a meaningful assessment.

As with any system, there can be problems with the implementation of 360-degree feedback systems. It is important to note that more information does not necessarily create better results. A 360-degree review takes a lot of time in designing and is complex in administration. Typical 360 reports may be long with charts, graphs, and comments. Sometimes it is difficult for an employee to tell which items are most important to focus on. Issues of anonymity and breach of privacy can also become major problems because of many people being involved in the process.

Gaps between self-perceptions and other's perceptions may cause confusion. A feedback experience that leaves an employee confused or angry creates a huge barrier to taking action. Feedback can be useless if it is not carefully and smoothly dealt with. A 360-degree feedback system is supposed to be more appropriate for developmental purposes than for appraisal purposes. When used for appraisal purposes, there is much room for internal politics and self-serving behaviours because anonymous evaluators, especially coworkers, could intentionally evaluate a manager lower in order to increase their own chances for a promotion. Differences among raters can present a challenge, especially if a 360-degree rating is used for discipline or pay decisions. In addition, there are greater chances of rating biases creeping in during the process because of a number of evaluators being involved. Sometimes, it can lead managers trying to become 'nice' rather than effective in order to get good scores from subordinates or peers.

Making 360-degree appraisals work means making it as easy as possible for managers to take action on the results. The entire rating mechanism, scales, evaluation forms, and assessment criteria should be carefully structured and designed so as to avoid any chances of errors. A well-designed 360-degree report should include specific action points and bulleted suggestions from raters that describe exactly how the manager should change. 360-degree data should guide decisions related to rewards, promotions, or development. Organizations should train people in giving unbiased feedback.

In spite of the value of performance evaluation systems, such systems are not used very frequently for senior executives in most organizations.[6] More specifically, the higher one rises in an organization, the less likely one is to receive quality feedback about job performance. Several questionable beliefs exist regarding performance evaluation at the executive level. These myths could be that performance evaluation goes against a senior position's dignity and may be detrimental to executive creativity, innovative thinking, and autonomy. Nonetheless, executives desire feedback. Suggestions from subordinates may be helpful in encouraging the use of performance evaluation at executive levels.

Competency-based Appraisal

Some organizations appraise employees based on the competencies and skills the job requires. A competency-based employee appraisal process focuses on the skills and competencies necessary to be successful and appraises employees on the basis of actual and desired competencies. The performance targets may include strategically important behaviours, such as building trust or customer satisfaction. These strategically relevant core behaviours enable the managers to identify competencies to appraise employees. For example, in the chapter on job analysis, British Petroleum's (BP's) skill matrix was discussed. BP uses its skill matrix for a number of HR activities, such as job analysis, recruitment, appraisal, training, and rewards. This matrix shows the basic skills or competencies required to do a job and the minimum level of each skill that the job requires.

Competency-based appraisal systems allow managers and supervisors to identify gaps in competencies and deploy remedial measures. Developing competency-based performance management systems typically involves creating comprehensive competency models for all jobs and assessing employees against those models during performance reviews. By identifying core competencies that align with the company's mission, vision, and goals, management can consistently and fairly appraise employees. Assessment centres are an important tool for competency-based appraisal.

An assessment centre is a mechanism to evaluate an individual's potential and performance. This method tests a candidate in different social situations using a number of assessor and procedures. An assessment centre typically involves the use of methods such as social events, tests, exercises, and assignments to assess different competencies. Techniques such as business games, role playing, and in-basket exercises are also used in this method.

When an assessment centre is being set up, it must be designed with a specific purpose in mind. A preliminary statement of organizational objectives may be drawn up, indicating who is to be assessed, who the assessors will be, what target positions will be tested for, and other considerations. Trained evaluators observe and evaluate employees. After the assessors have completed their evaluations, all of the assessments are then pooled. Nowadays, assessment centres have taken the shape of development centres. These hybrid centres, which combine aspects of performance assessment and development, help provide participants with feedback on how to create their own personal development programme.

APPRAISAL FEEDBACK AND COUNSELLING

An important component of strategically linked performance management systems is the mechanism of feedback and performance counselling. Constructive and continuous feedback helps in changing behaviours to reach the desired state. It builds people's confidence to do better. A feedback interview is the process of sharing concerns and issues related to one's appraisal.

Feedback involves three important stages:

- **Pre-Interview Stage** Before the actual feedback interview, the supervisor or manager should do some preparations. Making sure to accurately define the problem helps in developing a solution. They must go through the details of the initial performance standards, actual performance, and gaps to decide what to discuss. It is important to identify the strengths and development needs of the employee. They must also make sure that the employee has sufficient advance notice for the interview so that he has time to do his own preparation.

- **Interview Stage**   This is the actual feedback stage. The concerned manager and the employee sit and discuss the results of the appraisal process. Constructive feedback helps share evaluation reports without making people feel bad. Feedback should be given at a time when the employee is in a receptive mood. A manager should avoid giving feedback when the employee is preoccupied with an important organizational assignment or is emotionally worked up.

  Feedback should be focused on the behaviour of the person rather than on the person himself, especially while conveying negative feedback. The employee needs to be encouraged to change behaviour and performance. Feedback should be non-judgemental and non-evaluative. It should be clear to the employee what is expected out of him. Feedback should be continuous. Most importantly, feedback interview must be a two-way communication. Getting the employee involved in the feedback process helps ensure they play an active role in improving their performance.

- **Post-interview Stage**   An appraisal does not end with just feedback. It is important to make a record of plans the manager and employee have made for the future. The key to successful employee appraisals is setting up review parameters in advance and communicating them to the workers. It is important to let the employee know whether or not he/she will be retained, promoted, or given a raise. The manager will also have to identify any problems to work on with the intention of developing an action plan for improvement of skills. The manager and employee can discuss a timeline for continued informal and formal reviews.

  After the appraisal takes place, plans for improvement can be implemented. During this time, managers can regularly keep records of employee performance. Periodically, the manager and employee can meet face-to-face to discuss employee progress. Employees can share how well they think they are progressing. The plans for the next period require an intensive follow-up.

POTENTIAL APPRAISAL

The framework of performance management also incorporates the idea of potential appraisal. Potential appraisal refers to the identification of the hidden talents and skills of a person. The person might or might not be aware of them. It is different from performance appraisal as it refers to the abilities of the employees that are not being used at the time of appraisal. It searches for the latent abilities of the employee in discharging higher responsibilities in future. The potential of the employees is judged on the basis of his present performance, personality traits, past experience, qualifications, and so on. It also looks at the hidden skills and knowledge of an employee. It aims at informing the employee their future prospects and helps the organization in drawing their successions plan. It also requires updating the training efforts regularly and advising the employees on things that they can do to improve their career prospects.

Potential appraisal is a future-oriented appraisal whose main objective is to identify and evaluate the potential of the employees to assume higher positions and responsibilities in the organizational hierarchy. Many organizations consider and use potential appraisal as a part of the performance appraisal processes. The purposes of a potential review are to inform employees of their future prospects and to enable the organization to draft a management succession programme. Potential appraisal also helps in updating training activities and to advise employees about the improvements required to enhance their career opportunities.

There are various techniques used for potential appraisal. Potential appraisal could be done with the help of 360-degree appraisal reports. MBOs, psychological and psychometric tests, management games such as role playing, and assessment centres for competency-based appraisals are all used for assessing future potential apart from assessing current performance. The potential for improving performance (PIP) measures the performance of the average worker versus the best person performing a particular task. Large differences suggest that performance can be improved by bringing average performance up closer to the best performance. Small differences suggest little potential for improvement.

A good potential appraisal system would be based on clarity of roles and functions associated with the new positions. This requires extensive job descriptions to be made available for each job. A good potential appraisal system provides opportunities for the employees to know their strengths and weaknesses and possibilities for future career progressions. Regular counselling and guidance sessions enable the employee to develop realistic self-perceptions and plan his own career and development.

The fundamental goal of performance management is to improve employee effectiveness. It is a continuous process where managers and employees work together to monitor and review an employee's performance and his or her overall contribution to the organization. The establishment of an effective performance management system requires time and resources and, therefore, the support of top management. Management support to act on the outcomes of the performance management process is necessary to ensure that good performance is rewarded, inadequate performance gets the necessary support and training to improve, and consistently poor performance results in a change of responsibilities or termination, as appropriate.

COMPENSATION AND REWARDS

Employees, in exchange of their work, generally expect some remuneration. The goals of compensation management are to design a pay structure that will attract, motivate, and retain competent employees. Compensation plays a major role in attracting talent from the market, and the compensation system of the organization is the key factor for creating an employer brand.

The objective of the compensation function is to create a system of rewards that is equitable to the employer and employee alike. The desired outcome is an employee who is attracted to the work and motivated to do a good job for the employer. Patten suggests that compensation should be adequate, equitable, balanced, cost-effective, secure, motivating, and acceptable.[7]

There are two main types of compensation.

1. **Direct compensation** The pay that a worker receives, such as wages, salaries, commissions, and bonuses
2. **Indirect compensation** All rewards that are not included in direct compensation (for example, benefits like vacations, housing subsidy, and medical allowance)

Another way to classify rewards is to consider it as monetary or non-monetary. As the name implies, a monetary incentive is a money-based reward given when an employee meets or exceeds expectations. Monetary incentives can include cash bonuses, stock options, profit sharing, and any other type of reward that increases an employee's compensation. Non-monetary rewards may include anything, ranging from restaurant coupons, movie tickets, supermarket discounts, paid sabbaticals, free cellphone or wifi, gym membership, spa services, healthcare benefits, life insurance, daycare and childcare benefits, and recognition certificates or awards.

TRADITIONAL COMPENSATION SYSTEM

Traditional compensation systems typically involve the use of job analysis to determine the knowledge, skills, and abilities (KSAs) required to perform jobs. Job analysis information is then used for job evaluation, which determines the relative standing of each job in the salary or wage hierarchy of an organization.

Job evaluation is a process to determine the monetary worth of a job based on job analysis data. Essentially, the process of job evaluation involves a review of each job to determine the extent to which compensable factors are present. Typically, jobs are evaluated on certain compensable factors, such as knowledge, know-how, accountability, effort, and problemsolving. Various types of traditional compensation methods are:

- **Job classification system**   Jobs are classified into a grade structure or hierarchy. Each level in the grade/category structure has a description and job titles. Each job is assigned to the grade/category providing the closest match to the job. To ensure equity in grading and wages, a common set of grading standards are used. Due to differences in duties, skills, and knowledge, grading standards are developed mainly along occupational lines.
- **Point system**   A variation of the classification system, it involves assigning points to each job on the basis of compensable factors, such as position in hierarchy, accountability, and number of tasks performed.
- **Factor comparison system or ranking system**   It involves comparing jobs to determine differences in the presence of compensable factors. Jobs are compared to each other based on the overall position of the job to the organization. The 'position' of a job is usually based on hierarchy/level, designation, number of hours, responsibility (supervisory and fiscal), and working conditions.

Limitations of Traditional Methods

The biggest drawback of the traditional compensation system is that compensation is for jobs, not individuals. It rewards position, not effort; seniority, not merit. Such a system of compensation promotes Parkinson's syndrome or Parkinson's law. The law, articulated by Cyril Northcote Parkinson, is based on the philosophy that 'work expands so as to fill the time available for its completion'.[8] People just do only things that are part of their job and spend most of the time on completion of basic tasks. It promotes a 'this is not my job' mentality. Traditional compensation, thus, does not leave any room for creativity, performance, or 'extra effort'.

A further criticism is that each employee is compensated only for the performance of a specific job. Thus, the compensation system introduces constraints on managers' flexibility in utilizing the workforce. When a person is asked to perform work outside of his or her job classification, there are problems in assignment of a pay rate to such jobs. In addition, traditional compensation systems do not work well with managers and professionals. With such employees, the job-based focus of traditional systems conflicts with the individualized nature of their work. With increasing professionalization of the workforce, the importance of this problem is magnified.

STRATEGIC COMPENSATION

One of the most important ways by which organizations implement their strategies is to reward employees for behaviours that lead to fulfilment of strategic goals. Strategically aligned rewards help reinforce desired behaviours repeatedly.

The purpose of strategic compensation is to:

- Align compensation with company strategy
- Attract and retain employees
- Reinforce positive behaviours
- Motivate desirable performance
- Link individual performance to company performance

The compensation plan should help advance the firm's strategic goals. Management should produce a reward strategy that is aligned with the corporate strategy. This means creating a compensation package that produces the desired employee behaviours that help the firm achieve its competitive strategy.

Figure 8.3 illustrates the idea of strategic compensation.

Figure 8.3   Strategic Compensation

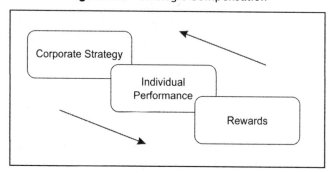

Approaches to Strategic Compensation

An effective compensation system makes employees put their efforts for achievement of organization's goals and objectives. Strategic compensation, thus, involves a focus on performance and contribution. This may apply at various levels: individual, team, or it may be organization-wide.

Compensation for Individual Performance:

- Merit pay
- Competency-based pay
- Broadbanding

Compensation for Team Performance:

- Team-based pay
- Gainsharing
- Team awards and bonus

Compensation for Organizational Performance:

- Variable pay plan (VPP)
- Performance bonus
- Profit sharing
- Employee stock option plan (ESOP)

Each of these plans is now discussed in detail.

Compensation for Individual Performance

Traditionally speaking, there are two basic ways to make direct financial payments to employees: based on increments of time or based on performance. Time-based pay is still the foundation of most employers' pay plans. Some blue-collar and clerical workers receive hourly or daily wages, for instance. Other shop floor workers may be paid weekly. Managers tend to be paid monthly. The second direct payment option is to pay for performance. Piecework ties compensation to the amount of production (or number of pieces) the worker turns out. Sales commission is another performance-based (sales-based) compensation. While time-based compensation does not reward performance directly, the second is directly linked to productivity or output. Thus, it can be considered as a basic form of strategic compensation. Other popular forms of strategic compensation or pay plans are discussed below.

Merit Pay

Merit pay or a merit raise is any salary increase the firm awards to an individual employee based on improvement in individual performance. Merit pay is a raise in base pay based on performance. Every year, the performance of employees is assessed and a raise is given to those employees who have improved their performance during the past year. Although the term merit pay can apply to the incentive raises given to any employee, the term is more often used for white-collar employees.

Merit pay is different from a bonus in that it usually becomes part of the employee's base salary, unlike bonuses that are one-time rewards. Merit pay is different from pay for performance, although the two are often considered as being similar. Merit pay incentive plans reward performance by increasing the employee's salary on a normally permanent basis. On the other hand, pay for performance (discussed later in the chapter) rewards employees using different criteria and formulae, without increasing their salary permanently.

Advantages and Limitations

Merit pay is designed to motivate employees to meet performance goals. It rewards employees for being good at their jobs. Sometimes the area of performance is easy to quantify. For instance, a car dealership can reward employees for consistently exceeding sales goals. In other cases, the company is trying to improve performance in less quantifiable aspects of the job, such as teamwork. In this situation, the incentive is tied to the supervisor's rating of employee performance at a scheduled review. Employees who receive higher ratings earn more incentive pay.

Merit pay is a subject of debate. Companies give raises based on the appraisal process. Since many appraisals are often biased and subjective, giving merit pay based on such appraisals will undermine the spirit of the process. Another problem with merit pay is that employees receive the increase in base pay even if their performance slips after the raise. Successful execution of merit pay requires establishing effective appraisal procedures and ensuring that managers tie merit pay to performance.

Competency-based Pay

Competency-based pay refers to a pay system in which pay increases are linked to the skills an employee acquires and applies. Under such a system, the company pays for the employee's skills and knowledge, rather than for the title he or she holds or the job's tasks and duties. In practice, competency-based pay usually involves *pay for knowledge* and *pay for skills*. Pay-for-knowledge pay plans reward employees for learning organizationally relevant knowledge. Pay-for-skills plans rewards around existing and evolving skills. It tends to be used more for workers with operational duties or manual jobs.

The impact of rapid technological change, globalization of product markets, and the emphasis on quality necessitate a frequent updating of skills. With skill-based pay, employees are able to increase their compensation as they acquire a broader range of skills. Skill-based pay or knowledge-based pay, thus, creates a strong motivation to learn and acquire new skills. Although there are variations in how skill-based pay is implemented, employees typically start out at the base rate and increase their compensation as they master a sequence of skill blocks. Assessment of skill mastery is done through various testing approaches. These may include observation of work, written tests, assessment centres, and so on.

The pay increases are usually tied to three types of skills:

- Horizontal skills, which involve a broadening of skills in terms of the range of tasks. Horizontal skill plans reward the acquisition of complementary skills (for example, individual learns how to do both accounts payable and accounts receivables) across several jobs.

- Vertical skills, which involve acquiring skills of a higher level in each skill block. Vertical skill plans measure the acquisition of input/output skills (for example, a drill press operator mastering preventive maintenance and in-process inspection) within a single job.
- Depth skills, which involve a high level of skills in certain specialized areas relating to the same job. Depth skill plans reward skill specialization (for example, computer programmer specializing in database programming).

For example, BP's skill matrix is used to determine the compensation of employees based on mastery of each skill level as shown in Figure 5.6. The concept of vertical, horizontal, and depth skills may be understood from the example. As shown in the figure, horizontal skills are technical expertise, business awareness, communication, and so on. The boxes indicated by letters A, B, C, and so on, are descriptors for each level of the skill denoting vertical skills; for example, in technical expertise, (A) might read 'basic knowledge of handling machine' while (H) might read 'conducts and supervises complex tasks requiring advanced knowledge of a range of skills'. Depth skills may imply acquiring in-depth knowledge of certain specialized skills. For instance, the dark boxes indicate minimum level of skill required in each vertical category in order to occupy this position.

Skill-based pay approaches have been frequently implemented in high-involvement manufacturing settings, and they also are being implemented in service environments. Skill-based pay works very well in organizations where promotional opportunities are less due to delayering. Such organizations give incentives by promoting skill enhancement. In certain companies, skill-based pay is implemented in conjunction with semi-autonomous work teams. In such companies, employees master the skills required for a job and then move to another job or role in the team until all the skills are mastered. Upon completion of the rotation, the employee can then move into another team and so on.[9] In a number of companies, skill-based pay is tied to acquiring a formal degree or on completion of a course or training programme.

Advantages and Limitations

Skill-based pay is a person-based and not a job-based system. It positively encourages skills development. Thus, the system is more performance-oriented and strategically driven compared with the traditional compensation system. It emphasizes developing a broad range of skills, which makes the employee multi-skilled. With skill-based pay, it is easy to fill in for absences because of the availability of cross-trained employees. It helps employees enhance their employability. The costs of higher wages are offset by enhanced learning, higher productivity, and increased efficiency. Further, because employees gain pay increases by expanding their skill sets, it enhances job satisfaction and self-esteem.

There are problems as well in implementing skill-based pay. One problem involves compensating employees who have moved up and progressed out on the skill block. They may have mastered all the levels and on account of organizations being flat, there may not be much scope for upward promotions too. For such employees, lateral promotions may be given to take advantage of their skills. One of the more difficult aspects involved in the administration of skill-based pay involves the determination of the amount of pay that should be assigned to skill blocks. Of course, competitor and industry data can be used to establish the range and values for skill blocks, but sometimes, it may be a little complicated to put it into action.

Broadbanding of Pay Scales

Most firms have pay plans that slot jobs into classes or grades, each with its own vertical pay rate range. Broadbanding is the term applied to having wide salary bands, which are much more encompassing than traditional salary structures. Broadbanding is defined as a strategy for salary structures that consolidate a large number of pay grades into a few 'broad bands'. Typically, broadbanding involves a reduction in the number of salary bands (pay grades), and the differential between one grade and the next is increased. It means collapsing salary grades and ranges into just a few wide blocks or bands, each of which contains a relatively wide range of salary levels. In flat organizations, fewer promotional opportunities exist. Thus, the broadbanding structure allows more latitude for pay increases and career growth without promotion. Broadbanding is strategic in nature as it is directed towards obtaining greater flexibility. Broadbanding may be clubbed with skill-based pay as well. For instance, an employee in a particular pay band can earn more by acquiring more skills.

Advantages and Limitations

Broadbanding has been successfully implemented in organizations that attempted to become flat. Broadbanding encourages internal mobility and potentially more developmental cross-functional assignments. The advantage of maintaining fewer bands is that employees' salaries can be raised substantially even without a promotion. Sometimes broadbanding can be unsettling, particularly for new employees. Broadbanding may also lead to perception of inequities. In a broadbanding system, it is relatively possible to have two people with the same responsibilities have earnings that are quite different. Often biased or reckless managers can tweak the system to favour their own people. Broadbanding is often seen as linked to reduction in opportunities for promotions. While moving towards a broadbanding approach, there must be sufficient employee understanding of the salary determination process and a culture based on communication and trust.

Compensation for Team Performance

For an increasing number of organizations, implementing a compensation plan that rewards employees for successful teamwork provides great synergy with their organizational model. Some of the popular mechanisms for rewarding team performance are discussed below.

Team-based Pay

With the growing importance of teams in organizations, compensation systems are being designed to reward team members for behaviours that facilitate team work. Typically, team-based pay involves specifying a team goal and then allocating to all team members a reward for its accomplishment.

In a team-based pay compensation structure, a portion of an employee's wages or bonus is tied to the success of team goals, with all team members typically receiving the same or similar incentive pay. Basing incentive pay on the performance of employee teams involves determining salary and/or bonuses based on the work of a group of employees rather than on individual contributions. To be effective, this type of approach must be clearly defined, achievable, and embraced by the participating team members. Team-based pay is a good way to ensure that the team is working together with shared goals. If instituted correctly, team-based incentive pay plans can have a positive impact on overall productivity and performance levels.

Gainsharing

Team-based pay often involves some form of gain sharing. The gains to be shared are often linked to the accomplishment of strategic objectives. Gainsharing involves sharing the gains from cost-savings, usually as a lump-sum incentive. Gainsharing is a system of management in which an organization seeks higher levels of performance through the involvement and participation of its people. As performance improves, employees share financially in the gain. It is a team approach. It is a technique that compensates workers based on improvements in the company's productivity.

The typical gainsharing programme involves measuring performance and then through a predetermined formula shares the savings with all employees. The organization's actual performance is compared with baseline performance (often a historical standard) to determine the gain. Employees have an opportunity to earn a gainsharing bonus generally on a monthly or quarterly basis. Gainsharing measures are typically based on operational measures (productivity, production cost, scrap rates, and error rates) that are more controllable by employees. Workers voluntarily participate in management to accept responsibility for cost-cutting reforms.

Gains are self-funded from savings generated by cost-cutting. It works best when company productivity levels can be easily quantified. Gainsharing applies to all types of business that require employee collaboration. However, gainsharing systems may vary widely in terms of their design and the degree to which they are integrated into the regular operating systems.

Team Awards and Bonus

In contrast to gainsharing plans, which typically reward the performance of all employees at a facility, bonuses for team performance tend to be for smaller work groups. These bonuses reward the members of a group for attaining a specific goal, usually measured in terms of physical output. Team awards are similar to team bonuses, but they are more likely to use a broad range of performance measures, such as cost savings, successful completion of a project, or even meeting deadlines. Team incentives, which are aimed at increasing productivity and improving morale, provide an opportunity for each member of the team to receive a bonus.

One benefit of team awards or bonus is that they often involve an element of improvement in calculating the bonus. For example, a sales group's team-based bonus might include incentives for improving new customer acquisition by a certain percentage over previous periods. Rather than being satisfied with consistent numbers year to year, a bonus for improving performance can motivate employees to constantly work harder and more efficiently.

Advantages and Limitations

Team-based compensation offers a number of advantages. The most important is that it promotes team spirit and facilitates cooperation. Further, incentives or bonuses to teams can be given immediately after completion of the project, thereby strongly linking desired behaviours with rewards. Another advantage of team-based incentive pay plans is that employees are motivated to work together towards a common goal. This can translate to greater unity at the workplace.

One concern with team-based pay systems is that some individuals may not do their share of work. This phenomenon is often explained through the concept of social loafing. The tendency of people to expend less effort when working collectively than when working individually, is called as social loafing. Some employees work less and prefer to be free riders on the efforts of more productive team members. Sometimes competition between teams can hurt the company as a whole. If not properly designed, employees have difficulty seeing how their individual performance affects their incentive pay.

To avoid this, it is important to have clear group goals as well as individual goals within that. The individual team member's compensation should vary according to the individual contributions to the team effort as a whole. Groups should promote cooperation as well as healthy competition. They must promote dialogue, team spirit, and motivation to make every member contribute. In order to be truly beneficial, it requires complete support for the team-based philosophy and a fair reward system.

Compensation for Organizational Performance

Organization-centric compensation approaches aim at directing employee performance towards attainment of organizational goals. Although all forms of strategic pay systems promote organizational performance indirectly, certain specific types of compensation systems are aimed at enhancing organizational performance more directly. These are:

Variable Compensation

Variable pay, also sometimes known as performance pay, is used to recognize and reward employee contribution towards company productivity and performance. Variable pay is often based on two main factors: an employee's performance and the company's performance. It involves target setting and actual payout based on that combination. Variable pay is an important component of total rewards in any organization nowadays. Variable pay plans are implemented with the intent to create among employees a sense of shared destiny. A common element of such plans is the concept of having a portion of employees' compensation tied to performance. Various popular forms of variable pay plans or performance-linked compensation are:

- **Increment to base pay** This is also called the add-on plan. Here, bonus or incentives constitute a form of add-on or addition over actual salary.
- **At-risk pay** It is normally operationalized by reducing employees' base pay by a certain percentage and then allowing them to receive various amounts of that percentage and more,

depending on performance measures. It means that one amount of pay is at-risk and is paid when targets are achieved.

- **Potential base pay at risk** This form of variable pay may exist where the company has a tradition of steady raises. This practice would be implemented by allocating only part of the pay as a regular raise. The remaining percentage is set aside for allocation with greater increases if performance targets are met or exceeded.

More organizations are replacing their annual salary increases and holiday bonuses with pay-for-performance plans. According to the HR consulting firm Hewitt Associates, about 78 per cent of multinational corporations (MNCs) use some form of VPP to reward employees. Variable pay started gaining importance in the Indian market in the last decade. It is becoming a common concept in the private sector. Even Indian public sector units are now moving towards it though the percentage there is typically not as high.

Advantages and Limitations

Variable pay has become an increasingly popular mode of compensation in most companies. To minimize business risk, companies are trying to reduce their investment in fixed costs and maximize the use of variable costs, which they incur only if they achieve certain results. Employee compensation in many industries is a company's single largest expense. Companies also use variable pay to drive performance culture and even leverage it to attract and retain talent. VPPs may help provide employment security because with part of employees' compensation being derived from the company's profitability, with declines in profits, total labour costs decline and employees may not need to be laid off.

Most criticisms of variable pay can be traced to concerns about the nature, implementation, and execution of such programmes rather than the principles on which they are based. Rewarding employees for superior performance ratings assumes that those ratings depend on employees' ability and motivation. However, sometimes performance may actually depend on forces outside the employee's control, such as biased appraisals, lack of cooperation from coworkers, or other organizational constraints. An element of complexity with variable pay involves the measures of performance to which pay is to be linked. The measures should be clear and must reflect the organization's overall strategies.

Despite these mixed results, business consultants agree that well-designed variable pay programmes that truly reward individual performance can be helpful. The purpose of a good VPP should be to make the company stronger and more competitive. Variable pay programmes that are not based on principles of employee empowerment are almost certainly doomed to fail. Business goals must be clearly defined and adequately disseminated to employees, and they should be arrived at with their assistance. It is also important that performance must be measured regularly and reliably through a fair system of performance appraisal and feedback.

Performance Bonus

Like merit pay or performance-linked pay, performance bonuses reward individual performance. However, bonuses are not rolled into base pay. In some cases, the bonus is a one-time reward.

Bonuses may also be linked to objective performance measures rather than subjective ratings. Performance bonus is an incentive for employees to share the company's good times. A performance bonus could be offered to:

- Salespeople who exceed their quotas for the year
- Employees who complete a higher than average number of procedures
- Accounts receivable staffers who achieve high levels of collections
- Production line workers who suggest product design improvements
- Employees who consistently report to work on time, or use less than their allotment of sick leaves, or suggest ways to reduce expenses, and so on

Advantages and Limitations

Performance bonus creates two winners: the employee receives the reward and the employer benefits from the worker's performance. Performance bonus encourages employees to become more productive or maintain high standards of performance. Bonuses for individual performance can be extremely effective and give the organization great flexibility in deciding what kinds of behaviour to reward. It gives a message that the company is trying to encourage certain types of behaviour by rewarding it.

However, bonuses often perpetrate an 'entitlement mentality'. Employees start relishing frequent bonuses and often expect that they will be given bonuses irrespective of performance. When bonuses are not granted, it leads to disgruntlement. This phenomenon is typical of public sector companies in India. Organizations need to convince people that bonus is for the overall betterment of the organization and they need to earn it.

Profit Sharing

Profit sharing is an incentive-based compensation programme to award employees a percentage of the company's profits. Profit sharing, when used as a special term, refers to various incentive plans introduced by businesses that provide direct or indirect payments to employees that depend on the company's profitability in addition to employees' regular salary and bonuses. When company profits are shared, it gives a feeling of belongingness and involvement in the company. Long before many western industrial nations followed suit, Jamsetji Tata introduced profit sharing in 1934 in India. About 40 per cent of companies in India today offer profit-sharing plans.

Under profit sharing, payments are a percentage of the organization' profits and do not become part of the employees' base salary. Profit-sharing programmes require setting up a formula for distribution of company profits. The formula is usually based on 5–6 per cent of the employee's salary. They usually include a vesting period of five–seven years. The company contributes a portion of its pre-tax profits to a pool that will be distributed among eligible employees. Generally, this is done on an annual basis. During less profitable years, the company may opt to not contribute. It lets companies control how the money is invested and is not as expensive to administer as other plans.

Advantages and Limitations

Profit sharing brings employees to work together towards the organization's profitability. It enhances commitment to organizational goals. It encourages employees to think more like owners, taking a broad view of what they need to do in order to make the organization more effective. They are more likely to cooperate and less likely to focus on narrow self-interest. In addition, profit sharing has the practical advantage of costing less when the organization is experiencing financial difficulties.

Disadvantages are that the pay for each employee moves up or down together, and there is no individual differences for merit. It focuses only on the goal of profitability which sometimes may be at the expense of quality. For smaller companies, these plans may result in drastic swings in earnings for employees, which the employees may find difficult to manage their personal finances. An organization setting up a profit-sharing plan should consider what to do if profits fall. If the economy slows and profit-sharing payments disappear along with profits, employees may become discouraged or angry. One way to avoid this kind of problem is to design profit-sharing plans to reward employees for high profits but not penalize them when profits fall.

Employee Stock Option Plan (ESOP)

An ESOP is when the company offers its shares to the employees. Often organizations give shares as part of their salary, rewards, or bonuses. The ESOP concept was started by George Eastman, founder of Kodak, in 1919. An ESOP may be in the form of an option to buy the company's share. This could either be at the market price (price of the share on the stock exchange—in this case, certain units of stocks are reserved for employees), or at a preferential price (lower than the current market price). Thus, ESOPs involve making the workers' shareholders of the company by inducing them to buy equity shares, usually at lower price. In many cases, advances and financial assistance in the form of easy repayment options are extended to enable employees to buy shares.

There are time limits for availing this scheme. For instance, one can acquire the shares after completing a particular period of employment. This is known as the vesting period and generally ranges from one to five years. A large number of Indian companies have implemented ESOP. The information, communication, and entertainment (ICE) sector dominates the ESOP space, followed by financial services and then manufacturing sectors. Information technology (IT) companies in India have been the main issuers of ESOPs. Infosys, in fact, is said to have pioneered the concept of ESOPs in India. The effectiveness of ESOPs as a retention tool has inspired large Indian business houses to offer them to employees, for example, Aditya Birla Group, ICICI Bank, HDFC Bank, Dabur, Bharti Airtel, ITC, Marico, and NIIT. NALCO has become the first public sector undertaking (PSU) in India to offer ESOPs.

Advantages and Limitations

Companies consider ESOPs as an incentive tool that enhances productivity, motivates employees, and increases employees' participation in the company's overall performance. It is a win-win situation for both employers and employees. The stock option is the most popular long-term incentive. It is often used as a tool to retain employees. ESOPs help improve bottom line through employees' involvement, interest, and loyalty.

However, employees may feel 'forced' to join, thus placing their financial future at greater risk. Both their wages or salaries and their retirement benefits depend on the performance of the organization. In some cases, the ESOP fable has been a source of disillusionment. In a number of companies, employees holding ESOPs were shown the pink slip even before the company went public. In that case, the employees were left with useless stocks and no option of selling them. The interest in ESOPs did not last long as the gains depended on the market prices of the shares. Despite this, ESOPs have never really lost sheen and continue to be preferred by companies and employees as a source of remuneration. As long as ESOP is treated as an incentive tool or the employer is genuinely interested in creating wealth for the employee, the situation is not all that bad.

Non-monetary Incentives and Benefits

Motivating employees can be challenging for any business owner or manager. Workplace motivators include monetary and non-monetary incentives. The purpose of monetary incentives is to reward employees for job performance through money. The purpose of non-monetary incentives is to reward employees for job performance through opportunities. This may include restaurant coupons, movie tickets, supermarket discounts, gym or spa memberships, healthcare benefits, childcare, day care, flexible work hours, sabbaticals, and recognition certificates or awards.

Recognition programmes are one of several types of non-financial rewards. Recognizing an employee's contribution is a powerful motivation tool. Motivational theories like those of Maslow and Herzberg show that recognition has a positive impact on performance. The term 'recognition programme' usually refers to formal programmes, such as employee-of-the-month programmes. Social recognition programme generally refers to informal manager–employee exchanges such as praise, approval, or expressions of appreciation for a job well done.

Although not usually considered an incentive, job design can have a significant impact on employee motivation and retention. Challenging work is an important driver for attracting employees. Job design is, thus, a useful part of an employer's total rewards programme. Overseas assignments are also seen as a form of reward. However, issues such as how to account for geographic differences in cost of living is a big policy issue. Employers handle cost-of-living differentials for transferees in several ways. One way is to pay a differential for ongoing costs in addition to a one-time allocation. Other way is to simply raise the employee's base salary. An employee may get allowances, including cost-of-living, relocation, housing, and education.

EXECUTIVE COMPENSATION

One issue that confronts organizations is designing compensation for top executives. Compensation or remuneration for senior executives is different from compensation for other employees in most organizations. Executive compensation refers to compensation for employees that include presidents of the company, chief executive officers (CEOs), chief financial officers (CFOs), vice presidents, directors of the company, and other upper-level managers.

Executive compensation packages are designed by a company's board of directors, typically by the compensation committee consisting of independent directors, with the purpose of incentivizing the executive team. The executives' total reward package must align with each other and with the goal of achieving the company's strategies. It requires first defining the strategic plan and context for the executive compensation plan. Next, it requires defining the strategic role behaviours the executives must exhibit to achieve the firm's strategic goals. Subsequently, it requires designing each component of the executives' compensation package and structuring them into a balanced plan that motivates executives to achieve these aims.

At the heart of most executive compensation plans is the idea that executives should be rewarded if the organization grows in profitability and value over a period of years. Therefore, their total compensation packages are more significant than their base pay. The key elements are:

- **Salaries**   Salaries of executives vary by type of job, size of organization, region of the country, and industry. On average, salaries make up about 40–60 per cent of the typical top executive's annual compensation total.
- **Executive bonus plans**   Bonuses for executives can be determined in several ways. A system whereby bonuses are awarded based on the judgement of the CEO and the board of directors is one way.
- **Performance incentives**   Performance-based incentives attempt to tie executive compensation to the growth and success of the organization. For instance, a stock option gives an individual the right to buy stock in a company, usually at an advantageous price.
- **Benefits and perquisites**   Executive benefits may take several forms, including traditional retirement, health insurance, and vacations. It may include additional benefit items that other employees do not receive. Executives also receive benefits called perquisites or perks. Whether it is a house or car, it is the status enhancement value of perks that is important to many executives.

Executive pay is determined using multiple, strategy-based performance criteria. Three main factors, namely *job complexity* (span of control, the number of functional divisions over which the executive has direct responsibility, and management level), the employer's *ability to pay* (company performance, profitability, and rate of return), and the executive's *human capital* (educational level, field of study, and work experience) account for most of executive compensation variance.

Recent public activism, shareholder vigilance, and government intervention have sent sharp signals on what companies pay top executives. The Occupy Wall Street movement essentially stood for the vast inequality between what is now famously called the elite 1 per cent and the 99 per cent of the society. *The Times*, UK, in its report '**High Pay Centre**,' which says an executive pay scam has developed with the earnings of chief executives growing to 180 times that of the average worker, compared with 60 times as much in the 1990s. In India, too, this has been a sensitive issue, with none other than Narayan Murthy, the founder of Infosys, asking the essential question 'how much is too much?' He argued that the reason why CEOs needed to be paid globally competitive compensation was that they had the capabilities of global standards and would find global opportunities for themselves.

Executive compensation plan characteristics and design are heavily influenced by elements of corporate policies and the legal framework of the country. The Sarbanes-Oxley Act of 2002 affects how employers formulate their executive incentive programmes in the United States. Sarbanes-Oxley injects a higher level of responsibility into the decisions of executives and board members. Historically, executive salaries in India had been tightly structured as per government regulations. The Indian Companies Act, 1956, contained provisions for managerial and executive remuneration, which embody a self-contained code in themselves. It has been replaced by the Companies Act, 2013. It states that companies have to ensure the level and composition of remuneration is reasonable. It makes it mandatory for firms to make additional disclosures and limit salary increase in tough times.

The dilemma associated with executive compensation is a worldwide phenomenon. Probably the first and most important step needed is to obtain alignment between company performance and compensation systems. It is true that mechanisms used to reward executives are likely to have an enormous effect on the company's future. Comparing pay to stock performance can help determine whether executives are overpaid.

DESIGNING AN EFFECTIVE COMPENSATION STRATEGY

Strategic compensation involves a focus on performance and contribution. As discussed above, it may apply at various levels: individual, team, or organization. Often the distinction may not be so categorical. For instance, skill-based pay may apply to individuals as well as teams. A performance bonus may sometimes be a team intervention, while in certain companies, it may be an organization-wide incentive plan.

Three basic issues need to be addressed while designing a strategic pay plan:

- What are the organization's strategic goals?
- What employee behaviours and skills does the organization need to achieve its strategic goals?
- What compensation policies and practices will help to produce the desired employee behaviours?

The compensation plan of an organization should help attain the firm's strategic aims. Management should design a compensation plan that is aligned to its overall strategy. This means creating a compensation package that produces the employee behaviours the firm needs to achieve its competitive strategy. Many organizations focus on formulating a total rewards strategy. Total rewards encompass the traditional pay, incentives, and benefits, as well as additional motivational elements as part of rewards, such as more challenging jobs, career progression, promotions, awards, and recognition.

Developing compensation plans for managers and professionals is similar in many ways to developing plans for shop floor or blue-collar employees. Professionals are people whose main duty must be the performance of work requiring advanced knowledge, and the advanced knowledge must be customarily acquired by a prolonged course of specialized intellectual instruction. Generational incentive differences are affected by career stage and proximity to retirement. The older the employee, the more the focus is placed on retirement benefits or supplementing retirement income with part-time or temporary jobs. The younger the employee, the more the focus is placed on job satisfaction and the work environment. The bottom line is that incentives must be tailored to the needs of the workers rather than using the one-size-fits-all approach, which is impersonal and sometimes ineffective. Some incentives can actually hamper employees and companies by decreasing motivation, interest, and job satisfaction. Incentives must take into account the workers for whom they were created. A balance between monetary and non-monetary incentives should be used to satisfy the diverse needs and interests of employees.[10]

The above discussed pay approaches are applicable to managerial and professional jobs as to production and clerical ones. However, there are some differences. Managerial jobs tend to stress hard-to-quantify factors such as judgement, reasoning, decision-making, and problem-solving skills more than basic operations or clerical jobs. For such jobs, there is also more emphasis on basing pay decisions on performance, rather than on static job factors. Similarly, compensating professional employees with specialized skills, like software engineers and scientists, presents unique problems. These jobs require highly abstract factors for success, such as creativity and problem solving, which are not easy to quantify, measure, or compare. Traditional job evaluation approaches to pay determination are no longer relevant. Although they are still important as a backbone to determine the basic structure of pay, they usually play a secondary role in the total rewards decisions.

Implementing such plans is not as easy as it may seem. Many such programmes are ineffective and many have turned out to be even disastrous. In a lot of cases, these plans failed to motivate employees.[11] Equally problematic is the fact that some incentives unintentionally promote wrong behaviours. Thus, a company that links pay to number of units sold of a particular product is simply incentivizing sales and not really quality or customer satisfaction. Often, such a strategy may influence employees to focus only on selling the product at the cost of corporate ethics and accountability.

Implementing a change in the current compensation system is not an easy task. It takes a great deal of consideration to communicate significant changes. Managers also need to address the issue of equity. Using a market-based approach to determine pay helps ensure that pay is competitive and provides equity. Organizations also deploy communication and feedback systems, suggestion schemes, grievance mechanisms, and pay satisfaction surveys to ensure that employees view pay as fair. Further, employers do not have free reign in designing pay plans. Various laws of the land lay down conditions that determine compensation decisions, such as minimum wages, overtime rates, and benefits. In India, there are several legal provisions that govern pay-related decisions.

HR Anecdote
Pygmalion and self-fulfilling prophecy

In his path breaking article titled 'Pygmalion in management', published in the *Harvard Business Review*, J. Sterling Livingston introduces the readers to the concept of self-fulfilling prophecy. He named this 1969 article after the mythical sculptor, Pygmalion, who carves a statue of a woman that was so beautiful and realistic that he fell in love with it. It was because of his love that the statue was brought to life and he married her.

His title also pays homage to George Bernard Shaw, whose play *Pygmalion* explores the notion that the way one person treats another can have transforming power. In the play, an underclass flower-girl, Eliza Doolittle, is metaphorically 'brought to life' by a professor who teaches her to refine her accent and conversation and conduct herself with sophisticated manners in social situations. This is what transforms her from a flower girl to a 'lady'.

Livingston notes that creating positive expectations produces positive results. The article provides insights for managers. If we set high expectations for employees, they are likely to achieve it. If managers' expectations are high, productivity is likely to be excellent. Self-fulfilling prophecies indicate that if a manager is convinced that the people in her group are good, they will reliably outperform a group whose manager believes the reverse—even if the innate talent of the two groups is similar.

Sources: Adapted from J. Sterling Livingston (1969), Pygmalion in management, *Harvard Business Review* (July–August): 81–89; J. Sterling Livingston (2009), *Pygmalion in management* (Boston, MA: Harvard Business Press).

News Grab
India may have a skilled talent surplus by 2030

As talent shortage takes hold across the Asia-Pacific region, salaries are set to surge for highly skilled workers, with India being the only country to buck the trend due to surplus talent. Indian is the only country that is expected to have a highly skilled talent surplus by 2030. This is unique because every other major country will witness a massive rise in company payrolls due to a shortage of highly skilled talent. These insights are a part of **'The Salary Surge Study'** conducted by **Korn Ferry**.

The study estimates the impact of the impending shortage between the future labor supply and demand on the payroll of 20 major global economies. The research is focused only on highly skilled labor to understand the impact on each economy at three future milestones: **2020, 2025, and 2030**. Although the focus is on all sectors, three crucial sectors are central to the study: financial and business services, technology, media and telecommunications (TMT) and manufacturing. The study uses educational qualification as a proxy for skills. The study essentially calculates the average pay premium, which is how much organizations could be forced to pay workers, over and above normal inflation increase.

India is the only economy that can expect to avoid upward spiralling wages, given its highly skilled talent surplus at each milestone. The surplus of extra manpower is driven by a growing, younger working population with the country's median age expected to be just 31 years by 2030. This is a huge supply of talent compared to the ageing population in China, Japan or the US. India's emphasis on affordable and accessible education will generate armies of college level talent.

The 20 countries included in the study are: the Americas (Brazil, Mexico, US), EMEA (France, Germany, Netherlands, Russia, Saudi Arabia, South Africa, UAE, UK) and Asia-Pacific (Australia, China, Hong Kong, India, Indonesia, Japan, Malaysia, Singapore, Thailand).

Sources: Adapted from https://www.peoplematters.in/article/skilling/why-india-will-be-the-only-country-with-a-skilled-talent-surplus-by-2030-18624; https://www.thehindubusinessline.com/news/surplus-talent-may-see-india-buck-the-global-salary-surge-trend-study/article24247475.ece.

CHAPTER SUMMARY

- Performance appraisal is the process of evaluating how employees perform their jobs compared to a set of standards.
- Traditional performance appraisal approach suffers from several limitations. These limitations make traditional performance appraisals merely an exercise in paper work without much utility.
- Performance management is a comprehensive, continuous, and flexible approach to the management of performance of teams and individuals.
- Performance measurement system that is strategically linked helps assess the degree to which the behaviour of employees contributes to attainment of strategic goals.
- 360-degree appraisal is a performance assessment tool that incorporates feedback from all who observe and are affected by the performance of a candidate.
- A competency-based appraisal process focuses on the skills and competencies necessary to be successful. Assessment centres are an important tool for competency-based appraisal.
- The framework of performance management also incorporates the idea of potential appraisal.
- Traditional compensation systems typically involve the use of job evaluation to determine the monetary worth of jobs based on job analysis data.
- The biggest drawback of traditional compensation system is that compensation is for jobs not individuals.
- Strategically aligned rewards help reinforce desired behaviours.
- Strategic compensation may apply at various levels: individual, team, or it may be organization-wide.
- Workplace motivators include both monetary and non-monetary incentives.

EXERCISES AND DISCUSSION QUESTIONS

1. How is 360-degree appraisal and feedback an important component of strategically linked performance managements systems? Discuss how 360-degree mechanism can be effectively implemented.

2. Discuss the various types of strategic compensation systems. Highlight how strategic compensation drives performance.

3. Think of any organization that is considered as a leader in its business segment. Search for information related to the organization and answer the following:
   i. Try to look for its performance appraisal process. Analyse whether it is following a traditional performance evaluation system or strategically linked performance management system.
   ii. Identify the major components of its compensation strategy. Comment on whether it has deployed a traditional or strategic compensation system.

CASELET

Performance Management and Rewards at Tata Consultancy Services

Established in 1968 as Tata Computer Centre, Tata Consultancy Services (TCS) is a pioneer in the IT arena in India. Headquartered in Mumbai, Maharashtra, it is an Indian multinational and operates in 46 countries. It is the world's 2nd-largest IT services provider. TCS is one of the largest Indian companies by market capitalization. It is among the most valuable IT services brands worldwide. TCS alone generates 70 per cent dividends of its parent company, Tata Sons. In 2015, TCS was ranked 64th in the *Forbes* World's Most Innovative Companies ranking. In 2017, it was ranked 10th on the Fortune India 500 list. In April 2018, TCS became the first Indian IT company to cross $100 billion market capitalization. Its focus on building a diverse workforce along with a supportive work environment has contributed to its immense popularity.

As part of the business mandate to become more responsive, TCS announced in the beginning of 2018 that it is adopting enterprise-wide Agile, a new delivery model that is focused on delivering outsourcing projects in increments within a well-defined short duration. This necessitated overhauling its HR strategy. The move was intended to support the new shorter and quicker delivery model demanded by clients today.

Agile systems are typically comprised of smaller teams who work on a finite set of clearly defined items. The teams' goals and composition change as the project evolves. It is like a fleet of small but powerful motorboats steering more efficiently than a giant ship. Becoming agile has implications for core processes like HR. One significant impact of building agile systems was on the performance appraisal mechanism at TCS. Agile philosophy is changing the way TCS measures the performance of its employees, manages talent development, and budgets for recruitment. Previously, workforce planning, budgeting, and goal-setting were easier to do as IT projects were longer and more predictable in nature.

Scrapping the bell curve model, TCS set about redesigning its appraisal system. The bell curve system of performance appraisal is a forced ranking system. Through this system, the organization tries to segregate the best, mediocre, and worst performers and nurture the best and discard the worst. This segregation is based on relative comparison of the performance of the workforce against those engaged in similar activity and ranking them accordingly. TCS has decided to give up this model for a more agile system. Its appraisal system will be redesigned from scratch. To build a flawless model, the company would be assessing its employees on a more regular basis, instead of periodic appraisal. The appraisal system will be separate for IT and BPO employees. TCS announced that the company will modify an existing platform for its IT appraisals, while for the BPO employees it would be more of a social media system. Along with that, appraisal of senior executives is also being closely examined.

This new system was planned to be implemented in a stage-wise manner covering one sub-set of employees at a time. Gradually, the company would be ready to move towards continuous appraisal and feedback cycle round the year applicable for all employees. Instead of half-yearly appraisal system, targeted employees would move to a project end appraisal cycle—and that the projects could last anywhere from two months to a year. It is a more continuous feedback system.

The entire workforce is being trained in Agile methodology. TCS is also changing the way it budgets for workforce planning by involving business heads and being continuously flexible about hiring budgets. The company is gearing to get the business fully involved in the workforce planning side, so that it does not end up hiring the kind of competencies they may not need for a long time. Learning and development is another major area that is going through change. The company is moving certain people from business functions to talent development so they can bring in the right expertise. There is cross functional movement to nurture expertise and promote learning. There is a need to have continuous upgradation of competencies. Employees need to reinvent themselves continuously, with relearning and new skill sets. The new performance management strategy is synchronized to support continuous learning and improvement. This also calls for an overhaul of its reward strategy to match with the new performance appraisal agenda. Both monetary and non-monetary rewards have always been part of the total rewards strategy at TCS. The company has been quite inventive in the past in terms of pioneering new reward systems such as work from home and flexible timings as part of its non-monetary incentives. The new 'agile' philosophy may require further reinventing its rewards game plan.

However, the new system is likely to face many challenges. Total employee count at TCS at the end of December 2017 stood at 390,880, making it the biggest IT firm by employee strength. It involves addressing key concerns such as: How will the new system apply to all employees? How to measure people as they are doing small projects? How will accountability get fixed? and so on. The company feels that the younger workforce is more aware of the way it works and are, thus, more receptive of the new system. The challenge is mid- to senior-level employees to also appreciate this process because they are accustomed to doing things in a specific way. Changing their mindset will require time.

IT service companies in India as well as across the globe will keenly watch how TCS manages its appraisal system, given the scale of the exercise. TCS is looking forward to adopting a system of continuous feedback and performance improvements, a goal that may be hard to achieve, given its sheer size and number of employees.[12]

Questions for Discussion

1. Discuss the key features of the new business model at TCS. What are its HR implications?
2. What are the challenges that TCS is likely to face vis-à-vis its new performance management and reward strategy? Suggest ways to overcome the initial hurdles.

NOTES

1. P. Drucker (1954), *The practice of management* (New York, NY: Harper).
2. For instance, G. Latham, M. Terence, and L. D. Dennis (1978), Importance of participative goal setting and anticipated rewards on goal difficulty and job performance, *Journal of Applied Psychology 63*(2): 163–171; C. A. L. Pearson (1987), Participative goal setting as a strategy for improving performance and job satisfaction: A longitudinal evaluation with railway track maintenance gangs, *Human Relations 40*(8): 473–488.
3. J. W. Fleenor and J. M. Prince (1997), *Using 360-degree feedback in organizations: An annotated bibliography* (Greensboro, NC: Center for Creative Leadership).
4. D. W. Bracken, M. A. Dalton, R. A. Jako, C. D. McCauley, and V. A. Pollman (1997), *Should 360-degree feedback be used only for developmental purposes?* (Greensboro, NC: Center for Creative Leadership).
5. P. Atkins and R. Wood (2002), Self-versus others' ratings as predictors of assessment center ratings: Validation evidence for 360-degree feedback programs, *Personnel Psychology 55*(4): 871–904.
6. C. O. Longenecker, A. J. Jaccoud, H. P. Sims, and D. A. Gioia (1992), Quantitative and qualitative investigations of affect in executive judgment, *Applied Psychology: An International Review 41*(1): 21–41.
7. T. H. Patten (1977), *Pay: Employee compensation and incentive plans* (New York, NY: Free Press).
8. C. N. Parkinson (1955), Parkinson's law, *The Economist*, London, 19 November; C. N. Parkinson (1957), *Parkinson's law and other studies in administration* (Boston, MA: Houghton Mifflin Company).
9. C. Greer (2001), *Strategic human resource management* (New Delhi, India: Pearson Education).
10. A. Kohn (1993), Why incentive plans cannot work, in *Ultimate rewards: A Harvard business review book*, ed. S. Kerr (Boston, MA: Harvard Business School Press).
11. G. Dessler (2013), *Human resource management* (Upper Saddle River, NJ: Pearson Education).
12. With inputs from https://www.peoplematters.in/site/interstitial, retrieved 17 October 2017; https://economictimes.indiatimes.com/tech/ites/tcs-plans-to-straighten-out-the-bell-curve-with-new-appraisal-system/articleshow/55611676.cms, retrieved 17 October 2017.

Employee Relations, Engagement, and Termination

Chapter Overview

This chapter deals with the idea of employee relations, engagement, and termination. It discusses the concept of employee relations and its evolution. Issues related to trade unions, collective bargaining, and employee participation in management are highlighted. The meaning and significance of employee engagement are then discussed along with the typology of engagement. Thereafter, the topics of retention and employee termination are covered.

Learning Objectives

1. To get familiarized with the concept of employee relations and the shift in its approach
2. To understand the meaning and framework of employee engagement and the strategies to improve engagement
3. To develop an understanding of the concept of employee termination and identify ways of improving retention

OPENING STORY

Industrial Relations Reforms in India

The Government of India has unleashed labour reforms to give a fillip to the Indian economy by rationalizing the plethora of labour laws. This paves the way for the long-awaited and much-needed restructuring of industrial relations in India. This reform is in line with the central theme of the government to boost manufacturing for job creation through its 'Make in India' initiative.

The Ministry of Labour and Employment has been taking steps for simplification, amalgamation, and rationalization of 44 central labour laws into four major labour codes—Code on Wages, Code on Industrial Relations, Code of Social Security, and Code on Occupational Safety, Health and Working Conditions. The government has taken several other initiatives as well:

Legislative initiatives of Government of India

- **Payment of Bonus (Amendment) Act, 2015**: Eligibility limit for payment of bonus is enhanced from ₹10,000/- to ₹21,000/- per month.

- **Payment of Wages (Amendment) Act, 2017**: Allowed payment of wages to employees by cash or cheque or crediting it to their bank account.
- **Child Labour (Prohibition and Regulation) (Amendment) Act, 2016**: Provides for complete ban on employment of children below 14 years in any occupation or process.
- **Maternity Benefit (Amendment) Act, 2017**: Increases the paid maternity leave from 12 weeks to 26 weeks.
- **The Employee Compensation (Amendment) Act, 2017**: Seeks to rationalize penalties and strengthen the rights of the workers under the Act.
- **The Payment of Gratuity (Amendment) Act, 2018**: Provides flexibility to the central government to increase the ceiling limit of gratuity to such amount as may be notified from time to time.
- Under governance reforms, the Ministry has notified '**Ease of Compliance to maintain Registers under various Labour Laws Rules, 2017**', which has in effect replaced the 56 Registers/Forms (under 9 Central Labour Laws and Rules) by 5 common Registers/Forms. This will save efforts, costs, and lessen the compliance burden by various establishments.

Source: National Portal of Government of India (https://labour.gov.in/initiatives-central-government).

EMPLOYEE RELATIONS

The term 'employee relations' refers to the relationships between employers and employees. Traditionally, the term 'industrial relations' has been commonly used. It is used to denote the employment relationships concerning management and employees or among employees and their associations. Industrial relations originated in the 20th century and has its roots in the industrial revolution, which created the modern employment relationship in large-scale industrial organizations with thousands of factory workers. These industrial enterprises were marred with problems related to low wages, long working hours, and exploitative labour practices. Industrial relations thought emerged as a middle ground between classical economics and Marxism with Sidney Webb and Beatrice Webb's *Industrial Democracy*, published in 1897, being a key influencing work.[1]

Industrial relations refers to the pattern of relationship that exists because of the necessary collaboration of men and women in the employment processes of industry.[2] Industrial relations is concerned with maintaining harmonious relations at the workplace and to maintain industrial democracy. It is characterized by forces of conflict as well as compromise. Individual differences and disagreements are resolved through constructive and democratic means. Industrial relations are dynamic and changing to keep pace with employee expectations, trade unions, and other economic and social institutions of society. It is influenced by a complex set of institutional, economic, and technological factors.

The scope of industrial relations is wide. It includes both *preventive machinery* (for example, grievance redressal, disciplinary measures, standing orders, code of conduct, ethics, discipline procedures, collective bargaining, and participatory schemes) and *settlement machinery* for dispute settlement (for example, mediation, conciliation, arbitration, and adjudication).

With evolving times, the playing field of industrial relations has changed. Business organizations are no longer the same industrial houses they used to be in the yesteryears. Industrial relations as a term originated out of the traditional manufacturing settings of the industrial era. In the present times, the service economy has become dominant, and with it the nature of workplace has changed. The key players have metamorphosed in terms of demographic profile, education, ideologies, and philosophies—thereby the priorities too have changed. Today's organizations are global in nature and so is the workforce. This mandates a completely new way of managing employees. All these changes mark a paradigm shift in this domain—one which emphasizes a shift from traditional 'industrial relations' to a broader, more pluralistic 'employee relations' orientation. The shift highlights a change in philosophy regarding workplace relations, with a focus on 'conflict' to a focus on 'cooperation'. As evident from Table 9.1, the number of reported industrial disputes in India has gone down over the years.

Table 9.1   Industrial Disputes in India

Year	No. of Disputes	No. of Workers	No. of Man-days Lost
2001	674	687,778	23,766,809
2002	579	1,079,434	26,585,919
2003	552	1,815,945	30,255,911
2004	477	2,072,221	23,866,367
2005	456	2,913,601	29,664,999
2006	430	1,810,348	20,324,378
2007	389	724,574	27,166,752
2008	421	1,579,298	17,433,721
2009	345	1,867,204	17,622,055
2010	371	1,074,473	23,130,527
2011	370	734,763	14,458,038
2012	318	1,307,454	12,936,795
2013	258	1,838,160	12,645,371
2014	317	1,155,599	11,087,715
2015	184	627,132	2,920,536

Source: Labour Bureau, Government of India, www.labourbureau.nic.in.

Industrial relations is increasingly being called employment relations or employee relations because of the importance of non-industrial employment relationships. Broadly speaking, industrial relations is used to refer to the relationships between an employer and their employees collectively through their union, with a strong influence of the government and legal structure. The use of the term 'industrial relations' to describe workplace relations is no longer as prevalent due to the widespread deindustrialization of economies and declining union membership and government interference. Instead, employers now prefer to use the term 'employee relations', referring to relationships that exist in both unionized and non-unionized workplaces. Despite change in orientation, on many grounds workplace problems and issues remain the same as ever. Both the terms continue to be used interchangeably.

TRADE UNIONISM

A trade union is an association of workers or employees formed mainly to negotiate with the employers on various workplace issues and improve the terms and conditions of work. It is an organized association of workers in a trade, group of trades, or profession formed to protect and further their rights and interests. A trade union, through its leadership, bargains with the employer and negotiates labour contracts. A trade union is supposed to be internally democratic, have a strong and popular leadership, and work to promote industrial peace and harmony. There are various types of trade unions depending on membership, structure, goals, and style of functioning.

In India, the formation and working of trade unions is regulated by the Trade Union Act, 1926. According to the Act, a trade union refers to any combination, whether temporary or permanent, formed primarily for the purpose of regulating the relations between workmen and employers, between workmen and workmen, or between employers and employers for imposing restrictive conditions on the conduct of any trade or business and includes any federation of two or more trade unions.

Industrialization brought about new economic and social order in societies. Trade unions emerged as a result of the new social order. Originating in Great Britain, trade unions became popular in many countries during the industrial revolution. They grew as a result of the efforts of social reformers who felt that workers need to organize in order to come out of their plight. By the 1810s, the first labour organizations to bring together workers of divergent occupations were formed. Possibly, the first such union is believed to be was the General Union of Trades, also known as the Philanthropic Society, founded in 1818 in Manchester.

N. M. Lokhande is said to be the founder of organized labour movement in India. He founded the first trade union in the country, namely the Bombay Mill Hands Association, in 1890. Beginning of labour movement in the modern sense started after the outbreak of World War I. Economic, political, and social conditions influenced the growth of trade union movements in India. The Russian Revolution in 1917 and the establishment of International Labour Organization (ILO) in 1919 influenced the formation of trade unions in the country. In 1920, the All India Trade Union Congress (AITUC) was formed—the 1st national-level trade union. Various other unions emerged subsequently.[3]

Trade union movement in India as also elsewhere has faced major ups and downs. It was at its peak during the mid-20th century. Various important collective bargaining agreements were reached at in different industries. Trade unions have played a very active role in textiles, cement, iron and steel, railways, and the banking sector, among others. Proliferation of trade unions, many of them affiliated to political parties, has been a distinguishing feature during the post-independence period.

However, with time, their membership has started to dwindle. Small size of unions, weak leadership, poor financial position, low-level of knowledge of union members, mutual strife, and fear of victimization and political interference are some of the reasons behind the slowing down of trade union movement in India. Further, corporatization and welfare capitalism led to a new employment equation at the workplace, obviating the need for industrial-era mindset ridden trade unions. Changing organizational culture and employment dynamics have resulted in creating a competitive workplace with international work values. The erstwhile dominant 'blue collar' workforce has evolved into 'knowledge assets', with very different work orientation and aspirations. Under such settings, the need for trade unions has lost its relevance to some extent.

Trade unions have transformed their working styles. A number of unions and associations have recently come up in new sectors such as retail, IT, and hospitality in India. In 2017, the states of Karnataka and Tamil Nadu saw the first IT/ITES union registering under the Trade Union Act, 1926. Pantaloon employees formed a union under the banner of the Bharatiya Kamgar Sena (BKS). Unions at Big Bazaar and Metro AG played an active role in the recent past. Unions have started emerging in BPOs, quick service restaurants, and the hospitality industry too.

These new-age unions have undergone attitudinal transformation. With increasing education and awareness of workers, trade unions have become more mature, rational, and realistic. These unions are depoliticized and are different in their working and ideology. They are more professional and are partnering with social and civil rights activists, media, academics, equality campaigners, international bodies, and social movements in order to shun their militant image and to look for ways of more inclusive growth of the working class. They are deploying new *modus operandi*, such as use of Internet and social media. They are attempting to reach out to larger audiences through campaigns on social media and Internet. The 'Our Walmart' campaign in the United States in 2012 was a major campaign rooted in social media to effectively organize large workforces around the world. Today, trade unions are more diverse in terms of membership. Amarjeet Kaur of the All India Trade Union Congress (AITUC) became the first woman general secretary of a central trade union in India. All these changes forebode an emerging new role of trade unions in the 21st century.

COLLECTIVE BARGAINING

ILO defines collective bargaining as negotiation about working conditions and terms of employment between employers and employees. Collective bargaining is a collective process in which representatives of both the management and employees participate. There is mutual give and take leading to a win–win agreement. It helps in bringing about compromise for establishing peace. ILO's Collective Bargaining Convention, 1981 (No. 154), states that all the member nation states of the ILO should have a mechanism in place to promote collective bargaining for determining working conditions and terms of employment.[4]

Collective bargaining develops a sense of self-respect and responsibility among the employees. It results in the establishment of a harmonious industrial climate. Collective bargaining may take place at various levels, such as national-level involving union confederations, central employer associations and government agencies, sectoral or industry-level focusing on terms of employment in one industry, company/enterprise level involving one establishment, and plant/unit/departmental level involving issues related to a particular plant or unit.

Chamberlain and Kuhn identify two major forms or models of bargaining, namely cooperative bargaining and conjunctive bargaining.[5] Cooperative bargaining involves negotiation of an issue on which both the parties may gain, or at least neither party loses. It is truly complementary or integrative in nature. Both accept that 'neither will gain unless the other gains too'. Therefore, there is willingness to concede and be pliant. It is a win-win bargain. Conjunctive bargaining arises from the requirement that some agreement may be reached so that the operations on which both are dependent may continue. It is competitive in nature. It may be characterized by mutual coercion and hostility. It is based on a zero-sum game—'my gain is your loss and your gain is my loss'. It is more a win-lose or even a lose–lose solution as the final outcome may lead to more hostility in future. Most bargains in reality tend to become a conjunctive bargain where one party tries to dominate the other.

The collective bargaining process typically involves three stages:

Pre-negotiation phase

- *Preliminary request*   Both parties try to develop the issues that they believe are most important. This phase involves placing initial demand by one party and consideration of the demand by the other party.
- *Preparation of collective bargain*   This involves determination of issues for bargain. Composition of negotiation teams may be required. Determination of scope and level may also take place and agenda of bargain may be spelled out.

Negotiation phase

- *Setting the stage/Ice-breaking*   Negotiations may start with setting the tone to start discussions. It may also necessitate attitudinal restructuring. This involves shaping some attitudes such as trust, developing a congenial bargaining environment, and working out the modalities.
- *Propose*   This phase involves the initial opening statements and the possible options that exist to resolve them.
- *Discuss*   Issues are discussed in a threadbare fashion. Each party may discuss pros and cons in detail. This phase could be described as 'brainstorming'.
- *Bargain and decide*   Negotiations are easy if a problem-solving attitude is adopted. This stage comprises the time when 'what ifs' and 'supposals' are set forth. Give-and-take is decided and final decision taken.

Post-negotiation phase

- *Final documentation*   Once bargaining is done, the contract agreement is written down. The agreement should include the agreed matters as also the frequency of its review.
- *Arbitration clause*   The agreement must include an arbitration clause. Whenever the parties have any differences pertaining to the matter, an arbitration clause can be resorted to.
- *Implementation of contract agreement*   This stage is described as consisting of effective joint implementation of the agreement. Both parties must respect the agreement and see that it is implemented in a fair and justifiable manner.

In India, collective bargaining has a long history. Way back in 1918, Mahatma Gandhi—as the leader of the Ahmedabad textile workers—advocated the resolution of conflict through collective bargaining. Collective bargaining agreements became popular after Indian independence. V.V. Giri, a prominent labour activist who later became the President of India, espoused that collective bargaining be used to settle disputes between labour and management. Significant agreements have taken place in several industries such as chemicals, petroleum, tea, coal, oil, aluminium, banking and insurance, and textile at various levels.

In 2011, the country's largest passenger car manufacturer, Maruti Suzuki India, witnessed one of the most violent incidents of labour unrest in modern times. A senior executive lost his life and several others were injured as a result of the violence. The protests continued for several days when finally, with the intervention of the government, a collective bargain agreement was reached. In 2015, the agreement was further renewed. A number of other significant bargains have taken place in recent times in Hyundai Motor India, MRF Tyres, and Nokia India, among others. Despite setbacks in some sectors, collective bargaining continues to play an important role in industrial democracy.

EMPLOYEE PARTICIPATION IN MANAGEMENT

Participation in management refers to participation of employees in the decision-making process of the organization. It is known as labour participation or workers' participation in management. Participation refers to the involvement of a person in a group situation that encourages him to contribute to group goals and share the responsibility of achievement.[6] Participation in management gives the employee a sense of importance, pride, and accomplishment. It involves sharing responsibility and authority along with a sense of accountability. It helps to establish industrial democracy and strengthen cooperation, and, thus, maintain industrial peace and harmony. Participation may be viewed as a mechanism for increasing the efficiency of enterprises, developing social education, and elevating the status of a worker in the society. The ILO has been encouraging member nations to promote employee participation.

Employee participation in management may exist at different levels:

- *Information participation*   It ensures that employees are able to receive information pertaining to the matter of general importance.
- *Consultative participation*   Here, workers are consulted on the matters of employee welfare, such as work, safety, and health. However, final decision always rests with the top-level management.
- *Associative participation*   It is an extension of consultative participation as management here is under the moral obligation to accept and implement the unanimous decisions of the employees.
- *Administrative participation*   It ensures greater share of workers' participation in the administration of various functions that concern them (for example, canteens, welfare facilities, and employee benefits).
- *Decisive participation*   This is the highest level of participation where decisions are jointly taken by employees and managers.

Employee participation may take various forms. It may be voluntary or statutory; direct or indirect; formal or informal. The most common forms of employee participation schemes are:

Indirect/Informal Participation

This refers to mechanisms that indirectly provide employees a sense of involvement and participation. Some of the common forms of indirect participation schemes are:

- *Collective Bargaining*   This involves mutual negotiations on matters of common interest. The process of bargaining can at best be considered as a basic level of participation where workers have a platform to express, discuss, and negotiate.
- *Job enlargement and enrichment*   Job enlargement refers to expanding the job content or adding task elements horizontally. Job enrichment refers to adding 'motivators' to the job (for example, status and autonomy) to make it more rewarding. This is participation in the sense that it offers freedom for employees to use their judgement and be more creative.
- *Suggestion schemes*   Employees' views are invited and incorporated in final decisions and rewards may be given for the best suggestion. It gives the employee a sense of self-fulfilment. It provides the employee with an outlet to vent his concerns.
- *Total quality management and quality circles*: Also known as continuous process improvement, total quality management (TQM) represents a long-term effort to orient all activities around the concept of quality. It is based on the belief that quality can be improved by everyone through participation. Quality circle (QC) is a mechanism to improve quality. It is based on the premise that quality control planning could only succeed with 'quality-mindedness' at every level. A QC has 7–10 people from the same work area who meet regularly to analyse and solve quality-related problems in their area. They are called participative because they involve every employee in the organization in improving quality continuously.
- *Autonomous/empowered teams*   Autonomous teams are established to manage projects or specific tasks. Authority and responsibility are passed on to the employees who then experience a sense of empowerment, ownership, and control. They are given latitude to establish their own internal goals and work practices.

Direct/Formal Participation

This refers to mechanisms that directly promote participation through formalized schemes. They may also be statutory in nature. Some of the common forms of direct participation schemes are:

- *Board-level participation*   This refers to representation of employees at the board of directors' level. The workers' representative on the board can play a useful role in safeguarding the interests of workers. This is seen as the highest form of industrial democracy.
- *Work councils and joint committees*   Various organizations have staff councils or work councils that are bodies of employee representatives. Such councils play varied roles, which

range from seeking information on the management's decision to carrying out administrative responsibilities such as managing canteens, crèche, and rest rooms. Joint councils or committees are bodies comprising of representatives of employers and employees. Such committees take decisions on a wide range of topics connected to welfare and working conditions.

- *Financial participation*   It involves a stake of the employee in the finances of the organization. The logic behind this is that if an employee has a financial stake in the organization, he/she is likely to be more positively motivated and involved. It gives the employee a sense of 'shared destiny'. Some popular schemes of financial participation are performance-linked pay, profit sharing, gain sharing (sharing gains from productivity improvements or cost reductions), employees' stock option schemes, and performance bonus.

In India, various kinds of participative schemes exist. Financial participation schemes such as ESOPs, profit sharing, and gain sharing are common in Indian organizations. Likewise, QCs, suggestions schemes, and job enlargement and enrichment have been adopted successfully in companies like BHEL, Maruti, and Tata Group of companies, among others. Many of the schemes are statutory in nature. The Industrial Disputes Act, 1947, requires industrial establishments employing 100 or more workmen to constitute works committees. In 1958, joint management councils were introduced. These have to be compulsorily provided in all organizations with more than 500 employees. The worker–director scheme was adopted in 1977. Apart from this, there are many other schemes of participation, such as shop councils or unit councils, to be provided at different levels in an establishment.

However, the implementation of participative schemes in India has been ridden with ups and downs. Financial participative schemes such as ESOPs, which were initially very successful, saw a dip in their popularity. In some cases, joint boards or councils have been dealing with inconsequential matters rather than with real issues of production and efficiency. Worker directors have also often become puppets in the hands of management. In order for the schemes to be successful, participation should be real. A peaceful atmosphere should prevail that promotes trust and authenticity. Employees need to be educated to enable them to think rationally and contribute effectively to the process.

Issues related to employee relations merit detailed discussions in the light of legal and regulatory mechanisms. They are usually dealt as a separate subject matter and embody a complete discipline in itself. They are, thus, covered extensively in books on industrial relations or employee relations.

EMPLOYEE ENGAGEMENT

Employee engagement is the commitment and involvement an employee has towards the organization and its values. Employee engagement is about understanding one's role in an organization, and being energized it. Engagement at work is conceptualized as the 'emotional connection of organizational members' to their work roles and tasks. Engagement means involvement—physically, cognitively, and emotionally—during role performance.[7]

Engagement has two important elements:

- ***Job involvement***　It is the degree to which the job situation is central to the person and his or her identity. Job involvement is a 'cognitive or belief state of psychological identification'. Job involvement is thought to depend on need identification and the potential of a job to satisfy these needs. Jobs are tied to one's self-image. It is concerned with how the individual involves himself during the performance of his job.
- ***Flow***　It refers to the 'holistic sensation' that people feel when they act with total involvement. Flow is the state in which there is little distinction between the self and work. When individuals are in 'flow state', little conscious control is necessary for their actions. Because of job involvement, an individual may experience natural flow of work abilities— things seem to just fall in line as per an individual's requirements. Work becomes part of an individual's interest.

Employee engagement is an intrinsic attitude that denotes an employee's enthusiasm for his or her job. An engaged employee is one who is involved in work and enjoys doing it. Employee engagement is a barometer that determines the association of a person with the organization. It creates positive attitudes and behaviours leading to improved business outcomes. Engaged employees are likely to stay with the company, be an advocate of the company, and contribute to bottom line success. Engaged employees form an emotional connection with the company. It builds passion and commitment for the organization's goals. Engagement requires a two-way relationship between employer and employee.

Typology of Employee Engagement

Employees can be categorized into various types depending on their level of engagement. Two important dimensions can be used to create the employee engagement typology. The first dimension is 'behaviour', which can be mapped along a continuum ranging from active to passive. The second dimension is 'outcome', which can be mapped as constructive or destructive. Based on these two dimensions, a 2 × 2 matrix can be constructed, delineating four types of employees based on the level of engagement. Figure 9.1 illustrates the matrix.

Figure 9.1　Employee Engagement Typology

	Behaviour	
	Active	Passive
Constructive	Engaged	Not Engaged
Destructive	Actively Disengaged	Disengaged

The four categories of employees are:

- **Engaged**   These are employees who are active and constructive. These employees are the builders of an organization. They show high level of engagement. They perform at consistently high levels. They work with passion and innovation and move their organization forward. They have a strong connect with the company. They are the champions, catalysts of high performance, and are star employees.

  Strategy: Organizations should uphold them as opinion leaders, change agents, and brand ambassadors. They typically exert a positive influence on the performance of their coworkers and subordinates. It is important to reward their contribution and give them opportunities for growth.

- **Not Engaged/Enrolled**   These employees are passive but constructive. They tend to concentrate on tasks rather than the goals and outcomes. Employees who are not engaged tend to feel their contributions are being overlooked. They choose to silently keep working and are not actively involved in any negative activity. They show up for work but do little beyond the minimum effort required to complete their job. The 'Employee Engagement—Global Workforce' study by Towers Perrin has revealed that this category comprises the biggest segment of employees.[8]

  Strategy: Not engaged employees may need careful and empathetic counselling and mentoring to shed their complacent behaviour. Most 'not engaged' employees neither improve nor detract from current performance, as they tend to do their jobs quietly. It is important to recognize their small contributions and build a conducive environment for them to get engaged.

- **Disengaged/Disenchanted**   They are passive and destructive. There is a very subtle distinction between 'not engaged' and 'disengaged' employees. While not engaged employees tend to concentrate on their tasks, disengaged employees frequently ignore tasks and may be involved in serious negligence at work. They are unhappy employees. Their behaviour may be passively destructive.

  Strategy: It is important to address the cause of their apathy. They require motivation and counselling. It is not about healing disengagement, but about preventing it. By the time disengagement translates into active disengagement, the damage is already done.

- **Actively Disengaged**   These employees are actively destructive. They are not just unhappy at work, rather their unhappiness gets actively manifested. They create problems, indulge in uncivil behaviour, and sow seeds of negativity. They undermine what their engaged coworkers accomplish. They are problem creators and spread a sense of disgruntlement.

  Strategy: Ignoring actively disengaged employees is dangerous. Their lack of commitment and the negative effect they have on the performance of others is too great to be ignored. Management should make efforts to identify these employees and take appropriate actions to correct the problem. They either need disciplining or training, or they may even be fired in case of repetitive offence.

The Cost of Disengagement

Disengagement can be a huge cost to the company. Actively disengaged employees are a more serious cost. They hamper the working of an organization. Disengagement may bring with itself many types of costs.

- **Direct Cost** Disengaged employees generally take more leaves, are often absent, are negligent, miss deadlines, and show poor results. Gallup, a leading research agency, has found that a disengaged employee costs the organization $3,400 for every $10,000 of salary, or 34 per cent.[9] Disengaged employees create disengaged customers because they naturally pass on their negativity. Disengaged employees cause damage to company property and indulge in theft of office equipment.
- **Decrease in Company Performance** Employee disengagement leads to lowering of company performance. Highly profitable companies have more engaged employees versus unprofitable companies. Disengaged employees drag down overall company performance.
- **Turnover and Training Costs** Disengagement leads to talent loss. There is a huge cost of employee turnover. Further, the cost of fresh recruitment and training is also high. There is also a hiatus or gestation period involved in this process. This is also a serious cost.

Disengagement costs companies huge losses every year. The psychological costs of disengagement may be even greater than the financial costs. Poor performance by disengaged coworkers is an important reason that engaged employees leave their jobs. It is critical for managers to be sensitive to and be aware of every employees' job satisfaction. Frequent communication with employees is a must. Management needs to know the exact root of the disengagement and define the focus of improvement.

Measuring Employee Engagement

A lot of organizations conduct frequent employee engagement surveys to identify the level of engagement and unearth potential problems. The following four-step approach helps measure employee engagement.

Step I: Communication The employer must regularly interact with employees and listen to them in order to identify potential problems and concerns. Regular communication and feedback helps build trust and enables managers to get a feel of the undercurrents.

Step II: Measure employee engagement Employee engagement needs to be measured at regular intervals. Engagement surveys may be designed to know the current levels of engagement and classify employees into various categories of engagement typology. Various kinds of survey tools exist to aid organizations in mapping engagement. Gallup, has developed a survey tool called *G12-Employee Engagement Survey*, which is commonly used by business organizations.

Step III: Identify the problem areas Based on survey findings, problem areas and causes of disengagement may be identified.

Step IV: Take action   Once the issues and concerns have been identified, it is important to initiate action plans to take corrective steps. Surveys may be meaningless if the results are not analysed for remedial action.

Action plans must also have an in-built monitoring and review mechanism. Engagement surveys without visible follow-up action may actually decrease engagement levels, suggesting that organizations must think twice before measuring engagement without commitment for action planning.

Fostering Employee Engagement

Organizations need to create a culture that fosters employee engagement. The following action points may be taken care of to build a culture of engagement.

- Listen to the employees: Most people want to work for an employer who listens to their problems and takes care of their needs.
- Provide clear, consistent expectations: Vague policies and unclear expectations can make employees feel disengaged. Organizations must spell out clearly what they expect from employees.
- Give employees a sense of importance: Valuing people and giving them a sense of importance has a greater impact on loyalty and engagement.
- Develop opportunities for advancement: The chance to work the way up the corporate ladder is a tremendous incentive for productivity and employee engagement.
- Create good relationships: Organizations need to build relationships around trust and authenticity.
- Celebrate and reward successes: Managers must set realistic targets, and then reward and celebrate when they are attained.
- Create a sense of belongingness: Managers must move from 'the company' to 'our company' orientation. Employees have to be seen as partners in everything.
- Identify causes of disengagement: Organizations need to have smoke detector mechanisms in order to identify causes behind any form of disengagement and take remedial action.

When employees feel that the organization cares, they are bound to be engaged. Their commitment to the organization rises.

EMPLOYEE RETENTION AND TERMINATION

Employee retention refers to the policies and practices that let employees stick to an organization for a longer period of time. Every organization invests time and money in employees in terms of recruitment, training, or rewards. The organization suffers when the employees leave their job once they are fully trained. Retaining skilled employees is a significant issue for any business. The cost of losing an employee includes not only lost productivity but also the expense of recruiting, selecting, and training a new employee.

Despite efforts to retain employees, terminations are inevitable. Termination of employment is an employee's departure from a job, willingly or unwillingly. Terminations are a necessary part of business life and must be carried out promptly when the need for such actions become obvious. A wise employer will always follow proper termination procedures and carry out systematic termination planning.

Termination Planning

Termination planning involves assessing termination/separation causes on a periodic basis. There may be two primary causes of termination:

- **Voluntary termination**   This is termination of employment by the employee (for example, attrition/turnover and voluntary retirement). Attrition is a serious problem affecting all business organizations. Voluntary turnover cannot be planned; it can only be anticipated. Past trends and data as well as the present industry scenario helps in anticipating this. Frequent feedback, surveys, and candid exchange with employees helps in identifying the possibilities. Identifying causes of previous turnovers and remedying the shortcomings may alleviate the problems to some extent.
- **Involuntary termination**   This is termination of employment as part of the company policy or other circumstances not in the hands of the employee (for example, termination of contract, retrenchment, dismissals, retirements/superannuations, and death). Retirements are more planned and natural. Termination of contract is also expected. Other forms of involuntary termination, such as retrenchment (often called 'golden handshake' or 'giving pink slip') or dismissals (often called 'firing') may cause animosity and, hence, have to be properly handled.

Whether voluntary or involuntary, termination is a sensitive matter. Often organizational reputations may suffer because of wrongful terminations especially in case of retrenchments or dismissals. Terminating an employee is often a stressful process for employees and employers alike. Considerable care and good judgement must be used to ensure that the termination complies with the requirements of employment law as well as keeps the 'employer image' of the company intact. There are legal, ethical, and social underpinnings of termination, especially retrenchment or dismissal. How one dismisses an employee sends a powerful message to the remaining staff. Terminating employment is, thus, never an easy task.

Maintaining an updated database of existing and past employee demographics and work profile is absolutely essential to do termination planning and fill vacancies on time. Companies must make sure to keep records of all past warnings, actions, employee dissatisfaction data, performance progress, and so on. Monitoring of workplace activity, feedback, and employee surveys helps company management to be aware of what employees feel to get a pulse of intentions to quit. All termination plans should consider the long-range risks, given that many incidents of workplace violence may occur after the termination.

Issues in termination planning and strategy

There are various critical issues in termination planning that need to be taken care of:

Termination target selection   In case of retrenchment, it is important to determine who is to be terminated, when, and how. Key employees have to be valued. A lot of organizations follow last-in-first-out (LIFO) method to identify targets for termination. However, inadequate performance report will always be a basis of retrenchment. Dismissals for misconduct will target problem employees after carrying out the due process of disciplinary action. It is important to provide initial feedback or warnings so that the targeted employee knows that he is failing.

Termination notice and etiquette   It involves carefully handling issues such as detailing causes of termination, selection of person-in-charge who gives the notice, timing of termination, and language and timing of notice. It is advisable to at least give the employee some notice period or compensation in lieu of that. Due consideration has to be given to legal and ethical issues at the time of termination.

Preparing for reactions   Often employees react in unexpected ways after hearing about their termination. They may become violent or agitated. Companies should try to be sensitive to how they might be feeling but not get swayed emotionally. Care has to be exercised that the employee's impulsive reactions may not cause dismay among others.

Informing the team   Once it is decided to terminate an employee, it is important to inform the team or unit about the action as well as intimate them about plans for filling the vacancy. The staff will appreciate being kept in the know so that they can adjust their priorities as necessary.

Compensation and benefits of separation   Employees should be handed the benefits they are entitled to—often called a severance package. This should be done fairly, judiciously, and as compassionately as possible. In case of retirement, passing on retirement benefits may take place. In case of termination by death, compensation may be given to family, as ordained by the company policy.

Handing over charge   Employee may be asked to hand over the charge to a designated person, often the supervisor. It may involve handing over all documents and possessions.

Protecting data   One should make sure that adequate security measures are taken after terminating any employee. Before the employee leaves the premises, any keys or company document or property must be returned immediately. Moreover, changing any necessary passwords or access code information is essential.

Exit interview   An exit interview, especially in the case of voluntary turnover, is important. This helps gain insights into the employee's perception of his work, team, and the company. It also helps get feedback about potential problems at the workplace.

Post-termination formalities and strategies   Termination does not always involve complete severing of ties. Some high-performing employees who are retiring may be offered extensions.

A number of companies maintain alumni networks to keep in touch with old employees who may be willing to come back. Companies may often rehire these employees who may bring richer experiences with them. The concept of boomerang employees has already been discussed in the chapter on staffing.

Once termination has taken place, the vacancy may have to be filled—this restarts the manpower planning and career planning loop.

Improving Employee Retention

Employee turnover or attrition is a serious problem in business organizations nowadays. Turnover results in loss of corporate knowledge or memory. Retaining employees, especially the top talent is a priority for every organization. The following strategies may help curb turnover and improve retention:

Strategic HR planning and staffing   A carefully designed staffing approach helps hire the right people with the right skills. When there is a match between people and the organization, it helps improve retention rates.

Onboarding and orientation   Every new hire should be oriented to fit with the organization's culture. Right onboarding and orientation helps acclimatize the incumbent to the organization. Pairing new employees with mentors helps in ensuring that the employee feels comfortable in the new settings. Mentors can offer guidance and be a sounding board for newcomers.

Recognition and rewards systems   Every person wants to feel appreciated for what he/she does. It is important to show appreciation to employees. Both monetary and nonmonetary rewards are important. These recognition programmes go a long way in arresting employee turnover.

Work–life balance   A healthy work–life balance is essential for employees. Organizations need to have in place work–life balance policies. Flexible work arrangements, time-offs, vacations, recreation, child care support, and elderly care support are some of the work–life balance initiatives.

Learning and development   Employees always look forward to learning opportunities and possibilities of career advancement. Organizations need to invest in their employees' professional development and provide opportunities for them to grow.

Communication and feedback   Keeping open lines of communication is vital for employee retention. There must be upward, downward, and lateral communication. A culture of open communication and feedback builds trust in the system and helps improve retention.

Fostering teamwork   When people work together, they can achieve more than they would have individually. Fostering a culture of teamwork and collaboration that accommodates individuals' working styles encourages everyone. It is also important to celebrate major milestones for individuals and for the team.

Managers need to develop strong working relationships with their employees and stay attuned to individual motivations or frustrations. This helps address issues that could impact retention. Just like 'exit interviews', a lot of organizations are now going for 'stay interviews'. A stay interview is a meeting with an employee to discuss things like what they like and dislike about their role, their strengths and weaknesses, and expectations they have from the company. This helps tailor organizational strategies to retain them.

One of the best ways to put an effective employee retention strategy in place is to track past turnover metrics. Segmenting turnover data helps chalk out effective retention plans. By examining turnover data by location, department, and level, one can identify trends, uncover root causes, and take appropriate action. Segmenting turnover data will help identify areas that seem to have a problem. This approach also helps identify areas with a stellar record for retention in order to share best practices across the organization. One important metric that is important to track is the turnover of top talent compared with low performers. Higher turnover rates for top performers can signal serious organizational problems that need to be addressed.

Turnover is not always a bad thing. It is important for any organization to see an ongoing, regular influx of new talent that brings fresh ideas and experiences along with a different perspective. Turnover can help rejuvenate an organization and invites everyone to continually examine and challenge common practices and assumptions, looking for ways to improve. However, too much turnover can harm the organization. As a general rule, while turnover rates vary with the economic climate, most organizations try to keep turnover below 15 per cent. When turnover exceeds this, it signals serious problems that merit serious attention.

HR Anecdote

When Moses led the people of Israel away from the Red Sea, they moved out into the desert of Shur. They traveled in this desert for three days without finding any water. When they came to the oasis of Marah, the water was too bitter to drink. So they called the place Marah (which means 'bitter'). Then the people complained and turned against Moses. 'What are we going to drink?' they demanded. So Moses cried out to the Lord for help, and the Lord showed him a piece of wood. Moses threw it into the water, and this made the water good to drink (Exodus 15:22–25).

For Moses, his life was concerned with leading the people of Israel to the Promised Land. From the very beginning, Moses' mission was clear. He was unwavering in his commitment to take his people along. Moses grew up with a silver spoon in his mouth, having been raised by the Pharaoh's daughter. Yet he truly related to and understood the slave's life of misery. His life was devoted to freeing his people and listening to their issues.

Lesson: The people complained to Moses because water did not taste good. As their leader, he is the one they looked up to and complained to. Even if the leader or manager might not be responsible, he has to listen to complaints and look for possible solutions, even if those complaints are beyond his control.

News Grab
Digital Attrition: Imbalance in IT Industry

As IT companies train employees in digital skills, some are beginning to reckon with a new problem—there are more trained employees than jobs, an imbalance that is resulting in employee attrition. These companies are investing in reskilling their talent and need to retain them to recoup their investment. Companies are seeing higher attrition levels with digitally trained people. The dilemma for the IT services companies is that if they do not reskill employees, it will be difficult to deliver the services for digital technology projects; and if they are re-trained but not utilised, they may leave the company eventually.

The endeavour is not only to keep people ready but to give them the right deployment. One way to ensure that employees stayed was to show strong growth in new businesses that would lead to trained employees being deployed. The largest IT services company has trained over half its nearly 400,000 workforce in digital skills. It gets under a quarter of its revenue from the new technologies. Companies are looking at hiring talent with the right digital skills to avoid some of these issues. Training employees on digital skills helped create a deeper bond with the company as employees value the investments that are being made to keep them relevant.

Source: Adapted from //economictimes.indiatimes.com/articleshow/64023624.cms? utm_source=contentofinterest&ut.m_medium=text&utm_campaign=cppst.

CHAPTER SUMMARY

- The term 'employee relations' refers to the relationships between employers and employees. Traditionally, the term 'industrial relations' has been commonly used.
- Industrial relations as a term originated out of the traditional manufacturing settings of the industrial era. In the present service economy, the nature of workplace has changed, mandating a shift from 'industrial relations' to 'employee relations'.
- A trade union is an association of employees formed to negotiate with employers on various workplace issues and improve their terms and conditions of work. The new-age unions have undergone attitudinal transformation.
- Collective bargaining refers to negotiation about working conditions and terms of employment between employers and employees.
- Participation in management refers to participation of employees in the decision-making process. There are various levels and forms of participation.
- Employee engagement is the commitment and involvement an employee has towards the organization and its values. It has a positive impact on business outcomes.
- Termination of employment is an employee's departure from a job, willingly or unwillingly.
- Employee retention refers to the policies and practices that let employees stick to an organization for a longer period of time.

EXERCISES AND DISCUSSION QUESTIONS

1. Discuss the difference between industrial relations and employee relations and examine how the paradigm shift has taken place.
2. What is employee engagement? Discuss the engagement typology and suggest strategies for managing each category of employee.
3. Highlight the major issues and concerns in employee termination. What are some of the ways to improve retention?

CASELET

Employee Relations and Engagement at Taj Hotels

Since its establishment, the Taj Group had a people-oriented culture. The group aimed at making the HR function a critical business partner. To achieve 'Taj standards', all employees are placed in intensive training programmes. In order to show its commitment to and belief in employees, the Taj Group developed the 'Taj People Philosophy' (TPP), which focused on employees' learning and career planning. The concept of TPP, was based on the key points of the Taj employee charter:

- Every employee would be an important member in the Taj family.
- The Taj family would always strive to attract, retain, and reward the best talent.
- The Taj family would commit itself to communication and transparency.

As part of the TPP, the Taj Group introduced a strong performance management system, called the Taj Balanced Scorecard System (TBSS) that linked individual performance with the group's overall strategy. As an extension of the TBSS, Taj created a unique employee loyalty and reward programme, called the Special Thanks and Recognition System (STARS). STARS was an initiative aimed at motivating employees to transcend their usual duties and responsibilities. The STAR system also led to global recognition of the Taj Group of hotels when the group bagged the Hermes Award for 'Best Innovation in Human Resources' in the global hospitality industry.

The TPP and STARS were not only successful as an HR initiative, but brought many strategic benefits to the group. The service standards at all hotels of the group improved significantly because the employees felt that their good work was being acknowledged and appreciated. Reportedly, customer satisfaction levels increased significantly.

The 26/11 Attacks at Taj

On 26 November 2008, 175 people died in Mumbai, India, when terrorists simultaneously struck five locations—all well-known landmarks. The Taj Mahal Palace and Tower was one of them. Nobody had ever thought that the beautiful domes of the hotel would become closely associated with the horrific attacks. However, it was also a saga of extraordinary heroics by the hotel staff for their customers, and in a way, for their country. The sense of duty and service was unprecedented.

The terrorists started firing inside the hotel. The hotel staff displayed exemplary presence of mind, courage, and sacrifice to protect the guests. A young lady who was a relations executive stopped many of the guests going out and volunteered to go out several times and get stuff such as water for the guests when the situation outside the hall was very explosive and she could have easily been the target of the bullets. The young lady had no instructions from any supervisor to do what she did. She took just three minutes to rescue the entire team through the kitchen. People exhibited extraordinary courage to save guests included janitors, waiters, directors, artisans, and captains—all levels of people. Thomas George, a captain, escorted 54 guests through a backdoor staircase and when he was going down last, he was shot by the terrorists. General Manager Karambir Singh Kang's wife and two young sons died in a fire that swept through their apartment on the hotel's top floor. Even after receiving the news, he insisted on staying at his post to direct response to the ongoing attack.

The heroic response by employees of Taj Hotel focuses on the staff's selfless service for its customers and how they went beyond their call of duty to save lives. The multimedia case study 'Terror at the Taj Bombay: Customer-Centric Leadership' by Professor Rohit Deshpande from Harvard Business School documents the bravery and resourcefulness shown by employees during the attack. The study mainly focuses on 'why did the Taj employees stay at their posts during the attacks, jeopardising their safety in order to save guests?' and 'how can that level of loyalty and dedication be replicated elsewhere?' A dozen Taj employees died trying to save the lives of the hotel guests. Not even the senior managers could explain the behaviour of these employees.

Deshpande says even though the employees 'knew all the back exits' in the hotel and could have easily fled the building, they stayed back to help the guests. The natural human instinct would be to flee. These are people who, on the other hand, decided to stay. In the process, some of them, unfortunately, gave their lives to save guests. This is exemplum of customer-centricity, employee commitment, and leadership at its best. It focuses on the hotel's approach to the Indian culture of 'guest is God' philosophy. It is believed that in India there is a much more paternalistic equation between employer and employee that creates strong kinship. However, Taj employees' sense of loyalty to the hotel and responsibility towards the guests goes beyond expectations. No amount of training could have prepared them for such an unprecedented situation.

This was the most trying period in the life of the organization. Senior managers, including Ratan Tata, were visiting funeral to funeral over the next 3 days. Various benefits were extended to the families of the deceased, including full salary for life for the family, complete responsibility of education of children and dependents, and full medical facility for the whole family and dependents for rest of their lives. All employees, including casual employees, were treated as being on duty during the time the hotel was closed. Relief and assistance was extended to all those who were injured. Employee outreach centres were opened where all help, food, water, sanitation, first aid, and counselling was provided.

Despite the terrorists' attack on 26 November, the Taj Mahal Hotel opened her doors to guests by Christmas Eve the same year. At a commemorative event, Ratan Tata, the then group chairman, broke down in full public view, saying, 'The company belongs to these people.' Ratan Tata personally visited the families of all the 80 employees who in some manner—either through injury or death—were affected.

The question that remained unanswered, however, was how did Taj employees manage to demonstrate such loyalty and dedication. How was such passion created among the employees? This level of engagement goes beyond any theoretical framework or a 2 × 2 matrix. It cannot come through training and development. Some people say that it has to do with the DNA of the organization, with the way Tata's culture and value system is; its stand on ethics, duty, sincerity, and above all—its philanthropic philosophies. 'It's all of those very specific things that build a customer-centric culture', Deshpande says. 'This example far exceeds anything I've seen before.'

A definitive answer to the question of why the Taj employees behaved as they did may not be possible; however, students of management will likely get a new perspective to the concept of employee relations and engagement.[10]

Questions for Discussion

1. What are the key features of Taj's people philosophy?
2. In light of the concepts of employee relations and engagement, discuss the 26/11 attacks and the behaviour exhibited by the employees. How do you explain the situation?

NOTES

1. S. Webb and B. Webb (1897), *Industrial democracy* (London, UK; New York, NY; Bombay, India: Longmans, Green & Co.).
2. D. Yoder (1942), *Personnel management and industrial relations* (New York, NY: Prentice Hall Inc.).
3. C. B. Mamoria, S. Mamoria, and S. V. Gankar (2012), *Dynamics of industrial relations* (Mumbai, India: Himalaya Publishing House).
4. For details of the convention, see C154 - Collective Bargaining Convention, 1981 (No. 154), retrieved from https://www.ilo.org/dyn/normlex/en/f?p=NORMLEXPUB:12100:0::NO::P12100_INSTRUMENT_ID:312299, retrieved 3 March 2018.
5. N. W. Chamberlain and J. W. *Kuhn* (1965), *Collective bargaining* (New York, NY: McGraw-Hill).
6. K. Davis (1962), *Human relations at work* (New York, NY: Mc-Graw Hill).
7. W. A. Kahn (1990), Psychological conditions of personal engagement and disengagement at work, *Academy of Management Journal* 33(4): 692–724.
8. For details of the survey findings, see https://employeeengagement.com/towers-perrin-employee-engagement.
9. For details of the report, see https://www.theemployeeapp.com/gallup-2017-employee-engagement-report-results-nothing-changed.
10. With inputs from https://hbr.org/product/terror-at-the-taj-bombay-customer-centric-leadership-multimedia-case/511703-MMC-ENG and https://www.thehindu.com/news/Taj-staff-heroism-defies-Harvard-study/article15535482.ece, retrieved 6 July 2016.

Strategy Evaluation

Part I

THE FRAMEWORK OF STRATEGIC HUMAN RESOURCE MANAGEMENT
Chapter 1: Concept of Strategic Human Resource Management

Part II

CONTEXT OF SHRM
Chapter 2: Environment of SHRM
Chapter 3: Technology and HRM

Part III

STRATEGY FORMULATION
Chapter 4: Strategy Formulation and HRM
Chapter 5: Work Flow Analysis and Strategic Job Analysis

Part IV

STRATEGY IMPLEMENTATION
Chapter 6: Strategic Human Resource Planning and Staffing
Chapter 7: Strategic Training and Development
Chapter 8: Performance Management and Compensation
Chapter 9: Employee Relations, Engagement, and Termination

Part V

STRATEGY EVALUATION
Chapter 10: Strategic HR Evaluation

Strategic HR Evaluation

Chapter Overview

This chapter discusses the concept of strategic human resource (HR) evaluation. It identifies the need for measuring human resource management (HRM) activities and taking informed business decisions. Various approaches and techniques of HR evaluation are discussed. Methods of evaluation of an individual HRM subsystem as well as an HRM system as a whole are discussed in detail. The concept of HR analytics and its use in strategic HR evaluation is also highlighted at the end of the chapter.

Learning Objectives

1. To understand the concept of strategic HR evaluation
2. To identify the various approaches and techniques of HR evaluation
3. To understand the metrics and methods of evaluation of individual HRM practices as well as the HRM system

OPENING STORY

HR and Finance—Marriage on the Clouds

The changing business environment is making cross-functional collaboration more important than ever before. However, no partnership could have a more immediate impact on corporate performance than finance and HR departments working together. Traditionally, the two have not really worked together. The fact is many HR professionals do not necessarily appreciate a balance sheet or hard accounting data. Finance professionals may not really understand the value of things like motivation and soft skills.

However, things are changing. With the digitization of the economy and the emergence of analytics, finance and HR managers are coming together. With an eye on business transformation, both are now focusing on using business metrics and analytics to contribute to the bottom line. They are coming out of their cocoons and working in tandem. Just as the chief finance officer (CFO) helps the chief executive officer (CEO) lead the business by allocating financial resources, the chief human resources officer (CHRO) should help the CEO by building talent. The link between financial numbers and the people who provide productivity to reach those numbers should be inseparable. CHROs need to understand finance, and CFOs need to be more people-centric. When CFOs and CHROs work together, they can significantly impact the business.

An Ernst & Young survey shows companies with high collaboration between HR and finance experience an increase in topline revenue, an increase of 10 per cent or more in operational cash flow, and an increase in employee productivity and engagement. Moreover, according to the survey, 80 per cent of the global HR and finance professionals interviewed said their relationship had become more collaborative over the last three years.

CFOs and CHROs are collaborating to evaluate the financial impact and business risks of various HR interventions. Utilizing the data gained through analytics, they can design effective strategies. Using unified technology for both finance and HR is like a marriage made in the clouds. Not only does this create harmony, it can help drive analytics where HR and finance aid each other.

Finance people need to think holistically about the business, which includes the people component as well. Likewise, HR managers need to understand that they are not there just to give people a joyful time. They are there to drive the business. Both need to forge a strong relationship with each other.

Source: Adapted from https://www.forbes.com/sites/oracle/2015/09/29/cfos-and-chros-the-collaboration-imperative/#132de72b500b and https://www.hcamag.com/hr-news/how-can-hr-and-finance-work-more-effectively-together-252009.aspx.

MEASURING HRM

With the increasing emphasis on strategic HRM (SHRM), there has been a greater need to explain and show the contribution of HR departments. The evaluation of HR programmes and activities is now becoming a priority in a number of organizations. Evaluation of HR practices helps in elucidating how HRM actually contributes to overall organizational productivity and performance. The strategic role of HR managers requires them to work with line managers and executives to create a vision for the organization's future and establish an HR strategy that enables the strategic plan to be executed.

The idea of valuation of human resources is said to have started with the resource-based view (RBV). The RBV owes much of its genesis to a remarkable book by a Professor of Economics at University of London, Edith Penrose published in 1959. Penrose conceptualized the firm as a collection of productive resources.[1] This work was later rediscovered by a string of other researchers who agreed that human resource is the most important resource for competitive advantage.[2] In the 1960s, Rensis Likert, along with other social researchers, made an attempt to define the concept of human resource accounting (HRA).[3] HRA is the process of identifying and reporting investments made in the human resources of an organization. The term 'human capital management' (HCM) started to be used in this context. It refers to the comprehensive set of practices for recruiting, managing, developing, and optimizing the human resources of an organization. It views employees as assets that can be invested in and managed to maximize their business value. It was suggested that HR managers need to have an investment perspective to human resource.

HR evaluation helps in justifying the existence and contribution of the HR function. It helps in showing the bottom-line contributions of the HR department. It also helps in demonstration of efficiency and accountability in utilization of human resources. It provides assessment tools to identify lacunae in HR practices to enable remedial action. Most importantly, it enables us to understand the role of the HR function in the accomplishment of company goals. Thus, strategic HR evaluation requires measuring whether HR function, programmes, and activities have contributed to the company's strategic objectives. It helps in showing the HR deliverables. It is believed that 'what can't be measured can't be managed'.

SHRM requires moving away from looking at the HR department as a cost centre to an investment centre. The benefits resulting from HR programmes such as reduced turnover or improved percentages of good hires can be determined in monetary values. In such cases, the effectiveness of the function can be measured as a profit centre. A profit centre or investment centre approach requires a shift in perspective from perceiving HR as a cost centre to an investment that can achieve bottom-line results. Adoption of this approach requires the HR department to become client-oriented and quality conscious in delivering services and programmes. The profit centre approach allows management to effectively measure return on the resources invested in the HR department.

Figure 10.1 illustrates the framework for strategic HR evaluation.

Figure 10.1   Framework for HR Evaluation

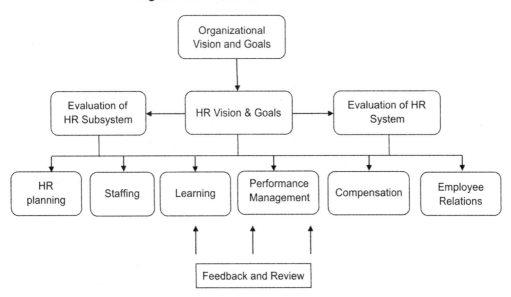

APPROACHES TO HRM EVALUATION

There may be various approaches to HR evaluation depending on what is being evaluated and how. Some of these issues need discussion.

Scope of Analysis   The domain or scope of strategic HR evaluation may vary from focus on individual HR practices to evaluation of the overall HR system.

- Individual HR practices: Evaluation of HR practices may focus on single practices as subsystems of HR. Thus, an evaluation of recruitment, selection, training, and performance appraisal may take place separately. Measures like recruitment time, recruitment advertising cost, training cost, and training effectiveness focus on evaluating individual HR areas.
- System of HR practices: Evaluation of system of HR practices entails a comprehensive broad-based evaluation of the entire HRM system. It involves designing a mechanism to evaluate the overall performance of the HRM function.

Criteria of Analysis   The priority of evaluation programmes may be on efficiency-based criteria vis-à-vis HRM or it may be on effectiveness.

- Efficiency-based measures: These are primarily productivity-based measures that basically aim at assessing quantity and cost of production. It seeks to evaluate 'how well' the productivity targets were achieved. Some of the efficiency measures could be per head expenditures, staffing ratios, or training costs.
- Effectiveness-based measures: Effectiveness is generally viewed as a multidimensional construct and typically involves multiple criteria, such as goal attainment, adaptability, and flexibility. Quality of work, employee satisfaction, and engagement could be some effectiveness measures.

Focus of Analysis   An important evaluation issue is whether the criteria will involve outcomes or processes.

- Focus on outcomes: Outcomes are results or end products of any activity. They focus on 'what' is attained. They are rational, objective criteria for evaluation. Examples of outcome criteria could be productivity ratios, sales, and profitability for a company.
- Focus on process: Processes concern behaviours or how activities are performed. They focus on 'how' something is attained. An example of a process criterion could be whether a unit meets the planned time schedule or an employee handles customer query satisfactorily. The process-oriented approach focuses on the types of activities performed by the department and the degree of efficiency in administering those activities.

Indices of Analysis   Strategic HR evaluation may be done using quantitative or qualitative measures and indices.

- Quantitative measures: Quantitative measures of HR are specific, quantifiable criteria. These include absenteeism, turnover, job acceptance rates, number of strikes, revenue per employee, production per employee, sales per employee, HR budget per employee, time to fill vacancies, training hours, and so on. Quantitative measures can sometimes be combined in the form of composite indices to measure the overall performance of HR as an investment centre.
- Qualitative measures: Qualitative indices include those dimensions that cannot be exactly quantified but can nevertheless be measured using behavioural instruments such as questionnaires and interview check-list. These measures include employee morale, satisfaction, commitment, motivation, perception about HR programmes, equity, and so on.

Techniques of Analysis Two major techniques of analysis may be identified.

- Audit techniques: An HR audit is an investigative and comparative process that attempts to measure the effectiveness of the HR function. Like financial auditing, it involves compiling and analysing data (usually a year) to reveal how HR is performing. It also provides baseline data to improve the performance of the organization. Audit approaches, also sometimes referred to as stakeholder approaches, determine the satisfaction of key users of HR services. Audit approaches may include personnel indices, such as per capita costs or absenteeism rates and service user reactions, such as employee surveys regarding job satisfaction, pay satisfaction, and so on.
- Analytical techniques: Analytical procedures are used for evaluating specific data, mainly financial, and looking at variations that occur in the data. Analytical procedures are evaluations of information through analysis of plausible relationships among both financial and nonfinancial data. The analytical approaches to HR involve either experimental designs, like those used in training assessment, or cost-benefit analysis and utility theory.

Level of Analysis Another dimension of evaluation involves the level of analysis. Typically there are three levels of analysis:

- Strategic level: The objective of evaluation at the strategic level is to determine whether HR policies and programmes are consistent with the company's strategy and have been able to attain the organizational goals.
- Managerial level: At the management level, the focus is on managerial outcomes, such as the cost-benefit of a training programme and recruitment cost.
- Operational level: At the operational level, the focus is on the day-to-day operationalization of HR programmes, namely implementation of safety provisions and dispensing with rewards.

Time Period of Analysis The time horizon involved in the assessment may vary. It is often related to the level of analysis undertaken.

- Long-term: Corporate-level evaluation focuses on assessing the strategic activities of HR departments. Thus, they tend to place greater importance on activities, such as human resource planning (HRP), which have long-term strategic implications.
- Medium-term: Middle management and nonsupervisory employees tend to place importance on the department's ability to provide services on matters of mid-term importance.
- Short-term: Operating line executives, who have production responsibilities, focus on issues of immediate priority.

Thus, the HR function has to be evaluated at different levels involving different time frames that need to be taken into account in an evaluation strategy.

Various organizations have started deploying cost–benefit analysis for the quantification of any HR intervention. The cost–benefit approach compares the cost of HR programmes and services to the benefits derived from them. While programme costs are usually easy to identify, it is difficult to determine the benefits. In most cases, subjective data is used to assign a monetary value. This tends to decrease the reliability of the process. This approach, thus, needs to be used with caution. It may work well with individual short-term activities where quantification is easy, rather than evaluating the entire HR function.

Often the above limitation is taken care of by using utility analysis. Utility analysis is a specific type of cost-benefit analysis, which has applicability to HR issues. Utility analysis has the advantage of expressing evaluations in terms of not just explicit costs and benefits but also implicit costs and benefits, which are of much greater interest to general managers in assessing the contribution of HR to strategy. Several HR activities are evaluated using utility analysis, most commonly recruitment and selection. For instance, utility analysis of selection procedures deals with projected cash flows, such as in the form of savings from increased productivity.

EVALUATING HR SUBSYSTEMS

Major HR functions of strategic importance are HRP, staffing, performance evaluation, compensation and reward systems, training and development, and employee relations.

Evaluating HRP

Evaluating HRP is complex. Its effectiveness can be evaluated from a behavioural and qualitative perspective. The process of strategic HRP is more important than its outcome. This is because managers from different areas come together and reexamine fundamental assumptions to lay down a viable plan for the future. Such deliberations and the resultant collaboration are often valuable take-aways of the process.

Since HRP is the starting point in the HR flow, its effectiveness determines the effectiveness of all other HR subsystems. Potential inaccuracies in HR forecasts have a negative spill-over effect on all other HR domains.

Measures Used for Evaluating HRP

Some of the measures that can be used as indicators for evaluating HRP are:

- The accuracy of forecast in terms of correct supply analysis, demand analysis, and gap analysis is an indicator of the success of HR plans.
- An important criterion of HRP effectiveness is the concept of *just-in-time talent*, which means that vacancies can be filled quickly by a person as and when they arise. Whether vacancies have to be filled internally or externally, HRP efforts must help fill positions at just the right time.
- In cases where vacancies have to be filled from within through promotion, the holding pattern and time is indicative of the effectiveness of HRP. Holding time refers to the time an individual has to wait for promotion after becoming eligible. Waiting time results in underutilization of skills, leading to dissatisfaction reflecting on a shoddy planning effort.
- The degree to which functional area managers accept HRP as an activity that helps them perform their jobs well is a measure of the effectiveness of HRP.

- For external hires, the ability to get right candidates in right time is an indicator of the success of HRP. It is important that candidates hired should match with the organizational requirements. Absenteeism and turnover rates are indicators that the right people were not hired.
- For companies that have a preference to hire from internal sources, the extent of satisfactory placements by promotions may be an indicator of the effectiveness of HRP. To the extent that shortages in skills are forecasted and prepared for through proper development of employees, the organization has less need to hire from external labour market.

Evaluating Staffing

A company's recruitment and selection procedures are critical to its ability to acquire the right HR in order to attain its strategic objectives. Companies are now placing primary emphasis in matching applicants with the culture of the organization. Thus, evaluations may need to focus on developing measures of staff compatibility with organizational characteristics.

Measures Used for Evaluating Staffing

Staffing basically involves three important activities, namely recruitment, selection, and placement. Thus, evaluation measures need to apply to all these areas. Some of the commonly deployed measures are:

- **Number of resumes** received in response to recruitment advertisements or any other recruiting effort is an indicator of the reach and efficacy of the effort.
- **Number of unsolicited walk-ins and applications received** (both online and offline) also speak about the employer image of the organization, which is in part formed by how the organization carries out its recruitment and selection.
- **Selection ratio** (SR) is often used as an indicator of recruiting effectiveness. An SR is the proportion of job openings to applicants. An SR of 1/10 means there are 10 applicants for 1 job opening. A lower SR is more desirable because it enables the organization to choose job candidates from a larger pool, thereby increasing selectivity.
- **Time lapse data** (TLD) is another such measure. TLD is the average time that elapses between points of decision in recruiting. Let's assume, that the job is filled an average of two months after publication of the recruitment advertisement. Thus, the advertisement should be placed at least two months before the job has to be filled. Data also may be available on the time lapse between interviews and offers and between offers and acceptances. A low TLD is preferred.
- **Yield ratio** is another measure of HRP. The yield ratio for any recruiting step reflects the number of candidates available at a step and the next step.
  - a. Let us say a company assessed that newspaper advertisements may result in 1,000 applications.
  - b. Of these 1,000 applications, 100 are judged to meet some minimum qualifications. Thus, the yield ratio at this initial stage is 10 per cent.

c. Of the group of 100 candidates, 50 accepted invitations to be interviewed (yield ratio is 50 per cent at this stage).

d. Of the 50, 10 were given job offers (20 per cent yield ratio).

This ratio then can be used as a basis for planning future recruitment efforts. By going backwards from the yield ratio, the recruiter can estimate how many applicants will be necessary in order to fill a certain number of positions. The recruiter then can adjust the recruiting effort accordingly.

- **Cost per hire** is another popular mechanism for assessing hiring efforts. The cost of the recruitment source and selection technique deployed may include advertising expenditure, cost of campus visit, designing psychometric tests, administering test, interview, and so on. This may be assessed on per hire basis to get an idea of the average cost of hiring.

- **Cost–benefit analysis** deals with comparing cost of the staffing process (for example, cost of a test and advertisement expenditure) with projected cash flows, such as savings from increased productivity of new hires compared with old incumbents, expressed in net present values or candidates' future production rates, error rates, and other outcomes.

- **Utility analysis** may also be used for assessing the effectiveness of selection processes. Utility analysis is a specific type of cost-benefit analysis. Utility analysis has been quite successfully used in assessing selection mechanisms. It involves assessing implicit costs like time spent and effort involved and benefits like quality of new hires.[4]

- **Match between candidate and organization** is another indicator of how good the selection mechanism is. It is reflected in satisfaction, quality of work, and retention rates after a certain time period. If a company performs staffing functions poorly, the impact may get potentially manifested in HR problems later, such as absenteeism and turnover.

- **Composition or mix of candidates** selected is another indicator of a selection process carried out well. Diversity is an important variable for organizational success. Employees from diverse backgrounds bring individual talents and experiences in suggesting ideas that are flexible in adapting to fluctuating markets and customer demands.

Evaluating Learning and Development

Organizations design learning programmes in order to enhance skills to increase productivity, improve morale, and develop talent. Evaluating training and development involves an assessment of how learning and skill development is taking place.

Measures Used for Evaluating Learning and Development

- Donald Kirkpatrick's criteria serve as one of the most popular frameworks of training evaluation.[5] He suggested four criteria for training evaluation:
  - *Reactive criteria*   It aims at mapping a trainee's satisfaction with training or the perceptions of its quality or relevance. It is assumed that the best training results occur under conditions in which trainees are highly motivated to learn and have a positive reaction towards training. It is important to measure reaction, because it helps one understand how well the training was received by the audience.

- *Learning criteria*   This aims at assessing whether trainees have adequately learned what they were supposed to learn. Learning criteria are concerned with whether participants have absorbed the content of training. Since the basic purpose of training is skill building and to enhance learning, measuring whether this has been achieved is critical to any successful training programme.

- *Behaviour criteria*   This focuses on assessing whether the training programmes have translated into changes in behaviour such as decision-making, communication, and interpersonal relations. Usually, it is recommended that some time should elapse between the completion of training and measurement of resultant behaviour.

- *Results criteria*   This seeks to evaluate the impact of training on bottom-line performance, for example, more units produced, reduction in scrap rates, reduction in errors or breakage, and improvement in absence rates. Similarly, an effective training programme could also get reflected in improvement in morale or reduced absenteeism.

The type of criterion to be used in the evaluative process would depend on training methods adopted. For example, for technical skills training, results criteria may be more meaningful. On the other hand, for a management development programme, behavioural or learning assessment may be more valid.

- **Experimental designs**   Two experimental designs have particular relevance to the assessment of training effectiveness:

  - *Pretest-posttest control group design*   This involves two groups of subjects or participants in the experiment, namely the control and experimental groups. The experimental group is the group that receives training while the control group does not. Members of the control group are employees with similar work profiles as the experimental group, who may also undergo the same training in future, but are currently not doing so. Assignment of participants to the two groups is done randomly so as to control for such extraneous influences as differences in ability, experience, and skill. The two groups are tested on certain common parameters before training is imparted to the experimental group. The parameter chosen for assessment should be related to the theme of training. The experimental group then undergoes training, while the control group does not. After training and appropriate time lag, both groups are posttested. The statistical approach for assessing the significance of results involves the computation of gain scores, in which each individual participant's pretest score is subtracted from the posttest score. Mean value of gain scores (posttest-pretest) is evaluated within the experimental group and the control group, and their significant differences are assessed using appropriate statistical tools like independent samples T-test. If differences exist, it may indicate that the group that has undergone training has shown some change.

  - *Posttest-only control group design*   This design also utilizes experimental and control groups with randomly selected participants having similar work profiles. However, in this case, there is no pretesting. After the experimental group has undergone training, a test is administered on both groups and scores obtained. The posttest difference between the scores of both groups are assessed using T-test. This design is useful where a pretest cannot be used for reasons that it will reveal the hidden purpose of training.

For instance, training on ethics may sensitize employees on this aspect if they are asked questions during pretest and cause them to become overcautious during training.

- **Quasi-experimental design**   This design is based on time series analysis. There is no control group. Performance of the group that undergoes training is evaluated at certain periods before training and again periodically after training. A time series trend line may be generated to see changes in performance or behaviour. This design may be appropriate in situations in which no control group can be obtained having similar characteristics.
- **Cost-benefit analysis**   Like any other HR activity, cost-benefit analysis applies to training as well. It involves assessing the cost of training, for example, trainers' fee, training material, equipment, and man hours of work lost, and benefits such as improved output and productivity.
- **Human resource development audit**   Organizations now evaluate the human resource development (HRD) system rather than focus on just training. HRD is the long-term overarching framework for helping employees develop their skills, knowledge, and abilities. HRD audit is a comprehensive evaluation of the current HRD strategies, structure, systems, styles, and skills in the context of business plans of a company. It then seeks to answer whether the current skill base of the employees in the company is adequate to achieve business plans.
- **Service user reactions**   It is also important to assess the reaction of stakeholders towards the training participant. These stakeholders may be the trainee's manager or supervisor, coworkers or peers, subordinates, team members, suppliers, or customers with whom the trainee may be interacting closely. Assessing stakeholder reaction will help understand whether they perceive any change in the trainee's performance or behaviour post training.

Evaluating Performance Management

Maintaining an effective performance measurement system requires proper training to evaluators, adequate time internals for evaluations, performance-linked incentives and rewards, and well-planned performance counselling to improve performance.

Measures Used for Evaluating the Performance Management System

- **Number of performance targets attained**   Performance goals should be SMART—specific, measurable, attainable, relevant, and timely. The number of performance goals achieved after the prescribed time period helps assess the effectiveness of the performance management system.
- **Duration and frequency of appraisal**   Performance management has to be a continuous process, with regular appraisals and feedback. Too frequent appraisals may stress out employees, while appraisals given after a long duration may go against the spirit of continuous feedback. Thus, the duration and frequency of appraisal should be appropriate so as to result in clearly perceived changes.

- **Technique of appraisal used**   The technique of appraisal also reflects the efficacy of the performance management system. 360-degree appraisal is preferred to traditional top-down evaluation.
- **Opinion surveys**   Opinion surveys involve conducting surveys of stakeholders to elicit their opinions regarding efficacy of the performance appraisal mechanism. This involves assessing employee satisfaction with their performance ratings.
- **Linkage between ratings and rewards**   Another effectiveness indicator can be obtained by correlating employees' ratings with the percentage increases in compensation.
- **Frequency of litigation**   Litigation is common in Western countries when employees feel that their appraisal reports are biased.
- **Manager-wise audit**   To identify a general pattern in the ratings given by a manager (towards extremes) in order to determine the scope for biases, prejudice, or subjectivity.

Evaluating Compensation

A good compensation system is one that is consistent with organizational strategies. Such a compensation system helps reinforce strategically congruent behaviours. Evaluating compensation system involves assessing whether compensation and reward is equitable and competitive so as to have motivating value.

Measures Used for Evaluating the Compensation System

- **Assessing compensation mix**   The compensation mix is a critical issue that reflects on how good the compensation system is. Traditional compensation relies on a fixed salary system, where wages are given based on position and not on merit. When profits decline, the cost of compensation goes up, often resulting in employee lay-offs. A good compensation package is one that combines both fixed and variable pay components. When profitability declines, compensation costs also decline.
- **Degree of flexibility**   While compensation systems based on job valuation promote rigidity and pigeonholing, flexi pay plans such as cafeteria benefits and variable pay promote flexibility and innovative behaviours. The degree of flexibility in pay plans also help the company adjust its compensation cost.
- **Pay equity**   Compensation should be fair and equitable. The equity theory of motivation by Stacy Adams puts forward the idea that individuals are motivated by their perception of equity and fairness.[6] There are two components of equity that a good compensation system focuses on:
  - *Distributive Justice*   The perceived fairness of the amount and allocation of rewards among individuals. This affects job satisfaction.
  - *Procedural Justice*   The perceived fairness of the process to determine the distribution of rewards. This affects organizational commitment, trust, and intention to quit.

  Communicating how performance was evaluated and how rewards were decided helps build trust and equity. Pay satisfaction surveys help in measuring the sense of equity.

- **Cost of compensation**   The cost of compensation package vis-à-vis employee productivity measured in terms of sales, revenue, and so on, provides an idea of how well the rewards are reinforcing desirable behaviours.
- **Market competitiveness**   Comparisons of the company's wages for various jobs with those in relevant labour markets help provide an assessment of how the company's wage system is fairing.
- **Compliance to legal requirements**   Organizations often have to comply with labour laws and legal requirements vis-à-vis minimum wages or equal opportunities. Noncompliance will result in undesirable consequences. Compliance with legal provisions conveys honesty and integrity. This in itself is a strong indicator of the effectiveness of the compensation system.
- **Number of payroll complaints received**   The number of payroll complaints that an organization may receive (for example, wrong computation of salary or benefits, inadequate rewards, and unequal pay for equal work) indicates fallacies in the reward disbursement process. This reflects that the compensation system needs correction.
- **Timeliness of pay**   The timeliness of payment is an extremely vital factor in pay satisfaction. If employees receive pay checks on time, it suggests that the compensation system is efficient.
- **Completeness of pay package**   Pay package has to be complete in all respects as promised; otherwise, it is bound to create inequity and dissatisfaction. Benefits and rewards should be complete and not given in a fragmented manner.

Evaluating Employee Relations

Employee relations has always been a critical area of concern for all organizations. It has a bearing on all other HR activities. Any problems on the employee relations front are bound to act as stumbling blocks in the way of the smooth functioning of the organization. Thus, employee relations climate has to be monitored and evaluated on a regular basis.

Measures Used for Evaluating Employee Relations

- Number of strikes, work stoppages, disputes, and so on
- Number of complaints and grievances reported
- Absenteeism and turnover
- Number and type of legal cases filed
- Unionization and union activities
- Number of layoffs and retrenchments
- Company rankings and HR awards received
- Inspection requirements fulfilled and certifications received
- Health, safety, and welfare provisions existing in the organization
- Surveys on employee motivation, satisfaction, commitments, and so on

The above discussed measures focus on both quantitative and qualitative approaches to evaluating the different HR subfunctions. By evaluating these activities, HR departments can show what its deliverables are.

EVALUATING THE HR SYSTEM

While the above measures focus on evaluating individual HR subsystems, organizations are increasingly deploying overarching measures of effectiveness of the HR function in totality. These frameworks help in assessing the overall performance of the HR function. Although numerous measures have been proposed for evaluation of the HR function, there is still a lack of a robust and comprehensive framework.

Anne Tsui and Luis Gomez-Mejia's comprehensive conceptual framework addresses this to some extent.[7] Their framework differentiates between outcomes or processes affected by line management and those under control of the HRM function. In order to evaluate broader HR performance, a company might examine turnover, grievance rates, or workers' compensation claims, which are largely affected by the actions of the company's line managers.

Jac Fitz-enz, who is often acknowledged as the father of human capital strategic analysis and measurement, is credited to have developed the first HR metrics in 1978. His award-winning book, *The ROI of Human Capital*, suggests a reliable way to quantify the contributions of people to corporate profit.[8] He suggests that HR professionals need to gauge human costs and productivity at three critical levels: organizational (contributions to corporate goals), functional (impact on process improvement), and HRM (value added by HR department activities). The return on investment of human capital shows how to integrate these levels into a single, end-to-end system of human capital valuation reporting. He demonstrates how to link specific HR objectives to operational improvements and corporate financial gains. He also invented the idea of human performance benchmarking.

The HR Scorecard

In 1992, Robert S. Kaplan and David Norton introduced the balanced scorecard, a concept for measuring a company's activities in terms of its vision and strategies, to give managers a comprehensive view of the performance of a business.[9] The key new element is focusing not only on financial outcomes but also on the human issues that drive those outcomes.

The balanced scorecard suggests that we view the organization from four perspectives. The scorecard for an organization should focus on developing metrics for each of the four perspectives:

- The learning and growth perspective
- The business process perspective
- The customer perspective
- The financial perspective

The balanced scorecard is a management system (not only a measurement system) that enables organizations to clarify their vision and strategy and translate them into action. It provides feedback around both the internal business processes and external outcomes in order to continuously improve strategic performance and results. The balanced scorecard methodology is based on the premise 'what gets measured gets managed'.

Based on the concept of the balanced scorecard, Brian E. Becker, Mark A. Huselid, and Dave Ulrich proposed the idea of the HR scorecard.[10] As senior managers turn the spotlight onto HR's contribution to the organization, the HR scorecard plays a powerful role in enabling HR to reposition itself as a key strategic business partner. It talks about creating a scorecard for the overall performance of the HR function. The HR scorecard is a mechanism for describing and measuring how people management systems create value in organizations.

The scorecard attempts to provide a link between HR operations and a company's business targets. HR scorecards are tied to corporate goals or strategic plans and are designed to track and measure the efficacy of HR activities and enable managers to make targeted investments in HR. It involves both financial and nonfinancial aspects.

Developing the HR scorecard typically involves the following steps:

1. Review existing measures and identify their strengths and weaknesses
2. Identify corporate goals and HR's contribution towards these goals
3. Create a list of results that HR produces to support the organization
4. Define measures for each result
5. Prepare two reports to communicate actual versus planned performance
6. Review performance and take corrective steps

HR scorecard helps show how HR is contributing to the business. For example, if a key corporate goal is to improve customer service, then elements like customer service training should be part of the HR scorecard. Similarly, if a company wants to innovate products, the HR department can align its focus to gain talent that embraces innovation. The HR scorecard is, thus, a good way to strategically align HR with the company by showing how HR metrics are improving the overall business.

A number of organizations use the HR scorecard to benchmark against industry leaders. HR benchmarking is a process of collecting data on various aspects of HRM systems from world-class or highly comparable organizations and setting that as a standard to emulate. Organizations may use industry best practices as benchmarks. This data is then used to set standards and evaluate the performance of one's own firm, and thereby identify areas that need improvement. Some organizations have developed a human resource index (HRI) to compare progress over time with other organizations. The HRI is said to be effective for measuring attitudes, overall satisfaction, and commitment to organization goals.

STRATEGIC HR EVALUATION: CHALLENGES

Despite its benefits, HR evaluation remains a challenge. There is still a lack of proper implementation of measurement tools for HR processes. Human capital is largely intangible and difficult to measure as a component in a company's business success. Most companies neither have the capability nor systems in place to adequately document and measure HR activities. HR professionals often lack financial or business acumen to show the HR deliverables.

Broader approaches to HR evaluation tend to focus on the effectiveness of the HR function. In contrast, a narrower evaluation of the HR function would focus on its efficiency in administering a certain programme. Isolated evaluations of the HR function lead to lack of congruence between HR sub-functions. In addition, another problem in HR evaluation is with respect to the time frame involved. It takes time for the results of an HR programme to manifest themselves. There are problems when evaluation is performed on only a one-shot basis instead of a continual and systematic basis. There are obvious advantages with longitudinal approaches as opposed to cross-sectional approaches because of the latter's inability to provide insights into causality.[11]

Another issue in HR evaluation is whether to look at short-term benefits and problem-solving capacity of a programme or to look at the long-term impact on business processes. For example, a new reward programme may result in improvement in motivation but may make the employees more dependent on monetary incentives. Likewise, a company may note that its overall turnover rate has gone down, suggesting a seemingly positive outcome, but a more careful scrutiny may reveal that it is losing its star employees and high performers. Strategic approaches to evaluation recognize the organizational interdependencies of HR policies with business processes.

One of the most important dimensions missed out in most discussions on HR evaluation is the issue of ethics. In the pursuit to determining the impact of HR practices on financial or operational measures, the importance of ethics often gets underrated or ignored altogether. It is sometimes said that it is unethical on the part of an organization to place a monetary value on its HR. In fact, people are shown as 'assets' or 'resource', thus, often undermining the fact that they are human beings. Further, there could be concerns related to the creditability of the numbers reported. Sometimes, companies inflate figures to project a positive image. The urgency to improve HR metrics often goes against the notion of ethical business practices. Compliance with the law or regulations is not enough. It also requires setting high standards of ethical behaviour. HR managers should not get obsessed with numbers and data, they have a moral duty too—to ensure that HR systems are fair and based on ethical principles.

HR ANALYTICS

In recent times, the concept of big data analytics has drawn attention of businesses. Big data is a term that describes the large volume of data—both structured and unstructured—that businesses encounter on a daily basis. Big data analytics is the use of advanced analytic techniques for large, diverse data sets. Using advanced analytics techniques, such as text analytics, content analysis, machine language learning, data mining, and statistical analysis, businesses can analyse data to make better decisions.

In the case of HR, organizations have huge amounts of talent or people-related data (for example, skills, performance ratings, age, tenure, performance, and educational background), which can be used to better understand HR dynamics. Big data analytics for HR is the process of looking at HR data in search of trends, patterns, correlations, and insights about human behaviour. All this can enable a much more meticulous and objective evaluation of the HR function.

HR analytics refers to applying analytic processes to the HR function for getting better returns on investments. HR metrics is the quantification of HR programmes and processes. HR analytics examines the effect of HR metrics on organizational performance. HR analytics helps correlate business data and people data. It helps in establishing a relationship between what HR does and business outcomes and then creating strategies based on that information. HR analytics is the systematic identification and quantification of the people drivers of business outcomes. It uses HR metrics data to address questions like how high the annual employee turnover is, or how much losses will employee turnover lead to. It helps to evaluate and improve practices such as talent acquisition, development, retention, and overall organizational performance by applying the idea of predictive analytics.

HR analytics helps improve organizational performance through identification of high quality talent. It can help forecast workforce requirements and utilization for improved business performance. It can also help identify the primary reasons for attrition and identify high-value employees likely to leave. Further, it can aid in recognizing the factors that affect employee satisfaction and productivity. Analytics can help companies track absenteeism, turnover, burnout, performance, and much more. By applying complex statistical analyses, HR can predict the future of the workforce.

Imagine if one can predict which employees are most likely to leave the company using HR analytics. This information will help in succession management and strategic workforce planning. For instance, algorithms created by HR analytics solutions identify individuals likely to leave by studying the employees' online activity, profile updates, employment history, job performance, and payroll data. If the computer red-flags a valued employee, it is time for a raise or a promotion in order to keep them from leaving. Companies like Xerox and Wal-Mart are already using this to control attrition.

Domains of HR Analytics

HR analytics can be used in various HR areas such as:

- Capability analytics: It is a talent management process that allows one to identify the capabilities or competencies one has. It helps keep track of current and required skills and competencies.
- Competency acquisition analytics: It is the process of assessing the competencies required now and in the future. A company can monitor how effective it is at developing these competencies in-house or recruiting candidates with those competencies.
- Capacity analytics: It seeks to establish how efficient people are, for example, through time-motion study, and online tracking one can assess whether people are spending too much time on administrative work and not enough on more profitable work.
- Employee churn analytics: It is the process of assessing staff turnover rates in an attempt to reduce employee churn. Tools such as trends analysis, time-series analysis, historical mapping/extrapolation, exit interviews, employee surveys, social media content analysis, and psychographic profiling can be used to identify potential employees likely to leave.

- Corporate culture analytics: It is the process of assessing and understanding the corporate culture. This then allows one to track changes in culture one would like to make; for example, an analysis of customer service conversations can provide a rich vein of data to assess corporate culture.
- Recruitment channel analytics: It is the process of working out where the best employees come from and what recruitment channels are most effective.
- Employee performance analytics: It seeks to assess individual employee performance. The resulting insights can identify who is performing well and who may need some additional training.

HR analytics can help to dig into problems and issues surrounding the HR function, and using analytical workflow, guide managers to gain insights from information at hand and then make relevant decisions. HR analytics is about analysing an organizations' people problems. HR analytics is a data-driven approach towards HR. This data-driven approach that characterizes HR analytics is in line with the SHRM thought. It enables HR to make better decisions using data and create a business case for HR interventions. The alignment between what the business needs and how HR can supply that need can be done with the help of HR analytics. By emphasizing the business impact of HR, it helps the HR department move from an administrative expert to a strategic partner.

HR Anecdote
Jonathan Livingston Seagull

Jonathan Livingston Seagull is a seagull who is bored with daily squabbles over bits of food. He wonders why he can't fly. Seagulls have large wings, because of which they can't fly very high. He questions the idea of leading a pointless life and just struggling to survive. Driven by a passion for flight, he pushes himself, rising, falling—he eventually learns to fly. But his unwillingness to conform to group norms results in his expulsion from the flock. An outcast, he still continues to learn, setting higher standards and trying to reach them. He evaluates his progress and then makes efforts to improve each time.

One day, Jonathan meets two gulls who take him to a 'higher plane of existence'—a better world found through perfection of knowledge. He discovers that his sheer tenacity and desire to learn make him 'pretty well a one-in-a-million bird'. Here, Jonathan befriends the wisest gull, Chiang, who takes him beyond his previous learning, teaching him how to move with natural ability to any place. The secret, Chiang says, is to 'begin by knowing that you have already arrived'. Jonathan then returns to Earth to spread his love and knowledge for flight. His mission is successful, gathering around him others who want to excel and not just survive.

This fable is about life and flight; about passion and vision; about growth and learning; about challenging rigid norms and stereotypes; about self-perception and evaluation; about setting higher goals and achieving them; about benchmarking and excelling. It is about continuous evaluation and improvements. Business organizations too need a 'Jonathan' spirit.

Source: Adapted from R. Back (1970), *Jonathan Livingston Seagull* (New York: Macmillan).

News Grab
India witnesses 77% growth in HR analytics professionals in 2018

LinkedIn's report 'The Rise of Analytics in HR: An Era of Talent Intelligence' shows that in India, 14 percent of jobs in HR are now analytics. In the past five years, there has been a 77 percent increase in specialized analytics professionals in HR in India. These professionals are known to fill various specialized job titles such as 'Data Scientist', 'Talent Analytics Director' and 'Diversity Analytics Specialist'.

AI and automation are transforming the way companies hire, develop and retain talent. Recruiters are increasingly relying on real-time, actionable and on-demand insights. The top three industries to adopt talent analytics in India are financial services & insurance, technology-software, and professional services.

In fact, financial services leads the pack as the top industry to adopt talent analytics in seven countries in Asia-Pacific, including Australia, India, Indonesia, Singapore, Hong Kong, New Zealand, and Taiwan. However, priority areas where talent analytics is leveraged in different countries vary. For example, in India and China where people switch jobs often, talent acquisition is a priority. However, in Southeast Asia and Australia where the attrition level is lower, focus is more on talent development and workforce planning.

With the increasing demand for high-performing talent, HR leaders are turning to analytics to answer critical questions about workforce planning, identifying skills gap, employee retention, and evaluation of HR systems. Analytics and data-driven decision-making is enabling HR managers to add more value to the business. Analytics is helping HR and organizations in finding the solutions related to talent management.

Source: Adapted from https://www.peoplematters.in/news/jobs/india-witnesses-a-77-growth-in-hr-analytics-professionals-report-18278?utm_source=peoplematters&utm_medium=interstitial&utm_campaign=learnings-of-the-day.

CHAPTER SUMMARY

- Evaluation of HR practices helps in elucidating how HRM actually contributes to overall organizational productivity and performance.
- There are various approaches and techniques to carry out HR evaluation.
- Various metrics have been developed to evaluate HRP, staffing, training and development, performance management, compensation, and employee relations.
- Organizations are now increasingly deploying overarching measures of effectiveness of the HRM system in totality.
- An HR scorecard is a mechanism for describing and measuring how people management systems create value in organizations.
- Despite its benefits, HR evaluation remains a challenge due to lack of proper implementation of measurement tools for HR processes.
- HR analytics helps in HR evaluation by applying analytic processes to HR data for getting better returns on investments.

EXERCISES AND DISCUSSION QUESTIONS

1. What is the rationale behind HRM evaluation? Is the statement *'what gets measured, gets managed'* true? Give your arguments.
2. Discuss the various approaches to HR evaluation with examples.
3. Choose a top-ranking global organization and collect information on use of HR evaluation. Identify various techniques and methods and comment on their effectiveness.

CASELET

Valuing Human Resource at Infosys

Infosys Limited is an Indian multinational corporation that provides business consulting, information technology (IT), and outsourcing services. Infosys was established by seven engineers with an initial capital of $250 in 1981. It has its headquarters in Bengaluru, India. Infosys is the second-largest Indian IT company by 2017 revenues. It provides software development, maintenance, and independent validation services to companies in finance, insurance, manufacturing, and other domains.

Infosys had 82 sales and marketing offices and 123 development centres across the world as on 31 March 2018, with major presence in India, the United States, China, Australia, Japan, Middle East, and Europe. It has several credentials to boast of. It was the first Indian-registered company to list employees stock options schemes (ESOPs) and American depository receipts (ADRs) on NASDAQ on 11 March 1999. It has more than 200,000 employees, of which 36 per cent are women. Its workforce consists of employees representing 129 nationalities. It has managed to build a rich and diverse set of workforce. Its attrition rate is also among the lowest in the industry.

Infosys is credited with having introduced the most innovative practices in HR and finance domains, being ranked as one of the most innovative companies in the world by Forbes. In the 1990s, Infosys pioneered the concept of systematic HR valuation in India. In the financial year 1995–1996, Infosys became the first software company to value its human resources in India. It recognized human resource costs as an investment rather than as expenses, and added the dimension of 'value' to human resources. Infosys, started showing human resource as an asset in its balance sheet.

It adopted the Lev and Schwartz Model for HR accounting. According to this model, an organization's HR is divided into groups of employees like skilled, semi-skilled, and unskilled workforce, and different categories of engineers, managerial cadres, and sales force. Based on the data, average earnings profiles are created and the present value of the future earning capacity of an employee, from the period of joining the organization up to retirement, was computed. Infosys calculated the compensation of each employee at retirement by using an average rate of increment. The increments were based on industry standards, and the employee's performance and productivity. This value was discounted at the rate per cent per annum, which was the cost of capital at Infosys. Finally, the total compensation of each group was calculated. The amount of present values over the various employee groups indicates the total human value of the organization. In the first year of valuation, Infosys valued its HR assets at ₹1.86 billion. Narayana Murthy, the then chairman and managing director of the company, said 'Comparing this figure over the years will tell us whether the value of our human resources is appreciating or not'.

HR valuation enabled the company to understand whether the skill sets of its human capital was appreciating or not. Analysts felt that it was an investor-friendly disclosure and assured stakeholders that the company had the right human capital to meet its future business requirements. It also helped Infosys to decide the compensation of employees. The company ensured that it compensated each employee according to his/her net worth.

By adopting HR valuation, the following information could be obtained:

- Cost per employee
- The amount of wealth created by each employee
- The profit created by each employee
- The ratio of salary paid to the total revenue generated

It helped Infosys in identifying the right person for the right job based on the person's specialized skills, knowledge, capabilities, and experience.

It was an investor-friendly disclosure and assured stakeholders that the company had the right human capital to meet its future business requirements. When the HR were quantified, it gave the investors and other clients true insights into the organization and its future potential. Proper valuation of HR helped organizations to eliminate the negative effects of redundant labour. It helped them to channelize the available skills, talents, knowledge, and experience of their employees more efficiently. It started adding more employees and the value of its employees started to increase.

Although total revenue to the HR value in the year 2002 declined considerably due to may be an increase in cost (training or salary or in form of any other monetary benefits), the ratio of total revenue to number of employees increased. It increased after that continuing till 2007. In the year 2008, return on the HR value was the least due to the economic crisis and the global downturn. In 2011, an official release from Infosys claimed that each employee at Infosys was worth over ₹1 crore. According to company experts, not only does an exercise like this help to build external customer relations, it also helps create internal equity in the company and manage the workforce better. For instance, if an employee were to leave, companies would also be able to measure how much value had gone out of the system.

By 2018, however, not everything was good with Infosys. Foreign institutional investors' ownership of Infosys Ltd dropped to 34.87 per cent at the end of 30 June, the lowest since March 2009. By June 2018, it saw an attrition level of 20.6 per cent, the highest in its history, while its 23.7 per cent profitability was the lowest. Behind the headline numbers and valuations of HR, there is a bigger challenge faced by Infosys. Some feel it is due to management failure to invest enough in newer and more profitable technologies and arrest flight of labour to companies offering better opportunities. There have been a host of internal problems at Infosys. Charges of fraud in visa for employees being sent abroad is another reason why Infosys saw a dip in its popularity. All this has affected employee morale, leading to high turnover. Infosys was always considered to be an aspirational employer. The IT bellwether and a pioneer of some of the most innovative HR practices seems to have lost its sheen, making it a daunting task to return the company to its former glory.[12]

Questions for Discussion

1. Discuss the benefits of adopting HR valuation at Infosys.
2. Infosys is losing its tag as the bellwether of IT industry in India. Comment with suggestions for improvement.

NOTES

1. E. T. Penrose (1959), *The theory of the growth of the firm* (New York, NY: Wiley).
2. The leading researchers in the domain of RBV are: J. B. Barney (1991), Firm resources and sustained competitive advantage, *Journal of Management 17*(1): 99–120; J. B. Barney and P. M. Wright (1988), On becoming a strategic partner: The role of human resources in gaining competitive advantage, *Human Resource Management 37*(1): 31–46; B. Wernerfelt (1984), A resource-based theory of the firm, *Strategic Management Journal 5*(2): 171–180.
3. R. Likert (1961), *Patterns of management* (New York, NY: Mc-Graw Hill).
4. C. Greer (2001), *Strategic human resource management* (New Delhi, India: Pearson Education).
5. D. Kirkpatrick (1996), Revisiting Kirkpatrick's four-level-model, *Training & Development 50*(1): 54–57.
6. J. S. Adams (1963), Towards an understanding of inequity, *Journal of Abnormal Psychology 67*: 422–436.
7. A. S. Tsui and L. R. Gomez-Mejia (1988), Evaluating human resource effectiveness, in *Human resource management: Evolving roles and responsibilities*, ed. L. Dyer, pp. 187–227 (Washington, DC: Bureau of National Affairs, Inc.).
8. J. Fitz-Enz (2009), *The ROI of human capital: Measuring the economic value of employee performance* (New York, NY: Amacom).
9. R. S. Kaplan and D. P. Norton (1996), *The balanced scorecard: Translating strategy into action* (Boston, MA: Harvard Business School Press).
10. B. E. Becker, M. A. Huselid, and D. Ulrich, (2001), *The HR scorecard: Linking people, strategy, and performance* (Boston, MA: Harvard Business School Press).
11. Greer, *Strategic human resource management*.
12. With inputs from https://www.infosys.com/investors/reports-filings/annual-report/annual/Documents/AR-2011/ai_13.html, retrieved 7 July 2017.

Index

24/7 customer 176
3M 180
absenteeism 180, 193, 211, 225, 294–295, 297–299, 302, 306
Accenture 100, 106, 175
achievers 220
ADDIE model 210
Aditya Birla Group 258
Adler, A. 64
administrative: expert 26, 307; linkage 15, 115, 118
Adobe 99
adrenalin 86
agile 93–94, 130, 142, 152, 160, 265–266
AIDA principle 170
Air India 179
Aircel 75–76
Alibaba 93
All India Trade Union Congress 271–272
Almond, G. A. 56
alternative-form reliability 184, 193
Amazon 93
ambidextrous 91, 95–96
American Express 87, 167, 210
analysers 15, 118
Ansoff, H. I. 8–9
Aon Hewitt 4
Apple Inc. 92, 214
Apple University 214
appraisal: free-form method 237; career-oriented 166, 223–224; feedback 238, 245; potential 225, 246–247, 264; self 242; 360-degree 144, 242–243, 247, 264, 301
apprenticeship 213
arbitration 269, 273
Arthur, J. B. 15, 106
assessment centre 245

AT&T 87, 242
at-risk pay 255
attrition 134, 151–152, 176, 182, 281, 283, 285, 306, 308–310
autonomous teams 275
Azim Premji University 214
Azmi, F. T. 90, 221

Back, R. 307
Baird, L. 115
Bamberger, P. A. 17
Bechtel 182
Becker, B. E. 304
Beer, M. 11
behaviour modelling 215
behavioural description interview (BDI) 194
Behavioural expectation scales (BES) 238
Behavioural observation scales (BOS) 237–238
behavioural: competencies 144; flexibility 215 methods 237; orientations 64; rating approaches 237–238; rating techniques 238; training 151
behaviourally anchored rating scale, (BARS) 237
best fit school 7–8, 14, 17
best practices school 7, 17
Bharatiya Kamgar Sena 272
Bharti Airtel 75–77, 258
Bharti Infratel 76
BHEL 276
Big Bazaar 272
big data 101–103, 305
blur effect 90
body shopping 174
Boeing 214
Bombay Mill Hands Association 271
boomerang employees 175, 283
Boudreau, J. 31

British Petroleum 146, 226, 245
broadbanding 250, 253
business environment 42–45, 55, 73, 76–77, 206, 221, 291

Cadbury India 24, 31
capability analytics 306
capacity analytics 306
capitalist economy 52
career: centre 223; development 88, 128, 222–224; ladder 147, 168, 225–227; management 167, 223; map 223; path 30, 88, 119–120, 223–224, 226–227, 243; planning 88, 164, 222–224, 227, 234, 283, 286; plateau 167, 225; transition 227
CareerBuilder.com 177
category rating methods 236, 238
Chamberlain, N. S. 272
change agent 26, 28
Charan, C. 4
Chief Human Resource Officer 32, 104
Cipla 178, 200
Citibank 175
coaching 84, 99, 103, 151, 212–213, 224, 241
Coca-Cola 59, 134, 168, 176
Coleman, J. S. 56
collective bargaining 269, 271–275
compensation mix 301
compensation: direct 247; executive 259–261; indirect 247; performance-linked 255; strategic 232, 249–250, 261, 264
competency: acquisition analytics 306; profiling 88, 143–144, 146, 211
competency-based: appraisal 244–245, 264; pay 250–251; training 88, 212, 216–217
configurational perspective 7, 14–15, 17
content plateau 225
contingency perspective 7
contract: agreement 273; recruiting 171
Convergys 170
corporate culture analytics 307
cost per hire 298
cost–benefit analysis 20, 295–296, 298, 300
critical incident technique 182, 194, 237
Crompton Greaves 31

D'Aveni, R. A. 73
Dabur 258

Daimler Benz 150
Davidow, W. H. 93
Davis, S. 90
defenders 15, 118
dejobbing 142–143, 146
Delery, J. E. 14
Deloitte 168
Delta Airlines 166
demand analysis 161, 163, 296
Dessler, G. 147
Devanna, M. A. 9–10
DHR International 172
digital convergence 84
Directorate General of Employment and Training 172
disengagement 278–280
distributive justice 301
doers 220
Doty, D. H. 14
Drucker, P. 66, 238
dual career paths 226–227. *See also* career; career path
Dyer, L. 17

economic: environment 42, 46, 54; policies 46, 52–54; structures 46, 49–50; systems 46, 52, 54
Economist Intelligence Unit 65
Effron, M. 112
E-HR 24, 85–87, 97
Eisenstadt, S.N. 56
e-learning 88, 216–218. *See also* learning; mobile learning; virtual learning
electronic arts (EA) 178
emotional intelligence (EI) 30, 141
employee: champion 26; churn analytics 306; engagement 100, 222, 276–280; learning matrix 219; referrals 168–169; relations management software 88; retention 34, 182, 280, 283–284, 308; stock option plan 250, 258; turnover 107, 124, 164, 182, 279, 283, 306
employment agencies 71, 171–173
Entelo 98
Ernst & Young 100, 292
Esso Research and Engineering Company 242
Evans, P. 93–94
executive search firms 172
exit interview 282, 284, 306

experimental designs 295, 299
expert software systems 88
external fit 7, 15, 18–19, 45
Exxon 242

Facebook 98, 177, 218
factor comparison system 248
Federal Express 166–167
Federation of Indian Chambers of Commerce and
    Industry 169
feedback, 360-degree 243–244. *See also* appraisal
field review 237
Filler, E. 30
financial participation 276
fiscal policy 53
flow state 277
flypaper approach 181
Fombrun, C. J. 9–10
Forbes 4, 265, 292, 309
forced distribution method 237
forced ranking 237, 265
Ford 91
foreign investment policy 54
forgetting 221–222
formal participation 275
Fortune 100 companies 178
Fortune 500 companies 24, 98
Fortune 1,000 companies 99
Fortune India 500 companies 265
Future Innoversity (Future Group) 214
Future of Work 127–129

gainsharing 250, 254
Gallup 279
gamification 218–219
gap analysis 161, 163, 296
Gartner 99, 101
GE 3–5, 168, 175, 210, 242
General Motors 94
General Union of Trades 271
German military 242
Gild 98
GM 24, 31
Godrej Consumer Products 180
golden handshake 281
Golden, K. 115, 281
Gomez-Mejia, L. R. 303
Google 19, 96, 168, 202

Government of India 41–42, 177, 203, 268, 270
graphic rating scale 236
Gratton, L. 6
Guest, D. 7

Hackman, J. R. 133
Hall, L. 115
Hamburger University 214
Hamel, G. 8
Harley-Davidson Motor Company 105–106
Harvard Business School 26, 287
Harvard Model 11, 13, 17, 20
Harvard University 11
HCL Technologies 179
HDFC Bank 258
Head Hunters India 172
Hendry, C. 5
high performance work practices (HPWP) 14
Hindustan Unilever Limited 114

Hofstede, H. 66–67
Holder, G.W. 17
Honda 210
horizontal fit 18, 45
HR analytics 291, 305–308
HR audit 295
HR generalist 29–30
HR scorecard 303–304
HRD audit 300
HSBC 177
human assets 5, 10–11, 19
human resource management 5, 9–11, 128, 291
humanistic approach 9, 11, 17, 113, 115
Huselid, M. A. 14, 304
Hyland, M. A. 7
hyperarchy 91, 93–94, 96–97
Hyundai Motor India 274

IBM 81, 167–168, 170, 175, 180, 200, 214, 226, 242
ICICI Bank 258
Idea Cellular Ltd 75
Idlers 220
Ignatius, A. 112
Ikya 174
in-basket exercise 215
increment to base pay 255. *See also* compensation
Indian Armed Forces 157–158
Indian Staffing Federation 174
industrial policy 53

informal participation 275
informality 90, 148
information culture 90–91, 97
Infosys Global Education Centre 214
Infosys Limited 31, 134, 170, 178, 200, 214, 258, 261, 309–310
Instagram 98
instantaneity 90
instrumental approach 9, 17, 113, 115
intangibility 90
integrative linkage 115
Intel Corporation 134, 160
intelligent tutoring systems 213
interactivity 90, 217
internal fit 7, 18, 45, 129
International Labour Organization 65, 127, 271
International Monetary Fund 41
Internet of Things 101
Internet recruiting 179
Internet-based services 243
inter-rater reliability 184, 193, 196, 238–239
involuntary termination 281. *See also* attrition
ITC 258

Jac Fitz-Enz 303
Jackson, S. E. 16, 25
Jet Airways 176
Job Instructional Technique (JIT) 213
job: acceptance rate 294; analysis 87, 128–129, 131, 133–147, 149, 151, 153, 182–184, 189–190, 193–194, 196, 245, 248, 264; characteristics model 133; classification system 248; content 135–136, 275; context 135–136; description 98, 136–137, 139, 141, 143–144, 170, 172, 177, 193, 211, 234; design 22, 133–134, 259; enlargement 134, 168, 275–276; enrichment 134, 168, 225–226, 275; evaluation 139, 248, 262, 264; fairs 171, 173, 178, 200; involvement 277; postings 166–167, 182; redesign 133–134; requirements 135–136, 144, 196; rotation 14, 134, 141, 166–168, 212, 226; specification 136–137, 139, 211
job-hazyness 142
jobs and skills audit 161
Johnson & Johnson 220
joint committees 275
just-in-time talent 296

Kaplan, R. S. 303
Karen, L. 6
Khan, M. N. 90
Kirkpatrick, D. 298
Kirloskar Group 230
knowledge management 209–210
Kodak 82, 258
Kuhn, J. W. 272

labour market 11, 54, 64, 119, 161, 297
last-in-first-out 282
lateral: moves 29–30, 167–168; promotion 29–30, 53, 157, 167–168, 225–226, 252, 283
Lawrence, P. R. 11
layoff 234, 302
learning iceberg 208–209
learning needs analysis 210–211
learning: action 213; asynchronous 217; game-based 217–218; mobile 218; multimedia 216; off-the-job 214–216; on-the-job 212–214; organization 8, 113, 207–209, 211, 229–230; organizational 27, 207–209, 230; plateau 225; programmed 213; strategy 211–212, 219–220; synchronous 216
leasing agencies 173
Legge, K. 6
Lengnick-Hall, C. A. 115
Lengnick-Hall, M. L. 115
Lepak, D. P. 15
LG 134
life plateau 225–226
LinkedIn 98, 177, 218, 308
Livingston, J.S. 263, 307
Lockheed Missile & Space Company 170

macro environment 44–46
Mafoi 174
Malone, M. S. 93
management by objectives 238
management games 215, 218, 247
Manpower Inc. 174
manpower planning 87, 117, 119–120, 157–159, 240, 283
Marico 31, 258
Maruti Suzuki India 274
matching philosophy 181
Mattel 205
McDonald's 214

McKinsey 176
McMahan, G. C. 6
mentoring 84, 151, 199, 212, 224, 278
Merck 180
merit pay 250–251, 256
Merrill Lynch 77
Meshoulam, I. 17, 115
Metro AG 272
Michael Page India 172
Michigan Model 9–10, 13, 17, 20
micro environment 44–45, 70–71
Microsoft 98, 134, 168, 176, 178, 200
Microsoft India 178
Miles, R. 15, 18, 118
Mills, D. Q. 11
Ministry of Defence, India 157
Ministry of Labour and Employment, India 177, 268
Ministry of Social Justice and Empowerment, India 172
Mintzberg, H. 8
Mirakle Couriers 201, 203
mixed economy 52
mobile recruiting 178
Mohandas Pai, T. V. 31
monetary policy 53
Monsanto 175
Monster 171
Morgan Stanley 75
Motorola 214
MRF Tyres 274
multiskilling 167
Myer, C. 90, 192

NALCO 258
narrative method 237
NASA 210, 222
NASSCOM 169
National Employment Service 172
National HRD Network 169
Naukri.com 171
negotiation 61, 99, 146, 236–237, 272–273
Nerolac 31
NIIT 258
Nike 134
Nokia India 274
non-monetary incentives 22, 259, 262, 264, 266. *See also* compensation
Norton, D. P. 303

O'Reilly III, C. 95
Oldham, G. R. 133
onboarding 98–99, 180, 198–199, 202, 283
on-demand recruiting services 172
ONGC 28
opinion survey 301
Oracle 86, 292
Organization for Economic Cooperation and Development 47
Ort, M. 112
Oxford University 201

P&G 87
paired comparison method 236
Pantaloon 272
Parkinson, C. N. 140
Parkinson's law 140, 248
participation in management 274
Patten, T. H. 247
pay equity 301
Peiperl, M. 15, 118, 120
Penrose, E. 8, 292
PeopleSoft 86
Pepsi 176
performance: analysis 211; bonus 250, 256–257, 261, 276; measurement system 241, 264, 300
person–job fit 133, 183
Peter, L. J. 17, 31, 66, 180, 207, 238
Philanthropic Society 271
Philips India 31, 134
Pieperl, M. 118
Pizza Hut 170
podcast 218
point system 248. *See also* compensation
politico-legal environment 55, 59–60
Porter, M. 16, 83, 118, 120
posttest-only control group design 299–300
potential base pay at risk 256
Prahalad, C. K. 8, 92
pretest-posttest control group design 299
procedural justice 301
Procter & Gamble 176
profit sharing 14, 248, 250, 257–258, 276
promotion: horizontal 225; vertical 167, 225
prospectors 15, 118
Purcell, J. 7, 16
PwC 31, 130

quality circles 14, 243, 275
quasi-experimental design 300
Quik Wok 170

Ramanujam, V. 115
Ramaswamy, R. 92
Ramstad, P. 31
R-Com 75–76
reactors 15, 118
realistic job preview 181–182
recruitment: advertising 169–170, 294; channel
    analytics 307
relearning 221–222, 266. *See also* learning
reliability 183–184, 239, 296
Reliance Industries Ltd 75
Reliance Jio 75–77
resource-based view (RBV) 8, 292
retrenchment 119–120, 281–282
revenue per employee 294
role playing 215, 245, 247

Sahara 176
sales per employee 294
Samsung 75
Satyam Marico 31
Schippman, J. S. 146
Schuler, R. S. 16, 25
selection ratio 297
self-assessment 223, 240. *See also* appraisal
Senge, P. 207, 216, 274
Shell Oil 242
Siebel Systems 88–89
Siemens 86, 200
simulation exercises 88, 190, 193, 215, 217
skill: based pay 251–253, 261; depth 252; horizontal
    252; vertical 251–252
Snow, C. C. 15, 18, 118
social media 80, 98–101, 177–179, 200, 218, 266,
    272, 306; analytics 98, 178; learning 218. *See
    also* learning
socialist economy 52
Society for Human Resource Management 99, 169
sociocultural environment 62–64, 66–67
socio-economic stratification system 62
Sodexo 100
soft HRM 5–7, 9, 11, 13–15, 17–24, 28–29, 31,
    43–45, 47, 49, 51, 71–73, 113–115, 128–129,
    292–293

Sonnenfeld, J. 15, 118, 120
special events recruiting 172
Spector, B. 11, 15, 118
stakeholder 11, 20, 295, 300
Starbucks 177
Storey, J. 7, 25
strategic: human resources planning 159; job
    modeling 146; management 5–6, 8–9, 11, 17–
    18, 25, 32, 34, 45, 112–114, 120, 221; partner
    6, 26, 31, 121, 307
strivers 220
structural plateau 225
succession planning 34, 119–120, 123, 164, 211,
    220, 224, 226–227, 234
suggestion schemes 262, 275. *See also* feedback
summer internships 175
Sun Bank 182
Sun Microsystems 92, 214
superannuations 281
supply analysis 161–162, 296
systems concept 43–44

Taj Hotels 286
talent: acquisition 98, 116, 178, 200, 306, 308;
    management 98–99, 128–129, 143, 147, 151,
    160, 166, 200, 306, 308; poaching 176
TalentBin 98
task analysis 211
Tata Consultancy Services. *See* TCS
Tata DoCoMo 75–76
Tata Motors 150–152
Tata Sons 265
Taylor, F.W. 91
TCS 31, 200, 265–266
team bonus 254
team-based pay 250, 253–255
TeamLease 174
technological environment 67, 81–82
Telecom Regulatory Authority of India 77
Telenor 75–76
temping 173–174
termination 11, 60, 73, 119–120, 129, 164, 234,
    269, 271, 273, 275, 277, 279–283, 285, 287;
    planning 119–120, 164, 281–282. *See also*
    layoff
test–retest reliability 184, 193
thesocialCV 98
Thomson Reuters 31

Tichy, M. N. 4, 9–10

time lapse data 297

The Times, UK 260

Torrington, D. 115

total quality management 243, 275

Towers Perrin 278

Toyota Kirloskar Motor Pvt. Ltd 230

Toyota Motors 240

trade policy 53

training: evaluation 298 (*see also* appraisal); cross-functional 221; Internet-based (IBT) 216, 218; sensitivity 215; T-group 215; vestibule 214

transactional analysis 216

Truss, C. 6

Tsui, A. S. 303

turnover 34, 119–120, 124, 161, 164, 179, 182, 188, 279, 281–284, 293–94, 297–298, 302–303, 305–306, 310

Tushman, M. 95–96

Twitter 98–99, 177

U.S. Department of Labor 172

Ulrich, D. 25–26, 31, 111–112, 304

understudy 199, 213

Unilever 114

unit raiding 179

United Nations 46–47, 63, 65, 74

United Nations Development Programme 47

United Nations Educational, Scientific and Cultural Organization 63

universalistic perspective 7, 14

University of London 8, 292

University of Michigan 31

unlearning 206, 221–222, 229. *See also* learning; relearning

utility analysis 296, 298. *See also* analysers

validity 183–186, 189–190, 193, 196, 239; concurrent 186, 193; construct 185; content 184–185; criterion-related 185–186; predictive 185–186, 193

variable pay plan 250

velcro organization 91, 94–95

Verreault, D. A. 7

vertical fit 7, 18, 45

virtual: jobs 143; learning 216 (*see also* e-learning; learning; mobile learning); organization 91–92, 97; reality training 217 (*see also* training); technology leasing 174

vision 4, 6, 11, 18–19, 21–23, 25, 112–13, 121, 124, 150, 160, 192, 196, 303, 307

Vodafone 75–77

voluntary: retirement 281 (*see also* superannuation); termination 281. *See also* layoff

VRIO framework 8

Wal-Mart 24, 29, 306

Walton, R. 11, 24

Webb, B. 269

Webb, S. 269

WhatsApp 178, 202

Wipro 31, 134, 176

Wipro Infrastructure Engineering 31

work councils 275

workflow analysis 128–133, 135, 137, 139, 141, 143, 145, 147, 149, 151, 153

work–life balance 34, 67, 283

World Bank 42, 47–49

World Economic Forum 65

Wurster, T. S. 93–94

Xerox 31, 306

yield ratio 169, 297–298

YouTube 99, 104, 177, 218